Reproduced from a bookplate made in 1796 for
the Blue Hill Library by Jonathan Fisher,
the first "settled minister" in Blue Hill and
one of America's earliest wood-engravers.
No.
Bluehill
Library.
Know thyself
JF

# James K. Polk

## A POLITICAL BIOGRAPHY

# James K. Polk

## A POLITICAL BIOGRAPHY
### *To the Prelude of War*
### *1795 - 1845*

By

EUGENE IRVING McCORMAC

Biography in two volumes
To the Prelude of War, 1795 - 1845
To the End of a Career, 1845 - 1849

Published by American Political Biography Press

Newtown, CT

All publications of
AMERICAN POLITICAL BIOGRAPHY PRESS
Are dedicated to my wife
Ellen and our two children
Katherine and William II

This particular book is
Dedicated to:

Edward Crimmins
iconoclast
North Fort Myers, FL

Professor McCormac dedicated his work to:
"The memory of My Mother"

# PREFACE

In the two standard sets of American biographies—namely, the *American Statesmen Series* and the *American Crisis Biographies*—the name of James K. Polk does not appear in the list of titles. Evidently the editor of the first set did not consider Mr. Polk to have been a statesman worthy of serious consideration, and the editor of the second set seems to have been unaware that Polk had played a conspicuous part in any of the crises of American history.

Although it is not my purpose to criticize the selection made by these editors, I believe that the character and success of Polk's political career entitled him to a place in either series. I believe that the following pages will show Mr. Polk to have been a constructive statesman—a statesman possessed of vision, sound judgment, and unusual executive ability. Surely he was a ''crisis'' President. He extended our national boundaries to the Pacific Ocean and determined the political destinies of the future population of the vast area lying west of the Louisiana Purchase. His request for an appropriation with which to conduct negotiations with Mexico called forth the Wilmot Proviso; and this proviso precipitated the ''irrepressible conflict,'' which was one of the greatest crises in American history.

When nominated for the Presidency in 1844, Polk was neither unknown nor inexperienced in national affairs. He had been selected to conduct Jackson's bank war in the House of Representatives, and he had performed this task to the entire satisfaction of the President and the Democratic party. As Speaker of the House of Representatives, he had displayed alertness of mind, sound judgment, and ability as a party leader. And when, in 1844, Van Buren announced his opposition to the annexation of Texas, General Jackson urged that Polk be nominated, for, as he said, Governor Polk was the ablest exponent of Democratic doctrines and the one who would be most capable of carrying them into successful operation. The General did not overrate the political ability of his protégé. As President, Polk formulated his policies with precision and confidence; and despite many obstacles, he succeeded in carrying them into effect.

It has not been my purpose to write a personal biography. Therefore this volume deals almost entirely with Polk's political career. In the discussion of the events of his administration I have attempted to show the part played by the President in formulating the policy of the nation. In the field of foreign relations I have been concerned mainly with the President's foreign policy and with the motives, viewpoints, and exigencies which led to the adoption of that policy. For this reason the history, policies, and motives of other countries concerned have been treated incidentally only. Polk's policies were influenced by what he believed to be the facts concerning those countries, and not by the facts which have subsequently been found to be true. For example, I did not feel that a biography of President Polk called for an exhaustive discussion of conditions in Mexico, either before or during our war with that nation. For similar reasons, the discussion of the Oregon question is confined to the official acts of Great Britain and to the interpretation of those acts by the government of the United States.

The material used in the preparation of this volume has been gathered mainly in the University of California Library, the Tennessee State Library, and the Library of Congress. I am indebted to Dr. John W. Jordon, Librarian of the Historical Society of Pennsylvania, for placing at my disposal the Buchanan Papers, and to Professor St. George L. Sioussat for assistance of various kinds. I am under especial obligation to Dr. Gaillard Hunt and Mr. John C. Fitzpatrick, of the Manuscripts Division of the Library of Congress. Their never-failing courtesy and valuable suggestions facilitated my research work in many ways.

Dr. Justin H. Smith's valuable work entitled ''The War with Mexico'' was published soon after the manuscript of my volume had been completed. Although it appeared too late to be used in the preparation of my manuscript, I am gratified to note that on most points covered by the two works we have arrived at substantially the same conclusions.

BERKELEY, CALIFORNIA,<br>
   December, 1919.

CONTENTS



⌊ix⌋

## CHAPTER I

## ANCESTRY AND EARLY LIFE OF JAMES K. POLK

The pedigree of the Polk family has been traced back to 1075—to Fulbert, who was born in the reign of Malcolm III, of Scotland. In 1153 Fulbert was succeeded by his son Petrius, who took the surname Pollok from the estate which he inherited. In 1440 Sir Robert de Pollok, a "younger son" of the family, inherited an Irish estate and removed to Ireland. By common usage the name of this branch was soon contractd into Polk. Sometime between 1680 and 1687[1] Robert Bruce Polk, or Pollok, second son of Sir Robert II, left Ireland with his wife, six sons, and two daughters, and settled in Somerset County, Maryland. Their oldest son, John Polk, married Joanna Knox and established that branch of the family whence came our subject, James K. Polk.

William Polk, the only son of John and Joanna, after living for a time in Carlisle, Pennsylvania, removed with his family to Mecklenburg County, North Carolina. Colonel Ezekiel Polk, the seventh child of William, married Mary Wilson, and the fourth child of this union was Samuel Polk, the father of the future President. The President's mother was Jane Knox, a great-grandniece of John Knox, of Scotland. Her father, James Knox, of Iredell County, North Carolina, was a captain in the Revolution. Mrs. Polk was a rigid Presbyterian, and a woman of keen intellect and high character. From her James inherited many of his well-known traits. She lived to witness the whole of his successful career, and to assist, during his last moments, in preparing him for "a future estate."[2]

---

[1] Authorities differ as to the date.

[2] Garrett, *Pedigree of the Polk family*. Richardson, *Messages*, IV, 371. Nelson, *Memorials of Sarah Childress Polk*, 150 and *passim*. Chase, *History of the Polk Administration*, 475.

James Knox Polk, oldest of the ten children of Samuel and Jane Knox Polk, was born on November 2, 1795, in Mecklenburg County, North Carolina.[3] The Polk family had settled in this frontier region some time before the Revolution, and tradition has credited Polk's ancestors with a leading part in promulgating the much-mooted Mecklenburg Declaration of Independence. His grandfather, Colonel Ezekiel Polk, whom the Whigs in 1844 accused of Toryism, was an officer in the Revolutionary army.

James's father, Samuel Polk, was a plain but enterprising farmer. At an early age he had been thrown upon his own resources and had met with the hardships incident to frontier conditions. With the hope of improving his fortunes, he followed the trend of emigration westward, and in the autumn of 1806 settled in the valley of the Duck River, Tennessee. He was one of the first pioneers in a region then a wilderness; but the valley proved to be fertile and Mr. Polk in time was rated as a prosperous farmer. He was an ardent supporter of Jefferson, and his faith in the soundness of Republican doctrines was inherited by his son James. The correspondence in the Polk Papers indicates that the entire family, including the President's mother, took a keen interest in politics and that all of them were firm believers in the maxims of Jefferson.

James was but eleven years old when his father located in Tennessee. Had he possessed a strong physique, doubtless he would have shared the fate of the average eldest son and have been trained to cultivate the family estate. But he was not strong[4] and his first years in Tennessee were spent in making

---

[3] On November 2, 1846, Polk noted in his diary: "This is my birthday. According to the entry in my father's family Bible I was born on the 2nd day of Nov., 1795, and my mother has told me that the event occurred, as near as she could tell about 12 o'clock, Meridian, on that day." (*Diary*, II, 216.)

[4] "I closed my education at a later period of life than is usual, in consequence of having been very much afflicted and enjoyed very bad health in my youth. I did not commence the Latin Grammar until the 13th of July, 1813." (Polk, *Diary*, IV, 160.)

good use of such limited educational advantages as were afforded in a pioneer community.

Young Polk was studious and ambitious, but Fate seemed determined to deprive him of the opportunity for satisfying his desire for an education. His health did not improve, and his father, believing that a more active life than that of a student would be conducive to health, determined to make a business man of his son. Accordingly, much to the son's disgust and over his protest, he was placed with a merchant to learn the business. After remaining but a few weeks with the merchant, however, the earnest appeals of the son overcame the resistance of the father, and in July, 1813, James was permitted to continue his education under the guidance of Reverend Robert Henderson at a small academy near .Columbia, Tennessee. For about a year Polk "read the usual course of latin authors, part of the greek testament and a few of the dialogues of Lucian," and, according to the testimony of his preceptor, he "was diligent in his studies, and his moral conduct was unexceptionable & exemplary."[5] After spending nine months at Murfreesborough Academy, where his "literary merit and moral worth" won the approval of the rector, Samuel P. Black,[6] James entered the University of North Carolina at Chapel Hill in the autumn of 1815. He was naturally drawn to the university of his native state, and the fact that his cousin, Colonel William Polk, had for many years been one of its trustees, may have been an additional reason for selecting this institution.

At college Polk manifested those peculiar traits which later characterized his career as a statesman. Eschewing the less profitable, but usually more attractive, side of college life, his time was occupied with hard and well directed study. "His ambi-

---

[5] A recommendation dated December 31, 1814. MS in Tenn. Hist. Soc. Library.

[6] Recommendation dated October 5, 1815. MS in Tenn. Hist. Soc. Library.

tion to excel,'' wrote one of his political friends,[7] ''was equalled by his perseverance alone, in proof of which it is said he never missed a recitation nor omitted the punctilious performance of any duty.'' Numerous remarks in the diary written while he was President show that, in Polk's own opinion, time spent in mere pleasure was so much time wasted. He seems to have been equally serious-minded during his college days. Neither at college nor at a later time did Polk deceive himself or attempt to deceive others by assuming great native brilliancy. He never posed as one whose genius made it easy for him to decide great questions offhand. He never attempted to conceal the fact that his conclusions were reached as the result of unremitting labor. And if his conclusions were sometimes attacked as unsound, he was, on the other hand, spared the embarrassment of ridicule, which often fell to the lot of his more brilliant competitors during his long political career.

Polk was graduated from the university in 1818 and enjoyed the distinction of being awarded first honors in both mathematics and the classics. He was very fond of both subjects, as each appealed to his taste for industry and precision. Of his classical training he retained the substantial and discarded the ornate. ''So carefully,'' wrote the friend above cited, ''has Mr. Polk avoided the pedantry of classical display, which is the false taste of our day and country, as almost to hide the acquisitions which distinguished his early career. His preference for the useful and substantial, indicated by his youthful passion for mathematics, has made him select a style of elocution, which would perhaps be deemed too plain by shallow admirers of flashy declamation.''

After his graduation Polk returned to Tennessee with health impaired by close application, and early in 1819 began the study of law in the office of Judge Felix Grundy. A warm personal and political friendship resulted, which was severed only by the death

---

[7] *Democratic Review*, May, 1838. Polk says that this sketch was written by J. L. Martin, later *chargé d'affaires* to the Papal States (*Diary*, IV, 132).

of Grundy in 1840. The pupil studied hard, and late in 1820 he was admitted to the bar. He immediately began the practice of law at Columbia, in his home county of Maury, among friends and neighbors whose confidence in his ability assured him, from the beginning, a profitable practice. ''His thorough academic preparation, his accurate knowledge of the law, his readiness and resources in debate, his unswerving application to business, secured him, at once, full employment, and in less than a year he was already a leading practitioner.''[8] His account books show that he continued to enjoy a lucrative practice although much of his time was spent in public service.[9]

For three years the young attorney's time was occupied exclusively in the practice of his profession. His only active participation in politics was to serve for one term as clerk of the state senate. In 1823, however, he was chosen to represent his county in the state legislature, and, having thus entered the political arena, he continued in a very active, and for the most part successful, political career to the close of his term as President. He spent two years in the legislature, where he soon established a reputation for business capacity and for superiority in debate. He took an active interest in all measures for developing his state and gave special attention to the providing of better educational advantages. He enjoyed the personal and political friendship of General Jackson, and it afforded him much pleasure to assist by his vote in sending that military hero to Washington to represent the state in the Senate of the United States. Few acts of his life gave him, in later years, greater pride than his participation in launching Jackson in his political career; and, as the General was ever mindful of the welfare of his political supporters, this incident was no impediment to Polk's own political advancement. His friendship for Jackson was natural, although the two men differed widely in personal characteristics and in

---

[8] *Dem. Rev., sup. cit.*

[9] His account books are in the Library of Congress.

their attitude toward authority. From early youth Polk had been an ardent advocate of republicanism. He was a firm believer in the teachings of Jefferson and shared with his patron an unbounded faith in individual freedom. Pioneer conditions also are conducive to a strong belief in practical democracy, and Jackson seemed to be a leader who understood the people's desires and sympathized with them.

On January 1, 1824, Polk married Sarah Childress, whose father was a prosperous farmer near Murfreesborough, Tennessee.[10] Mrs. Polk was a lady of refinement and ability. Her sound sense and personal charm aided materially the political fortunes of her husband and later caused her to be regarded as one of the most popular ladies of the White House. Many who rated her husband as inferior, even contemptible, joined in the unanimous verdict that Mrs. Polk was a lady of culture and attractive personality. This fact is attested by numerous private letters. Judge Story was ''thunderstruck'' to hear of Polk's nomination in 1844, but he admired Mrs. Polk. When her husband was leaving Washington in 1839 to enter the campaign for the governorship of Tennessee, Story expressed his admiration for Mrs. Polk in a poem written in her honor.[11]

One of the young men who attended Polk on his wedding day was his law partner, Aaron V. Brown, later United States senator and governor of Tennessee. Their friendship continued to the end, and to no one else, except Cave Johnson, did Polk more frequently confide his usually well concealed political plans.

Two years in the state legislature increased the young attorney's natural taste for politics, and his success in that field made him determine to seek a wider opportunity for satisfying his political ambitions. In 1825 he offered himself as a candidate, and in August of that year was chosen to represent, his district in Congress. When elected, he was not quite thirty years of age,

---

[10] Nelson, *Memorials of Sarah Childress Polk*, 17.
[11] *Ibid.*, 54.

and on entering Congress, he was, with one or two exceptions, the youngest member of that body.

Mrs. Polk did not accompany her husband on his first trip to Washington. The journey was made on horseback, in company with several other members of Congress. At Baltimore they took the stagecoach, leaving their horses until their return in March.[12]  On his second journey to Washington, Mrs. Polk accompanied him in the family carriage. The money paid to members as mileage in those early days was small compensation for the hardships encountered on a journey from remote western states. Still, the pioneer statesmen endured such hardships without complaint; they even extracted pleasure from these tedious overland journeys.

There was little ostentation in Washington in this early period. The life of the average congressman's family was extremely simple. It was customary for two or more families to rent a single house for the season and "mess" together.[13]  Among the "messmates" of the Polks were Hugh L. White, of Tennessee, and John C. Calhoun, of South Carolina, both of whom later became Polk's bitter political enemies.

Although in politics a disciple of Jefferson and an ardent supporter of Jackson, Polk was wholly unlike either man in personal peculiarities. Jefferson was a born leader of men, and his exuberant optimism and personal charm attracted hosts of disciples. He advertised his democracy by extreme informality and slovenly garb; and he delighted in shocking the "well born" by disregarding the rules of social etiquette. Jackson, also, was a born leader of men. He commanded the multitude because he insisted upon doing so,[14] but the "plain people" approved him

---

[12] *Ibid.*, 27–28.    [13] *Ibid.*, 30–31.

[14] Judge Catron has given such an excellent description of Jackson's will to command that it seems desirable to rescue his letter from oblivion in spite of its length. It was written on the day after the General's funeral.

"One thing may be safely said of Gen¹ Jackson—that he has written his name higher on the Temple of fame, than any man since Washington,

mainly for the reason that they regarded him as one of themselves. Polk, on the contrary, had few intimate friends. His
associates recognized his ability, but he lacked that magnetism
which alone can attract a wide personal following. He was
naturally formal and punctilious, and he seldom sacrificed his
dignity in the pursuit of popular applause. While he was

of those belonging to History in this country. And what is more remarkable in him than any other American is, that he maintained his power
from seventy to *eighty*, when he had nothing to give. This he did by the
force of will and courage, backing his thorough out & out honesty of
purpose. His intuitive faculties were quick and strong—his instincts
capitally good. The way a thing should be done struck him plainly—&
he adopted the plan. If it was not the best, it would still answer the purpose, if well executed. Then to the execution he brought a hardy industry,
and a sleepless energy, few could equal—but this was not the best quality
he brought to the task. He cared not a rush for anything behind—he
looked ahead. His awful *will*, stood alone, & was made the will of all he
commanded; & command it he would and did. If he had fallen from the
clouds into a city on fire, he would have been at the head of the extin-
guishing host in an hour, & would have blown up a palace to stop the fire
with as little mis-giving as another would have torn down a board shed.
In a moment he would have willed it proper—& in ten minutes the thing
would have been done. Those who never worked before, who had hardly
courage to cry, would have rushed to the execution, and applied the match.
Hence it is that timid men, and feeble women, have rushed to onslaught
when he gave the command—fierce, fearless, and unwavering, for the first
time. Hence it is that for fifty years he has been followed, first by all
the timid who knew him—and afterwards by the broad land, as a match-
less man—as one they were ready to follow wherever he led—who with
them never was weary—and who could sweep over all opposers abroad or
at home, terrible and clean as a prairie fire, leaving hardly a smoke of the
ruin behind. Not even death could break the charm. The funeral yesterday was a great mass meeting—of women, children, men, black, white
colored—of every grade, mixed up by the acre outside—the House crammed
within. There was not a loud word nor a smile so far as I heard or saw.
See him they would and did—nay they would see the cof[f]in cased in
lead. It was just possible to have room for the soldiers, (a rather tedious
process) they claimed it as a *right* to see the thing done. The [illegible]
crowd followed him to the Tomb; a stone grave by the side of Mrs.
Jackson's—laid there in 1828—covered with a copper roofed canopy some
ten feet high resting on stone pillars. He was tediously put in, and the
tomb-stone left off, so all could look once more. It was a scene for a
painter to see the dense crowd at the particular spot—the slave women
in an agony of grief laying their heads on the shoulders and backs of the
lady friends of their old master; leaving laces wet with tears—nor did
the circumstance elicit a single remark so far as I heard. Death did not
make all equal, more completely than did this funeral'' (Catron to
Buchanan, Nashville, June 11, 1845, *Buchanan Papers*).

Speaker of the House, a press correspondent gave the following sketch of his personal appearance:

I have never seen a man preside over a popular legislative body with more dignity and effect than Mr. Polk. In person he is rather below the middle size, and has a firm and upright carriage which gives great self-possession and command to his manner. His head is finely formed, with a broad and ample forehead, and features indicative of a character at once urbane and decided. He is scrupulous in his dress and always appears in the chair as if he were at a dinner party.[15]

---

[15] *United States Magazine,* quoted by Nashville *Union,* July 17, 1839.

## CHAPTER II

## OPPOSITION MEMBER OF CONGRESS

On questions of governmental policy which divided the people of his day Polk entered the political field, as he left it, a consistent Jeffersonian Republican. Like his illustrious patron, however, he found, when entrusted later with the highest executive responsibilities, that theories, however good, must sometimes yield to the practical solution of the problem in hand. On such occasions, as in his expansion policy, he did as Jefferson had done; he assumed far-reaching power for the executive branch of the central government, leaving himself thereby open to the same criticisms which he and Jefferson had hurled at the Federalists.

Polk began his career in Congress as an opponent of the existing administration, and republicanism is always most vigorous when relieved of responsibility. During his first years in Congress his republicanism could have free play. He took a definite stand at once on the side of the states and the people, and vigorously assailed the autocratic powers alleged to have been assumed by President Adams, as well as the centralizing tendencies of that administration.

At a later day Polk's political opponents ridiculed him as being Jackson's *alter ego* and asserted that he had ascended the political ladder on the coat-tails of the "old hero." However effective such allegations may have been as campaign arguments, the fact remains that as early as 1825 Polk's political views were already freely promulgated in Congress, while those of Jackson on most questions were yet unformulated, or at least unannounced. As to the tariff, the only important question on which the General seems at that time to have formed a definite idea, the two men differed widely. That Polk, like others, humored the whims of General Jackson for political reasons need not be denied, that he profited by his friendship is beyond question; but priority in advocating measures later championed by both men would seem to absolve Polk from the charge that his opinions were derived ready-made from his more conspicuous chief. It does not appear that he gripped more firmly to the General's coat-tails than did others of his party.

Since the Tennessee land question was the theme of Polk's first formal speech in Congress, and since this subject was destined to acquire great political significance, it seems desirable to give a summary of its history in order to show its political importance.[1]

North Carolina, the former owner of Tennessee, when ceding this territory to the United States, had reserved the right to dispose of certain lands included in the ceded area. Other tracts were reserved for the Indians. These reservations necessarily limited the amount of land left at the disposal of Tennessee. Under the so-called compromise agreement of 1806, much of the Indian land was procured for the state, and one-sixth of it was to be reserved for educational purposes. In 1821, however, the provision relating to school lands was found to be invalid. As a result, the Tennesseans decided to ask Congress for certain government lands (in Tennessee) which might be disposed of for educational purposes. As the lands in question were those which settlers had declined to purchase at the price asked by the federal government, they were commonly called "waste" lands, although they were far from being worthless.

Although the legislature considered the subject as early as 1821, no definite action was taken until 1823, when it was referred to a select committee of which Polk was made chairman. From

---

[1] For a more detailed account, see Professor Sioussat's interesting article, ''Some Phases of Tennessee Politics in the Jackson Period,'' *Am. Hist. Rev.*, Oct., 1908.

this committee the chairman reported resolutions which, in addition to asking Congress to grant the lands in question, requested the senators and representatives from Tennessee to work for this end.[2]

In 1825, Polk was transferred from the state legislature to the federal House of Representatives. Realizing that the school land question was of prime importance to the people of his state[3] he embraced the earliest opportunity (January 23, 1826) to call up the Tennessee memorial—which he had prepared in 1823—and moved that it be referred to a select committee rather than to the Committee on Public Lands; and despite considerable debate this course was followed. Polk was made chairman of the new committee.[4] The bill which he reported soon afterward failed to pass the House. As will appear later, however, this Tennessee land question was revived from time to time by both Polk and "Davy" Crockett, and it was one of the rocks on which the Jackson party in Tennessee split into fragments.

Questions less local in character soon presented themselves. All of Jackson's supporters asserted, and doubtless many of them believed, that their hero had been virtually, even if not legally, cheated out of the Presidency in 1824 by "bargain and corruption" on the part of Adams and Clay. The well-known fact that the House of Representatives, whenever it might be called upon to select the chief magistrate, was intended by the Constitution to

---

[2] Printed copy of the resolutions in *Colonel Wm. Polk Papers.*

[3] "You cannot be too industrious," wrote one of his constituents a year later, "in endeavoring to effect the object contemplated in your Report of the last session on the subject of those govr n ment lands. To get this matter through 'is a consumation devoutly to be wished' for it will in a great measure disarm the opposition." The writer told Polk that the press did not tell the people very much about his work in Congress, and he advised Polk to send personal communications to many friends to counteract any assertions by enemies that he is inefficient. He also urged Polk to make a "thundering speach" against Haynes' bankrupt bill. "I do not know what your sentiments are on this subject but I think I know what your *interest* is" (Jim R. White to Polk, Dec. 30, 1826, *Polk Papers*).

[4] *Register of Debates,* 19 Cong., 1 sess., 1075–1077.

have a free choice, irrespective of the popular vote, did not in the least appease their wrath. They resolved at once on two lines of policy—to alter the Constitution of the United States in order to deprive the House of the privilege of choosing a President in any case, and in the meantime to make it as uncomfortable as possible for the one who had been so chosen. It is not easy to determine the degree of their sincerity in the first part of their program, but in the second part they were in deadly earnest.

The first move toward altering the Constitution was made by McDuffie, of South Carolina. On December 9, 1825, he offered resolutions which were referred to the Committee of the Whole House. His resolutions declared that the Constitution ought to be so amended that in electing the President and Vice-President of the United States "a uniform system of voting by Districts shall be established in all the States," and in no case should the choice of these officers devolve upon the respective houses of Congress. The resolutions provided also that the subject should be referred to a select committee "with instructions to prepare and report a joint resolution embracing the aforesaid objects."[5] On December 29, Cook, of Illinois, offered resolutions much like those of McDuffie, but providing in addition that the voters in the districts should vote directly for both officers. If by employing this method no election resulted, the choice should "be made by States" from the two highest on the list.[6] The last part was not clear, for it did not specify the manner in which the states should make the choice.

The resolutions of McDuffie and Cook caused considerable debate, and afforded an opportunity for others to air their views on constitutional questions. Some thought that the people were already intrusted with more power than they could use with intelligence, while others vigorously expounded the doctrine of *vox populi vox dei*. McDuffie was not, he said, "one of those visionary

---

[5] *Register of Debates,* 19 Cong., 1 sess., 797.
[6] *Ibid.,* 866.

advocates of the abstract rights of man, that would extend the power of the people further than is conducive to the happiness of the political society." Patriotic intentions, he admitted, would furnish no adequate security for the wise selection of a chief magistrate, in the absence of sufficient intelligence. "It would be a vain and delusive mockery, to invest them with an elective power, which they could exercise to the destruction of that which is the end of all government—the national good.'"[7] Although McDuffie himself believed that the people were sufficiently intelligent to make a proper choice, the conservatives could not be convinced that he was not playing with fire.

Polk spoke to the resolutions on March 13, 1826.[8] He apologized for departing from his usual custom of giving a "silent vote," and for extending a debate already prolonged. But as the subject was national in scope and vital in character, he could no longer remain silent. He attempted no flights of oratory, but he displayed at once more than ordinary ability as a debater. His remarks were clear and incisive, both in declaring his own views and in refuting the arguments of others. Jefferson himself never gave more unqualified endorsement to the doctrine of majority rule. The resolutions involved, said Polk, the question of the people's sovereignty. *"That this is a Government based upon the will of the People; that all power emanates from them; and that a majority should rule;* are, as I conceive, vital principles in this Government, never to be sacrificed or abandoned, under any circumstances." In theory, all "sound politicians" admit that "the majority should rule and the minority submit," but the majority, in his opinion, did not always prevail under the existing system of elections.

In his zeal for the popular cause Polk attempted to refute an assertion made by Storrs, of New York, that it was not intended by the framers of the Constitution to intrust the choice of

---

[7] Feb. 16, 1826. *Abridg. of Debates,* VIII, 992.

[8] *Abridg. of Debates,* IX, 8–16.

dent and Vice-President to direct popular vote. He made the rather astonishing statement that, if Storrs were right, ''I am free to admit that I have been wholly mistaken, and totally wrong, in my conceptions upon this subject.'' With a shade of sophistry he held that it was not reasonable to suppose that the people, having ''recently broken the chains of their slavery, and shaken off a foreign yoke,'' should in drafting their Constitution have voluntarily disfranchised themselves. In spite of well-known facts to the contrary, he tried to prove his contention by quoting parts of the preamble,[9] and rather unsuccessfully from the *Federalist*, Randolph, and Monroe, to show that election by the people had been intended by those who framed the Constitution. He was on surer ground when he asserted that it mattered little whether Storrs were right or wrong, inasmuch as the question before them did not concern elections under the present provisions of the Constitution but an amendment for changing the present method of selecting a President.

In Polk's opinion, there were several good reasons why the President should never be chosen by the House of Representatives. He is not an officer of the House. He is the chief magistrate of the whole people and should therefore be responsible to them alone, and dependent upon them for reëlection. Election either by the House or the Electoral College always makes choice by a minority possible, and there is danger that such elections will become more frequent. Representatives are chosen a long time before, and not for the purpose of selecting a President. A Representative may be ignorant of the wishes of his constituents, or he may willfully ignore their preference. The long period between the election of Representatives and their choice of a President affords ample time to influence their votes by bribery or by executive patronage.

Election by districts, as proposed in the resolutions, was, Polk believed, better than a continuation of the present system under

---

[9] ''We, the People etc. do ordain and establish this Constitution.''

which some electors were chosen by state legislatures, others by districts, thereby making it possible for one-fourth of the people to elect a President. But he concurred with Livingston, of Louisiana,[10] who preferred to dispense with electors altogether. "Let the people vote directly for the President without their intervention . . ." then ". . . there can be no division between contending candidates for elector, in favor of the same candidate, and the majority of the people of each district can control and give the vote of that district . . . the sentiment of each mass of the community throughout the Union, composing a district, is fairly elicited, and made to have its due and proportional weight in the general collected sentiment of all the districts in the Union.''

Although he offered no resolution embodying his ideas he suggested one[11] for the committee's consideration. His suggestions were more explicit and covered the ground more completely than the resolutions already before the House. Some of his arguments on this subject were partisan and sophistical; but in no case did he indulge in such absurdities as did one of his opponents, Edward Everett, who tried to convince his fellow-members that any attempt to amend the Constitution was itself unconstitutional. Each member, said the sage from Massachusetts, had taken an oath to support the Constitution as it is, and could not propose to alter it without violating that oath.[12] Neither George III nor John Tyler could plead a more tender conscience nor display a greater respect for oaths of office than Everett did on this occasion. No wonder Polk asked if "the gentleman [were] serious in this puerile conception?''

---

[10] McDuffie favored this also.

[11] Each state was to be divided into as many districts as it had members in both houses of Congress. The people in each district were to vote directly for President and Vice-President, without the intervention of electors, and a plurality in each district was to count as one vote. If no election should result, the matter was to be referred back to the people, who were then to select from the two highest on the list (*Abridg. of Debates,* IX, 16).

[12] *Ibid.,* 18.

In attempting to show that members of the House were not the proper persons to elect a President, Polk supported the extreme democratic view which would divest a member of Congress, even as a legislator, of his representative character and make him a mere delegate. "It has been openly avowed upon this floor," said he, "that there is no connection between the Representative here, and his constituent at home; that the Representative here is not bound to regard or obey the instructions of those who send him here. For myself, I have never entertained such opinions, but believe, upon all questions of expediency, that the Representative is bound to regard and obey the known will of his constituent." Any other view would intrust the rights of the people to "the accidental interest, or capricious will of their public servants." He no doubt had Jefferson's inaugural in mind when he added: "Shall *we* assume to ourselves the high prerogative of being uncontaminated and incorruptible, when the same attributes are denied to all the rest of mankind? Is immaculate purity to be found within these walls and no other corner of the earth?" Whether representatives endowed with "immaculate purity" or "angels in the form of kings"[13] can be intrusted with the government of their fellows may be open to question, but both Jefferson and Polk must have known that the framers of the Constitution had consciously placed more reliance on the discretion of the public officials than on the efficacy of a count of heads.

A remark made by Everett gave Polk an opportunity to pay tribute to General Jackson as the champion of the people. If the government were ever destroyed, said Everett, "it would not be by a President elected by a minority of the people, but by a President elected by an overwhelming majority of the people; by some 'military chieftain' that should arise in the land." "Yes, sir," answered Polk, "by some 'military chieftain,' whose only crime it was to have served his country faithfully at a period

---

[13] See Jefferson's inaugural address.

when that country needed and realized the value of his services.''
If the government were ever destroyed, it would be, in his opinion,
by ''the encroachments and abuse of power and by the alluring
and corrupting influence of Executive patronage.'' This was
intended, of course, as a thrust at President Adams; but in lending his support to the elevation of the ''old hero,'' Polk was help-
ing to hasten the demoralizing influence of patronage which he
so much feared.

Some of the northern members objected to the proposed
amendment on the ground that under it slaves would be represented. During his whole political career, slavery was a subject
which Polk avoided whenever possible. It is interesting to note,
however, that his opinions now expressed for the first time in
Congress were never substantially modified. He regretted exceedingly ''that scarcely any subject of general concern can be
agitated here, without having this important subject of slavery,
either collaterally, or incidentally, brought into view, and made
to mingle in our deliberations.'' His views now expressed were
reiterated in substance when he had to deal with the Wilmot
Proviso. Both now and later he was unable to see why this
irrelevant topic should be dragged into discussions of public
policy.

In answering his opponents Polk declared his firm belief in
state rights. Storrs and others had alleged that the proposed
amendment would tend to consolidate the people of the Union.
Polk denied this and said that he would oppose the amendment
if he had any idea that it would produce any such result. ''No
man,'' said he, ''deprecates more than I do, any violation of
rights secured to the States by the Federal Constitution,'' and
no one more fears ''the yawning gulf of consolidation.''[14]

Polk always referred to himself as a Republican, but it is
plain that he was not a believer in true representative govern-

---

[14] ''When I speak of State rights, I mean, as I understand the constitution to mean, not the rights of the Executives of the States, but I mean
the rights of the people of the States.''

ment, and was in fact a democrat.[15]  His remarks show clearly the influence of Jefferson's teaching.  He was an admirer of General Jackson, and used his influence both publicly and privately[16] to promote the General's interests, but there is no evidence that he relied on Jackson for political opinions.  On the contrary, Jackson read with approval Polk's speech on the constitutional amendment and assured him that it was well received by his constituents and would give him a strong claim to their future confidence.  "I agree with you," wrote the General,[17] "that the District System is the true meaning of the Constitution, but as this cannot be obtained any uniform System ought to be adopted instead of leaving the election of President to Congress."

As a critic of the Adams administration Polk did not rise above the political claptrap of the day.  All that can be said in his favor in this respect is that he spoke less frequently than did some of his colleagues.  Even his private letters are tinctured with a bias and a bitterness that do him no credit.  A letter written to Colonel William Polk concerning the subserviency of the Speaker and of congressional committees is of special interest, for in it Polk makes the same charges which were later made against himself when he became the leader of the administration forces.  "The 'factious opposition' as they are termed," said the letter,[18]

who really consist of the friends of the Constitution, & who do not support upon the fashionable doctrine of *faith* every measure emanating from the administration, merely because it is an administration measure, are to the extent of the power of the administration, and its friends literally proscribed."

Senate committees have been "arranged for effect," although there is but a small administrative majority in that body.

---

[15] There was, of course, no Democrat party at this time.

[16] For example, in a letter to Colonel William Polk, Dec. 14, 1826, he urged the latter to induce the legislature of North Carolina to give some public expression in favor of Jackson on January 8 (*Colonel Wm. Polk Papers*).

[17] Jackson to Polk, May 3, 1826, *Polk Papers*.

[18] Polk to Col. Wm. Polk, Dec. 14, 1826, *Colonel Wm. Polk Papers*.

''Studied majorities in favor of the administration have been placed on each, regardless, it would seem in some instances, of qualifications, talents, or experience. The selections were no doubt made, in conformity to a previous secret understanding, among the favorites at Court.''

In the House, also, ''some remarkable changes have been made in committees by the Speaker. They too have all been arranged for effect.'' The power of patronage, he continued, is corruptly used to ''sustain an administration, who never came into power by the voice of the people.'' How could a man who felt thus, within three short years, give his unqualified support to the administration of General Jackson? The answer is simple. Polk was, despite his ability and generally sound judgment, above all a party man.

At the close of his first term in Congress, Polk, in his appeal to his constituents for reëlection, laid special stress on his opposition to the Panama mission. Soon after taking his seat, he said it became his duty to act upon a proposition emanating from the executive, ''as novel in its character as it was believed to be in consequences.''[19] Not believing in entangling alliances, ''I was opposed to the Mission in every possible shape in which it could be presented, believing, as I did, that the United States had nothing to gain, but much to lose, by becoming members of such an extraordinary Assembly.'' The administration, lacking popularity, was trying to extend the powers of the federal government ''to an inordinate and alarming extent . . . and substitute patronage for public will.'' He was reëlected without difficulty and was, at the beginning of the next session of Congress, made a member of the Committee on Foreign Affairs.[20]

Throughout the Adams administration Polk corresponded with General Jackson. He not only supplied the hero of the Hermitage with information on passing events, but offered welcome suggestions and advice. ''I feel greatly obliged to you,'' wrote

---

[19] Polk's circular letter to his constituents, dated March 4, 1827. Printed copy in *Colonel Wm. Polk Papers.*

[20] *Jour. of H. R.*, 20 Cong., 1 sess., 25.

Jackson on one occasion,[21] ''for the information contained in your letter [on internal improvements] . . . and I truly appreciate those feelings of friendship which dictated the communication.''

When, in the spring of 1828, the subject of Jackson's execution of the six militia men was under investigation in Congress, Polk and Judge White procured and published a statement from General Gaines and a copy of Governor Blount's orders to Jackson.[22] It was Polk who first notified Jackson of his vindication by a committee, and it was to Polk that the General forwarded additional documents to be used in case it should become necessary.[23] Jackson approved Polk's advice that the attack of the opposition relating to this subject should be met by an active campaign of refutation, but that there should be no defense on the Burr episode until there had been some definite charge.[24] To another letter from Polk offering advice on political matters, Jackson answered: ''I have read your letter with great interest & attention—the reasons therein contained leaves no reason to doubt of the correctness of your conclusions, it is such as I had long since concluded to pursue.''[25] It is evident that the General already recognized the soundness of Polk's judgment and his shrewedness as a practical politician.

During the session of 1828–29 the Tennessee land bill again became the subject of animated discussion in the House. When he first introduced it, in 1825, Polk had the unanimous support of the people of Tennessee, and of the entire delegation in Congress from that state. But it now met with opposition from an

---

[21] Jackson to Polk, Dec. 4, 1826, *Polk Papers.*

[22] Polk to Jackson, April 13 and 15, 1828, *Jackson Papers.*

[23] Jackson to Polk, March 23, 1828, *Polk Papers.*

[24] The six militia men are made a hobby by the opposition, said Jackson, by which they ''can impose upon the credulity of the ignorant. . . . The plan there that you have suggested is the only one that can fairly meet, and effectively put down their hobby.'' ''I think your reflections on the Burr business is correct, no defence, without a charge'' (Jackson to Polk, May 3, 1828, *ibid.*).

[25] Jackson to Polk, Sept. 16, 1828, *ibid.*

unexpected quarter—an opposition which resulted in a bitter political feud. The eccentric David Crockett, for reasons best known to himself, had come to the conclusion that the "waste" lands, instead of being sold at a higher price for the support of schools, should be given or sold at a nominal price to poor settlers. He therefore offered an amendment to effect this purpose, and thus assumed the rôle of champion of the poor, as opposed to the rich who, as he said, could alone afford to take advantage of schools. Whatever his motives may have been, his opposition to a bill which he had ardently supported at the last session was at once attributed to the influence of Jackson's political enemies. The Tennessee delegation, wrote Polk,[26] were mortified to think that Crockett "should have coöperated with some of our bitterest and most vindictive political enemies, men, some of them of 'coffin hand bill' and 'six militia men' memory, and joined them in denouncing the Legislature of his state on the floor of Congress." Gales and other "Adamsites," Polk continued, are urging him on and reporting speeches that he never made, while he, it is said, will vote for Gales and Seaton for public printers and against Duff Green. They are making a tool of Crockett in order to deal a blow at Tennessee. Other members of the Tennessee delegation, said Polk, will furnish evidence against Crockett, but prefer not to do so, because the people might regard such action as persecution.

Crockett differed from his colleagues not merely on the land question; he opposed, also the attempt made by the Jackson party to introduce *viva voce* voting in the House so that they might brand the unfaithful. Several members, including Polk, Judge White, R. Desha, and J. C. Mitchell prepared statements concerning the boasts and the conduct of Crockett, and addressed them to Pryor Lea, one of their colleagues. The statements were based largely on assertions made by Crockett at White's lodgings in the presence of the men who had prepared them. Crockett

---

[26] Polk to McMillan, Jan. 16, 1829, *ibid.*

there produced his amendment and boasted that it would be adopted. When asked if he were willing to imperil the entire land bill by insisting upon his amendment, he replied in the affirmative. His constituents, he said, wished the land bill to be killed, for so long as the land continued to be property of the United States the people might use it free of charge. He went so far as to avow that, regardless of his instructions from the legislature, he would support the measures of any man who would vote for his amendment. All agreed that he had been fraternizing with Adams men in an effort to procure their votes. To Mitchell, Crockett openly admitted that Gales had printed— under Crockett's name—a speech which had never been delivered, so that the latter might distribute it among his constituents.

As a result, it was thought, of Crockett's opposition, the House laid the entire land bill on the table. Not satisfied with his victory, however, the incorrigible ''Davy,'' after returning to his district in western Tennessee, continued his attacks upon his colleagues. In public addresses he told the people that the land bill, had it passed, would have sacrificed the interests of the poor settlers. He was especially enraged by what he termed Polk's ''officious interference'' in the affairs of West Tennessee.[27] Apparently, Polk retaliated by publishing articles hostile to Crockett in a local paper of the latter's congressional district.[28]

Although Crockett did not succeed in his efforts to obtain cheap land for his constituents, he nevertheless had the pleasure of blocking the attempt made by his colleagues to procure school

---

[27] Adam R. Alexander to Polk, April 25; Polk to Alexander, May 1, 1829; *ibid.*

[28] In volume 80 of the *Polk Papers* is a series of five undated articles in Polk's handwriting headed ''Col. Crockett & his course in Congress.'' They are signed ''Several voters,'' and as Crockett is spoken of as ''our immediate representative,'' it is evident that they were to be understood as coming from his constituents. They were probably written for publication in some West Tennessee newspaper. They point out that Crockett had been elected as a friend of General Jackson, but that he has been supporting the old Adams-Clay party, ''under the orders of Daniel Webster'' and other Hartford Convention Federalists. He has been absent from duty in the House and has done ''literally nothing'' for the poor settlers of his district.

lands for their state.[29]  Until his defeat by Adam Huntsman in
1835 he remained in Congress and continued to oppose all measures championed by the followers of Jackson.  The importance of
his defection lies in the fact that it was the first breach in the
solidarity of the Jackson party in Tennessee.  One of the chief
critics of Crockett's apostasy in 1829 was Judge White, a man
destined ere long to become the center of a political storm that
would overthrow Jackson's supremacy in his state and seriously
weaken it in the nation.  For the time being Crockett stood practically alone.  Tennesseans generally were proud to uphold the
standard of their warrior hero.

As General Jackson entered the White House the specter of
executive usurpation vanished through the window and Polk,
like other critics of President Adams, now became a loyal supporter of executive policies.  In a letter to his constituents, dated
February 28, 1829,[30] Polk congratulated them on the recent
political victory, and dwelt at length on the significance of that
victory.  The contest had been "between the virtue and rights
of the people, on the one hand and the power and patronage of
their rules [rulers] on the other."  The people, said he, have
spoken with a voice of warning to future aspirants who may seek
to elevate themselves by bargain and intrigue.  The country is
still destined to be divided into political parties, and already
there is evidence that the partisans of Adams and Clay are preparing under the leadership of the latter to oppose the incoming
administration.  But Jackson has nothing to fear from his
enemies.  "He is expected to produce reform, correct abuses, and
administer the Constitution in its purity, and upon Republican
principles contemplated by its wise framers."  He has been chosen
by the people, and his administration will be both prosperous and
popular.

---

[29] By the acts of 1841 and 1846 Congress finally granted these lands to
Tennessee (Sioussat, "Some Phases of Tennessee Politics in the Jackson
Period," *Am. Hist. Rev.*, 1908, 58).

[30] Pamphlet in Tenn. State Library.

Having pronounced this encomium on the new régime, Polk reminded his constituents that he had contributed his ''feeble aid'' to the Jacksonian cause because he believed the General's principles to be orthodox and his purpose to be to serve the whole Union. According to others, however, the aid which he had contributed was not so *feeble* as his modesty had led him to assume. The Adams men in Tennessee gave him ''grate credit'' for compassing their mortifying defeat, and resolved, on that account, to defeat him if possible at the next election.[31]

Despite efforts of his enemies Polk was re-elected by a large majority. On his return to Washington he soon became leader of the administration forces in the House and, as will appear in the following chapter, acted as Jackson's aide-de-camp in the war on the Bank of the United States. With his customary discretion he declined to join with those who felt impelled to give unsolicited advice to the President regarding his social and his executive duties. Toward the end of Jackson's first year in office, and after political Washington had been arrayed in hostile camps by the crusade against Mrs. Eaton,[32] certain members of Congress met, by invitation of C. A. Wickliffe, of Kentucky, for the purpose of discussing the situation. Some of those who attended proposed that the President should be urged to remove Eaton from the cabinet, and that he should be advised to hold regular cabinet meetings. When consulted, Polk, White, Grundy, and other members from Tennessee declined to participate. They even refused to enter into a correspondence with Wickliffe concerning the subjects which had been discussed at the meeting.[33] By thus declining to assume the rôle of guardian over the President, Polk and his associates retained his confidence and good will. While each did his part in supporting Jackson's legislative program, Polk, more than any other, aided in his war against the Bank of the United States.

---

[31] Yell to Polk, Sept. 9, 1829, *Polk Papers*.

[32] See Parton, *Life of Andrew Jackson*, III, chap. xvii.

[33] Letters from Wickliffe to White, Grundy, Polk *et al.*, Dec. 24, 1831. Also other letters on this subject in the *Polk Papers*.

CHAPTER III

## POLK AND THE BANK OF THE UNITED STATES

In the bank controversy of Jackson's administration, which Sumner has called "one of the greatest struggles between democracy and the money power,"[1] Polk bore a prominent and difficult part. It was a part which required a thorough knowledge of the subject, alertness of mind, industry, and sound judgment. It required, also, an intimate knowledge of the plans and purposes of the President, and a certainty on Jackson's part that his confidence would not be misplaced. As this is a biography of Polk, not of Jackson, no attempt will be made to treat the bank war in all of its phases. Yet it seems necessary to consider certain aspects of this controversy in order to make clearer the part played by Polk as a member of the Committee of Ways and Means.[2]

It is generally held by historians that Jackson, when he became President in 1829, harbored no special hostility to the Bank of the United States, but that he was later won over by his friends, who had grievances of their own against the bank. But if Jackson's memory may be relied upon, this belief is contrary to the facts in the case. In 1833, in reply to a letter of inquiry from Polk, Jackson stated that the original draft of his inaugural address, written at the Hermitage, contained a paragraph giving his views on the bank, and another, his views on surplus revenue. After he had reached Washington, he said, he was persuaded by friends to omit both of these paragraphs, as it was thought that the subjects were better suited to an annual message to Congress.

---

[1] Sumner, *Andrew Jackson*, 227.

[2] The summary of the beginnings of the bank war, unless otherwise noted, is drawn largely from Sumner.

"Every one knows," he added, "that I have been always opposed to the U. States Bank, nay all Banks."[3]

In his first annual message Jackson questioned both the constitutionality and the expediency of the existing bank, and vaguely suggested the desirability of a bank "founded on the credit of the government and its revenues." This part of the message was referred by each house to a regular committee. In the Senate, Smith, of Maryland, reported from the Committee on Finance in favor of the bank. In the House, April 13, 1830, McDuffie, of South Carolina, reported from the Committee of Ways and Means, also in favor of the bank. McDuffie declared that the constitutionality of the bank had already been settled by decisions of the Supreme Court, that its expediency was beyond question, and that a bank modeled on the President's suggestions would be both inexpedient and dangerous. On May 10, the House, by a vote of eighty-nine to sixty-six, tabled resolutions which declared that the House would not consent to renew the charter of the bank, and on May 29 it likewise tabled resolutions calling for a report of the proceedings of the bank. It was evident that Congress would not support the President in his opposition to the bank. The defection of McDuffie, who had taken a leading part in the attack of the Jackson forces on the Adams administration, made it necessary for the President, when the time came for forcing the bank question to an issue, to look elsewhere for a leader on whom he could rely.

In his message for 1830, Jackson again proposed a bank as a "branch of the Treasury Department." This seemed to indicate a desire for something like the sub-treasury which was later recommended by President Van Buren. But Jackson's suggestions were vague and Congress gave them little serious consideration. An attempt of the Secretary of War, in July, 1831, to remove the pension funds from the New York branch of the bank,

---

[3] Polk to Jackson, Dec. 23, 1833. Jackson's reply is undated and written on the back of Polk's letter (*Polk Papers*).

met with opposition and failure.  By the end of 1831 the President's message was more pacific in tone, and the report of his Secretary, McLane, even spoke in favor of the bank.

The tone of the message only encouraged his political opponents, who were already making plans for the next Presidential election.  The bank took the initiative by addressing a memorial to Congress, asking that the bank be rechartered.  On January 9, 1832, this memorial was presented in the Senate by Dallas and in the House by McDuffie, both "bank Democrats."[4]  The committees of the two houses to which the subject was referred both reported in favor of a new charter, but with certain modifications.  The Jackson supporters now determined to fight a recharter with every possible weapon and demanded a searching investigation of the bank's conduct.  On February 23, Clayton, of Georgia, presented a motion in the House asking for the appointment of a select committee to conduct the investigation.  Technical objections were raised by friends of the bank, but Polk met their objections point by point and defeated them with their own weapons.[5]  In a speech delivered on this occasion, Polk condemned the bank for having the audacity to ask for a charter and then trying to prevent an investigation.  The inference to be drawn from such shrinking from scrutiny, said he, was that there was something "rotten in the state of Denmark."  In justification of his motion for a select committee, Clayton presented two lists of charges, which had been prepared for the purpose by Benton.[6]  The first specified seven instances of charter violation, involving forfeiture; the second gave fifteen instances of abuse, which required correction, though not involving forfeiture. The investigating committee which the Speaker selected submitted three reports (that of the majority unfavorable to the bank), but our present purpose does not warrant a discussion of either the reports or the charges.

---

[4] *Register of Debates*, 22 Cong., 1 sess., 54.

[5] Benton, *Thirty Years View*, I, 236.

[6] *Ibid.*, 237.  The charges are given on the next page.

In the Presidential campaign of 1832, Clay, seeing the *availability* of the bank question, made it a leading issue. In so doing he acted contrary to the better judgment of many friends of the bank, including its president, Nicholas Biddle. A bill passed Congress, providing for a recharter of the bank, and Jackson must now either admit defeat or kill the bill by his veto. He accepted the challenge, vetoed the bill, and appealed to the people to sustain him. He was reëlected by a large majority. Jackson's triumph at the polls was not in reality an endorsement of his veto, but he so regarded it and resolved to exterminate the "monster."

When the bank question first became prominent, the opinions of the administration party were not yet clearly defined. This party "was still only that group of factions which had united in opposition to Adams."[7] A large number of Jackson's most enthusiastic supporters were friends of the bank. Some of the political leaders, including Van Buren, had even signed petitions for the establishment of branch banks. Many politicians, as Niles said, had to "turn a short corner," when Jackson came out against the bank. More independent spirits, like McDuffie, refused to see the light and braved the executive wrath. Opposition in Congress made Jackson only the more determined to wage a relentless war upon the "corrupt institution," but his success would depend, to a considerable degree, on the orthodoxy and ability of the leaders of the administration forces in that body. Obviously the administration program could not be intrusted to the recently converted, whose past record would surely be held up to embarrass them. The fight must be led by those whose record was unassailable. Such was James K. Polk, of Tennessee, the friend and neighbor of the President. He gave to the administration his unqualified support, and, to quote his eulogist,[8] "in

---

[7] Sumner, *Andrew Jackson*, 248.

[8] Eulogy delivered at the time of Polk's death, by L. M. Smith, Newman, Ga. (*Papers of Mrs. Polk*, I).

the hour of darkness and danger, was unquestionably its chief reliance.''

When Congress convened in December, 1832, Polk was transferred from the Committee on Foreign Affairs to the Committee of Ways and Means. A confidential letter written by Jackson to Polk on December 16 discloses the temper of the President as well as the intimate relations of the two men:

The president with his respects to Col. J. K. Polk, of Congress, encloses him a note from Mr. Page of Philadelphia, a man of high character & in whom confidence may be placed. This is done to add to the information heretofore given the Col. *to show* him that the hydra of corruption is only *scotched, not dead*, and that the intent is thro' Wolf's recommendation, to destroy the vote of the people lately given at the ballot boxes & to rally around the recharter the present Session of Congress *two thirds*. . . . Call upon the Sec. of the Treasury who must agree with me that an investigation by Congress is absolutely necessary.

A postscript instructed Polk to have Sullivan, a government director, brought before the committee, and ended with a peremptory order ''Attend to this.''[9] Polk did ''attend'' to it, and the Secretary of the Treasury seems to have been persuaded that an investigation was necessary.

Though Jackson in his annual message, December 4, 1832, informed Congress that the report of the Secretary of the Treasury ''will exhibit the national finances in a highly prosperous state,'' nevertheless he advised the sale of all corporation (bank) stocks held by the government. He also urged that the safety of public deposits in the Bank of the United States was worthy of ''serious investigation'' by Congress. In response to these suggestions, the Committee of Ways and Means, of which Polk was a member, undertook an investigation of the charges which had been brought against the bank. The directors were summoned to Washington and examined upon oath,[10] and other testimony was taken to supplement the information which had

---

[9] *Polk Papers.*
[10] *Dem. Rev.*, May, 1838.

been gathered by the President. Reuben M. Whitney, the political scavenger of the administration, wrote to Polk from Baltimore, February 9, 1833, urging him to hasten the investigation, and warning him that Adams and Sergeant had been consulting with members of the committee. On February 11 Whitney wrote from Philadelphia advising Polk that the bank relied much on the ability of Verplanck[11] to outgeneral his opponents on the committee. While the investigation was in progress, Polk, on February 13, reported a bill to sell the bank stock owned by the government, but it failed in the House by a vote of one hundred and two to ninety-one. On March 1, Verplanck, for the majority of the Committee of Ways and Means, reported the bank to be sound and the public deposits safe, although it was admitted that in interfering with the plan of the government to pay off the three per cent securities the bank had exceeded its lawful powers. This report was adopted by the House. The *Globe* charged the majority with forcing the adoption of its report without having considered or presented the evidence which had been collected by its minority members. Many members, it said, who were not in favor of the bank had voted for adoption because, on the showing of the majority report, they could not conscientiously say that the bank was *not safe.*[12] Anticipating the character of the majority report, Polk prepared and submitted a minority report for himself and two other members of the committee. After criticizing the majority of the House for wishing to force the adoption without adequate consideration of evidence, and intimating with some justice that the committee had passed lightly over certain damaging testimony, Polk went with considerable detail into the question of the ''three per cents.'' These were securities bearing three per cent interest issued by the government

---

[11] Chairman of Ways and Means Committee and a friend of the bank. Whitney urged Polk to see that Gilmore, another member of the committee, should not be tampered with. Verplanck, he said, was not to be trusted and should not be permitted to have access to the testimony already taken, unless accompanied by ''one of our friends'' (*Polk Papers*).

[12] Washington *Globe*, March 6, 1833.

in 1792 for accrued interest on the Revolutionary debt.  The
government had decided to pay off about $6,500,000 of these, and
on March 24, 1832, the Secretary of the Treasury notified the
bank of his intention to pay this amount on the first of July.
Biddle requested the government to postpone payment until
October 1 and agreed to reimburse the treasury for the extra
three months' interest.  To this the government agreed.  When
asking for postponement, Biddle based his request largely on two
special reasons, neither of which implied that the bank wished any
accommodation for itself.  The assigned reasons were: (1) that
$9,000,000 of duty bonds would be payable on July 1, and mer-
chants would be inconvenienced should the three per cent debt
also fall due on that date; (2) should the much feared cholera
appear, business would be deranged, and if, in addition, the bank
should have to call in its money loaned to merchants, in order
to pay off the three per cents, great distress would result.

The government having agreed to delay payment, the bank
made secret but unsuccessful attempts to arrange with Thomas
W. Ludlow, New York agent of foreign holders, to postpone payment of part of this debt.  It then sent General Cadwallader, a
director of the bank, to Europe.  He made an agreement with
Baring Brothers & Co., of London, by which the Barings were
to arrange with certificate holders to postpone payment for one
year.  The Barings were to pay all holders who were unwilling
to wait and themselves to assume the debt to that amount.  As
a result of Cadwallader's agreement adjustments were made to
the extent of nearly five million dollars.  Every effort was made
to keep the transaction a secret, but it leaked out, and an account
of it was published in a New York paper.  Biddle then dis-
avowed the arrangement.

In his minority report Polk showed conclusively that the real
reasons for the bank's desire for postponement could not have
been those assigned by its president.  He gave a very clear
analysis of the evidence which had been collected by the committee

and made it plain that the bank had no intention of applying any of its money to the purpose for which it had said it desired these funds. He reached the inevitable conclusion that the bank had desired postponement because of its own weakness.

In his entire report, but especially in his arraignment of Biddle, Polk displayed those qualities which ever distinguished him in debate, and which fully justified the confidence reposed in him by General Jackson. His preparation was exhaustive and his arguments clear cut and logical. His language was well chosen and dignified, but at the same time scathing and merciless. "When the President of the Bank," said Polk, "not only induces the board to act for reasons unknown to themselves, but conceals even from the committees acts done in their names, something stronger than doubt almost seizes on the mind. When, to the consideration that the committees know little of the proceedings had in their names, is added the fact that every Government director is excluded from even that little, by being excluded from every committee, the Government at least has grounds to doubt whether its interests are safe in such keeping. When a show of the strength of the Bank is made, consisting of sums in specie and amounts in exchange, while the debts are secretly contracted, which have enabled the Bank to accumulate these funds, are concealed even from those who make the exhibition, there is just ground to doubt whether there be soundness in the institution, or proper precaution and responsibility in its management."[13]

When, in the spring of 1832, Benton prepared his catalogue of charges against the bank for Clayton to present in the House, he strained his imagination in order to make his list as long and as formidable as possible. Such a course may have been effective for campaign purposes, but many of Benton's charges were easily shown to be exaggerated or unfounded. For this reason his arraignment lost force and failed to convince the doubtful. Polk, on the contrary, confined his denunciation to points on which the

---

[13] *Reports of Committees*, 22 Cong., 2 sess., No. 121.

bank could offer no legitimate defense of its conduct.  His arguments were then, and are today, unassailable.[14]  Polk well knew
that neither his report nor his arguments on the floor would have
much weight in the House, as a majority of the members were
resolved to stand by the bank in spite of its faults.  He was
speaking to a wider audience and may have been already seeking
popular support for the impending executive assault on the bank.
However this may have been, he significantly pointed out that
the institution might be reached by the executive without any
assistance from Congress.  "Whether the existing facts," said
Polk in his report,

> are sufficient to justify the Executive in taking any steps against the
> Bank, authorized by its charter, is a matter for the decision of the proper
> officers, acting upon their own views and responsibility: any opinions by
> Congress can make it neither more nor less their duty to act.  Whatever,
> therefore, the opinions of the members of this committee might be as to
> the justice or policy of any Executive action, they deem it unauthorized
> and improper to express them officially.

In other words, it was for the executive alone to determine
whether the bank had violated its charter or had been guilty of
mismanagement, and, if so, to apply the remedy.

Whether, at the time Polk made his report, Jackson had resolved upon a removal of the deposits from the bank as a proper
remedy, we are unable to say.[15]  If he had, Polk, who was certainly in his confidence, was doubtless aware of the fact.  Polk's
remarks on executive responsibility and his indifference to the
opinions of Congress seem to indicate that such was the case.
He may even have suggested removal of the deposits to the President, but of this there seems to be no direct evidence.  It is

---

[14] "Its facts and reasonings," said the *Globe* (March 6, 1833), "are
perfectly irresistible.  It exposes the subterfuges and self-contradicted
testimony under which that corrupt and corrupting institution has shel-
tered itself, in a manner so clear and convincing, that it must satisfy
every honest man who reads it, of the utter profligacy of its management."

[15] To quote Sumner on this point:  "Lewis says that he does not know
who first proposed the removal of the deposits, but that it began to be
talked of in the inner administration circles soon after Jackson's second
election" (Sumner, *Jackson*, 297).

worthy of note, however, that the well-known paper of September 18, 1833, in which Jackson announced to his cabinet his intention to remove the deposits, makes use of many of the same facts and employs much the same reasoning that Polk had already used in his minority report.

The minority report arrayed against its author all the power and the venom of the bank party, and measures were taken to prevent his reëlection to Congress. Friends of the bank held a meeting at Nashville and denounced his report. He was accused of destroying credit in the West by proclaiming that the people were unworthy of mercantile confidence. Handbills signed ''Muhlenging'' were circulated, alleging that Polk as a member of Congress had been opposed to pensioning Revolutionary soldiers.[16] Polk met the issue squarely as a foe of the bank, and during the campaign stress was laid on the bank affiliations of Bradford, his opponent. Under the circumstances, Polk's success or defeat was regarded as of more than local importance. ''Your friends here,'' wrote Donelson from Washington, ''take a deep interest in your election and are all well apprised of the instruments which are employed to defeat you.''[17] Donelson showed his own interest by inclosing in his letter evidence to be used against Bradford. In 1827 Bradford had applied to Adams for an appointment as marshall. His friends had sent letters of recommendation representing him to be a friend of Adams and an opponent of Jackson. From the files in the State Department, without the knowledge of the Secretary, Donelson had copied extracts, and now sent them to Polk, to be used at his discretion so long as Donelson's name was not mentioned. A speech made by Bradford in the Tennessee Senate in 1831, in favor of rechartering the bank, was also reprinted and circulated among his constituents. It was a spirited contest, but Polk was reëlected by a majority of over three thousand votes.

---

[16] *Dem. Rev.*, May, 1838. Polk's ''Circular Letter'' to his constituents.

[17] A. J. Donelson to Polk, May 30, 1833, *Polk Papers*. The letter was marked ''*Private and for your eye alone.*'' There is nothing to indicate whether Jackson was cognizant of Donelson's act.

As soon as he was safely elected, Polk, with the assistance of Cave Johnson, began a quiet campaign for the Speakership.[18] He received encouragement from his political friends, but the expected vacancy[19] did not occur and he continued his labors as a floor member.

The adoption by Congress of Verplanck's report did not in the least alter Jackson's opinion of the character of the bank. On August 31, 1833, he[20] sent Polk a confidential letter in which he inclosed a report of the bank directors. Polk was authorized to use the facts contained in the report, but not to divulge that they had come from the President. Jackson regarded these facts as proof positive that Biddle had been using the people's money for purposes of corruption.

By September Jackson was ready to carry into effect his plan to deprive the bank of the use of government money. Duane had in May succeeded McLane in the Treasury Department and was expected to do the bidding of the President. On September 18, Jackson read to his cabinet the well-known paper in which he asserted that the deposits ought to be removed. Among the reasons assigned for the proposed action were the political activities of the bank, its attempt to postpone payment of the three per cents, and the fact that it had come into existence by an unconstitutional law. He would not, he said, dictate to the Secretary, but the President himself, assuming all responsibility, had

---

[18] This subject will be considered at length in another place.

[19] Stevenson was expected to accept a foreign mission and not be a candidate for reëlection. He resigned later for this purpose.

[20] The signature is cut off, but the letter is in Jackson's unmistakable hand. He says: "You will find from the inclosed that I have at last thro the Government Directors got a *Small peep* into their expense account, and the corruption on the morals of the people.

"In two years $80 odd thousand expended to corrupt the people & buy a recharter of that mamoth of corruption. I think when these scenes of corruption are made known to the people and that by an order of the board of directors, the whole funds of the Bank are placed at the disposal of Mr. Biddle to appropriate as he pleases [cut out with signature] most bold specious of corruption ever practiced by any body of people in the most corrupt governments" (*Polk Papers*).

decided that, after October 1, government money should no longer be deposited in the bank, and that all money there on that date should be drawn out as needed.  Duane declined to give the necessary order to effect Jackson's purpose and later refused to resign. He was dismissed and Attorney General Taney commissioned to take his place, September 23, 1833.[21]  Taney gave the order, and the "hydra of corruption" was at last more than "scotched."

Jackson's high-handed act produced much excitement throughout the country.  The bank issued a paper[22] in reply to the President's charges, and a bitter conflict was inevitable as soon as Congress should assemble.  "At such a crisis it became important to have at the head of the Committee of Ways and Means a man of courage to meet, and firmness to sustain, the formidable shock. Such a man was found in Mr. Polk, and he proved himself equal to the occasion."[23]

Congress met on December 2, 1833, and, as a result of the recent election, the administration forces were in unequivocal control of the House.  Jackson's message, dealing among other topics with his removal of the deposits, and accompanied by a report of the Secretary of the Treasury on the same subject, was sent to Congress on the third of December.  A contest at once arose over the reference of both message and report.  Friends of the bank wished them referred to the Committee of the Whole House, where the enormity of the President's conduct might be discussed without limit.  The Jackson supporters, on the other hand, wanted them referred to the Committee of Ways and Means, of which Polk had recently been made chairman.  On the tenth, McDuffie succeeded in carrying a resolution to refer Taney's report to the Committee of the Whole.  On the eleventh, Clay, of Alabama, presented a resolution to refer that part of the President's message relating to finance to the Committee of Ways and Means, but to this McDuffie and others offered vigorous

---

21 Mosher, *Executive Register*, 113.

22 *Niles' Reg.*, XLV, 248.          23 *Dem. Rev.*, May, 1838.

objections. On the same day, Polk moved a reconsideration of the vote which had referred Taney's report to the Committee of the Whole, and he was at once accused by the opposition of aiming to have it referred to his own committee so that he could smother the question. Chilton, of Kentucky, who was especially opposed to a reconsideration, did not wish to see "the whole weight of this massive Government imposed on the shoulders of his friend from Tennessee,"[24] and urged that the question ought to be left with the larger committee so that all might discuss it.

Discussion was the last thing which Polk desired, and precedent supported his contention that the reference made under McDuffie's resolution had been entirely irregular. Never before, he said, had a great subject of national policy been referred, in the first instance, to the Committee of the Whole on the state of the Union. The course which he advocated was simply the usual one. In the argument Polk was the equal of any of his opponents. When they told him that the Secretary's reasons had been stated in his report, thereby making investigation by a committee unnecessary, Polk replied that the report contained various statements of fact which might involve the bank's charter, and that these facts should be carefully investigated. He also reminded them of their assertions that the state banks in which the President had deposited public money were unsafe, and that the public faith had been violated. "Is it not proper, then, for a committee of the House to inquire by which party the contract was violated?"[25] After much discussion the House, on December 17, decided, by a yea and nay vote of one hundred and twenty-four to one hundred and two, to reconsider its vote on McDuffie's resolution.

Having won on the question of reconsideration, Polk now fulfilled Chilton's prophecy by moving that Taney's report be

---

[24] *Cong. Globe*, 23 Cong., 1 sess., 24. All arguments made in the House, unless otherwise noted, are taken from the *Globe,* and may be found under dates mentioned in the text.

[25] *Ibid.*, p. 25, Dec. 12, 1833.

referred to the Committee of Ways and Means. McDuffie immediately moved that Polk's committee be instructed to "report a joint resolution providing that the public revenue hereafter collected be deposited in the Bank of the United States, in conformity with the public faith pledged in the charter of the said bank." It is not at all likely that McDuffie expected his motion to carry, but he gained what was doubtless his main object—an opportunity for a discussion of all phases of the question. This move on the part of the opposition brought from the President a letter instructing Polk to make a short reply and then to call for the previous question;[26] but two long months of debate had yet to elapse before Polk's committee would be able to consider the Secretary's report, unhampered by annoying instructions.

Binney, of Pennsylvania, interrupted the discussion on December 18 by presenting a memorial from the bank. The substance of this document was a declaration that the bank was entitled to the deposits unless Congress should decide otherwise. On Polk's motion, the memorial was referred to his committee. On the same day, Chilton moved to instruct the Committee of Ways and Means to report a joint resolution directing the Secretary of the Treasury to restore the deposits to the bank, but, on the request of McDuffie, this motion was withdrawn.

On the main question of referring the Secretary's report with instructions to Polk's committee, McDuffie made the opening speech (December 19). The gist of his remarks was that removal of the deposits was illegal because the President had usurped authority in performing it. Even the President, he said, had admitted that the authority rested with the Secretary, and, if so, Jackson could not lawfully assume it. On December 30, Polk replied in defense of the administration. As usual he had thoroughly prepared himself for his task. He was ready with authorities and precedents to support his own contentions as well as to refute those of his opponents. So thorough and

---

[26] Jackson to Polk, Dec. 18, 1833, *Polk Papers*.

inclusive was his array of facts and arguments that, although the debate lasted nearly two months longer, there was little for any other administration member to add. Every opposition member who spoke to the question devoted most of his time to answering the arguments of Polk. He was regarded by all as the chief supporter, in the House, of the President and his policies. Jackson himself, on his next visit to Tennessee, told the people of Nashville that ''Polk for the hard service done in the cause deserves a Medal from the American people.''[27]

So far as a reference of Taney's report to the Committee of Ways and Means, as well as the attempt to instruct that committee, were concerned, Polk showed without difficulty that the opposition members were clearly in the wrong. The memorial of the bank setting forth its grievances, and likewise the charges of the government directors against the bank, had, after full deliberation, been referred by the House to the Committee of Ways and Means; there was consequently no good reason why the Secretary's report should not be sent to the same committee. Polk intimated that the real reason for this attempt to interrupt the normal procedure was the desire of his opponents to ''flood the country with inflammatory speeches,'' telling the people that panic must result from the removal of the deposits. Should the committee be compelled, said Polk, to act under the instructions proposed by McDuffie, it would be prejudging the question; investigation would be superfluous, and a report made under such instructions would be absurd. The task of justifying the arbitrary conduct of the President was more difficult. By many, Polk's argument on this subject may not be regarded as convincing.[28] But whether Jackson had acted within his rights or had

---

[27] Robert M. Burton to Polk, Aug. 27, 1834, *Polk Papers*. Polk's speech may be found in *Cong. Deb.*, X, 2.

[28] When Polk was a candidate for the Presidency, the *National Intelligencer* (Sept. 21, 1844) said: ''Throughout the whole of Mr. Polk's course in Congress in relation to the Bank of the United States, there was exhibited a zeal not only without knowledge, but often, we must think, against conviction.''

been guilty of gross usurpation, no one could have defended his course more ably than did the chairman of the Committee of Ways and Means. A slightly new turn was given to the discussion by the motion of Jones, January 14, 1834, to substitute instructions for those submitted by McDuffie. McDuffie's instructions, as Polk had pointed out, prejudged the whole question, and were mandatory as to the findings of the committee. Those now offered by Jones simply instructed the committee to "inquire into the expediency of depositing the revenues hereafter collected," not in the Bank of the United States, but in state banks.[29] It was now a question of compulsory restoration of the deposits, on the one hand; on the other, discretion for the committee as to its findings, after the expediency of deposit in state banks had been investigated.

While the question of reference with instructions was being debated, memorials from groups of individuals, some for and some opposed to the bank, were sent to the House. One came from the Maine legislature, upholding Jackson and pronouncing the bank unconstitutional. Efforts were made to refer some of the memorials to select committees, but, usually, on Polk's motion, they were all sent to the Committee of Ways and Means. Polk and his committee were therefore the objects of much criticism and even abuse. The sole purpose of both Taney and Polk, according to Binney, was to sustain the administration, without thought of the country's welfare. Polk's object in wishing to get possession of Taney's report, in the opinion of Moore, of Virginia, was to stifle debate, to put the stamp of approval on the report, and then to send it forth to deceive the people and prejudice them against the bank. A motion made by Hubbard to refer to Polk's committee the President's message on the re-

---

[29] On February 19, Mardis, of Alabama, offered a resolution, "That the Committee of Ways and Means be instructed to inquire into the expediency of reporting a bill requiring the Secretary of the Treasury to deposit the public moneys of the United States in State banks." There was much debate on this resolution, but, as it was later withdrawn by the mover, it will not be considered in the present discussion.

fusal of the bank to surrender its books and papers as pension agent, caused Watmough, of Pennsylvania, to think that "the Committee of Ways and Means have got a voracious appetite, and seem desirous to devour all that comes before the House." It was a question of law, he said, and should be referred to the Judiciary Committee. He was supported by Barringer, of North Carolina, who asserted that Polk's committee was trying to grasp all important legislation so that it might be shaped in the administration mold. But oppositon was futile; the message went with the memorials to appease the "voracious appetite" of Polk and his colleagues. There, too, went Taney's report, the main subject of discussion. On February 18, 1834, the two months' debate was closed by invoking the previous question, and Polk's original motion (of December 17, 1833) to refer to his own committee Taney's report on the removal of the deposits was at last carried by a yea and nay vote of one hundred and thirty to ninety-eight. All motions to instruct the committee had already been voted down, and the House now refused to hear new resolutions for this purpose. The victory of the committee was complete, and it could proceed, unhampered, to perform its part in the executive program. Polk's successful defense of the administration brought him letters of commendation from all parts of the country, and especially from his own state. Governor Carroll wrote from Nashville to compliment Polk on his "temperate, able and successful vindication of the President," and added that "this is almost the universal sentiment here."[30] Polk's services

---

[30] Governor Carroll to Polk, Jan. 23, 1834, *Polk Papers.* John H. Dew, member of the Tennessee legislature, wrote to Polk, Jan. 21: "Your argument in defence of the Executive for the exercise of an ordinary power, expressly conferred on him by the Constitution of the U. S. and fully sanctioned by precedent & custom evinces a most intimate acquaintance with the multifarious movements that have been made upon the great American political *Chess board* from the organization of the Government to the present *Crisis.* You have shown most incontestibly, from laborious research into public records and documents that the President and his Cabinet have in all things acted strictly within the sphere of their Constitutional duty and rule of action." There are many similar letters among the *Polk Papers.*

as guide in the proposed constitutional convention of his state were eagerly sought, and he was much talked about as a desirable candidate for Governor of Tennessee, and for Speaker of the national House of Representatives. Even your enemies say, said a letter from his home town, that "you could be elected for anything in Maury."[31]

Before the vote on the reference of Taney's report had been taken, the Committee of Ways and Means had already made it quite clear that nothing favorable to the bank might be expected from them. On February 11, Polk reported for the committee on Jackson's message against the bank—the message in which the bank was denounced for not surrendering the books and money held by it in its capacity as pension agent. Polk fully sustained the President and refuted every contention of the bank. "The committee," so read the report, "cannot condemn, in terms too strong, the conduct of the bank in this transaction." He reported a bill to the effect that, in future, pensions should be paid by officers of the government, and not left in "the hands of an irresponsible corporation."

By March 7, the committee was ready to submit its opinions on the removal of the deposits. These opinions were placed before the House on that date, and it was generally understood that they had been drawn up by the chairman. They held that both the removal of the deposits and the placing of this money in state banks were unquestionably legal. The committee believed the bank to be unconstitutional, but, even if it were not, its conduct had been such that it ought not to be rechartered, and therefore, the deposits ought not to be restored. They expressed full confidence in the competence of state banks to perform all necessary services for the government, and revived Jefferson's well-known arguments to prove that such an institution as the Bank of the United States had never been contem-

---

[31] T. H. Cahal to Polk, Jan. 2, 1834, *Polk Papers*. Maury was Polk's county.

plated by the framers of the Constitution. For his own reputation, Polk might well have stopped here; but he repeated the
arguments of the day that ''none can doubt the power of the
bank to create embarrassment,'' and he proceeded to show that
this had been done by loaning money at a given place during one
month, and then calling it in during the next. Such action may,
indeed, have been within the power of the bank, but banking
institutions seldom resort to that form of amusement. This may
have been one of the occasions noted by the *National Intelligencer*[32] on which Polk's zeal was not supported by either
''knowledge'' or ''conviction.'' However this may be, Polk had
not been found wanting in his defense of the President. His
services as a party leader of the House were none the less efficient because history may pronounce some of his arguments
untenable.

The House, on March 12, suspended the rules so that Polk
might have his report made a special order and thereby hasten
its adoption. This action was denounced by Adams, who said
that Polk, acting under royal prerogative, would soon close all
debate by the previous question and deprive the minority of its
constitutional right of discussion. But Adams could not very
well complain, as Polk pointed out, because Adams himself had
voted for the previous question when the bill to recharter the
bank had been forced through the House.

Polk did not, however, immediately call for the previous question, and his critics made the most of the opportunity afforded
them. Instead of reporting on Taney's reasons for removing the
deposits, said Wilde, of Georgia (March 19), the committee had
reported an argument—that the bank ought not to be rechartered. They had ''gone beyond the President and the Secretary,
in claiming power for the Executive.'' Harden, of Kentucky,
admired the ''master-stroke of policy'' of the committee in pronouncing against recharter when that question was not before it,

---

[32] *National Intelligencer*, Sept. 21, 1844. See above, note 28.

but it had given no information except a reëcho of Taney's report. McDuffie criticized Polk for shutting off debate, but he gave him full credit for acting "with a tact and skill and zeal worthy of a better cause."[33] McDuffie concluded his argument on April 4, Mason called for the previous question, and the debate on Polk's report was closed. Resolutions prepared by the committee, providing among other things for a select committee to investigate the bank, were quickly adopted. The new committee, appointed by the Speaker on the seventh, repaired at once to Philadelphia whence Mason, one of its members, kept Polk informed of its proceedings by confidential letters.[34] But the bank refused to submit its books for examination, and the special committee soon (May 22) reported that it had been unable to perform the duty assigned to it by the House. While investigation thus ended in failure, nothing was left undone which in any way depended upon the vigilance or activity of Polk. On June 13, he succeeded in sending to the table two joint resolutions from the Senate: one, disapproving of the removal of the deposits; the other, directing that the deposits be restored to the Bank of the United States.

By adopting Polk's report the House had put its stamp of approval on the President's act in removing the deposits, but the question of depositing this money in state banks had still to be considered. Jackson's opponents had always contended that, without the authority of Congress, the President had no right to intrust public money to such banks. On April 22, 1834, Polk reported from his committee a bill for regulating these state deposit banks. It was based on the report of the Secretary of

---

[33] McDuffie said he had criticized Jackson in the hope of bringing out Jackson's supporters. "The honorable member from Tennessee did come out boldly and manfully, took his position, and, whatever views I may entertain of his generalship, I am ready to bear testimony that the position which he has assumed is the only one he could assume, without leaving unprotected and undefended the very part which it was his duty to defend" (April 3, 1834). I have converted this into direct discourse. It is reported *indirectly* in the *Cong. Globe*.

[34] Mason to Polk, May 5 and May 10, 1834, *Polk Papers*.

the Treasury.  Adams (June 7) attempted to filibuster by moving a resolution to call on the Secretary of the Treasury to lay before the House the names of officers and stockholders of such banks, as well as numerous unimportant details.  Polk promptly met this by moving an amendment which required a similar statement from the Bank of the United States.  A request made by Adams (June 13) that Polk should withdraw his amendment gave the latter an opportunity, not only to defend the administration, but to employ that sarcasm and scorn which ever made him feared as a debater.  It was far more necessary, Polk believed, to require information from the old bank than from the new banks, because the government was a stockholder as well as a depositor in the Bank of the United States.  It was also more necessary, he said, because that bank

had set itself up in antagonistic position to the Government, had denounced the Executive as a tyrant, usurper, and despot, and more recently, had denounced and insulted the representatives of the people, because they had sustained him in his measures.  But, according to the gentleman, this immaculate and inoffensive Bank of the United States must not be looked into, though the affairs of the State banks must be thoroughly probed.[35]

Polk's bill for regulating the deposits in state banks passed the House, June 24, 1834, by a vote of one hundred and twelve to ninety, but it was now near the end of the session and the Senate at its last meeting, June 30, laid the bill on the table.  In the House, at least, the friends of the bank had been defeated on every point, and the acts of the President had been fully vindicated.  The completeness of this vindication was due, in no small measure, to the industry and vigilance of the chairman of the Committee of Ways and Means.

---

[35] Polk here read from the *National Gazette* an article in which the bank directors had denounced Jackson and the House.

## CHAPTER IV

## POLK-BELL CONTEST FOR THE SPEAKERSHIP

During his canvass for reëlection to Congress in 1833, Polk seems to have decided to become a candidate for the Speakership in the event of his success at the polls. Public attention had recently been called to this office by a rumor that the Speaker of last session, Andrew Stevenson, was to be given a diplomatic appointment and would therefore not be a candidate for reëlection.

Whether Polk's idea of becoming a candidate originated with himself or was suggested to him by friends is uncertain. There are among his papers letters which show that, soon after his election early in August, he began to sound his friends on the subject. Other letters make it equally clear that he was being considered for the office by men who knew nothing of his own initiative in the matter. Cave Johnson, his most intimate friend, aided him by soliciting the support of their political associates.

His first campagn for the Speakership was soon abandoned, for Stevenson did not go abroad as soon as had been expected. However, his aspirations met with some encouragement. In answer to a letter from Polk on the subject, C. C. Clay, of Alabama, wrote: "Should the vacancy, of which you speak, occur, I know of no other member, whose election to fill it would be more agreeable to my own feelings than yours." On the same day Clay said in a letter to Cave Johnson: "I am pleased with your suggestion of Polk as the successor of Stevenson, and hope we may be able so to manage, as to effect the object."[1] A week later Leavitt, a member from Ohio, informed Polk of Stevenson's

---

[1] Clay to Polk, Aug. 19, 1833; same to Johnson, same date, *Polk Papers*.

rumored appointment to a foreign mission.  He did not know, he said, whether Polk had been approached, but he hoped that he would be chosen to fill the vacancy.[2]  Other letters of similar import were received; one from Cave Johnson[3] said that he had been writing letters to members of the House in an effort to bring about concerted action in Polk's behalf.

At this early date Jackson seems to have taken no special interest in Polk's political promotion, although he was ready to give it his approval.  Having corresponded with the President on the subject, Grundy informed Polk[4] that he had "received an answer from the highest quarter of the most satisfactory & encouraging character."  He advised Polk to induce his friends to write to members of the House, but to avoid writing such letters himself.  James Walker, a brother-in-law of Polk, went to Washington in October in quest of a mail contract.  After an interview with the President in relation to Polk's aspirations, Walker reported that *"he gives in to them I think decidedly and frankly."*[5]  Jackson told Walker that some persons believed it would not "look very modest" to solicit the Speakership for Tennessee, as well as the Presidency.  The President himself ridiculed this objection and assured Walker that Polk's election would in no respect embarrass the administration.  Walker got the impression, however, that William B. Lewis was in favor of Bell.  Here may have been the beginning of Polk's intense dislike for Lewis.  Another interview with Jackson convinced Walker that the President was not only willing but eager to have Polk chosen Speaker of the House.  He was charmed with the Vice-President and advised Polk to make it known to Van Buren that he would support him for the Presidency.[6]

---

[2] H. H. Leavitt to Polk, Aug. 26, 1833, *ibid.*

[3] Johnson to Polk, Aug. 26, 1833, *ibid.*

[4] Grundy to Polk, Sept. 13, 1833, *ibid.*

[5] Walker to Polk, Oct. 22, 1833, *ibid.*

[6] Walker to Polk, Nov. 7, 1833, *ibid.*  From Yell, also, came a letter (Dec. 1) stating that in his opinion Van Buren could throw the Speakership to whom he pleased.

The twenty-third Congress convened on December 2, 1833, and Stevenson was reëlected Speaker on the first ballot—virtually without opposition. As Polk's candidacy had been contingent upon Stevenson's refusal to stand for reëlection he accepted the party program without evidence of disappointment. The committees were announced on the ninth, with Polk at the head of the Committee of Ways and Means—the appointment having been made, it was said, upon the suggestion of General Jackson. The chairmanship of this committee is an important position under normal conditions. At this time, when the President was preparing for his last and greatest contest with the bank, it was undoubtedly the most responsible position in the House. But Polk was not the man to shirk responsibility, and his success in outgeneraling the bank party soon demonstrated that the administrtaion had been fortunate in its choice of a leader.

Polk had scarcely accepted his new appointment when letters came from friends at home urging him to become a member of the proposed Tennessee constitutional convention. "A great number of people," wrote James Walker,[7] "will be satisfied in no other way than for you to be in the Convention."

While there seems to have been a general desire for Polk's services in the convention and a feeling that he of all men in the state was best fitted to draft a new constitution, yet some, even among his friends, appear to have doubted his ability to cope with his new duties in Congress. His brother-in-law, A. C. Hayes, wrote from Columbia, Tennessee, that Polk's friends were pleased, and his enemies mortified, by his elevation to the chairmanship of the Committee of Ways and Means. But he added: "I have, however, heard it suggested by some of your *good friends,* that you may not leave the present congress with the same reputation with which you entered—'they fear, that there is too great weight of talent against you on the Bank Question.' "[8]

---

[7] Walker to Polk, Dec. 18, 1833, *Polk Papers.*
[8] Hayes to Polk, Jan. 10, 1834, *ibid.*

Polk himself had no such fears, for self-confidence was one of his chief characteristics; difficulties never appalled him when party services were to be performed. He was already occupied with his committee and therefore declined to serve in the convention.

On June 2, 1834, Speaker Stevenson presented to the House his long expected resignation. On the same day John Bell, of Tennessee, was chosen to succeed him. On the first ballot Polk received forty-two votes to Bell's thirty. Both men gained as the balloting proceeded, but Bell's gains—due to accessions from the anti-Jackson camp—were larger than those of his rival. When the tenth ballot was counted the tellers reported that Bell had received one hundred and fourteen votes—more than enough to elect—while his nearest competitor, Polk, had received but seventy-eight.

The brief official record of this day's proceedings which one finds in the *Congressional Globe* gives not the slightest hint of the heartburnings and bitterness which were associated with this choice of a Speaker. From this election, however, resulted a political feud which split the Jackson party in Tennessee, and materially weakened it in other states. From this day forth Polk and Bell were uncompromising enemies—each determined to overthrow the political power of the other. As the opponents of the President had helped to elect Bell, the new Speaker was forced to ally himself more and more with this element. His endorsement of Judge White's candidacy aroused the ire of the President. Regarding both men as apostates and traitors, Jackson resolved to employ every means at his disposal for the purpose of crushing them. Polk profited much by this new turn of affairs. He was already fighting the battles of the President in the war on the bank. He had always enjoyed the confidence and good opinion of Jackson; but Bell's defection still more identified the Speaker's rival, Polk, with the party of the President. In a greater degree than ever was Polk now regarded as the administration leader of the House.

The antecedents of the Speakership election and the attitude of Polk and Bell toward adhering to a party program are told in a statement prepared, at Polk's request, by Cave Johnson. Johnson was, of course, one of Polk's closest friends, but his statement seems credible and is corroborated by the testimony of other members of the House. It reads as follows:

It was supposed many months before the vacancy actually happened, that it would take place & several individual friends of the administration were spoken of as suitable to fill the vacancy, among the number you & Col. Bell were esteemed the most prominent. None seemed to doubt that if so many friends of the administration were run, that the election would be finally settled by the votes of the opponents of the administration, who would of course cast their votes upon the man least acceptable to the President & his friends. This was a result the friends of the administration wished to evade—and therefore it was proposed, that the friends of the administration should have a meeting that the strength of the several candidates should be ascertained, that the strongest should be run as the candidate of the administration party & the others should yield their pretensions & support him. You unhesitatingly determined, that you was willing to have the election submitted to the friends of the administration & let them decide who should be the candidate & that you would support the man thus selected. You was considered I believe finally by all parties as the administration candidate & so far as I knew, heard or believe every vote which you received except one was given by the friends of the administration. . . . I understood, from members who conversed with Col. Bell upon the subject whose names I can give if necessary, that he refused to submit his claims to the Speakers chair to the friends of the President, & in consequence of his refusal no such meeting was holden. He received the votes of the opponents of the administration & was elected by them in conjunction with a few votes received by him among the friends of the administration.[9]

In a similar statement,[10] John McKintry, of Alabama, charged Bell with having refused to submit his claims to Jackson's friends and with having stated "that he did not expect to be elected by the administration party in the House, that he did not expect to get of that party more than 25 or 30 votes, [and] that he was supported by the opposition & elected by them." McKintry was

---

[9] Johnson to Polk, Sept. 12, 1834, *ibid.*

[10] McKintry to Polk, Aug. 13, 1834, *ibid.* C. C. Clay, of Alabama, in a letter to Polk (Sept. 13) says that Bell was generally considered to be an opposition candidate.

equally positive that Polk had readily consented to submit his claims to his party friends and to abide by their decision.

Up to the time that Bell became a candidate for Speaker, he was considered to be a loyal supporter of General Jackson. He was so regarded in his own state as well as in the House of Representatives. When the rumor that Stevenson would not be a candidate for reëlection was first circulated, it will be remembered that Jackson was consulted as to his attitude toward Polk's candidacy. Although the President was willing to give his approval, he did not appear to have any special interest in Polk's elevation. There is no evidence that the General, at that time, harbored any ill feeling toward Bell. Indeed, James Walker gathered from various conversations that Major Lewis preferred Bell for Speaker. But Bell's conduct during his recent campaign for the office changed all this. He was first distrusted, then openly denounced, by the President and his friends.

Congress adjourned shortly after the election of a Speaker, and in the final rush of legislation little attention was given to the contest between the two candidates. It was not apparent at the time that the controversy would have any vital significance in national politics. The first important result of the victory of Bell over Polk was its effect upon the influence of the two men in their home state.

For some time past Polk had been considered a desirable candidate for governor, and after his defeat by Bell his friends in Tennessee renewed their offer to support him for this office. His ever loyal brother-in-law, James Walker, began on his own initiative to agitate Polk's claims to the office and to assure him of the certainty of success. He informed Polk[11] that he had not lost prestige on account of his recent defeat, and that he could beat any man in Tennessee if he would consent to run. Letters offering support and encouragement came from Cave Johnson and other party leaders of the state. James Standifer assured

---

[11] Walker to Polk, June 30, 1834, *Polk Papers*.

Polk that he had not ''seen the first man but what says they would rather have James K. Polk's standing than John Bell's Speaker's place and all, the people are for the man that stands up boldly for the President and his measures, they are for no other sort of man these times.''[12] The sentiment expressed in this letter was becoming general in Tennessee, namely, that Polk and Grundy were the administration leaders in the state, and that Bell had deserted to the enemy. This view was impressed upon the President, who was then spending his vacation at the Hermitage, and it was about this time that he declared Polk to be deserving of a medal for ''the hard service done in the cause.''

Much resentment was aroused in Middle Tennessee by a speech delivered by Bell at Murfreesborough on October 6, 1834. The circuit court was then in session and Bell took advantage of the occasion to address the people there assembled. There are conflicting reports as to the substance of this speech, but in general the account of it given to Polk in a letter from his brother-in-law, John W. Childress, seems to be corroborated by the testimony of many who heard the speech delivered. According to this letter[13] Bell was very severe in his criticism of all who had questioned the propriety of his course in Congress, particularly during his contest for the Speakership. He asserted that all his competitors except one had treated him in a gentlemanly manner, leaving it to be inferred that Polk had not. ''He vaunted greatly,'' said Childress,

his adherence to principle, his unwavering support of the president, and said distinctly, and in these words, that had he not been true and firm to the administration, he could have changed the small majority in the house upon the Bank question by going over and taking his friends with him and thereby have defeated all the measures of the President.

His enemies, he said, had managed to delay Speaker Stevenson's appointment to a foreign mission in the hope of weakening his

---



[12] Standifer (member of Congress from Tennessee) to Polk, Aug. 25, 1834, *ibid.*

[13] Childress to Polk, Oct. 7, 1834, *ibid.*

(Bell's) prospects and strengthening their own (i.e., Polk's), but of this the President was of course not aware. He alleged that although other tricks had been employed in an effort to defeat him, he still had the confidence of the entire party except six or seven individuals. He said

that he was willing to give Jackson's experiment [state banks] a fair trial and if it did not answer the wants of the people, that then he *might* be in favor of a National Bank. That he had no idea that a metalic currency would answer the purpose of a circulating medium and almost said it was Demagoguic in any one that would say so.

W. R. Rucker, another brother-in-law, said in a letter[14] that the speech was "most intemperate and ill advised" and that many of Bell's friends did not approve such "abuse" of Polk and General Jackson.

Under the circumstances, Bell's speech was certainly ill advised, even if every assertion made in it had been true. Moreover, even though reports of the speech may have exaggerated its abusive character, yet certain remarks attributed to the speaker were of such a nature that, if skillfully used, they would arouse the ire of General Jackson against the man who had uttered them. Protestations of loyalty to the administration had an unwelcome ring in the General's ears when accompanied by boasts of Bell's great influence over party members and of the ease with which he might have defeated administration measures in the House. The truth of such an assertion would make it all the more galling to a man of Jackson's temperament. One can imagine his exclaiming: "By the Eternal, I'll show John Bell!" Then, too, Bell's remark concerning the President's *experiment,* and his *quasi* endorsement of a national bank, were most unfortunate for any man who wished to retain the friendship of "the old hero."

Polk's answer to Rucker indicated clearly the use that was to be made of Bell's speech. If the address has been accurately reported, said Polk, "it places him clearly and unequivocally at

---

14 Rucker to Polk, Oct. 12, 1834, *ibid.*

issue with the policy of the administration.''[15]  He wished the speech to be reported accurately and published to the world; then he would be fully prepared to meet its author on the issues which it had raised.

Before Bell's Murfreesborough speech had been delivered, Polk, as we have seen, had already been collecting statements from his friends concerning Bell's conduct in Congress.  Both men had also been exerting themselves to get control of the press in Middle Tennessee.  Local newspapers at that time wielded great influence, and the success of a politician depended in a great measure on his control over the reading matter of his constituents.

Polk's home was in Columbia; therefore the *Observer,* a local paper of that place, supported its townsman and criticized Bell's maneuvering in the late Speakership election.  The two leading papers of Nashville at that time were the *Republican* and the *Banner.*  The *Republican* defended Bell, and many of Polk's friends promptly administered the customary punishment of canceling their subscriptions to that paper.  One of these was Colonel Archibald Yell, an ardent admirer of Polk and an orthodox party man.  In answer to his protest, Allan A. Hall, editor of the *Republican,* defiantly predicted that Polk would soon lose the friendship of Jackson, Grundy, and Governor Carroll, and would be driven from power if he should dare to persist in his opposition to Bell.[16]

Bell succeeded in getting control of the *Banner,* also.  Until the middle of September, 1834, this paper had been edited by

---

[15] Polk to Rucker, Oct. 16, 1834, *ibid.*

[16] Yell to Polk, Sept. 25, 1834, *ibid.*  One part of Hall's letter, as quoted by Yell, read: ''and now mark me Yell for a prophet in less than six months there will be a split between Carroll & Polk nay there will be a split between Polk & the President!!  Coming events cast their shadows before.  Col. Polk by no earthly possibility can continue to maintain his present *position,* in the event of Certain future Contingencies which are *obliged* to take place.''  Yell took this to mean that Polk was to be driven from the chairmanship of the Committee of Ways and Means.  Carroll denied that he was hostile to Polk (Carroll to Polk, Dec. 19, 1834).

Samuel H. Laughlin, a friend of Polk, but who, unfortunately for both men, had been made extremely unreliable by a passion for strong drink.[17]  His contract as editor expired at this time and the proprietor, Hunt, formed a partnership with Bell.  A new editor was installed and the paper henceforth championed the cause of the Speaker.[18]  For the time being Polk had to rely mainly on the support of the Columbia *Observer* and the Murfreesborough *Monitor*.

Bell seems to have become somewhat alarmed at the result of his Murfreesborough speech, for both of his Nashville papers maintained that he had been misquoted, and that he was still a loyal follower of General Jackson.  Thereupon, William Brady, of Murfreesborough, set about collecting statements from various persons who had heard Bell deliver the address.  These Brady published in an extra number of the *Monitor*.  Copies of this number were sent to the President, to members of Congress, to leading political journals, and to prominent individuals, for the purpose of removing the "veil which now covers the political hypocrite [Bell]."[19]

Polk and his associates saw the necessity of establishing in Nashville a paper which would promulgate their own views.  "I think it more desirable," wrote A. C. Hays, of Columbia,[20]

that a Newspaper should be established in Nashville, that will fearlessly speak the sentiments of the people of the State, at this time than it has ever been, because I believe that the Press is at this time more under the influence of the *Bank & Bell & Foster* faction than it has *ever been*.

Laughlin had offered to serve as editor of an administration journal, but Brady[21] was not alone in thinking that "poor Sam" had already proved himself to be a total failure.  "The trouble

---

[17] One becomes accustomed to reading in private letters: "Laughlin has been drunk for a week."

[18] John W. Childress to Polk, Sept. 18; Wm. Brady to Polk, Dec. 26, 1834, *Polk Papers*.

[19] Brady to Polk, as cited above.

[20] Hays to Polk, Dec. 24, 1834, *Polk Papers*.

[21] Brady to Polk, as cited above.

is," said he, "Sam lacks moral courage; and when the sound of the Bugle is heard—and the enemy shall appear in force—Sam's in the straw." In Brady's opinion, some editor ought to be found who would be "wholly *de Nashvilleized*," who would stand by the President and support Van Buren as his successor.[22] For his own purposes, said Brady, Bell is putting Judge White forward to succeed Jackson, with the hope of succeeding White in the Presidential chair.

Bell's success in getting control of the Nashville papers was disconcerting enough to Polk's Tennessee friends, but they were still more chagrined because the Washington *Globe* seemed also to be lending its support to the Speaker. "How is it with the Globe?" wrote Brady in the letter above cited,

if that print is with the President and his friends, to me it has an awkward way of shewing of it. It is true that Blair sanctions the President personally, and in the main the measures of his administration; but how is it, that every apologetic article, which has appeared in the Nashville papers or elsewhere, in relation to Bell's election to the Speaker's chair, or his Murfreesboro Speech have found their way into the columns of the Globe?

Brady thought that Blair ought to give both sides or neither; Polk should compel him to show his colors by presenting for publication in the *Globe* the account of Bell's speech which had appeared in the extra *Monitor*. "Why is the Globe either silent— or giving support to Bell?" asked Childress.[23] People in Tennessee, he added, are beginnig to believe that the President prefers Bell to Polk; this is what Bell's adherents claim, and the attitude of the *Globe* lends color to their assertions. By all means, urged Childress, Polk must have his side of the argument published.

By courting the enemies of the administration and by subsequent indiscretions, Bell had engendered feelings of distrust

---

[22] On December 28 General Samuel Smith, in a letter to Polk, dwelt on the necessity of starting a new paper. Many in Tennessee, said he, whom Jackson believes to be his friends are in reality against him.

[23] Childress to Polk, Dec. 20, 1834, *Polk Papers*. Polk received other letters of similar character.

and hostility that were destined to involve others in serious political difficulties.  Polk was a man who did not easily forget, and
by lending aid to Bell in 1834 Blair was paving the way for his
own downfall, when Bell's rival became President ten years later.
Polk's friends believed that they saw the sinister as well as
successful influence of the Speaker in every quarter.  Polk himself alleged that Bell's exertions in behalf of Judge White were
not due to any love for the judge, but for the sole purpose of
promoting his own political advancement.[24]

The project of founding an administration newspaper in
Nashville now absorbed the attention of party leaders.  As no
really suitable man could be found to edit such a paper, Laughlin
was considered, although not without misgivings.[25]  Many politicians who had hitherto shouted for Jackson had deserted to
White, and nearly all of the papers of Middle Tennessee, including even the Columbia *Observer*,[26] had come out for the
judge.  This fact made it all the more necessary to have an
orthodox journal which would *enlighten* the people, and Laughlin,
despite his weaknesses, was a loyal party man.  After many
tribulations capital was collected, an outfit purchased, and in
March, 1835, Laughlin was installed as editor of the Nashville
*Union*.  Polk and Grundy were the guiding spirits of the new
paper, and to them and Cave Johnson ''poor Sam'' appealed for
aid in increasing his subscription list. He reported to Polk that
the editor of the *Banner* was ''wallowing in the mire,'' entirely
under the influence of Bell and Foster; and that efforts were
being made to retard the progress of the *Union*.''[27]

During the excitement which was created by Bell's Cassedy
letter, Laughlin—being ''himself again''[28]—with his ''sharp pen''

---

[24] Polk to James Walker, Dec. 24, 1834, *Polk Papers*.

[25] Sam'l G. Smith to Polk, Jan. 6, 1835, *ibid.*

[26] James Walker to Polk, Jan. 17, 1835, *ibid.*

[27] Laughlin to Polk, April 17, 21, 1835, *ibid.*

[28] Grundy to Polk, June 25, 1835, *ibid.*  For the Cassedy letter, see
p. 84.

did effective service for Polk by heaping odium upon Bell. ''That Cassedy letter,'' wrote Grundy to Polk, ''will make you Speaker, I think.''[29] It did, indeed, contribute to this result, but in Tennessee the combined influence of Bell and White could not be overcome. In spite of heroic efforts on the editor's part, the *Union* could not pay expenses, and the list of political ''apostates'' was steadily growing. Although Laughlin labored without salary, he was not without hope,[30] and his pungent editorials undoubtedly aided Polk in his campaign for reëlection.

President Jackson viewed with alarm the disintegration of the administration party in his home state. He was especially interested in the election of members of Congress. From his retreat at the ''Rip Raps'' he asked Polk[31] for reliable information concerning the political situation, and directed him to coöperate with Grundy and Cave Johnson in combating the schemes of Judge White and John Bell. He was able to get some news from the *Union,* although it came irregularly; ''the other Nashville papers, like base coin, circulate freely, but they have become the mere echo of Duff Green & other opposition prints.''

White's candidacy had irrevocably split the Jackson party in Tennessee. The President now considered White, Bell, and all their supporters to be his political and personal enemies. Polk, Grundy, and Johnson were to a greater degree than ever looked upon as the administration leaders in the state. It was certain that Polk would have the President's backing in his next contest with Bell for the Speaker's chair. From Washington, Donelson[32] wrote to congratulate Polk on his triumphant

---

[29] *Ibid.*

[30] ''I am now fairly in a State of belligerancy with my worthy neighbors. I have them, I think, in a good way if I can keep them so. A gradual but sure work of reformation in public sentiment is in progress here, and I hope the same work is going on throughout the State'' (Laughlin to Polk, July 5, 1835, *ibid.*).

[31] Jackson to Polk, Aug. 3, 1835, *ibid.*

[32] Donelson to Polk, Aug. 28, 1835, *ibid.*

reëlection in spite of the ''intrigues'' of Bell, and he reported the President to be in good spirits, notwithstanding the defeat of Governor Carroll. Donelson had, he said, conversed with many politicians, all of whom wished Polk to be chosen Speaker.

In Nashville, Laughlin, through the columns of the *Union* and by letters to individuals, was doing his utmost to discredit Bell and to present Polk's claims to reward for his loyalty to General Jackson. Polk had been the intended victim of Bell's ''treachery,'' wrote Laughlin, and therefore ''ought to be made the instrument of his defeat.''[33]

While the rivalry between White and Van Buren was of greater interest in national politics, yet administration leaders in all parts of the Union had come to feel that Bell—the alleged instigator of the party schism—was, after all, more guilty than White, and consequently deserving of punishment. Polk, on the other hand, was clearly entitled to the support of the administration forces in Congress. As chairman of the Committee of Ways and Means he had borne, in the House, the brunt of the President's war on the bank. In his home state he had done more than any other, with the possible exception of Grundy, to oppose the Bell-White coalition and to uphold the standard of General Jackson.

When Congress convened in December, Polk's election to the Speaker's chair was practically assured, and he was chosen on the first ballot by a majority of thirty-nine votes. His triumph over Bell was regarded by all as a distinct party victory. A

---

[33] Laughlin to Polk, Aug. 30, 1835, *ibid.* He quoted several reasons which he had assigned when urging Polk's election, among them:

''That your election will prostrate Bell and the White influence in this State, by showing to the people the true position of Bell, and how his position is received by the Republican party every where else, and that they are only sustained now by the false opinion which prevails that they are friends of Gen. Jackson.

''That your election will unmask the White party and exhibit them as the opponents of the Administration.

''That much is due to you. That you have stuck when others failed. . . . That your confidential relation to the President ought to be considered both as a merit and as a necessary qualification in a Speaker &c &c.''

"White" member of the Tennessee legislature, when writing to congratulate Polk on his election,[34] said that, although Bell's own friends hardly expected him to win, they did not think that he would be beaten so badly; they "attribute Mr. Bell's defeat to the influence of the President." Although a White supporter, the writer said that Polk had gained by his firm stand and that he was now stronger in his district than either White or Van Buren. "The election of Speaker," wrote Judge Catron,[35] "had an uncommonly great effect on the country people. They had been lead to believe great strength existed elsewhere—this is now admitted to be a mistake, and what must follow [defeat of White] is certain, as I believe." Bell himself had not been sanguine. He predicted his defeat by Polk before Congress had convened.[36]

Before proceeding with Polk's career as Speaker of the House of Representatives it seems desirable to retrace our steps in order to consider, in the following chapter, Judge White's unsuccessful campaign for the Presidency. The rivalry between White and Van Buren was the dominant factor at the time in both state and national politics. It played an important part in making Polk the presiding officer of the House, and it helped to shape many of the issues with which Polk, as Speaker, had to deal.

---

[34] H. M. Watterson to Polk, Dec. 21, 1835, *Polk Papers.*

[35] Catron to Polk, Jan. 8, 1836, *ibid.* "The effect of the news [Polk's election] upon the White cause," wrote Nicholson, December 20, "has been blighting." Many White men, said he, now think that their candidate should be withdrawn.

[36] W. H. Polk to J. K. Polk, Dec. 21, 1835, *Polk Papers.* He had seen a letter written by Bell to Judge Kennedy before the opening of Congress.

## CHAPTER V

# JUDGE WHITE AND THE PRESIDENCY

No biography of a statesman of the thirties—particularly of a prominent Tennessean—would be complete that did not include a chapter on the far-reaching effect of Judge White's decision to become a candidate for the Presidency. The importance of this decision lay in the fact that General Jackson had made other plans. In the parlance of the day, "King Andrew" had decreed that the "little magician" must be his successor, regardless of the will of the subjects—the "consent of the governed." When, therefore, the friends of White brought him forward as a rival to Van Buren, harmony in the Jackson camp was at first threatened, and finally destroyed. "Davy" Crockett had driven the first wedge into the solidarity of the Jackson domination of Tennessee; the White movement split it asunder. The result was the birth of the Whig party and a national political realignment.

When White was first mentioned in connection with the Presidency, Jackson's feelings were those of regret that his old friend should have been deluded by designing politicians; but when the judge was found to be a willing victim—independent even to the point of defying the President's wishes—the old-time friendship changed to bitter hatred. It was soon made apparent to politicians that they could not support Judge White without forfeiting all claim of loyalty to General Jackson. Assurances on their part that the two things were not incompatible availed nothing; all were forced to choose between the two men.

It is not easy to determine just when and by whom Judge White was first brought forward as a candidate for President, but his nomination for that office was considered by the Tennessee legislature as early as December, 1833. Up to this time, so far as Tennessee politics were concerned, Judge McLean, of Ohio, seems to have been regarded as Van Buren's most formidable rival. Some of the local papers had hoisted the McLean banner, with either Governor Carroll or Judge White for Vice-President.[1] But before adjourning in early December, 1833, the legislature seriously considered the feasibility of presenting a Presidential candidate from their own state. A resolution to nominate White was actually drawn up; but it was made known by a member that White opposed such a proceeding, and the matter was dropped. None of the members manifested any interest in nominating either Van Buren or McLean.[2]

Several causes coöperated in fixing the attention of politicians on White as a possible candidate. It was well known that Jackson had decreed that the Vice-President should succeed him; in spite of this, however, Van Buren had never been popular in Tennessee. Many of the President's most loyal supporters did not, and could not, share his admiration for the "heir apparent." State pride caused many to feel that, if possible, another Tennessean should be chosen to fill the office, and, next to Jackson, White was generally conceded to be the most able and popular son of the state. It is probable that Jackson's preference for Van Buren would have been sufficient to cause a split in the party as soon as the White movement assumed serious proportions, but the rivalry between Polk and Bell, and the support of White by the latter, lent an added bitterness and political significance to White's candidacy. The plan to nominate White was alleged to have been conceived by Bell for the purpose of advancing his own political fortunes in both state and national politics. Whether this allegation was true or false is a matter difficult to determine; but whatever Bell's motives may have been,

---

[1] Yell to Polk, Dec. 1, 1833, *Polk Papers*.

[2] A. O. P. Nicholson to Polk, Dec. 5, 1833, *Polk Papers*. Orville Bradley to White, Aug. 23, 1836 (Scott, *Memoir of Hugh Lawson White*, 302).

it seems clear that White's conduct was at all times aboveboard
and commendable.  He was too honest to seek political prefer-
ment by underhand methods, but he was, also, too brave and
independent to step aside simply because General Jackson willed
that he should do so.

Up to the time when White and Van Buren had been formally nominated and party lines definitely drawn, there was
quite a diversity of opinion in Tennessee, even among Jackson's
friends.  On December 22, 1833, A. V. Brown wrote to ask Polk
"the signs as to the 'successorship to the throne,'" and spoke
of McLean's popularity.  "Personally," said Brown, "I like
McLean myself but *politically* I fear he is *too far off* from us in
the South—and how will Van Buren help that matter in the
least?"  Between Clay and Van Buren, he continued, "might
not one find refuge in the personal worth & virtue of McLean,
although he would prefer some other than either, if chance or
destiny had not thrown him too far in the rear of probable success?"[3]  Other passages in the letter indicate that it was Calhoun
to whom he referred.  Generally, however, those of Polk's correspondents who were "not satisfied" with Van Buren were of
opinion that White was the only man who would bring success to
the party.[4]

On June 2, 1834, Bell defeated Polk in the contest for the
Speakership.  He was supported by many who were openly opposed to the administration.  In the House Polk had, during the
entire session, been leading the battle against the bank, and when
Congress adjourned on June 30 he had won a signal victory for
the administration.  In his defeat by Bell, Polk could easily be
made to assume the rôle of a martyr who had suffered for his
loyalty to the President and the party.  He seems sincerely to
have regarded himself as a victim of the treachery of Bell, who
had solicited opposition votes.

---

[3] *Polk Papers.*

[4] E.g., John W. M. Breazeale to Polk, March 21, 1834, *Polk Papers.*

As soon as Congress had adjourned, both men returned to Tennessee to air their grievances on the platform and in the public press. Polk, as we have seen, applied to his congressional friends for statements which would prove the perfidy of Bell, while Bell proceeded to get control of the Nashville papers, the *Republican* and the *Banner,* in order to defend himself and to overthrow the influence of Polk. Many of Polk's friends were desirous of nominating him for Governor, but he preferred to continue in national politics.

General Jackson, also, spent his summer vacation in Tennessee. The bank question was uppermost in his mind, and in a speech delivered in Nashville he made it clear that any new federal bank would be quite as objectionable as the one now in existence. As yet he seems to have taken no active interest in the quarrel between Bell and Polk, but he naturally felt grateful to the latter for his loyal support of the administration during the last sesssion. It was at this time that he declared Polk to be deserving of a medal from the American people for his services in Congress. Bell had not yet broken with the party and gave the President new assurances that he would continue to support the administration.[5] Indeed after Jackson's return to Washington there was, as we have seen, complaint in Tennessee that the *Globe* seemed to show a preference for Bell.[6] But during the fall of 1834 the political situation in Tennessee became such that the interests of Polk and the President were closely identified, while Bell cast his lot with the opponents of the administration. The main cause of the party cleavage was the renewed effort to nominate Judge White for the Presidency.

While Jackson was still in Nashville a caucus was held in that city—by friends of the bank, it was said—for the purpose of considering the nomination of White.[7] White was informed that

---

[5] Gen. Sam'l Smith to Polk, Sept. 20, 1834, *Polk Papers.*

[6] See above, p. 57.

[7] Burton to Polk, Aug. 27, 1834, *Polk Papers.*

the President threatened to denounce him should he express a willingness to become a candidate.[8]  Jackson doubtless noted many evidences of the popularity of White and of the unpopularity of Van Buren, but at this time it is probable that he had hopes of preventing disaffection.

While the President was passing through East Tennessee on his way to Washington, Orville Bradley, a member of the legislature, told him of the attempt made by the assembly in 1833 to nominate White — an attempt which Bradley, acting under White's directions, had been able to defeat.  He told the President, also, that two-thirds of the legislature had been unfavorable to Van Buren.  Jackson vigorously defended Van Buren.  He said ''that White could hardly get a vote out of Tennessee, and that Tennessee must not separate from the rest of his friends.''  He was willing to compromise by supporting White for Vice-President, and it would be time enough for White to run for President after Van Buren had retired.[9]

Jackson did not at this time harbor bitter feelings toward White, personally.  These did not come until later, and even then, as will appear, he regarded the judge more as a dupe of political intriguers than as his personal enemy.  His feeling in 1834 was one of annoyance that White should be made the instrument in an attempt to thwart the plans he had made for Van Buren.

White and Jackson had long been close personal friends.  The judge had loyally supported the ''old hero'' in his campaigns for the Presidency and during the first part of his administration was regarded as one of his most able advisers.[10]  But White was no sycophant, and he was too independent to follow any man's program, even though the man might chance to be

---

[8] White to Polk, Aug. 26, 1834 (Scott, *Memoir of Hugh Lawson White*, 254).

[9] Bradley to White, Aug. 23, 1836 (Scott, *Memoir of Hugh Lawson White*, 302).

[10] See letters of Jackson, Overton, Coffee, Polk *et al.*, in Scott, *Memoir of Hugh Lawson White*, 267–269.

General Jackson. As early as 1831, when Jackson was reconstructing his cabinet so that Van Buren might, under the President's own rule,[11] be made eligible to succeed him, he had invited White to become Secretary of War, while Eaton, the outgoing Secretary, was to have White's place as Senator from Tennessee.[12] The judge declined the offer, and although no breach between the two men resulted, White was henceforth made to feel that he was no longer in good standing in administration circles.[13]

Jackson was irritated by various manifestations of White's independence, and especially so by his disregard of the President's wishes when Clay's compromise tariff bill was before the Senate in 1833. The Senate had voted to refer Clay's bill to a select committee. Before White, their presiding officer, had appointed the committee, he was invited to a conference with the President. Preferring Clay's bill to one which had been sent to the House by the Secretary of the Treasury, and anticipating that Jackson had sent for him for the purpose of dictating the membership of the committee, White, before going to see the President, selected a committee which he thought would support Clay's measure. A majority, which included Clayton, of Delaware, were rated as anti-administration men.[14] The President was much ''mortified'' and told Grundy in a letter that ''it is an insult to me, & the Sec. of the Treasury that such a man as

---

[11] This rule was that none of his cabinet should succeed him if he could prevent it.

[12] White's testimony before the House Committee (Scott, *Memoir of Hugh Lawson White*, 299; Washington *Globe*, May 25, 1831).

[13] ''The true reason why nothing I have said is noticed in the Globe, I have no doubt is, because I have never assured any man that as soon as Gen. Jackson's terms of service are at an end, I will use all my endeavors *to elect the favorite of those who direct the operations of the paper*. I am for Gen. Jackson; but am not either a Calhoun Jackson man, or a Van Buren Jackson man, and therefore it is pleasing to the Globe and Telegraph not to notice favorably anything I can say or do; and as I am opposed to Mr. Clay, his papers will of course speak disrespectfully of me.'' White to F. S. Heiskell, editor of the Knoxville *Register*, May 18, 1832 (Scott, *Memoir of Hugh Lawson White*, 269).

[14] Testimony of Judge White before the House Committee (Scott, *Memoir of Hugh Lawson White*, 299).

Clayton should be upon it [the committee].''[15]   Nevertheless, Jackson held White in high esteem, and, despite this ''insult'' and other similar vexations, the two men continued amicable relations.  White was still rated as a Jackson man, and, in the judge's opinion, it was not until the President visited Tennessee in 1834 that he became convinced that White would not support his political program.[16]   Jackson was willing to compromise by letting White have the Vice-Presidency, but the judge must not stand in the way of Van Buren.

Up to the time that Polk returned to Washington for the opening of Congress, there is nothing in his correspondence, except his letter to White, to indicate that he took an active interest in the movement to nominate Judge White.  His thoughts were centered on Bell, and the suggestion made by C. C. Clay[17] to *''take good care to put your adversary in the wrong''* was entirely superfluous.  His task was made comparatively easy by the indiscretions of the adversary himself.  Bell's Murfreesborough speech[18] proved a boomerang to its author, for in it he had criticized the President and given quasi support to the national bank.  Then, too, Hall, of the Nashville *Republican*, had boasted that there would be ''a split between Polk and the President,'' and that Polk would be driven from power[19] by the political influence of Bell.  Such arrogance, when duly reported to the President, was sufficient to arouse his resentment, and, when it soon developed that Bell was one of the most ardent supporters of White, he was denounced as a political apostate.

The determination of White's Tennessee friends to nominate him, and Jackson's strenuous opposition to such a nomination, placed Polk in an awkward position.  White's friends have always

---

[15] Jackson to Grundy, Feb. 13, 1833, *Am. Hist. Mag.*, V, 137.

[16] ''He no doubt believed that whenever he and those he could control changed their creed, I would change my creed likewise, and he was never convinced to the contrary, until after his attempt upon me through Mr. Bradley, which was in the autumn of 1834.''  White to the ''Freemen of Tennessee'' (Scott, *Memoir of Hugh Lawson White*, 320).

[17] Clay to Polk, Sept. 23, 1834, *Polk Papers*.

[18] See above, p. 53.          [19] Yell to Polk, Sept. 25, 1834, *Polk Papers*.

assumed that Polk treacherously turned against White simply to please General Jackson, and White himself appears to have held this view. Even now, after Polk's entire correspondence has become available, it is difficult to determine to what extent this charge is true. His friendship for Judge White he never attempted to conceal, and that he desired the support of Jackson is beyond question; but after his defeat by Bell the political situation, both in Tennessee and in Congress, was such that for reasons of his own, and irrespective of Jackson's wishes, he could not support a candidate whose chief sponsor was his rival, John Bell. He liked White and, like many of his Tennessee friends, he probably did not share the President's admiration for Van Buren; but he was a firm believer in party loyalty; and besides, the men who were taking the lead in promoting White's interests were at the same time endeavoring to undermine Polk himself.

Polk's habitual reticence adds to the difficulty of determining his thoughts and motives. If possible, he always avoided controversies which did not immediately concern himself, and to his best friends he was guarded in expressing his opinions. When, in 1831, there was discord in Jackson's cabinet, Polk discreetly declined to participate in the effort to force Eaton from the cabinet, or even to discuss the matter in writing.[20] When the break between Jackson and Calhoun occurred, he forwarded Calhoun's ''defense'' to his friends, but without disclosing his own views. One of his closest friends complained that '' I write you my opinions freely as I am not disposed with you to conceal my views, but I must acknowledge that you have been more *prudent* with yours for I am not able to even conjecture how your feelings are after all your long letters.''[21]

---

[20] Several letters to C. A. Wickliffe declining to discuss the subject (*Polk Papers*).

[21] A. Yell to Polk, March 13, 1831, *Polk Papers*. Yell expressed his own opinions freely enough. He believed Calhoun's defense to be honest and sincere, and that Crawford was a scoundrel. He had a ''bad impression'' of Van Buren and hoped that he would not be nominated as Jackson's successor. The attempt to force Van Buren on the people would only aid ''Prince Hal.''

Polk and White had long been personal and political friends. There is nothing to indicate that their friendship had been in any degree affected by the coolness between White and the President. To this White's comments on Polk's defeat by Bell in 1834 bear witness. "Both are to me like children;" he wrote[22] "therefore I took no part in the contest." Polk's expression of "surprise and astonishment"[23] in September, 1834, when informed of Jackson's threat to denounce White, should he consent to become a candidate, was no doubt unfeigned. He was frequently evasive or noncommittal, but he was not given to flattery.[24]

Polk returned to Washington to assume his duties in the House in December, 1834. Up to this time there appears to have been no connection between his quarrel with Bell and Jackson's opposition to White. But he had not been in Washington long before these two controversies became merged by an effort on the part of Polk's opponents to bring White out as a candidate. Polk's own version of his attitude toward the judge's nomination is stated in a *"confidential"* letter to his brother-in-law, James Walker. As his motives in opposing White have often been questioned, it seemes desirable to insert this letter in spite of its length.

I have been so busily engaged in preparing the appropriation bills—and those connected with the Banks that I have not heretofore taken leisure to write to you. I have had nothing to do with the management—and undercurrents which I understand have been going on here in regard to the next Presidency. I have considered that it was my first duty to attend to the important measures committed to the committee of which I am a

---

[22] To editor of Knoxville *Register* (Scott, *Memoir of Hugh Lawson White*, 253).

[23] Polk to White, Sept. 2, 1834, *ibid.*, 254.

[24] White's biographer in commenting on this letter (of *September, 1834*) makes the rather astonishing statement that as soon as Polk ascertained "the sentiments of Gen. Jackson in regard to his successor" he shaped his "course according to the President's wishes, although motives of personal policy . . . decided him not to define his position until after his reëlection the ensuing August." She then goes on to show that Polk and Cave Johnson "had determined to pick a quarrel" with White in February, 1835!

member. This I have done and shall continue to do, and I am sure my constituents will appreciate my services more than if I were engaged in the intrigues of politicians with a view to my own personal advancement. I have no doubt that my constituents feel and think as I do, upon the subject of the succession,—but still they have not commissioned me here—either to engage their votes, to commit them upon the subject or to express their opinions. As a citizen I shall have a right to my own opinion,—and whenever there shall be occasion shall certainly exercise it. In regard to our countryman Judge White I have said this,—that there was no man to whom personally—I have ever had kindlier feelings, and that if he was brought forward, or taken up and run by our political party, it would give me pleasure to support him,—but at the same time I think that the party now dominant in the country, who have recently achieved so signal a victory, have fought the battle to little purpose, if in the moment of this triumph, they permit themselves to be divided & distracted about men, and thereby perhaps enable our political adversaries to take advantage of our divisions,—throw the election into the House, when there is danger that the money of the Bank and the patronage of the Government,—would corrupt & purchase votes enough to carry the election against us. It must certainly be the desire of our party, who are emphatically—from the policy we advocate, the party of the country,—if possible to continue united and not divide about men. I think the party should unite if it be possible and run but one man, and it would assuredly give me pleasure should Judge White be that man. Suppose we divide and select more than one candidate,—and suffer the friends of our respective candidates to become irritated & exci[ted] against each other; may not the opposition, and will they not take advantage of such a state of things, and at a moment when it shall be too late for us to retrace our steps, and re-unite our friends in favor of any one, suddenly push out a candidate of their own, defeat an election before the people, throw the election into the House and thus stand a fair chance to come into power against the popular will. To meet such a state of things I repeat we should continue united and if possible run but one man. Should Judge White be the man upon whom the party unite, none would support him with more pleasure than myself. Upon this subject, the present moment may be an important crisis. As soon as Congress assembled,—many of the opposition members expressed wishes that Judge White should be brought out and announced their intention to support him,—if he was &c. Their motive for this, the game they will play hereafter or the subject they hope to effect, I know not except—that they would doubtless do any thing in their power to divide & scatter us. That portion of our delegation in W$^t$ Tennessee, who manifested such unprovoked hostility to me during the past summer—I mean the Speaker, Dickinson &c. probably think they can make something out of this state of things to my prejudice, and for their own purposes,—have been zealous, or pretended to be so, to bring Judge White

out at once, and at all events, without waiting to consult any portion of
the democratic party—residing in other states with whom we have so
long acted,—and who have so long acted with us in supporting the administration of the present Chief Magistrate.  Ought they not to be at least
consulted before such a step is taken?  But that portion of our delegation
probably think that by taking this course they will gain an advantage of
me in Tennessee and that by uniting with the opposition Mr. B[ell] may be
enabled to retain his place here at the next Congress, in the same way he
originally obtained it.  The East Tennessee part of our delegation very
honestly and sincerely desire to see Judge White elected.  On the day before
yesterday I was informed by Col. Standifer that there was to be a meeting
of the delegation,—on the night following (last night) upon the subject
and was requested to attend.  On yesterday Mr. Lea spoke to me on the
subject & told me the meeting was to be at *Peyton's* room and urged us to
attend.  I told him that my attending or not attending was a matter of no
consequence;—that neither my own opinions or that of my constituents of
Judge White would be changed,—whether I attended or not; that I had no
commission from my constituents to speak for them; that, that was a matter
they would attend to for themselves, when the time came for them to act;
that I was very laboriously engaged in the discharge of my public duty as a
member of the House; and that I did not regard the proposed meeting as
any part of that duty.  I told him furthermore that I could not but suspect
that, that portion of our delegation who are, without cause given by me so
exceedingly hostile to me, were prompted in this movement more in the hope
of injuring me, than for any love they had for Judge White.  And furthermore I told him, that what was conducive against my attendance was this—
that I could not without losing all self-respect go into a consultation upon
any subject,—(unless public duty required it,) with that portion of our
delegation,—who had during the past summer through their organs and
tools so unjustly and wantonly assailed me, and especially when I was
informed that the meeting was to take place at the room of a colleague[25]
who was certainly unfriendly in his feelings towards me, and had never
invited me to come to it.  For these reasons I declined and did not attend.
The meeting was held, Grundy, Blair & myself absent.  Johnson attended—
but will probably communicate to the delegation his views in writing; they
entirely accord with mine.  I understand that *Dunlap* (though I have not
talked to him) agrees in his views with Johnson and myself.  I write you
very confidentially—that you may be apprised of what is going on here.
From the unfairness with which I have been treated in other things I have
reason to suspect that letters may be written home misrepresenting me upon

---

[25] Peyton, who was White's nephew, had opposed Polk in the Speaker-
ship election and had given as his reason, according to Cave Johnson, that
Polk had worked with the Nullifiers! (Johnson to Polk, July 15, 1834,
*Polk Papers*).

this;—probably representing from my absence from the meeting, that I am unfriendly to Judge White &c.—and I look for nothing else than to see some misinformation in regard to it, through the Nashville papers. I write you to put you in possession of the facts,—that you may in the proper way, and without using my letter publicly be enabled to put the matter right. I wish you to take so much of your time from your business—which I know to be pressing upon your time, as to write me your opinion fully & freely upon the subject;—and whether you think I have acted prudently or not. I have acted upon my convictions of what was proper,—and with feelings of most perfect friendship for Judge White. Can I be affected by it?

James Walker, Esq.,
    Columbia, Tenn.

Very sincerely,<br>Yr friend,<br>James K. Polk[26]

This letter seems to give ample reasons why a man of Polk's well-known belief in party loyalty should not support the apparently hopeless cause of Judge White. It is not fair to assume, as the friends of White have done, that those who did not come out for the judge were necessarily the abject creatures of General Jackson. There was only one man whose support could, by any possibility, have elevated White to the Presidential chair. That man was Jackson himself; and neither Polk nor those who acted with him could hope, even if they had so desired, to alter the President's determination to aid Van Buren. To support White, as Polk pointed out, would result in splitting the party and endangering its success, without benefiting the judge in any particular. It was too much to ask of Polk to coöperate with men whom he both distrusted and despised as he did Bell and Peyton in supporting a candidate who would inevitably be defeated. There is no reason for questioning the sincerity of Polk's belief that Bell was flirting with the opposition, as he had done when he was a candidate for Speaker. The assertions made by Polk, Grundy, and Johnson that they would gladly support White if he could procure the party nomination were said by their opponents to be pure cant and of course there was no possibility of his

---

[26] The letter is dated Dec. 24, 1834, *Polk Papers*.

procuring such a nomination unless Jackson should change his mind—but there is nothing in their private correspondence to indicate that they did not really prefer White to Van Buren.

On the day after the above letter was written Polk wrote[27] another *"confidential"* letter to Walker. Alluding to the former letter he said:

Since then the fact that a meeting took place and the objects of it has been communicated to ——————  ——————[28] and my course is highly approved. The meeting has attracted attention and things as they *really are in Tennessee,* are beginning to be well understood here. He says that if Judge White should be united upon and be a candidate of the party—that then he should be supported by the party—but any portion of those professing to be the friends of the administration who would bring him or any one else out—without consulting the wishes of the friends of the administration in other States, will eventually not only destroy him but themselves. The storm I apprehended is to burst upon us, and we in Tennessee must be prepared to meet it   Whatever our personal preferences for men may be, as patriots we should go for the good of the country,—and to that end should avoid divisions—and preserve if possible the integrity of the party.

The portion of the letter just quoted clearly indicates that Polk declined to attend the meeting without having a consultation with the President. Continuing, he told Walker that the person to whom he has alluded (Jackson ?)

says he has already heard that it has been dropped out by some one of the opposition, that the plan of their operation, is upon the *Bell* system, alluding to the Speaker's election. I will not be hasty or imprudent in this matter,—but may venture to communicate what is passing *to you.*[29]

He wished to know whether Tennessee would probably send delegates to the national convention of the party. He instructed

---

[27] Polk to Walker, Dec. 25, 1834, *Polk Papers.*

[28] Blanks in the copy in the Polk collection, but evidently mean Jackson.

[29] Cave Johnson, Polk told Walker, had written to the Tennessee delegation stating that he would not support White "if he is to be run by the opposition Nationals and Nullifiers,—aided by a small portion of the Jackson party." Polk, Dunlap, and Blair felt the same way, and "Grundy is more excited than I have almost ever seen him,—and seems almost ready to come out and denounce the whole movement,—as calculated to divide and destroy the party."

Walker to prevail upon the Columbia *Observer* to support the regular nominee in case its favorite should fail to procure the nomination. To this Walker replied[30] that he preferred White if he could be nominated by the party, but he feared that a split would make success doubtful. He promised to induce the *Observer,* if possible, to support the national ticket whoever might be nominated.

In a formal statement prepared by Polk[31] several items concerning the meeting of the Tennessee delegation in Washington are related which are not mentioned in his letters to Walker. According to this account, on the Sunday night before Congress convened, while Polk was calling on Grundy, Duff Green came in and urged that the Tennessee members should come out for White. Green expressed his own readiness to support the judge. Polk remained silent, but Grundy replied that he was not prepared to act on this subject. Although Polk had declined to meet with the other delegates, Lea, of Tennessee, came to the House a few days after the meeting had been held and handed Polk a letter which the delegation had prepared to send to Judge White. There were no signatures attached and Lea explained that the delegation had desired to have Polk sign it first. Polk replied

---

[30] Jan. 12, 1835 (*Polk Papers*). Walker had already written on January 7 that it had been reported in Tennessee that Bell and others intended to run White whether he is chosen by the national convention or not. ''I believe Judge White is the most popular man in Tennessee except Gen. Jackson, but I do not think it is certain that even he can get the vote of Tennessee in opposition to the regular nomination of the Republican party—it looks like suicide—and how can we mix with such men as Poindexter and others of the same stamp?'' He hopes that White will not lend his name to the scheme.

[31] It is addressed to J. B. & Co. (John Bell & Co.), but is changed into a letter to Cave Johnson. It is dated January 20, but relates to events that occurred as late as March 26. It probably is the first draft of his statement addressed to Johnson under date of March 26. In another letter to Johnson, dated March 28, Polk gives his reason for addressing him instead of Bell. Bell's criticisms of Polk had been contained in a letter written to Johnson, and, as Polk had received no communication directly from Bell, he could not write to him; or, if he should do so, Bell would not publish the letter. So it was sent to Johnson for publication at the proper time.

that he had nothing against White, but would not act with a portion of the party. A few days later Hubbard, of New Hampshire, informed Polk that Green was trying to interest members of Congress in the establishment of a White paper in Washington. Bell had tried to convince Hubbard that it would benefit New Hampshire to join with the South and West in forming a new party, but Hubbard declined to coöperate with him. May, of Illinois, told Polk that he had ''stumbled on a caucus'' composed of Bell, Peyton, and other Tennessee members. To May's protests against dividing the party, Bell replied that he saw no sacrifice of principle in winning opposition votes. In all of this Polk saw—or, at least, pretended to see—a plot of Bell, Green, and Crockett[32] to use Judge White for the purpose of overthrowing the Republican party.

The other side of the story is told in letters written to Cave Johnson by other members of the Tennessee delegation. These, White's biographer has published for the purpose of showing the ''duplicity of Johnson and Polk.''[33] The essential difference between these letters and those of Polk above quoted is that they state that Polk and Johnson had expressed a preference for White over any other man and had agreed to support him ''under any circumstances that he, Judge White, would permit his name to be used,'' while Polk maintained that he had promised support only in case White should be nominated by the party. Which of the two statements is correct we are unable to determine with absolute certainty, but Polk's version accords with his invariable practice of conforming to the party program.[34]

While Polk was declining to meet with Bell, his friend Brady was sending to Jackson and to members of Congress copies of the

---

[32] Crockett had signed the letter to White.

[33] Scott, *Memoir of Hugh Lawson White*, 259–262.

[34] Standifer asserted that the meeting of the delegation held for the purpose of considering White's nomination ''was a project of my own without being prompted by any one.'' Both Polk and Grundy, he said, after ascertaining that Bell would be there, declined to attend the meeting (*ibid.*, 260–262).

Murfreesborough *Monitor* containing Bell's Murfreesborough speech. He also urged upon Polk the necessity of establishing an administration paper in Nashville.[35] The plan of the bolters, he said, was White for eight years, and then "the Speaker will graciously condescend to take upon himself the burthens of State."

There is abundant evidence that Polk's Tennessee friends really believed that Bell and his adherents were plotting to divide the party. Daniel Graham of Murfreesborough wrote[36] that, while he preferred White to any other man, he distrusted his supporters. "No one here doubts," wrote Polk's brother-in-law, W. R. Rucker, "that he [Bell] is a thorough Bank man and at heart (though a dissembling hypocrite) one of Gen[l] Jackson's bitterest enemies."[37] In the opinion of James Walker, another brother-in-law, Van Buren was the only man who could lead the party to victory. "We justly esteem and appreciate Judge White, but cannot consent to become the tools of the opposition, or to be associated in political feeling with such as Poindexter & others."[38] A. V. Brown, one of Polk's closest friends, preferred White as a successor to Jackson but asked the question,

Do the Whigs really mean to do something finally for him—or is it a part of their policy to make a *present shew* in his favor to effect division in the Jackson ranks & so weaken Mr. Van Buren & then finally press some favorite of their own & so throw the Election in the House?[39]

Childress informed Polk[40] that it was rumored in Nashville that Bell and his friends were confident of throwing the election into the House, where White would have a majority, and that they

---

[35] Brady to Polk, Dec. 26, 1834, *Polk Papers.*

[36] Graham to Polk, Jan. 2, 1835, *Polk Papers.*

[37] Rucker to Polk, Jan. 5, 1835, *Polk Papers.* "Don't misunderstand me," he added, "I like White as well as any of these people, but I don't like these intriguing friends of his." He urged Polk to inform Jackson of the intrigues.

[38] Walker to Polk, Jan. 15, 1835, *Polk Papers.*

[39] Brown to Polk, Jan. 15, 1835, *Polk Papers.*

[40] Childress to Polk, Jan. 23, 1835, *Polk Papers.* Childress was Mrs. Polk's brother.

were equally confident of defeating Polk and Cave Johnson at the coming election.

The anomalous situation in Tennessee was aptly put by another of Polk's correspondents.

The more I reflect on the posture of affairs, the more am I provoked at the success of iniquity. Almost every man in the community who takes part in or cares for public doings, finds himself occupying a false position which he is compelled to defend. I shall find myself opposed to Judge White, which is not true, so of Doct Rucker & thousands of others—whilst thousands will find themselves opposed to Genl Jackson who are sincerely with him. Furthermore Genl Jackson & Judge White will find themselves in hostile attitude before the scene closes, whatever may be their hopes and expectations now.[41]

All agreed that John Bell was the man who had created this embarrassing predicament.

No doubt the intriguing of White's supporters was greatly exaggerated, but it seemed real enough to those who were striving to preserve party solidarity. Jackson's determination to force upon the people an unpopular candidate was after all the main cause of the difficulty, for many could not pass White by and support Van Buren without sacrificing their principles. Party loyalty alone kept others from espousing White's cause, and for some time many of Jackson's friends had hopes that he might yet drop Van Buren and acquiesce in White's nomination.[42]

The President, however, had no thought of abandoning his favorite. He vehemently condemned the activities of the Tennessee delegation, and he was beginning to regard Bell as an enemy.[43] Back of the encouragement given to White by political opponents was seen the hand of Henry Clay, who was believed to be ready to seize any advantage that might result from throwing the election into the House.[44]

---

[41] Daniel Graham to Polk, Jan. 29, 1835, *Polk Papers*.

[42] Gen. Sam'l G. Smith to Polk, Feb. 3, 1835, *Polk Papers*.

[43] Polk to Walker, Jan. 18, 1835, *Polk Papers*.

[44] Copy of a letter from Polk to somebody in Tennessee, dated February 7, 1835, *Polk Papers*. The letter was probably written to James Walker; see Walker to Polk, Feb. 24, *ibid*.

After the meeting of the Tennessee delegation, White of course realized that the members had divided on the question of supporting him. He regretted the discord that had arisen but nevertheless declined to forbid the use of his name.[45] On December 29, 1834, the delegation had addressed him a letter asking if he would accept a nomination, and he replied in the affirmative.[46] He said afterwards that he would never have consented to become a candidate but for Jackson's threat to make him "odious to society" if he did.[47]

Outwardly, at least, the judge remained on friendly terms with the Tennessee members of Congress who had opposed his nomination until a controversy arose over a question of patronage. Polk and Johnson had recommended, and Jackson had appointed, a district attorney for West Tennessee without consulting Senator White. In a letter to the two men[48] White intimated that there had been "secret contrivance" to bring about the appointment. If, as White's biographer asserts, these two Tennesseans "had determined to pick a quarrel with Judge White," they now had their opportunity—and they certainly made the most of it. They replied in a very caustic letter in which they repelled what they regarded as insinuations against themselves and the President. White's rejoinder was equally caustic, and the break was complete.[49]

It is quite possible that Polk may have welcomed such an excuse for openly breaking with the judge. The time had arrived when he must take a definite stand for one side or the other, inasmuch as it was now certain that the opposition intended to

---

[45] White to Alexander, Jan. 12, 1835 (Scott, *Memoir of Hugh Lawson White*, 255).

[46] Correspondence in Scott, *Memoir of Hugh Lawson White*, 329–331.

[47] Speech at Knoxville, Aug. 1, 1838 (Scott, *Memoir of Hugh Lawson White*, 359).

[48] Dated Feb. 24, 1835 (*Polk Papers*).

[49] The correspondence may be found in the *Polk Papers* under dates of February 24–26. Part of it is printed in Scott, *Memoir of Hugh Lawson White*, 256–259.

use White for the purpose of defeating the nomination of an administration candidate—that is a regular Republican nomination.[50] Such being the case, both self-interest and party loyalty beckoned in the same direction, for he could expect no favors from the men who were promoting the campaign for White's nomination.  Bell was his personal enemy and political rival; many letters warned him that the White adherents were scheming, as one put it, "to get White & the people upon one side & Van Buren & my friend Col. Polk on the other."[51]  Having made the inevitable choice, Polk endeavored, through James Walker and other local leaders, to hold his constituents in line for the administration, but White's popularity was already playing havoc with party solidarity.[52]  At a political meeting held in Columbia on February 12, Walker, by resolution, tried to pledge the meeting to the "party candidate."  The resolution was defeated by the aid of many who had hitherto been averse to White's nomination.[53]  Not long after this Walker felt certain that White would carry Tennessee and he cautioned Polk that "non interference may be your true position."[54]

Nearly all the newspapers in Tennessee favored White's nomination.  Bell controlled both Nashville papers, and late in February F. K. Zollicoffer, of the Columbia *Observer*, hoisted the White banner.  Polk and his friends in Middle Tennessee were without an organ of influence until they established, a month later, the Nashville *Union*, which White, in a speech in the Senate,

---

[50] Polk to —— (probably Walker), Feb. 7, 1835, *Polk Papers*.

[51] James H. Thomas to Polk, Feb. 12, 1835, *Polk Papers*.  J. W. Childress wrote (Jan. 23) that Polk and Johnson had been marked for defeat. Similar information came from Gen. Smith (Feb. 13), W. G. Childress and James Walker (both Feb. 14), *ibid*.

[52] Some in Tennessee, said W. G. Childress in his letter of February 14, "seem to think or to say that Jackson, the Jackson party and Jackson administration will soon be no more, that the whole will be swallowed in the White party."

[53] "The small politicians are all on the scent and expect to rise on the White excitement" (Walker to Polk, Feb. 24, 1835, *Polk Papers*).

[54] Walker to Polk, Feb. 28, 1835, *ibid*.

called a ''vehicle of slanders and falsehoods, gotten up in this city [Washington]'' for the purpose of distorting the truth.[55] This paper was edited by Samuel H. Laughlin; its policy was directed by Polk, Grundy, and Judge Catron, who were mainly responsible for its financial support.

Polk returned home after Congress had adjourned, only to find White's prospects daily growing brighter. In a speech delivered at Columbia, April 20, he justified his refusal to join other members of the delegation in asking White to run on the ground that he had not been sent to Washington for the purpose of making presidents. His personal preference had been for White, he said, if he could have been nominated by the Republican party.[56] Grundy approved this speech, but as to any further discussion of the subject his advice to Polk was that ''the judicious course is a plain one—say nothing.''[57]

In Washington, General Jackson was eagerly awaiting news from Tennessee. He was now fully convinced of Bell's ''perfidy,'' but apparently he did not yet realize the strength of the White movement. In a long letter[58] he expressed a fear that Polk's promised communication had been delayed by illness, '' for I am sure the little noise, and various meetings, got up by the instrumentality of Mr. Bell and Co. cannot have alarmed you.'' After delivering a homily on the iniquity of abandoning principles, and citing Clay, Calhoun, and Burr as horrible examples, he said that ''Mr. Bell, Davy Crockett & Co. has placed Judge White in the odious attitude of abandoning principle & party for office,'' and with the association of the nullifiers

The eyes of the people soon were opened to this wicked plan, to divide and conquer the Democracy of the union, prostrate the present administration by making it odious by crying out corruption and misrule, and being supported by office holders, and corruption, thereby to bring into power the

---

[55] Scott, *Memoir of Hugh Lawson White*, 292.

[56] Speech printed in the Washington *Globe*, May 29, 1835.

[57] Grundy to Polk, May 11, 1835, *Polk Papers*.

[58] Jackson to Polk, May 3, 1835, *ibid.* The letter was marked ''private for your own eye—it is wrote in haste.''

opposition, recharter the United States Bank, destroying the republican government & substitute in its stead, a consolidated government under the controle of a corrupt monied monopoly.

After scanning this doleful picture of a future possibility, Polk must have felt relieved when he read further on that "Mr. Bell & Co. have not succeeded—Virginia is erect again." "Surely," continued the President, "Tennessee will never put herself in the false position of joining the piedbald opposition of Whiggs, nullifiers, blue light federalists, and Hartford convention men. It cannot be—heaven and every principle of virtue and republicanism forbid it." Had White remained with his party, said Jackson, he might have procured the Vice-Presidency, but

he has been placed by Mr. Bell & Co. as the candidate of the opposition under the odious imputation of abandoning his old republican principles & party, for office, and whether he has or not the world has taken up that opinion, and he never can regain the confidence of that party again. The opposition never intended that he should be elected, they meant to divide, that they might conquer for Mr. Clay who, you may rely, is to be their candidate at last.

He had hopes that "judge White's eyes may be opened and he will *now* see that he is in a false position and abandon Bell, Davy Crockett & Co., and withdraw himself from the odious attitude intriguing apostates have placed him [in]."

It was doubtless pleasing news that Jackson thus fixed the blame for disrupting the party upon Polk's own enemies, Bell and Crockett. Equally pleasing must it have been to read that

You and Grundy, (by the true Republicans in Congress) are looked to, to take a firm and open stand in favour of the republican principles, a *national convention* by *the people*, and in toto, against nullification & disunion—and against *little* caucuses, of a few apostate members of congress, & preserve Tennessee from the disgrace of uniting with the piebald opposition to put down my *administration, and my fame* with it, and give the reigns of Government into the hands of those who have recently conspired to recharter the Bank.

In this fight for principles, said the President, all must take a definite stand; "do your duty (as you have done here) *at home,* and you will stand high with the republicans everywhere.'' Saving Tennessee proved to be a more difficult task than Jackson had anticipated, but, by attempting to do so, Polk and Grundy earned his undying gratitude.

In the President's opinion, two mutually antagonistic factions had joined forces for the purpose of destroying the Republican party. While Bell and Clay were aiming at consolidated government, Calhoun and his friends were using White's name ''to build up a Southern confederacy and divide the union.'' The President still spoke of White with regret more than anger. He did not charge him with being either a consolidationist or a nullifier, and he still had hopes that the judge would free himself from the influence of evil associates.

Jackson was much encouraged by the success won by his party in Virginia, Rhode Island, and Connecticut. As to Tennessee he had fears, but he also had hopes. ''Can it be,'' he said in closing his letter,

that Tennessee will abandon republican principles and be ranked with apostates, nullifiers & bluelight Federalist—Tristam Burges says she will— *forbit it virtue, forbit it heaven*—Tennessee has sustained me thus far, and I trust she never will abandon her principles for any person.

In another long letter written to Polk on May 12, Jackson vented his wrath upon those who held political control of the state for their refusal to participate in the national nominating convention.[59] ''How it is,'' he asked, ''that there is no man in the Republican ranks to take the stump, and relieve Tennessee from her degraded attitude?'' This question may have been intended as a hint for a more aggressive stand on Polk's part. ''If I was a mere citizen of Tennessee again,'' he continued, ''and wanted

---

[59] For example, the Nashville *Banner*, denouncing the national convention, said: ''So long as we live and breathe American air, we will resist the insidious proposition (whensoever and wheresoever it may originate), to lay at the feet of village politicians and placemen, who most usually fill *conventions*, the inestimable privilege of thinking and acting for ourselves in the choice of our rulers.'' Quoted in *Niles' Register* (March 28, 1835), XLVIII, 58.

everlasting fame, I would ask no other theatre to obtain it than before the people of Tennessee."[60] In this letter Jackson spoke of the seceders as "White Whiggs," and although both White and Bell still claimed membership in the Republican party, the press of both parties was beginning to class them as Whigs.[61] It was becoming the custom to apply this name to the National Republicans, of whom Clay was a recognized leader; they, with the White supporters, constituted the new Whig party.[62]

The desire of the Jacksonites to identify White and Bell with the Clay faction of the Whigs was aided materially by the discovery of Bell's "Cassedy" or "Bedford" letter of May 11, 1835.[63] There is nothing particularly damaging to either man in the letter itself, but as construed and placed before the people by their opponents, it was said to be a pledge that White, if elected, would not veto any law for rechartering the bank. The latter part of it was construed as a suggestion that Polk's

---

[60] In *Polk Papers*. Jackson's signature has been cut from this letter.

[61] "Elected, if elected at all, by the votes of the Whigs, he [White] will naturally and necessarily select his councillors from their ranks, and modify his measures according to their views." Richmond *Whig*, quoted by Richmond *Enquirer*, and reprinted in Washington *Globe*, May 4, 1835.

[62] In his letter of May 3 to Polk, above quoted, Jackson spoke of "modern Whiggs." He often omitted the h, and invariably used the double g.

[63] It was written to Charles Cassedy of Bedford County, Tennessee, and read as follows:

"Dear Sir: You will receive enclosed, the manifesto of the White cause and party. I think it contains our principles and the argument upon which they may be sustained briefly set forth.

"You will see by my letter all I know of Judge White's views about the Bank. He doubtless never will swerve from them, but it would be most unprecedented, and do him, and very justly too, a great injury, to be declaring before hand, that he would put his veto upon any measure whatever. It would be said to be an electioneering declaration, and besides Mr. Van Buren has given no such pledges.

"To defeat me for the Speaker's chair, is the main interest which Mr. Polk and Johnson have in this whole contest, as I believe.

"It would not do to ask Polk to vote for me against himself, but he might be made to pledge himself to go for me against any other candidate. My course in appointing him chairman of the Committee of Ways and Means could be used to show that I have not been influenced by personal considerations against him, when the country is concerned.

"Yours truly, "JOHN BELL."
Printed in Nashville *Union*, April 5, 1839.

constituents should pledge him to cast his vote for Bell in the election of a Speaker. Between the lines there was seen a threat to defeat Polk in his campaign for reëlection to Congress unless he should give such a pledge. The rumored contents—before its publication—were far worse than the letter itself, and its appearance in print failed to counteract the effect which the rumors had produced.[64]

Knowing that the people still believed in Jackson despite their loyalty to Judge White, Bell, who was himself a candidate for reëlection, published a long letter in the Nashville *Republican* denying that he had "brought White out" in the sense and for the reasons claimed by the Democrats. "I am not against Jackson or his administration," he wrote, "but I am opposed to Mr. Van Buren."[65] As a blow at Polk, however, he published in a McMinnville paper extracts from the correspondence which had passed between Cave Johnson and the Tennessee delegation at the time that White had been invited to become a candidate. Bell's adversaries now published the entire correspondence in the Nashville *Union,* and that journal highly commended the course which had been pursued by Polk, Grundy, and Johnson. From T. J. Pew, of Kentucky, Laughlin, the editor, learned that during the previous autumn Bell had urged Col. R. M. Johnson to become a candidate on the bank ticket[66] and this paper now claimed to have conclusive proof of Bell's affiliations with the bank. His "Cassedy" letter was published in the *Union* on June 26, and Grundy confidently assured Polk that "that letter will make you Speaker, I think."[67]

During this same month (May 20) Van Buren was nominated for the Presidency by the Baltimore convention, and a bitter

---

[64] A similar letter was written by Bell to a man in Giles County (Kincannon to Polk, June 1, 1835, *Polk Papers*). Kincannon said that he had seen the letter.

[65] Copied by the Washington *Globe*, May 28, 1835.

[66] Laughlin to Polk, May 30, 1835, *Polk Papers*. Pew said that he had seen Bell's letter to Johnson.

[67] Grundy to Polk, June 25, 1835, *ibid*.

national campaign was waged in Tennessee simultaneously with
the contest for supremacy between Polk and Bell. Although
Jackson had, in his "Gwin letter,"[68] asserted that it was to be a
convention "fresh from the people" to whose will all in the party
ought to submit, it was well known that this body had been called
together for the sole purpose of ratifying the "appointment"
already made by the President. His letter to Gwin had failed to
produce the desired effect, for Tennessee did not even send delegates to the convention at Baltimore. Still unwilling to believe
that the people of his state could fail to do his bidding, Jackson
caused a statement to be circulated to the effect that the contest
was really between himself and White, and not between the
judge and Van Buren.[69]

There was much vituperation on either side during the months
which preceded the congressional elections in Tennessee. Both
parties seemed to realize that, if elected, Polk would be chosen
Speaker of the House. Polk was popular in his district and many
of the "White Whigs" remained loyal to him. Toward the close
of the campaign, the Bell forces became more moderate in their
criticisms, for it had become apparent that by indulging too
freely in denunciations they had strengthened both Polk and
Van Buren.[70]

Confident of victory, Jackson, from his retreat at "Rip
Raps," was already planning work for Polk to do as soon as he
had been reëlected.[71] Polk, Grundy, and Johnson were to get up
meetings which would instruct Representatives in Congress to vote
against the chartering of any bank. They were also to induce the
state legislature to instruct the Senators from Tennessee to vote

---

[68] *Niles' Register*, XLVIII, 80–81..

[69] Scott, *Memoir of Hugh Lawson White*, 335.

[70] Polk to Jackson, Aug. 14, 1835, reporting his victory at the polls,
*Polk Papers*.

[71] Clay, said the President, is the real candidate of the opposition, and
Bell will sacrifice White and try to get votes for himself in the Speaker-
ship election. "The Judge will be left politically prostrate as ever, Aron
Burr was, and as few to sympathize with him on his downfall."

for Benton's expunging resolution and against a bank charter. In order to preclude the charge of persecution, he advised that the local meetings should draft their instructions before the legislature had convened and before either Bell or White had been nominated for reëlection as members of Congress. In any event, Bell's "Cassedy letter" would be a sufficient answer to any such charge.[72] And yet the man who wrote this letter vehemently denied that he ever interfered with the free choice of the people!

Some of the party politicians[73] were inclined to doubt the wisdom of having the members of Congress instructed by local meetings. They were not given much choice, however, in the matter of instructing Senators, for the President himself prepared an outline of instructions, which he sent to Governor Carroll. Major Guild was selected to present the instructions in the legislature. Jackson sent to Carroll, also, two volumes of the *Extra Globe* which contained Benton's speeches and other materials that might be useful for reference. He instructed Polk to repair to Nashville before the meeting of the legislature for the purpose of arranging everything for prompt action.[74] He also urged Polk to be in Washington a few days before the opening of Congress, and "there must be a meeting of the friends of the administration & select the candidate for Speaker and elect him the first ballott." He did not state explicitly that Polk would be that candidate, but his assurance that "the New England states will sustain you" indicates that Polk was the President's own choice for the office.[75]

---

[72] Jackson to Polk, Aug. 3, 1835, *Polk Papers.*

[73] For example, A. V. Brown (Brown to Polk, Aug. 27, 1835, *Polk Papers*).

[74] "You must be in Nashville some days before the Assembly meets, every arrangement ought to be made, and as soon as the House is formed the resolutions ought to be offered, or the opposition will forestall you by a set prepared for their own pallate be prompt and do not permit yourselves to be outgeneraled, the first blow is half the battle, and as they are preparing to elect a Senator, these resolutions will strike terror & confusion in their ranks—produce a panic, and blow up all their digested arrangements, and will add all the doubting members to your ranks."

[75] Jackson to Polk, Sept. 15, 1835, *Polk Papers.* "When you read & note burn this" was his final instruction.

Even if there had not already existed a strong personal friendship between Polk and the President, their common desire to overthrow the Bell-White faction was sufficient to identify their political interests.

For the next two months Polk kept Jackson well informed on passing events in Tennessee. With Donelson, also, he kept up a separate correspondence, concerning which they did not always take the President into their confidence.[76] Donelson did not share Jackson's belief that the legislature would adopt the Guild resolutions to instruct the Senators from Tennessee.[77]

In October, while the legislature was in session, Judge White visited Nashville and other nearby towns, where public dinners were given in his honor. Without assigning any reasons, Polk curtly declined to attend any of these, but he reported to the President that White had taken advantage of the occasions to electioneer for himself and to censure Polk, Grundy, and other supporters of the administration. Jackson was much incensed by this information, but he still believed that the effect of the judge's speeches would be counteracted by the debate in the legislature on the expunging resolutions. "Mark these words," he wrote to Polk, "have the yeas & nays taken upon them, and all who votes against them will be taught by the people of Tennessee that they have misrepresented them."[78] White, in Jackson's opinion, could not be too severely condemned for attacking Polk and other members of Congress; "rouse Grundy & Johnson into action, and I will vouch for the virtue of the people."[79]

The President's wish for prompt action on the expunging resolutions was doomed to disappointment; a wearisome discussion

---

[76] Both suspected that Bell had a spy in the President's household by whom he was supplied with administration secrets, but they give no clew as to whom they suspect (Donelson to Polk, Sept. 24, 1835, *Polk Papers*).

[77] Donelson to Polk, Oct. 20, 1835, *ibid.*

[78] "I cannot yet believe," he continued, "that the democratic republicans of Tennessee can be so unjust to me, as to unite with Clay & the opposition in condemning me for preserving the constitution."

[79] Jackson to Polk, Oct. 20, 1835, *Polk Papers.*

followed the introduction of the subject. On the other hand, the legislature very promptly nominated White for the Presidency, even before Jackson's above-quoted letter had reached Tennessee. In his letter of acceptance, White declared emphatically that his political principles had undergone no change; that the administration forces, and not he, had deserted the traditional party standards and become "a mere *faction.*"[80] After the formal nomination had been made the people regarded the campaign as a contest between Jackson and White, and the Presidency was the principal topic of discussion at every local gathering. The country people generally stood loyally by the President, while those living in towns were more apt to favor White.[81]

After the congressional delegation had set out for Washington—Polk to be elected Speaker over his arch enemy, Bell, and Johnson to frighten his friends by his near approach to a duel with the much hated Bailie Peyton[82]—the legislature continued the acrimonious debates on Jackson's expunging resolutions. To add variety, the White supporters in the legislature were accused by their opponents of fraud in connection with the public printing. While the debate was in progress, Jackson sent appeals for support to members of the legislature, and it was said that Polk had prepared the list to be thus solicited. White, also, corresponded with some of the members. He made no attempt to influence their votes, but his exposure of the methods employed by the President to defeat him undoubtedly brought him support. Strong language was used by both sides, and members did not hesitate to call General Jackson a "dictator" or to accuse him of trying to appoint his successor.[83]

---

[80] The documents relating to White's nomination are printed in Scott, *Memoir of Hugh Lawson White*, 331–334.

[81] J. W. Childress to Polk, Nov. 22, 1835, *Polk Papers.*

[82] Laughlin to Polk, Dec. 1; J. W. Johnson to Polk, Dec. 9, 1835, *Polk Papers.*

[83] A. O. P. Nicholson to Polk, Feb. 4, 1836, *ibid.* "It is declared every day & by the leaders, that to Mr. Van B's personal character they do not object—but their great objection is, to Pres' Jackson nominating his successor" (Catron to Polk, Jan. 8, 1836, *ibid.*).

Both Jackson and Bell were said to have flooded the state with ''franked'' political literature for the purpose of influencing both the legislature and the people. But the command of the ''old hero'' was no longer as of yore. The legislature which had so recently nominated Judge White now declined to instruct him to vote for Benton's expunging resolution[84]

Polk was elected Speaker of the House by a large majority, and both in Washington and in Tennessee the defeat of Bell for that office was expected to injure White's prospects in his own state. ''It was urged by the faithful,'' wrote White,

that by the election of Polk, the vote of Tennessee would be changed. The course of Alabama,[85] it was said, will be followed by the legislature of Tennessee, and in a very short time my name will be dropped everywhere. . . . Everything which can be done to my injury, within their power, is done by Grundy and Johnson, from my own State, and probably by Polk, also.[86]

Party leaders in Tennessee undoubtedly believed that White would now withdraw from the race, or that in any case Van Buren would carry the state. Polk received many letters expressing this opinion.[87] Their hopes of defeating the judge were somewhat disturbed by the refusal of the legislature to instruct him on the expunging resolutions, but they were revived by the expected effect of White's votes against some of Jackson's appointments and by his arguments and vote in favor of Clay's land distribution bill.[88]

----

[84] E. H. Foster to White, Feb. 26, 1836 (Scott, *Memoir of Hugh Lawson White*, 337).

[85] The legislature of Alabama nominated White, but on the condition that he should be ''the choice of the republican party throughout the Union.''

[86] White to Geo. W. Churchwell, Jan. 3, 1836 (Scott, *Memoir of Hugh Lawson White*).

[87] Among the rest Nicholson wrote (January 22) that since Polk's election the White men had practically given up the struggle; ''all excitement here has subsided, and the election of V. B. is given up by all but Gen. Barrow.''

[88] Walker to Polk, April 11, 1836. White's vote on the land bill ''must seal his fate,'' wrote Laughlin to Cave Johnson on May 9. One of White's admirers said at a political meeting that he ''had followed White to his grave when he [White] voted for the land bill—and that he could not stand to be buried with him'' (Herndon to Polk, May 25, 1836). All in *Polk Papers*.

One of the most serious handicaps of the administration party in Tennessee was the weakness of their press. The Bell-White faction had procured control of the leading newspapers in Nashville and elsewhere. The Nashville *Union* was the main Democratic organ and Polk was in constant receipt of letters from Laughlin, its editor, which stated that the paper was approaching bankruptcy. Laughlin himself was enthusiastic but unreliable. Many a letter from Nashville politicians reported to Polk that "Laughlin has been drunk for a week." Near the close of the campaign he became so untrustworthy that Judge Catron was obliged to edit the *Union*.[89]

For our present purpose it is unnecessary to follow in detail the remainder of White's campaign for the Presidency. By splitting the Democratic party and by bringing to Polk the powerful support of General Jackson, it was one of the principal factors in elevating Polk to the Speaker's chair. In his attitude toward White, Polk may have in some degree played the "unscrupulous partisan" which Parton says he was,[90] but the political situation which resulted from White's candidacy left him very little choice.[91] He could not coöperate with Bell, and it would have been political suicide to break with the President.

With the remainder of this campaign Polk's political welfare was not so intimately connected. It will therefore be treated incidentally only, in connection with his career as Speaker of the House.

---

[89] Catron to Polk, Sept. 6, 1836, *Polk Papers.*

[90] Parton, *Life of Andrew Jackson,* III, 617,

[91] That partisan Democrats really believed Judge White to have been made the tool of designing politicians and his own ambition is well indicated by Laughlin's entry in his diary on hearing of the death of White. "So, here is the end of ambition—of the ambition of an old politician who had been betrayed and deceived by his pretended friends, John Bell and others, into a course of intrigue and tergiversation, which had cast him from the Senate, had lost him the esteem of all good men in his state, and had embittered his latter days, and probably shortened his life. What a warning his example ought to afford to all thinking and candid men!" (*Diary,* April 14, 1840). As White carried the state by an overwhelming majority, there must inded have been a dearth of "good men" and a surplus of rascals!

CHAPTER VI

## SPEAKER OF THE HOUSE UNDER JACKSON

Following Jackson's advice Polk went to Washington late in November, 1835, in order to prepare the way for his election as Speaker.[1] The twenty-fourth Congress assembled on December 7, and, as the President had planned, Polk was elected on the first ballot. The coveted office was his reward for party loyalty, but he soon discovered that he must also pay the penalty of his success by being the object of more heckling and abuse than had fallen to the lot of any of his predecessors. The Democrats had a substantial majority in the House and were able to carry their measures; but the knowledge of this power only made their opponents more determined to goad the majority by obstructive tactics and by personal vituperation.

The entire period of Polk's speakership was one of political unrest, sectional discord, and personal animosity. Those who had so recently been friends and relentless in pursuing the common enemies, Adams and Tobias Watkins, hated one another all the more cordially now that the party was disintegrating, for each faction believed the other treacherously to have abandoned traditional party principles. On his own account, Polk had to suffer the slings and arrows of his brilliant but censorious rival, and of Peyton, Crockett, and other personal enemies. In addition, all who harbored grudges against the "military chieftain"— whether Nullifiers or Whigs—took keen delight in vitriolic attacks upon the administration, and in making it personally uncomfortable for the Speaker, whom they charged with being the President's creature and obedient slave. To this potpourri of

---

[1] Jackson to Polk, Sept. 15, 1835, *Polk Papers*.

discord was added the battle between Adams and the southern fire-eaters over the abolition petitions. Each side accused the Speaker of unfairness and harrassed him with hairsplitting questions of parliamentary procedure. Fortunately for himself his knowledge of detail, his methodical mind, and his habitual coolness under the most trying ordeals, enabled him to preside over the exciting debates with dignity and success when many a more brilliant man would have met with failure.

The disposition to humiliate Polk was manifested even before he had been elected. As soon as the House had been called to order, the clerk announced the first business to be the election of a Speaker by ballot. To this customary procedure Patton and others objected, and insisted upon a *viva voce* election. Except for showing a disposition on the part of the opposition to resort to annoying tactics whenever possible, this attempt to alter the mode of election was of little importance, for the House proceeded to ballot as usual, and Polk received one hundred and thirty-two votes to eighty-four for Bell—a vote which Benton says "was considered a test of the administration strength, Mr. Polk being supported by that party."[2]

The President's message was sent to Congress on the second day of the session. Evidently descrying the gathering war clouds, Jackson called attention to the dangers that would result from internal dissensions. He again recommended the adoption of an amendment to the Constitution which would prevent the election of a President from devolving upon the House. It is unlikely, however, that he had much hope that his suggestion would be followed.

The standing committees were announced by the Speaker on the fourteenth of December. In forming them, Polk followed the usual custom of placing safe party majorities on those which would have the shaping of important legislation. In so doing he simply followed precedent; but he had, when a minority

---

[2] Benton, *Thirty Years' View*, I, 569.

member, condemned the practice, and by adhering to precedent now he became the object of criticism and abuse.

The first difficult problem which confronted the new Speaker was the disposition of abolition petitions. On December 18, 1835, Jackson, of Massachusetts, presented a memorial in which citizens of his state asked Congress to abolish slavery in the District of Columbia. Hammond, of South Carolina, moved that the petition "be not received," but Polk ruled that such a motion had never before been presented to the House and that under the rules it was not in order. When Hammond offered another motion to "reject" the petition, Polk ruled that any petition might be rejected after it had been received. Although his rulings were logical and fair, they were assailed by the contestants on either side. The Speaker's motives were impugned and appeals were taken to the House, but even John Bell admitted that Polk had made the best disposition of a new and debatable question. This particular petition was sent to the table on Decemcember 21; but others like it soon appeared, and the "right of petition" became one of the most heated topics of debate. The *Globe* upheld the cause of the petitioners. Should the House, it said, yield to the demands made by Hammond and Wise and refuse to receive such petitions, it would be violating one of the most sacred constitutional guaranties.[3]

Nearly all of the northern members held that all petitions from American citizens must be received and that, after reception, Congress might dispose of them as it pleased. Southern members did not deny the right of petition, in the abstract; they were willing, they said, to receive "*bona fide*" petitions. But radicals from that section argued that, inasmuch as the petitioners in question were asking something which did not fall within the power of Congress to perform, there could be no obligation to receive requests to do the impossible.

---

[3] Washington *Globe,* Jan. 1, 1836.

On February 8, Pinckney, of South Carolina, presented a resolution which prescribed a method for dealing with anti-slavery petitions. After its passage by Congress it was popularly known as the "gag rule." It directed that all memorials, already presented or to be presented, praying for the abolition of slavery in the District of Columbia should be referred to a select committee. By the same resolution the committee was instructed to report that Congress possessed no power to interfere with slavery in states and ought not to interfere with it in the District. Regarded as a compromise, the resolution was passed by a large majority, but its provisions did not win the approval of extremists on either side. Slavery restrictionists condemned a measure which to them seemed a combination of cowardice and tyranny, while southern hotspurs like Hammond and Wise were dissatisfied because Congress would not reject all petitions relating to this subject. The recalcitrant members raised endless technical objections and appealed repeatedly from the decisions of the chair, but only in one instance did the House fail to sustain the rulings of the Speaker. Of all the objectors, Wise was the most abusive and unfair. Among other things he accused Polk of trying to force members to "vote like mules" without affording them an opportunity to consider the questions to be decided.

Pinckney's resolution did not succeed in precluding further debate on the subject of slavery. Briggs, of Massachusetts, presented another petition on February 15, and, in response to a question put by Wise, Polk decided that the Pinckney resolution applied only to petitions which had already been received. Thereupon Wise moved that the Briggs petition "be not received," and the Speaker ruled the motion to be in order. The ruling was clearly an error on Polk's part, and his decision was overruled by a vote of the House. His apparent concession to Wise was severely criticized by both northern and southern men. Among the latter, Manning, of South Carolina, said that the effect of the Speaker's decision would be to renew the angry sectional debates which the supporters of the Pinckney resolution had hoped to obviate; in addition, it was an arbitrary setting aside of the will of the House. "If the Speaker," continued Manning, "can by his decision reverse this resolution . . . then he has power to suspend, alter, or change, any deliberate act of this House, intended as a rule for its governance."[4] The vote of the House settled the question for the session at least. The effect of the reversal of Polk's decision was to apply the "gag rule" to all petitions that might appear, and to refer them automatically to the select committee. It was, of course, well understood that they would not be considered or reported back by the committee.

The Nashville *Republican* criticized Polk for being unable to keep order in the House. It contrasted him unfavorably with Bell, and *proved* his incompetence by citing numerous appeals that had been taken from his decisions. The *Globe* replied that the disorder and appeals were machinations of Bell's henchmen, who had been purposely trying to discredit the Speaker. It pointed with pride to the fact that only one of his decisions—a new rule which Polk had construed in favor of the Bell men— had been reversed by the House.[5]

The twenty-fourth Congress had not been long in session before the candidacy of Judge White entered into the debates of the House. On January 2, 1836, the *Globe* charged that Nullifiers, like Wise, and Abolitionists were supporting White for no other reason than to draw votes from Van Buren. For the same reason, it said, Webster was urged to run on a ticket of his own. In turn, Wise embraced every opportunity to attack the President and administration members, including the Speaker, and to accuse them of engaging in political intrigues.

---

[4] *Cong. Globe,* 24 Cong., 1 sess., App., 145.

[5] "The truth is, Mr. Polk has deserved the confidence of the House by a firm, faithful, industrious, and able discharge of his duties." This paper denied that Polk desired or had been offered a place in the cabinet, for the administration wished him to remain in the Speaker's chair (Washington *Globe,* March 16, 1836).

Such an opportunity was presented when Adams moved that a certain passage of the President's message be referred to a select committee. During the last days of the twenty-third Congress the House had passed, as part of the general appropriation bill, an item of $3,000,000 to be expended for national defense by order of the President. As the two houses had been unable to agree on certain details, the measure was defeated in the Senate. The President in his message deplored the failure of Congress to pass this necessary measure, and again recommended the appropriation. Adams moved that the subject be referred to a select committee for the purpose of ascertaining by whose fault the appropriation had been lost.[6] While debating the question, Wise sarcastically remarked that it was a most important subject, for "the fate of the presidential canvass is in part made to depend upon it." The President, he said, had intended to use the money as a secret service fund; had Cambreleng not refused to accept the reasonable amendments proposed by the Senate, the measure would have carried. He charged Polk with having solicited votes for the appropriation on the plea that the President desired it, and with having requested the members solicited to refrain from mentioning this fact.[7] Scarcely a measure came before the House that was not made by Wise the motif for an assault upon the administration. His criticisms of the Speaker were many and bitter, and frequent though futile were his appeals from the decisions of the chair. Polk's friends thought that Wise and Peyton were trying to provoke the Speaker into fighting a duel; even his own family feared that blood might be shed.[8]

---

[6] The *National Intelligencer* had asserted that the House, not the Senate, had been at fault—a charge which Adams resented.

[7] Jan. 21, 22, 29. *Cong. Globe*, 24 Cong., 1 sess.

[8] James Walker advised Polk to treat their abuse with contempt. No one, he said, would doubt the Speaker's physical courage. The whole matter was, in his opinion, a scheme of Bell to disgrace Polk by drawing him into a duel with either Wise or Peyton (Walker to Polk, March 14, 1836, *Polk Papers*).

Although Bell was less abusive than either Wise or Peyton, he frequently questioned the justice of the Speaker's rulings and accused him of partisan bias.[9]  On February 3, 1836, during a debate on the reference of a Senate bill for limiting the terms of certain officers, Bell said that never before had so many things of importance been excluded from the discussions of the House "by forms and decisions upon the rules."  His principal speech of the session was delivered while the naval appropriation was being discussed in the House.  He had little to say on the subject under consideration, but, having avowed his intention "to indulge the privilege of debate to the utmost limit of parliamentary license," he launched into an extended discussion of "the general policy of the present Administration, as lately developed."[10]  He employed the present occasion, he said, because those who were in control of the House took good care to exclude any resolution to which such remarks as he desired to make would be really germane.  After twitting the Speaker with having changed his opinions on the subject of patronage,[11] he arraigned the administration party for having abandoned the principles on which General Jackson had been chosen President.  It was not surprising, he said, that strange doctrines should appear, inasmuch as the single principle which is common to the present majority is unlimited devotion, not to any particular creed, but to *the party*.  He pointed out with remarkable precision the evils of abject partyism, and the inevitable abuses which result from

---

[9] Perhaps, as was later suggested by the Boston *Age* (Aug. 17, 1836), prudence led Bell to refrain from leading the assault and to delegate this function to his two associates.  Still, Wise needed little urging, and the fact that Bailie Peyton was a nephew of Judge White was sufficient to account for his animosity.

[10] March 16, 22, 25, 1836. *Cong. Globe*, 24 Cong., 1 sess., App., 722 ff.

[11] "It was, I believe, a private scheme [earlier] of my colleague, who is now the presiding officer of this House [Mr. Polk] to take from the Secretary of State the power of designating the publishers of the laws, and to vest it in the House of Representatives; so important at that day was the purity of the public press regarded by the Jackson party."

personal government by a popular hero.[12]  His own speech was no doubt intended for campaign purposes, but the picture which he drew of existing evils was none the less accurate on that account.  If it lacked in any particular, it was in being too charitable to the President himself, for after all Jackson was the individual most responsible for perpetuating those evils in the interest of party discipline.  There were other critics of the

---

[12] ''How has it happened that these abuses have not only been suffered to exist, but even to increase, under an Administration so decidedly popular and powerful?  When this problem shall be solved to the satisfaction of the public, the remedy will be supplied.  The true answer to the question, how these abuses came to exist under such an Administration, is, because the *Administration is such* as it is, because it is *popular*.  Every man of sound mind and lawful age knows that the President, nor any other being of created existence, can exercise a personal inspection and superintendence over all, or even a tenth part of the most important details of the public service.  Yet every important transaction connected with the public service is so managed by the subordinate officers, as to throw the responsibility upon the President.  If the delinquent officers do not do this themselves, their defenders in Congress and out of Congress do not fail, in effect, to fix the responsibility there.  Whether in Congress, or in the country, complaint is made of abuse in any branch of the public service, the answer is, eternally, that the charge is meant as an attack upon General Jackson!  His great name and popularity are the shield and buckler of every official delinquent, whether from incompetency or infidelity, from a clerk to the head of a Department—from the register or receiver of a land office, or an Indian agent, to a Minister Plenipotentiary!  The name and services of General Jackson, I repeat, are invoked to shield and cover, as with a mantle, every official transgression or omission, from the highest to the lowest, whenever it suits the interest of party to avail themselves of them.

''And the people are called upon to rally round—to stand by and defend—not the individual arraigned—not the delinquent department, but the President himself, who it is asserted through a thousand channels, is intended to be struck at and stabbed through the sides of the accused officer or Department.  The people cannot at once detect the artifices of party.  They are jealous of everything which savors of an attack upon General Jackson, and they in general act upon that suspicion.  Those, therefore, who dare, here or elsewhere, to find fault with the course of affairs, upon any ground, instead of finding countenance from those in power, or from the dominant party—instead of being cheered on in the ungracious task of reform, are met on the threshold, with the charge of secret and sinister motives—with anti-Jacksonism!  They are told, that their object is to assail the character of the hero of New Orleans, and the conqueror of the United States Bank; as if either one or the other of those victories could be of any worth now or hereafter, except to protect the Constitution, the country, and its liberties—as if those victories could be of any value, if as the price of them we are to surrender that very Constitution, those very liberties—those rich and glorious prizes for which

administration,[13] but none covered the whole ground so thoroughly and so accurately as did Bell.

The attacks made by Wise on the Speaker and the administration were capricious and, to his associates, extremely entertaining. His assertions, however, were more irritating than convincing. His own resolution, which called for an investigation of the method by which state banks of deposit had been selected, gave him an opportunity to vent his wrath upon Reuben M. Whitney, and upon those who had employed Whitney. His time was ill spent; assailing Whitney's reputation was like slaying the dead.

Throughout the session the Presidential campaign was a topic of absorbing interest. Few questions came before the House that did not elicit a discussion of the approaching election. This was natural, perhaps, for Van Buren had been nominated for the avowed purpose of continuing the policies of the present administration, and it was from these very policies that the White element of the party had revolted. On this subject personal animosity increased as the end of the session approached. As

those battles were fought and won. If those who venture to make charges against any department of the public service are not met precisely in this way, they are, at all events, told, that General Jackson is the head of the Government—that he is responsible for all the executive branches of the public service, and no attack can be made upon any branch of the public service, therefore, without attacking him, and everybody knows that he does his duty. A most shameful, egregious, and pernicious flattery. But the absurdity of the argument does not prevent it from being constantly interposed. The argument is, that because General Jackson is able, faithful, and patriotic, in the discharge of all his duties, therefore all the subordinate officers of the Government are so likewise. But more: if anyone shall reply to all this, and that he means no attack upon General Jackson, that he is willing to exonerate him from any agency in the abuses which are alleged to exist, he is forthwith denounced as a hypocrite—as a dastardly assailant, who wants the courage and independence to make a direct attack. He is dared to come forward like a man, and assail General Jackson as the author of all these abuses—his pride is appealed to—his feelings are chafed to draw him on to utter the fatal denunciation; and the moment he does so, the myrmidons of the party stand ready to hack him to pieces! These, sir, are the true *causes* of the continued abuses in the public service.''

[13] Robertson, of Virginia, when speaking (April 5) on the same bill, asserted that the administration desired a large appropriation for the navy so that there might be no surplus to distribute among the states.

if to make amends for the moderation displayed in his speech on the naval appropriation bill, Bell, when discussing the river and harbor bill on June 23, severely castigated both the Speaker and the administration. He charged the administration with deliberate extravagance, and said that the Committee of Ways and Means had been purposely organized by Polk ''upon a principle of extravagance.''[14] His purpose was to show, as Robertson, of Virginia, had tried to show when discussing the naval appropriation bill on April 5 that the administration hoped to nullify the effect of Clay's ''distribution bill'' by leaving no surplus for distribution among the states. However, it is difficult to see how Polk could have anticipated the passage of this bill when he appointed the Committee of Ways and Means.

Bell had little reason to complain of Polk's committees, for, as Gillet, of New York, pointed out (June 24), they were substantially the same as those appointed by himself.[15] In selecting his committees Polk had given no greater advantage to the majority than was customary, yet it is interesting to recall in this connection that he, too, during the Adams administration, had complained because ''studied majorities'' had been placed on committees, ''in conformity to a previous secret understanding,

---

14 ''I have said that I regard this bill as the result of a deliberate system of extravagance—of a plan for increasing the wants of the Government, and exhausting the Treasury. . . . I affirm that your Committee of Ways and Means of this House was organized upon a principle of extravagance. Look at the composition of that committee, sir, and then tell me it was not constituted with a deep design, and expressly with a view to the largest expenditure for which a pretext could be found, in every branch of the public service. Was there ever such a Committee of Ways and Means appointed in this House? Was there ever a more palpable desertion of the principle of representation—a more shameful abandonment of the interests of the entire interior of the country?'' (*Cong. Globe*, 24 Cong., 1 sess., App., 745).

15 Gillet scathingly denounced Bell's attitude toward Polk. He twitted Bell with not having defended his constituent (the President) when during the last Congress he had been called a *toothless tyrant* by a member of the opposition party. Repelling such attacks upon the President and declining to attend a caucus of the Tennessee delegation were the only crimes, said Gillet, of which Polk could be convicted, and as Speaker, ''even his political opponents bear testimony to his capacity, honesty, and impartiality.''

among the favorites at Court.''[16]   Both men advocated majority rule, yet neither accepted it with good grace when he chanced to be numbered with the minority.

In this same speech Bell reverted to the caucus of the Tennessee delegation, which had been called to consider the nomination of Judge White.  He said that the main object of the meeting had been to test the sincerity of certain members and that two of these gentlemen, Polk and Grundy, ''are at this moment in the enjoyment of the rewards of their hypocrisy and their treachery to their colleagues.''  He still spoke with respect of General Jackson and denied that he had ever called the President a tyrant or a crouching sycophant.  ''He may be the master of *slaves* and *menials*,'' said Bell, ''but nature has disqualified him from becoming one himself.''

The first session of the twenty-fourth Congress terminated on July 4, 1836.  Among its legislative acts were the admission to statehood of Arkansas and Michigan, and the reorganization of the general post-office along lines advocated by Amos Kendall.  Another law approved the President's order for removing public deposits from the Bank of the United States, and regulated for the future the method of depositing public money in state banks.  As a result of the payment in full of the national debt, Clay introduced in the Senate his well-known measure for distributing among the states the surplus revenue of the federal government.  As it was made to assume the guise of a deposit rather than a gift, the bill passed both houses of Congress and was signed— but with reluctance—by the President.  On June 7, while the bill was before the House, an attempt was made to refer it to the Committee of the Whole, for the purpose, said the *Globe,* of prolonging the debate and thereby defeating the admission of Arkansas and Michigan.  Polk blocked such a reference by casting his ballot in the negative and making it a tie vote.[17]

---

[16] Polk to Colonel Wm. Polk, Dec. 14, 1826, *Col. Wm. Polk Papers.*

[17] Washington *Globe,* June 10, 1836.

Although the Speakership is the most important and responsible position in the House, and although the Speaker's influence upon legislation is surpassed by few other officers of the federal government,[18] yet, from the very nature of his position, that influence is difficult to trace. By the personnel of his committees, by his decisions, by his control over debate by recognizing or refusing to recognize members who may desire to speak, one may trace in a general way the part played by the Speaker; but necessarily he takes little part in the discussions of the House. Polk did not even avail himself of the privilege of participating in debate when the House had resolved itself into a Committee of the Whole. For this reason his views on the various measures are not readily ascertained, and during this particular period his private correspondence affords little assistance. That he satisfied the party which elected him, there is abundant evidence in the records of the House, and in the public press. That he possessed the necessary knowledge and coolness of temperament to avoid the pitfalls prepared by his adversaries, is equally clear. "Never," said the editor of the Boston *Age,*

was man more rigidly and constantly assailed by a pack of untiring pursuers, than was Mr. Speaker Polk by his uncompromising assailants. They left no stone unturned that could be moved to his disadvantage. . . . But notwithstanding all the efforts that were made to destroy Mr. Polk, he passed the ordeal unscathed, and ultimately triumphed.

The editor said that he did not like Polk personally, and that he had preferred Bell for Speaker, still "it is but an act of justice to say of him, that he discharged his duties with great ability, promptness, and throughout the session was popular with an immense majority of the members," and self-respect compelled

---

[18] Mrs. Polk probably voiced her husband's sentiments when she said, years afterward: "The Speaker, if the proper person, and with a correct idea of his position, has even more power and influence over legislation, and in directing the policy of parties, than the President or any other public officer." Conversation with Samuel J. Randall. Quoted in Nelson, *Memorials of Sarah Childress Polk,* 206.

northern Whigs to support the Speaker in putting down Wise and his friends.[19]

After the adjournment of Congress on July 4, the great problem to be solved by the administration forces was not so much how to elect Van Buren, for that seemed certain, but how to save Tennessee. The prospect of losing the vote of the President's own state was most humiliating to himself and to the entire party. At first Jackson could not believe such a calamity possible; but, as the campaign proceeded, even he began to realize that, if the state could be saved at all, it could be done only by heroic efforts.

As usual, Jackson spent his vacation at the Hermitage, and during the summer he was honored with public dinners at various places. The people of Nashville entertained him with a barbecue to which "all creation" was invited.[20] The press and the platform of the respective parties vied with each other in regaling the people with political gasconade and personal abuse of the opposing politicians. On the President's side were Polk, Grundy, Cave Johnson, and Judge Catron, assisted by many lesser lights who followed their directions. Opposed to them were White, Bell, Peyton, and Foster, aided by a much longer and much abler list of second-rate assistants than could be rallied to the Jackson standard.

The most serious handicap with which the administration leaders had to cope was the want of an influential press. The Nashville *Union,* which had been founded after Bell had obtained control of the other Nashville papers, had never prospered, and was now in the final stages of bankruptcy. Long, the proprietor, had given up in despair and gone to Athens in East Tennessee to edit an obscure Van Buren sheet of precarious existence.[21] Due to drink, Laughlin, the editor of the *Union,* had become so unreliable that Catron, in the heat of the campaign, was forced

---

[19] Boston *Age,* Aug. 17, 1836; copy among *Polk Papers.*
[20] Laughlin to Polk, Aug. 8, 1836, *Polk Papers.*
[21] Long to Polk, Aug. 21, 1836, *ibid.*

to come to the rescue and edit the paper himself.[22]   The Washington *Globe* devoted considerable space to political affairs in Tennessee.  It tried to convince the people of the state that White could not by any possibility be elected, and that his nomination had been the work of instruments of Clay and Calhoun, who were conspiring against Jackson and Van Buren and attempting to deceive the people of Tennessee.[23]   Bell, of course, was charged with being the chief conspirator.  ''It is painful,'' said the *Globe* on October 7,

to a fair mind to deal with petty tricks—the offspring of low cunning— of a man educated as a pettifogger, and improved into a political Machiavel by a persevering study of the arts of deception in a seven years' apprenticeship in Congress.  John Bell has arrived at a point which entitles him to a diploma as a political imposter

who is trying to deceive the people of Tennessee.  As examples of Bell's hypocrisy, it cited his original opposition to White and his attempt to induce R. M. Johnson to run for President on a bank platform.

Much emphasis was placed on White's alleged affiliation with friends of the United States Bank.  Bell's ''Cassedy letter'' was said to have pledged White, in the event of his election, to sign a bill for rechartering the bank.  In several letters, Van Buren had already stated his unalterable opposition to such an institution, and by so doing furnished an excuse for the catechizing of his rival.  In a letter addressed to him by one of the local Democrats, White was asked the definite question whether he, if elected, would sign a bill to establish a bank of discount and deposit, or one of deposit only.  It was hoped that the letter would place the judge in an embarrasing position, but this hope was not realized. He met the issue squarely by stating that, while he considered the bank question to be obsolete, he would nevertheless give his

---

[22] After the campaign was over Catron, in a letter to Polk (Nov. 24) said that, while he hated to desert a man for ''that infirmity,'' they must have a reliable editor.

[23] Washington *Globe*, Aug. 27 and Sept. 5, 1836.

views on the subject. He had always believed, he said, that Congress did not possess the power to authorize any bank to transact business within the states; moreover, even if the power existed, it should not be exercised. This was still his opinion.[24]

In a speech delivered at Knoxville in August, White had already given a very complete statement of the principles for which he stood. He enumerated the doctrines which had been advocated by himself and the President at the time of the latter's first election. For advocating these same doctrines, said he, the President is now "openly denouncing me as a 'red hot Federalist,' having abandoned his Administration and being as far from him as the poles are asunder." The judge claimed to uphold the Republican creed of Jefferson, while the President is on "that side which leads directly to monarchy, although I hope he does not so intend it."[25]

Not even Jackson could shake the faith of Tennesseans in the ability and the integrity of Judge White. Even though the motives of his leading supporters may have been somewhat questionable, nothing that was ignoble or equivocal could be traced to White himself. He carried the state in spite of the misrepresentations of his traducers, and never again during the life of the "hero of New Orleans" was Tennessee to be found in the Democratic column at a Presidential election—although one of her own sons was the candidate in 1844.

The President was greatly mortified by the loss of his state. He declared that White had always been a hypocrite, and that the "morals of society" demanded his exposure.[26] But the mote in

---

[24] Andrew A. Kincannon to White, Sept. 14; White to Kincannon, Sept. 19, 1836, *Polk Papers.*

[25] Speech printed in Scott, *Memoir of Hugh Lawson White,* 346 ff. Excerpts in Washington *Globe,* Sept. 23, 1836.

[26] "Nothing but falsehood appears to be the weapons of our modern new born White Whigs of Tennessee in their late political crusade. White, Bell, Peyton, Murray & Co. appear to have abandoned truth, and now when the election is over, does not wish to be held accountable for their falsehoods . . . should I live to get home, a duty I owe to truth & the morals of society will induce me to expose Judge White, Mr. Bell, Mr. Peyton,

his brother's eye obscured the huge beam in his own own; his unfair treatment of White had been the determining factor in making the Judge a candidate and in winning for him the electoral vote of the state.

Congress reassembled on December 5 and, on the following day, received the last annual message of General Jackson. This document criticized the operation of the deposit act passed at the last session and advised the adjustment of revenue to the actual needs of the government. It informed Congress of the promulgation of the "specie circular" and asked that the policy therein adopted be made permanent by legislative enactment. It urged that the finances of the government should be put on a hard money basis. The tone of the message was optimistic, and indicative of the satisfaction felt by the President with the results of his administration. It contained no hint that he even suspected the country to be already on the verge of one of its most disastrous industrial and financial crises.

To carry the administration program through the House was a task of little difficulty for the Speaker. Polk arranged his committees on a political basis, and there was a safe majority in that body to insure the passage of desired measures. It required both skill and patience, however, to preserve order and to render harmless the assaults of an opposition whose animosity had not been lessened by their recent defeat at the polls.

Early in the session there appeared a new avalanche of memorials in which Congress was asked to abolish slavery in the District of Columbia. Generally, but not always, they were presented by John Quincy Adams. Polk decided that the "gag rule" had

---

Mr. Murray, and their falsehoods, so that the moral part & truth loving portion of the citizens of Tennessee may judge what credit can be reposed in those men, when they make assertions as to the acts & doings of others. I now believe that Judge White has been acting the hypocrite in politics, all his life, and individually to me—that he is unprincipled & vindictive I have full proof—that he will willfully lie, his Knoxville speech amply shows. I can forgive, & will, but I never can forget hypocrisy, or the individual capable of it" (Jackson to Rev. H. M. Cryer, Nov. 13, 1836, *Am. Hist. Mag.*, IV, 242–243).

expired with the last session, and so the whole question was once more open for discussion. After several heated debates, the rule was reënacted in an aggravated form which sent all such petitions to the table as soon as presented, without even the courtesy of a reference to a committee. Southern members looked upon these petitions as the work of fanatics[27] whose sole purpose was malicious mischief. They failed to realize that abolition was simply one among the many manifestations of the birth of a public conscience and of a desire to reform the world. The old idea that governments should not abridge personal privileges, even by eradicating admitted evils, was, during this period, rapidly giving way to a new belief that society as well as individuals possesses rights, and that governments are in duty bound to protect them. It was a period among which "isms" of various sorts flourished, and among the number, *abolitionism.* The most important and permanent product which resulted from this social unrest and striving for the ideal was the emergence of a public conscience and a determination to adjust individual conduct to the standards of public opinion. A feeling of responsibility for existing evil led the troubled conscience to seek power to eradicate it, and in seeking the necessary power the reformers naturally turned to the federal government. Calhoun understood the changed viewpoint far better than did his contemporaries. He realized that, on the subject of slavery, a national conscience had developed, although he may have exaggerated the part played in this development by the Nullification proclamation of General Jackson.[28]

---

[27] "Abolition," said Bynum, of North Carolina, Jan. 9, 1837, "is priestcraft [i.e. New England clergy], concocted and brought into existence by their unholy alliance with the superstitious and ignorant of both sexes."

[28] Speaking in the Senate on the Oregon bill, Aug. 12, 1849, Calhoun said: "The abolition of African slavery in its old form in the British West India Islands, and the long and violent agitation which preceded it, did much to arouse this feeling at the North, and confirm the impression that it was sinful. But something more was necessary to excite it into action,—and that was, a belief, on the part of those who thought it sinful, that they were responsible for its continuance.

"It was a considerable time before such a belief was created, except to a very limited extent. In the early stages of this Government, while

The enactment of gag rules resulted in more harm than good to the cause which they were intended to benefit. Many who had little sympathy with abolitionists disapproved of this drastic method of stifling public opinion. They regarded the gag laws as a fatal blow to the right of petition, although it is difficult to see why the southern members were not right in their contention that this right extended only to those who would petition about their own grievances, and not those of other persons. The right of the people to petition for a redress of their own grievances was never questioned by the most belligerent of the southern fire-eaters.

Polk was a slaveholder, but he did not let this fact influence his decisions. When objections were raised because Adams insisted upon presenting petitions from states other than Massachusetts the Speaker decided, on February 6, 1837, that "every member had a right to present a petition, come from what quarter it might." Adams thereupon informed the Speaker that he had a petition purporting to have come from slaves and asked if it would fall within the regular rule. The character of the petitioners presented a new point in procedure, which Polk did not attempt to decide; instead, he asked for a ruling by the House. Without seeking to ascertain the nature of the petition—which

---

it was yet called, and regarded to be, a federal Government, slavery was believed to be a local institution, and under the exclusive control of the Governments of the States. So long as this impression remained, little or no responsibility was felt on the part of any portion of the North, for its continuance. But with the growth of the power and influence of the Government, and its tendency to consolidation,—when it became usual to call the people of these States a nation, and this Government national, the States came to be regarded by a large portion of the North, as bearing the same relation to it, as the counties do to the States; and as much under the control of this Government, as the counties are under that of their respective State Governments. The increase of this belief was accompanied by a corresponding increase of the feeling of responsibility for the continuance of slavery, on the part of those in the North who considered it so. At this stage it was strengthened into conviction by the proclamation of General Jackson and the act of Congress authorizing him to employ the entire force of the Union against the Government and people of South Carolina." Having discovered the extent of *national* power, said Calhoun, the abolitionists have, since 1835, been striving to bring it into operation (Calhoun, *Works*, IV, 517–521).

turned out to be a hoax, and asked for the expulsion of Adams—
southern members wasted much time in an intemperate tirade
against the venerable ex-President. They at first demanded his
expulsion, and, failing in this, asked that he should be censured
''for giving color to an idea'' that slaves might address a communication to Congress. After Adams had riddled their arguments with sarcasm and ridicule, the House finally ended the
matter by deciding simply that slaves had no right to petition.
The charge made by Adams that Polk had exercised arbitrary
authority in his decisions on the subject of petitions seems to have
been wholly unwarranted, for the Speaker accorded him every
privilege which the rules of the House permitted.[29]

The Speaker's enemies tried on many occasions to confuse
him by propounding unusual and complicated questions, but in
this they were invariably disappointed. His thorough knowledge
of parliamentary procedure, and his ability to anticipate their
designs and to prepare for them, enabled him to render his decisions promptly and correctly. Never frustrated, he was quick
to see the bearing of an unusual proposition.[30] Although he
safeguarded the interests of the administration whenever possible,
yet his rulings were sustained—almost without exception, by a
considerable number of his political opponents.

The most severe charge which was brought against Polk during
the session arose out of the investigation of Reuben M. Whitney's
connection with the Treasury Department. It was alleged that
Whitney had given out advance information to speculators

---

[29] Polk's opinion of Adams' conduct and his complaints is recorded in
an undated manuscript in the *Polk Papers*. It is an answer to letters
written by Adams to the Quincy *Patriot*. ''The Speaker carries out and
enforces the decisions of the majority & therefore he represents in his
letter that the 'Speaker and the majority of the House' have undertaken
to exercise 'arbitrary authority.' If Mr. Adams is unwilling to submit
to the decisions of the majority of the House, he is unfit to be a member
of that body. . . . His complaints that his petitions were not read,—
shows either a total ignorance of the rules of the House, or is an attempt
to impose on the public'' (*Polk Papers*, undated, vol. 80).

[30] For example, Bell's motion of January 10 for leave to bring in a
bill to secure freedom of elections.

regarding the purport of Jackson's specie circular, and that he had been a partner in the resulting speculations. It was said, also, that he had levied blackmail upon the state banks which had been selected as depositories for government funds. A majority of the committee which Polk appointed to investigate these charges exonerated Whitney, but, in a minority report, Peyton, of Tennessee, accused the Speaker and the majority of the committee with having deliberately covered the fraud out of subserviency to the President. Nothing better, he said, could be expected from a Speaker who had crawled up to his office and had exchanged principle for power.[31] Even if these charges had been true, Peyton was not the man to throw stones. Hamer, of Ohio, forced him to admit that he had himself solicited for Bell the support of the President on the plea that Bell was a good party man and that Polk had been seeking votes from the Nullifiers.

The short but stormy session was adjourned by the Speaker on March 3, 1837. Although Polk had been severely criticized by some of his enemies, no one—as was done two years later—refused to join in extending to him the customary vote of thanks. The administration and its defenders had been denounced in violent language for alleged interference in elections, abuse of the power of patronage, and derangement of the finances of the country. Investigations had been demanded, and in some cases undertaken, but the charges had not been sustained. Indeed, so long as Polk had the selection of committees, there was small danger that any malfeasance would be *officially* unearthed.

For good or for evil, General Jackson had triumphed over all opposition. Van Buren had been chosen to succeed him, Taney

---

[31] ''The *price*, in *these days*, which must be paid for *power*, is the *sale* and *prostration* of *every principle* of *honor, patriotism, independence;* and I fear, sir, the day is distant when we shall see the *Speaker* of an *American Congress* dare to appoint investigation committees, a majority of which will be in favor of inquiry, how important soever it may be to the *preservation* of the *institutions* and *liberties* of *this country*. . . . Any man who *crawls* up to that point [Speakership] in *these days,* will never hazard the *consequences* of a *patriotic,* a *generous,* or a *noble* action; it would be fatal to him.'' March 1, 1837 (*Cong. Globe*, 24 Cong., 2 sess., App., 349–359).

had been confirmed as Marshall's successor, the mortifying censure of the Senate had been expunged, and the Bank of the United
States no longer existed as a federal institution.  On the last day
of the session Congress passed an act which not only carried out
another of the President's wishes, but which affected materially
the future career of the Speaker of the House.  Incorporated in
the civil appropriation bill was a clause providing for the outfit of
a minister to Texas, which meant, in effect, a recognition of Texan
independence.  The already approaching financial crisis made
Congress unwilling to continue by law the policy of the specie
circular, as Jackson had recommended in his message; instead,
that body sent him, on the last day of the session, a bill which
would virtually annul the celebrated circular.  But even in this,
"Old Hickory" had his way.  He declined to sign the bill on the
ground that its provisions were obscure and contradictory.[32]

[32] Richardson, *Messages*, III, 282.

CHAPTER VII

## SPEAKER OF THE HOUSE UNDER VAN BUREN

Judge White's victory in Tennessee humiliated, and for the time being discouraged, the Democrats of that state. Before the winter had passed, however, their hopes revived and they began to lay plans for the future. They were encouraged by the belief that White would never again be a candidate and that the main cause of defection would therefore be removed. In a letter to Polk, Nicholson said that the opposition leaders were determined to hold the state, and would do all in their power to injure Van Buren. But the people, said he, had gone over to White for purely personal reasons and would return to the Democratic fold.[1] Childress, also, had hopes that the people would renew their allegiance. He believed, on the other hand, that the leaders of the White party would vote for "Theodore Dwight himself" if he were run on the opposition ticket.[2] Still another informant discovered that the White faction was plotting to get control of the legislature for the purpose of ousting Grundy from the federal Senate. They were planning, he thought, to run Bailie Peyton for Governor; and should this be done, no one except Polk or Jackson could defeat him.[3] At the Hermitage Jackson was busily engaged in repelling slanders invented and circulated by the Whigs. One of these slanders was that, as a result of endorsing notes for relatives, the General had become financially ruined and now wanted a national bank. Protesting that he never had and never would favor a bank, Jackson announced his intention

---

[1] Nicholson to Polk, Jan. 22, 1837, *Polk Papers.*

[2] Childress to Polk, Feb. 17, 1837, *ibid.*

[3] J. H. Talbot to Polk, April 21, 1837, *ibid.*

to prepare an article on the subject which he desired Polk to see before its publication.[4]

Democrats were united in their desire to regain control of the state, but opinions differed as to the better method of procedure. Grundy advocated a conciliatory attitude toward the White supporters; this policy was adopted, and was voiced by John O. Bradford, the new editor of the Nashville *Union*.[5] But the seceders did not respond to kind treatment. Dunlap was badly beaten in his campaign for reëlection to Congress, and his district sent only bank supporters to the state legislature.[6] Cave Johnson was likewise unexpectedly defeated by an opponent who was as "bitter and malignant" as John Bell.[7] The result of the election caused a tempest at the Hermitage. Still blind to the real cause of the dissensions within his party, Jackson, in characteristic fashion, denounced the temporizing policy of Grundy and the *Union*.[8]

The outcome of the state elections and the fact that the sub-treasury plan was unpopular in Tennessee[9] led Catron and

---

[4] Jackson to Polk, May 22, 1837, *ibid.*

[5] Catron to Polk, July 7, 1837, *ibid.*

[6] Dunlap to Polk, Aug. 7, 1837, *ibid.*

[7] Johnson to Polk, Aug. 7, 1837, *ibid.* One gets an interesting glimpse of the prevailing professional ethics from his remark that he is going to Mississippi to practice law, for "I cannot charge my friends & my enemies will not employ me." In another letter to Polk, August 14, Johnson tells a story which indicates that election methods in his day were not unlike those of our own: "I was beaten in the last two days by the almost united action of the merchants & iron makers—who as if by concert upon my leaving a county for the last time went to work, under the pretence of collecting their debts, telling the people that they would be compelled to collect in gold & silver if I were elected—the price of property be reduced to almost nothing and the people ruined. Some of the iron makers, told their workmen, that they could not be employed if I was elected."

[8] "Davidson [County] has resulted as I expected, from the imbecile councils, of the Nashville politicians. The Union has been Muzzled by some unseen hands, and has been a great help to the enemy instead of benefit to the republican party. Mr. Grundy will feel the effects, of the combination, which has been produced by supineness & want of courage" (Jackson to Polk, Aug. 6, 1837, *Polk Papers*).

[9] James Walker informed Polk on August 27 that if the Van Buren administration should adopt the sub-treasury plan, it would find itself in

other prominent Democrats to believe that the state could never be regained by pursuing Grundy's conciliatory policy. It was a battle of numbers against wealth, said Catron,[10] and war to the knife was therefore the true Republican policy. He favored the sub-treasury plan, for "the Treasury is the arm of power" and must not be placed in private hands; the possession of government money by private banks "will convert the keepers into Federalists in principle & practice in a few years." Unlike Jackson and Van Buren, he advocated the emission of paper money by the Treasury, for the people want it and "numbers will govern in fact, in Congress, & out of it." Although he approved in general the idea of a sub-treasury, still, after reading the new President's message on the subject, he pronounced the plan there suggested to be sound in principle, but hardly possible in practice. The people, he said, demanded something more tangible, and unless provision were made for issuing paper money, the party would surely go down to defeat.[11] "Strike boldly," was his advice to Polk, "it is your habit, & the means of your elevation; it is expected of you."[12]

The echo of Jackson's farewell address had scarcely died away before the long-gathering financial storm burst upon the country, leaving in its wake the wrecks of shattered banks, ruined business enterprises, and a panic-stricken people. So desperate were

---

the minority in Tennessee, as the plan was too unwieldy and costly. White, he said, had announced that he was not opposed to a bank located in the District of Columbia, with branches in the states. Walker thought that this idea would win in Tennessee if states instead of individuals were made stockholders (*Polk Papers*).

10 "Open war, & to the knife, has ever been the course for the Republican side—no other position is left for it, nor has there been, since the days of Jefferson. It is the contest of Wealth against numbers; sapped by the statutes of descents when wealth consisted of Estates: but the European policy is here basing itself upon *incorporated* & merchantile wealth" (Catron to Polk, Sept. 2, 1837, *ibid.*).

11 Catron to Polk, Sept. 10, 1837, *ibid.*

12 "Go in for 30 or 40 millions, to be circulated fast as may be by the Govt—go for 20ties & over in gradations of tens. Strike out the interest feature—boldly declare that the farmers will hoard the notes bearing 5 per cent" (Catron to Polk, September 27, 1837, *ibid.*).

financial conditions that Van Buren felt constrained to convene the twenty-fifth Congress in extra session on September 4, 1837, for the purpose of laying before that body his plans for relief. His principal recommendation was the establishment of a sub-treasury; for experience had shown, he said, that depositing public money in state banks was little better than leaving it in the hands of the federal bank. The only safe custodian of the public funds was, in his opinion, the government itself. As a temporary remedy, he advised Congress to withhold further deposits with the states under the distribution act, and to authorize the emission of treasury notes. Although his recommendations were straightforward and sensible, they were, for that very reason, unlikely to be followed. Even the members of his own party were divided in opinion concerning the cause of the trouble, consequently they did not agree on remedies to be applied. Catron, as we have seen, was an advocate of paper money, while Jackson and the President still believed in hard money. Jackson received advance information concerning the character of the message and was delighted with the news that the President would recommend a separation of government finances from all banks, and the collection of public revenues in gold and silver coin.[13]

The members of Congress who had striven so hard to defeat Van Buren at the polls were not disposed to aid him now by sympathetic coöperation. In the House they were far more intent upon making life uncomfortable for the Speaker and the President than they were on relieving the financial stress of their fellow-citizens. It was known, of course, that Polk would be reëlected, and before the ballot had been taken, Mercer, of Virginia, proposed to transfer from the Speaker to the House itself the power to appoint committees. While the suggestion was not adopted, Mercer had the satisfaction of insulting Polk by implying that he could not be trusted. On the other hand, Patton, of Virginia, wished to have the rules so amended that the Speaker

---

[13] Jackson to Polk, Aug. 6, 1837, *ibid.*

might have a vote on all questions, but his amendment was rejected by the House.  As most of the business of the session would necessarily pass through the hands of the Committee of Ways and Means, Polk safeguarded the interests of the administration by selecting seven of its nine members from the ranks of his own party.

Although the President, when convening Congress, had definitely limited the scope of legislation, Adams was more terrified by the possible annexation of Texas than he was by the magnitude of the financial crisis.  On September 13, he moved to ask the President whether Texas had offered to join the United States, and, if so, what had been the reply made by our government.  Any proposition to annex it, declared Adams, would be unconstitutional—one which neither the President nor Congress "had any right to receive, entertain or consider."  It was his firm opinion that "a very large portion of the people of this country, dearly as they loved the Union, would prefer its total dissolution to the act of annexation of Texas."  The House, on September 18, curtailed his dissertations on the subject by passing a rule which limited discussions to questions included in the President's message.  Adams tried by various devices to inject the subject of Texas into later discussions, but Polk rigorously enforced the rule just adopted.

The rule for limiting discussion did not deter Wise from offering a resolution which provided that a committee be chosen by *ballot* to investigate the causes, delays, and failures of the Florida war.  Adams approved this method of selecting committees, for, said he, experience had proved that no real investigation would be prosecuted by any committee selected by the present Speaker.

Having failed in his attempt to deprive the Speaker of the power to make appointments, Wise welcomed the appearance in the House of the Senate bill for creating a sub-treasury.  This subject gave him an opportunity to vent his wrath and sarcasm not only upon the "Greatest and Best," as he called General

Jackson, but upon Van Buren and Polk as well. The late and present administrations, he said, ''have deliberately and wickedly, with malice aforethought, wrought this mischief'' and should be indicted by the people for their crimes. He took special delight in reading one of Jackson's messages which had incorporated a part of Polk's report—as chairman of the Committee of Ways and Means—highly commending the safety and efficiency of state banks. And now we read in the message of Van Buren, shouted Wise, ''that *the experiment has failed*''—the great chief, whom all had been taught to regard as a god, was after all a weak mortal whose wisdom was as fallible as that of other men.[14]

Little was accomplished during this brief session. The sub-treasury bill was defeated, and Congress contented itself with the enactment of emergency measures. The first three installments paid out under the operation of the distribution act were permitted to remain with the states, but the fourth was postponed and never paid. To meet the immediate needs of the government, the President was authorized to prepare interest-bearing treasury notes to be issued to an amount not exceeding ten million dollars. Having failed to agree upon any permanent financial policy, Congress, on October 19, adjourned until the regular session in December.

Before Congress had adjourned, the Tennessee legislature met in regular session. Governor Cannon assailed with some vehemence both Jackson and his successor. The Whigs began at once to formulate plans which they hoped might insure Polk's political downfall and prevent the reëlection of Grundy. Some of the Democrats were in favor of silently ignoring their critics, but Polk, who was still in Washington, urged the adoption of an aggressive course and the prevention of the election of a Senator, for the present at least.[15] Before he set out for Tennessee, Polk was authorized by Grundy to withdraw his name, as candidate

---

14 *Cong. Globe*, 25 Cong., 1 sess., App., 318.

15 Jonas E. Thomas to Polk, Oct. 5; Polk to Nicholson, Oct. 9, 1837; *Polk Papers.*

for Senator, should it develop that the interests of the administration might be promoted by so doing.[16]  Grundy was reëlected, but not without difficulty, for the ranks of the Whigs were steadily increasing.

The Democrats were alarmed but not disheartened.  A new editor, Cunningham, was put in charge of the *Union;* for to the moderation of Bradford, under Grundy's guidance, had Jackson attributed the recent defeats.[17]  Most hopeful of all was Jackson himself; he prophesied that Tennessee would be ''herself again'' in less than two years, in spite of Bell's New England tour, which was designed to transfer the state to Webster and the Federalists.[18]

When the twenty-fifth Congress met in December for its second session, a rather unusual problem was presented to the House for solution.  It was a question of settling a contested election of members from Mississippi, and, as the decision ultimately devolved upon the Speaker, Polk incurred the enmity of Sergeant S. Prentiss, a man quite as venomous as Wise or Peyton, and far more able than either.

In July, 1837, the Governor of Mississippi had called a special election in order that the state might send members to the extra session of Congress which had been proclaimed by President Van Buren.  Claiborne and Gholson, the men chosen at the special election, were, at the extra session, declared by the House to be members for the entire term of the twenty-fifth Congress.  Notwithstanding this decision of the House, Mississippi held another

---

[16] Grundy to Polk, Oct. 17, 1837, *ibid.*

[17] Although removed for the *moderation* of his editorials, Bradford was, on the other hand, dropped from the roll of divinity students by the Whig bishop for being so ardent a Democrat.  The incident well illustrates the political intolerance of the period.

[18] ''The course of Mr. Bell in attending the aristocratic, federal & shin-plaster meetings in Boston & New York, & his speeches at those meetings, which is a transfer of Tennessee to Mr. Webster & the blue lights, abolitionists and vagrants, is working well here—it has opened the eyes of the democracy of Tennessee, and none of his Whigg friends here will guarantee the sale.''  Jackson to Grundy, Dec. 16, 1837 (*Am. Hist. Mag.*, V, 138–139).

election in November and chose for Representatives S. S. Prentiss and T. J. Ward. Claiborne and Gholson were supporters of the administration, and their friends in Mississippi, relying on the decision made by the House, took no part in the November election. As a result, Prentiss and Ward were easily elected. Each side now claimed its representatives to have been lawfully elected and appealed to the House for a decision. After prolonged debate the House reversed its former decision and pronounced the election of Claiborne and Gholson void. It then proceeded to ballot on the validity of the second Mississippi election at which Prentiss and Ward had been chosen. On this question the vote stood 117 to 117. Polk cast his ballot in the negative, and the whole matter was referred back to the people of the state, who later reëlected Prentiss and Ward. The "glorious infamy" which attached to the Speaker's vote against him, Prentiss never forgot. In a flight of oratory he told the people of Mississippi that "the still small voice of James K. Polk deprived you of that which a hundred thousand bayonets could not have forced upon you."[19] On his return to Congress he had the supreme satisfaction, not only of harassing the Speaker on every possible occasion, but of opposing the ordinary vote of thanks to Polk on his retirement from the Speakership.

Slade, of Vermont, precipitated a stormy debate on slavery by presenting, on December 20, two memorials which asked for the abolition of slavery in the District of Columbia. After moving that the memorials be referred to a select committee, he entered into a prolonged and scathing discussion of the slavery question in its various phases. Having recognized the member from Vermont, Polk found it difficult to prevent his continuing, since Slade for some time was careful to keep within the bounds of parliamentary rules. When he finally launched into a discussion of slavery in Virginia, a member entered a protest and

[19] Clipping from some Philadelphia paper, dated Feb. 7, 1838 (*Polk Papers*).

Polk ordered Slade to his seat.[20]  Wise, Rhett, and other southern radicals were choking with rage.  Several exhorted their colleagues to leave the hall in a body.  After adjournment a meeting was held, and, although threats of disunion were freely made, few members were ready for so drastic a procedure.

On the following day Patton, of Virginia, introduced, as a "concession . . . for the sake of peace, harmony, and union," a gag rule more drastic than its predecessor.  It directed that all petitions on the subject of abolition should be laid on the table "without being debated, printed, read or referred," and that no further action should be taken thereon.  The rules were suspended, the previous question invoked, and the vote hurriedly taken.  When his name was called, Adams shouted that the resolution violated the federal Constitution, whereupon the Speaker forced him to take his seat.  Polk then ruled to be out of order the demand made by Adams that his reason for not voting should be entered in the journal.  A few days later, Polk even extended the new "gag-rule," by deciding that a resolution of the Massachusetts legislature asking for a repeal of the gag rule also came under the rule itself and could not therefore be considered.[21]

Sectional feeling was still more embittered during this session by the killing, in a duel, of Jonathan Cilley, of Maine, by another member of the House, William J. Graves, of Kentucky.  The demands made upon Cilley by Graves and his second, Wise, were held by many to have been extremely unreasonable.  By such members the killing of Cilley was regarded as little better than premeditated murder.  The appointment of a committee to investigate the circumstances of the duel with a view to punishing members who had taken part, led to a strange alignment in

---

[20] Polk said that, while his position would not permit him to state his own opinions on such agitation of this question, "they might readily be inferred by the House."

[21] January 3, 1838.  Polk seems, however, to have felt that he had gone too far in this matter, for on February 5 he ruled to be in order a petition of similar purport from citizens of Massachusetts.

defense of the participants.  Friends of Graves and Wise charged
that Polk had ''packed'' the committee to the prejudice of the
defendants; while Adams, declaring the investigation to be ''an
administration measure,'' not only condemned the committee for
having prepared an opinion, but objected to receiving their
report.  So intense was partisan feeling that Sawyer, of North
Carolina, objected to receiving a message from the President
which arrived while the clerk was reading the report of the committee, but Polk promptly decided that the constitutional right
of the President to send a message to the house at any time
transcended the rule which required unanimous consent to its
reception.

Hectoring of the Speaker continued to the end of the session.
On June 23, Adams reached the climax of absurdity by demanding that Polk should reduce to writing some irrelevant remarks
which Adams had made and which the Speaker had declared to
be out of order.  On Polk's refusal, Adams appealed from the
decision.  Needless to say, the House sustained the Speaker.

While Polk was successfully parrying the shafts of his enemies
in Congress, his friends in Tennessee were compassing the downfall of Bell, as well as formulating new plans for the Speaker
himself.  Donelson was indefatigable in his efforts to *expose* Bell's
*treachery*.  From his retreat at the Hermitage ''the chief'' forwarded documents to the Speaker and requested him to answer
Bell's charges against himself [Jackson], either in Congress or
through the *Globe*.[22]  Desirous of representing Polk's district in
Congress, Nicholson saw in the Speaker excellent Vice-Presi-
ential timber, but Polk was inclined to agree with other friends
that he might be able to accomplish more good in the governor's
chair.  Ex-Governor Carroll had announced to Polk his willingness to become once more a candidate for the office, and promised
to handle Cannon ''without gloves'';[23] but the politicians, fearing that he would be defeated, did not rally to his support.

---

[22] Doneldson to Polk, Jan. 4; Jackson to Polk, Feb. 2, 1838; *Polk Papers*.
[23] Carroll to Polk, Feb. 17, 1838, *ibid.*

Even before Polk had consented to run for governor, each party was striving to strengthen its own position in the state and to weaken the hold of its opponent. In Boston, C. G. Greene, under Polk's direction, collected evidence to prove that Bell, on his New England tour, had been entertained by Hartford Convention Federalists;[24] while in Tennessee, the Whig legislature instructed Grundy to vote against any sub-treasury bill that might come before the Senate. Although the purpose of this move was to force his resignation, he disappointed the Whigs by promptly announcing that he would obey his instructions. Much Whig literature was franked from Washington. White and Bell scattered widely the speech in which Wise had castigated Polk and the President.

From many sources Polk was importuned to accept the gubernatorial nomination, for it was believed that he could regain the state for the Democratic party.[25] Apparently the office was not attractive to him, yet duty to his party seemed to point in that direction. Late in the summer, after mature consideration, he finally consented to become a candidate. Many letters told him of the good effect which his acceptance had produced. One from Cave Johnson reported that in many places ''whole neighborhoods'' had returned to the Democratic party.[26]

The Democrats were still embarrassed by the weakness of their local papers, for Cunningham had proved to be quite as unsuccessful a journalist as Bradford. When seeking a more competent editor for the *Union,* Polk offered the position to

---

[24] Green to Polk, Jan. 18, 1838, *ibid.*

[25] One correspondent intimated that prospects of success might be better in the state than in Congress. Polk, he said, would redeem the state if any one could, and ''If there is any possible chance of the opposition getting the upper hand in the ensuing Congress, perhaps this course might be the prudent one; as your friends would as soon be annihilated at once, as to see that *most* INFAMOUS OF ALL INFAMOUS PUPPIES, John Bell, triumph over you in a contest for the Speaker's chair. Should the opposition succeed in their views, this must and will be the result, as you are now the most dreaded and consequently the most hated by them'' (W. S. Haynes to Polk, July 24, 1838, *ibid.*).

[26] Johnson to Polk, Nov. 2, 1838, *ibid.*

several persons in succession.  Among the number were Edmund Burke[27] and C. G. Greene, of Boston.  It was Greene, who, when declining the offer, suggested Jeremiah George Harris, then editor of the *Bay State Democrat*.[28]  For the Democrats this proved to be a most fortunate suggestion.  In Harris they found a man in every way suited to Tennessee politics—one who was more than a match for his adversaries of the quill, with the possible exception of Parson Brownlow.  The *Union* was enlarged, and on February 1, 1839, the proprietor, J. M. Smith, introduced the new editor to the people of Tennessee.  In the same issue Harris announced his policy: namely, to fight for the principles of Jefferson and his Republican successors, and for the overthrow of ''Federalism'' in the state.[29]  A week later Smith reported to Polk that a war of words with Hall, editor of the *Banner,* had already begun and that he [Smith] was much pleased with Harris.[30]

The proprietor of the *Union* had no reason to revise his opinion.  Harris launched at once into a campaign of vituperation and merciless denunciation of the Whigs which endeared him to his friends and made him dreaded by his opponents.  He was the type of editor in whom the people of the West delighted.  He and General Jackson became fast friends, but, in the main, it was to Polk that he looked for counsel and guidance.  He plunged with zeal into the campaign against Governor Cannon and announced that ''Tennessee has not seen so proud a day since the election of her own Jackson to the Presidency as will that on

---

27 Burke was later a Representative from New Hampshire.  In 1845, Polk put him in charge of the General Patent Office.

28 Greene to Rives of the *Globe*, Dec. 3, 1838, *Polk Papers.*

29 ''That tory federalism of 1798, Hartford convention federalism of 1814, and 'whig' Federalism of this day are identical, so far as they relate to the two grand party divisions of the country, is too susceptible of the clearest letter of proof to admit of a doubt.''

30 ''Mr. Hall of the Banner has commenced the war with the new editor of the 'Union' and if I am not mistaken he will find that he will have a little more to do than he at present imagines'' (Smith to Polk, Feb. 7, 1839, *Polk Papers*).

which the sovereigns of her soil shall by their unbought suffrage call Mr. Polk to the gubernatorial chair.''[31]

This is not, however, the place for a prolonged discussion of Polk's gubernatorial campaign. Reserving this for another chapter, we may follow his career through his last session as Speaker of the House. Selected by the Democrats for the avowed purpose of bringing Tennessee back into the party fold, Polk, as he called to order the third session of the twenty-fifth Congress, was more cordially hated than ever by Bell, Wise, Prentiss, and other enemies of the administration.

Van Buren's message, which reached the House on December 4, 1838, was optimistic in tone. He informed Congress that the rapid improvement of financial conditions and the resumption of specie payment by the principal banks had proved beyond question that a federal bank is not indispensable. Reiterating the belief that a sub-treasury would prove to be the best agency for collecting and disbursing the public revenue, he again recommended its creation by law. He alluded to Swartwout's defalcation and asked for legislation which would make such peculation in future a felony.

The lawmaking body of the nation paid little heed to the President's recommendations. Jockeying for position suited their present mood far better than constructive legislation. Having made gains in recent political contests, the Whigs had high hopes of carrying the next Presidential election. Without as yet announcing any program for themselves, they employed all of

---

[31] Nashville *Union,* Feb. 8, 1839. In the same issue Harris quoted an article from the Pennsylvania *Reporter* in which that paper urged that Polk should be made Vice-President. Concerning Polk's record the *Reporter* said: ''Knowing that the Bank of the United States was about to bring the whole of its mighty influence to bear against the administration of Gen. Jackson, it was deemed of the highest importance to be well fortified at the point where the attack was to be made, and the chairman of the Committee of Ways and Means, as the financial organ of the administration, became the most important position in the House. Col. Polk's known position in opposition to the re-charter of that institution, his intimate acquaintance with its history and transactions, and his powers as a ready and able debater, recommended him for its occupancy. And well did he justify the confidence so reposed in him.''

their energies in heaping odium upon the administrations of Van Buren and his predecessor. In the House the session was stormy from the beginning. When they could enlist the votes of the so-called conservatives, the Whigs were able to outvote the Democrats, and the task of the Speaker was made still more difficult.

On the second day of the session, and before the President's message had been received, Adams fanned the flame of sectional discord by moving that all petitions, remonstrances, and resolutions, for or against the annexation of Texas, should be referred to a select committee. His resolution was laid on the table by a vote of 136 to 61. His solicitude on this subject proved to be unwarranted, for the President in his message assured Congress that all proposals for annexation had been withdrawn. Adams then submitted a resolution which called for a committee to investigate the controversy of Andrew Stevenson, late Speaker of the House and present minister to England, with Daniel O'Connell, a member of Parliament. This also was sent to the table, but it had accomplished its intended purpose of attaching odium to the administration.

Abolition petitions again made their appearance. The persistence of the reformers aroused the fears as well as the wrath of southern members, and slaveholders required guaranties for the protection of their "peculiar institution." On December 11, Atherton, of New Hampshire, submitted a series of resolutions the purport of which was to declare unconstitutional any interference with slavery either in the states or the District of Columbia, and to reënact the gag rule regarding petitions. After a brief debate these resolutions were adopted by the House. The adoption of the gag rule did not, however, eliminate the slavery question. On the thirteenth, Adams tried to introduce a resolution to the effect that no enactment of Congress could add to or deduct from the powers of Congress which had been conferred by the Constitution. On the same day, Wise offered a series of resolutions which were designed to deprive Congress of all power

to interfere with slavery.   In both cases permission to introduce
the resolutions was denied by the House.   While Polk applied
the gag rule whenever possible, Cushing, of Massachusetts, won
applause from the reformers by forcing the Speaker to decide
that a protest against the constitutionality of the gag rule,
although itself out of order, must be inserted in the *Journal,* if
brought up on the following day in the form of a correction of
the minutes.[32]

For the Whigs, the news of Swartwout's defalcation was an
unusually sweet morsel, for it gave them an excuse to explore
with telescope and microscope the administrations of Jackson and
Van Buren.   And, as the Democrats no longer had a majority
in the House, it incidentally gave them a chance to humiliate
Polk by depriving him of the power to appoint the investigating
committee.   In disposing of the questions mentioned in the President's message, Cambreleng had moved that the part relating to
the defalcation be referred to the Committee of Ways and Means,
of which he was chairman.   On December 21, Garland, of Virginia, moved to amend by referring the question to a select committee of nine to be chosen by *ballot.*   In a scurrilous tirade,
Wise asserted that any committee appointed by the present
Speaker would conceal rather than disclose the facts.   He had, he
said, been chairman of another committee selected by Polk to
investigate the affairs of the General Post Office, and all his efforts
to ascertain the truth had been defeated.   Kendall, the Post
Master General,[33] had declined to furnish information on the

---

[32] Dec. 21, 1838. *Cong. Globe,* 25 Cong., 3 sess., 59.

[33] Wise called Kendall "the President's *thinking* machine, and his
*writing* machine—ay, and his *lying* machine!   Sir, if General Jackson had
been elected for a third term, one great good would have come of the
evil—*Amos Kendall would have been worked to death!*   Poor wretch, as
he rode his Rosinante down Pennsylvania avenue, he looked like Death
on a pale horse—he was chief overseer, chief reporter, amanuensis, scribe,
accountant general, man of all work—nothing was well done without
the aid of his diabolical genius."   Shielding Kendall, said Wise, was the
more reprehensible because Jackson had so relentlessly pursued Tobias
Watkins: "When the *indictments,* the *prosecutions,* were pressed unre-
lentingly against poor Watkins—when the Administration was crying,

ground that he was responsible to the President alone, and the
majority of the committee had excluded everything that might
reflect upon the administration. ''Now, sir,'' said Wise to the
Speaker,

I propose to show that *your* committee obeyed the will of their master.
Yes, as you had done, by *packing* and stocking the committee. It was *your*
committee—peculiarly and emphatically *yours*—its *appointment*, its *conduct*,
its honor or *infamy*, will forever attach itself, sir, to *your name*. In illus-
trating the conduct of that committee, I could consume days to show how
the plainest and most obvious and undeniable propositions were voted down;
how resolution after resolution, question after question to witnesses, going
into the very vitals of inquiry, were unblushingly rejected and stifled by
the majority of the committee . . . *you*, the Speaker, the President of the
United States, the heads of Executive Departments, *your* committee, and
your whole party, combined and conspired to stifle investigation.

Some of Wise's friends asked him to yield the floor for a motion
to adjourn. He declined on the plea that he might never get it
again, for, said he to the Speaker, ''I distrust you, sir.''[34] Polk
bore the onslaught with dignity and composure, and without
interference until Wise referred to Benton as the ''monster''
who was to perpetuate the present dynasty. On January 8, 1839,
he again assailed the Speaker and compared him to a gambler
who plays with loaded dice.[35]

It was believed by the Speaker's friends that Wise, Peyton,
and Clay were trying to provoke him into sending a challenge,[36]
for the ''murder'' of Jonathan Cilly had not been forgotten.

---

Shylock-like, 'my bond, my bond!' against one of Mr. Adams's default-
ers, then 'general and minute inquiries' were not only lawful, but a
duty; but, sir, the moment the band of investigation touched one of *his*
'little ones,' then inquiry was worse than a 'Spanish Inquisition.' ''

[34] Dec. 21, 1838. *Cong. Globe*, 25 Cong., 3 sess., App., 386–387.

[35] ''My colleague,'' said he, ''wants the committee appointed by
ballot, in order to avoid imputations on the *Speaker;* I want it appointed
by ballot, to avoid the Speaker himself.''

[36] According to a story printed in the *Globe*, August 21, 1844, on the
authority of General Jackson, Clay at one time appeared at the bar
of the House and said to Speaker Polk: ''Go home, *G–d d–n you, where
you belong!*'' In 1844 this ejaculation was made the theme of a campaign song. During a heated debate in the House, Wise shouted to Polk:
''*You are a damned little petty tyrant; I mean this personally—pocket
it!*''

But Polk treated their insults with silent contempt, and by so doing did much to establish a new precedent in such "affairs of honor." His personal bravery was questioned by none except his bitter enemies, and even the impetuous Jackson commended him for ignoring such flagrant indignities.[37]

The committee was chosen by ballot, and, needless to say, a majority of its members were opposed to the administration. The Democrats asked for the privilege of selecting the minority members, but their request was denied. Both majority and minority reports were tabled by the House on February 27, 1839. The investigation had been successful only in intensifying political discord. In a letter to Polk, Jackson asked for an account of the investigation, and expressed the belief that Swartwout could not have invested all of the million and a quarter which he had taken. "Where is the balance?" he asked, "The Whiggs have it."[38] To Grundy he suggested that William B. Lewis and Daniel Jackson, if put on oath, might tell how Swartwout had invested some of his money.[39]

Defalcations had been both frequent and brazen, and their cause, as Underwood, of Kentucky, pointed out,[40] could be traced to Jackson's policy of filling offices with those "whose subserviency to the will of the President, and devotion to the interests of party, constituted their principal recommendation." But undoubtedly Bynum's statement was equally true—that, when demanding that the select committee be chosen by ballot, the Whigs were less interested in political purity than in blasting Polk's prospects in his gubernatorial campaign.[41]

---

[37] Jackson to W. P. Rowles, Aug. 24, 1840. Printed in Washington *Globe*, July 19, 1844.

[38] Jackson to Polk, Feb. 11, 1839, *Polk Papers*.

[39] "I have no doubt," he continued, "if the truth can be reached, that the Whigg merchants of New York hold in their hands of the revenue chargeable to Swartwout, from $600,000 to $800,000 if not more, and it is suggested that he loaned to our little Whigg printer, Hall of the Banner, some thousands." Jackson to Grundy, Feb. 20, 1839 (*Am. Mag. of Hist.*, V, 141 142).

[40] *Cong. Globe*, 25 Cong., 3 sess., App., 375.

[41] *Idem*, 125.

Unquestionably disintegration of the Jackson party was due in part to the jealousy of ambitious politicians who had failed to obtain what they considered to be an adequate reward for services rendered.  But there was a deeper cause for defection—one based on the nature and ends of government itself.  For example, a man of Bell's type—one who believed in constitutional government, and one whose penetrating mind enabled him so clearly to see the inevitable results of administering the government according to Jacksonian methods—never logically belonged in the ranks of the party which followed so loyally the dictates of the "old hero."  Bell, and all others who viewed things as he did, were constitutionalists, and they gravitated naturally to the party which accepted the precepts of Hamilton, Marshall, and Webster.  During Jackson's first term, and to some extent during his second, there was much confusion of thought on governmental principles and functions.  Admiration for the man had obscured the vision of many who would otherwise have been quick to detect the inherent evils of Jacksonism.  By the time Van Buren became President, the personal element had, to a considerable degree, disappeared from politics.  In the party realignment which resulted, personal qualities were not entirely ignored; but of far greater importance was the attitude of statesmen and their supporters toward the fundamentals of government itself.  On this question the issue was clear cut.

Several speeches delivered during this session show that their authors fully understood the nature of Jacksonism and its paralyzing influence upon constitutional government.  The President in his message had attributed the success of our institutions to the "constant and direct supervision by the people over every public measure."  With this as a text, Bell assailed the "democratic tendencies" of which the administration boasted, and made an ardent plea for a return to constitutional government:

The People are told that our ancestors, who framed the Constitution in 1789, were half a century in the rear of the improvements of the present age; that they had not the benefit of the new lights which experience has shed upon the subject of government since that time, and which are now in full blaze around us. The science of government, we are told, has made great strides since our Constitution was framed; and, in deed, that instrument is beginning to be looked upon by many rather as a device of bad men, to advance the interests of the few at the expense of the many, and forming an actual obstruction to that full tide of happiness and prosperity which awaits us when the inventions of modern democracy shall be substituted for it. At all events, it is proclaimed to be the duty of every man who would improve the condition of the human family to strengthen the democratic tendencies of the Constitution, and to disrobe or rather strip it of those limitations and restrictions upon the popular will, with which our unimproved ancestors have thought it necessary to encumber it. . . . In truth, sir, it cannot be disguised that there are a class of politicians in the country at this moment, whose aspirations it does not suit that any restriction, any limitation whatever, shall exist in the practice of the Government upon the will or absolutism of the majority; and, in the estimation of all their followers, our Constitution is defective.[42]

Deploring the attempt to bring about more immediate control by the people, Bell boldly asserted that

according to our system, the People do not, and cannot, exercise any *direct* supervision over any public measure. Their power, their influence, their supervision, can be constitutionally exercised only by petition and remonstrance, and by the utterance of their voice at the ballot-box.

This was but a simple statement of facts; nevertheless, it required temerity to proclaim such a truth in the face of clamor for the exercise of popular will. To Van Buren's declaration that the extension of practical democracy had strengthened the Union, Bell replied that never before had there been such a relaxation of all ties which bind society together.[43] The power of the people, he said, had not in reality been increased, for party discipline had deprived them of all voice in public affairs.[44] The

---

[42] Dec. 26, 1838. *Cong. Globe*, 25 Cong., 3 sess., App., 360–361.

[43] "At no former period has so general a spirit of opposition to legal restraints or requirements manifested itself throughout the country, when they stand in the way of wilful passions or purposes of any kind. Slight regard for the Constitution and laws, commencing with the Government itself and its administrators, has gradually diffused itself over society."

[44] "Such is and has been the power of party discipline—such the despotic principle of party association for years, that the mass of the community have rather stood in the relation of subjects to be governed than the controlling elements of power."

truth of this statement, however, only made more deplorable the fact that the party which Bell himself had helped to organize should keep up the fiction of popular sovereignty, and even outdo their opponents in catering to the passions of the multitude.

When discussing an appropriation bill, on February 19, 1839, Kennedy, of Maryland, diverged from his subject to give a critical analysis of Jacksonism and to point out its disastrous consequences. Jackson, he said, had been singularly unlucky as a reformer, although he had been an innovator ''in the broadest and worst sense'':

> His administration was one ceaseless change: change, sometimes stealing along in noiseless advance, sometimes bursting forth in bold, open-day achievement; one while sweeping with the breath of spring, at another with the rage and havoc of the tornado. We had ever change of men, change of measures, change of principles. . . . The pervading characteristic of that most anomalous and extraordinary administration was mutation—uncertainty—experiment. It lived in perpetual motion, defying all hope of repose; it rejoiced in turmoil, and revelled in paradox. . . . The idea of political consistency never entered the President's head—he had no perception of the meaning of the term.

Jackson's idol, continued Kennedy, was popularity, and whatever sustained popularity constituted the theory of his conduct. It was not that wholesome popularity based on services rendered, ''but a domineering, wayward, arrogant popularity—an impatient, hectoring assumption of the right to lead, which repudiates all law, despises all observance, and maintains its supremacy by personal and party force.'' Jackson, said he, used his popularity to increase his power; and, in turn, he used that power to increase his popularity.[45]

---

[45] ''The very boldness of his designs seemed to fascinate the public admiration: he dazzled the popular mind by that fearlessness which we were, for a time, accustomed to interpret as a proof of his honesty and uprightness of purpose. . . . . He flattered the People with the address of a practiced courtier, startled and amused them by the thunderclaps of his policy, identified his success with the gratification of their favorite passions, grappled himself with wonderful adroitness to the predominant sentiments, wishes, and prejudices of the great and massive majority—

On February 22, Slade, of Vermont, obtained the floor for the purpose of discussing the general appropriation bill. His time was mainly occupied, however, in a masterful arraignment of Jackson and Van Buren, and of their methods. He attributed the gift of prophecy to Benton, Van Buren, and R. M. Johnson, who, in 1826, had reported to the Senate on the evils of executive patronage. Patronage, they said, would inevitably lead to one man power. By exchanging patronage for votes the President would soon control not only both houses of Congress, but the entire country.[46] "What was prophecy in 1826," said Slade, "has become history in 1839."

Under the caption of the "Pretensions of Democracy," he contrasted the now obsolete Republicanism of Jefferson with

---

and became a monarch, an autocrat, by the sheer concentration of republican suffrage."

Having discussed in detail the methods by which Jackson had arrogated all authority to himself while professing reverence for the Constitution, Kennedy depicted most admirably the effect of Jacksonism, not alone upon the character of the government, but upon society itself. It led not merely to corruption in official circles, but it demoralized the masses, as well. "We lived," said he, "in the midst of convulsions. The public taste was vitiated and fed by the stimulous of constantly recurring political eruptions; it delighted in strange conjectures—the heavings and spasms of that capricious power which displayed itself in such fantastic action at the capital. A spirit of insubordination, of misrule and riot became diffused through the community. Wild and visionary theories of political duty were disseminated abroad and showed themselves, in the most mischievous forms, in the proceedings of the State Legislatures. The most abstruse and difficult problems of political economy—questions of currency, finance, constitutional power—were summarily but authoritatively disposed of by the shallowest pretenders to statesmanship; and the oldest and best institutions of the country attacked and beaten down by political charlatans. Knowledge, deliberation, experience, all were obliged to give way to this newly-inspired intuition; and the greatest pains were taken by party leaders and demagogues to deceive the people into the belief that the profoundest questions of government might be consigned to the decision of men of the lowest scale of qualification in political science" (*Cong. Globe*, 25 Cong., 3 sess., App., 410–412). The whole speech is well worth reading.

[46] "We must look forward to the time when the nomination of a President can carry any man through the Senate, and his recommendation can carry any measure through the two Houses of Congress; when the principle of public action will be open and avowed—the President wants my vote, and I want his patronage; I will vote as he wishes, and he will give me the office I wish for. What will this be but the government of one man? and what is the government of one man, but a monarchy?" Quoted from their report by Slade.

the madness of Jacksonian Democracy—"*the* Democracy," as it
is called.  Its chief characteristic, said he, is sham, and it relies
for its success upon fomenting class prejudice.[47]  He read the
well-known letter to Monroe in which Jackson urged the President to crush the "monster, party spirit," and contrasted the
sentiments expressed in that letter with the practice of the administration of its author.  Hypocritical as had been the pretensions
to political virtue of those who had brought General Jackson
forward for the Presidency, Slade did not believe that even they
had fully realized the political debauchery upon which they were
entering.[48]

The Speaker, to whom this merciless, but for the most part
well-merited, arraignment of Jacksonism was officially addressed,
listened, undismayed by the perils which were being depicted.
None believed more thoroughly in party discipline than he, and
few had been more closely identified with the administrations of
Jackson and Van Buren.  He had effectively served his party
in many capacities, from conducting the bank war in the House
down to establishing local party newspapers.  His enemies fully
recognized his skill as a political strategist, even though they
denounced him as the tool of those whom he served.

---

[47] "Thus, the rich are made an object of jealousy to the poor.  The
laborer is excited against the capitalist—the indolent and improvident
against the industrious and frugal—the ignorant against the learned and
intelligent—and even the vicious and abandoned against the virtuous and
upright.  Associated wealth, no matter how widely it may embrace men
of small means, is declared to be monopolizing and dangerous.  Banks,
however prudently and safely managed, are denounced as the money
making machines of the wealthy, designed only to make the rich richer
and the poor poorer.  Factitious distinctions are created.  Jealousies are
excited.  An imaginary aristocracy is raised up in the midst of every
community; and nothing can be heard but the war-cry—down with
monopolies, and down with the aristocracy."

[48] "It seems impossible they should have dreamed that General Jackson, the author of the noble sentiments I have quoted, could ever be
brought to enact, in his own administration, an utter falsification of every
profession they contained—a falsification so complete, that there should
not be, as in truth, there is not, found a single one of his friends whose
face does not crimson with blushes at an exhibit of the contrast" (*Cong.
Globe*, 25 Cong., 3 sess., App. 323 ff).

Jacksonism was not without its defenders, although they failed to match their opponents in oratorical powers or in logical arguments. Crary, of Michigan, saw in the Supreme Court a political body "of the worst character," and he commended Jackson for having assumed the right to construe the Constitution as he pleased. As soon as men are elevated to that court, said Crary, they apply themselves to the study of British law and British precedents, and "they cannot be operated upon by the healthy influence of a sound public opinon."[49]  Rhett, of South Carolina, said that the country had always been divided into two great political parties—one which feared government and another which feared the people. Inasmuch as strength in the government could be attained only at the expense of popular freedom, he believed, like Jefferson, in restricting the functions of government within the narrowest possible limits.[50]

The entire session was characterized by intense party and personal recrimination. The Democratic party was no longer omnipotent. It was reaping the harvest of its own misdeeds, and, in addition, it was held accountable for the distressed condition of the country, although this had resulted from causes economic rather than political. Hope of success added boldness to the attacks of its opponents. Twelve years earlier, an attack upon Jackson and his policies would have meant political suicide for the assailant; it was now one of the surest means of acquiring popularity.

More than any other member of the House, Polk was given credit by one party, and blame by the other, for the success of the legislative part of the Jackson program. Consequently his adversaries were unwilling to permit him to withdraw from national politics without making one more attempt to humiliate him in the eyes of the nation. They had been unsuccessful in their efforts to confuse him in the complexities of parliamentary

---

[49] *Cong. Globe,* 25 Cong., 3 sess., App., 154.
[50] *Idem,* 134.

procedure. Their insulting invectives and their invitations to personal combat had been received with a dignity and composure that did credit to the Speaker. Unable to gratify their desire to injure the Speaker in a more effective manner, his enemies resorted to the petty and unprecedented course of opposing the ordinary vote of thanks on his retirement from office. Prentiss, who had, at a previous session, been deprived of a seat in the House by Polk's casting vote, was chief actor and stage manager in this puerile *opera bouffe*. The resolution which thanked the Speaker for "the able, impartial, and dignified manner" in which he had presided over the House, Prentiss moved to amend by striking out the word *impartial*. Prentiss did not "deny the capacity of the *Speaker,* his dispatch of business, or his full and thorough knowledge of parliamentary law," but he could not agree that he had been *impartial*. He argued that the House had expressed its distrust of the Speaker by taking from him the appointment of the Swartwout committee. On the other hand, he frankly admitted that his main objection to the resolution was the favorable effect it would have upon Polk's gubernatorial canvass in Tennessee. The Speaker, he said, was "playing a political game," in which this resolution would constitute an important part. Reviewing the personnel of the House committees, he condemned the Speaker for having put on all "political committees" a greater number of administration men than the small majority of that party would justify. He charged Polk with being a tool of the President and of the party. "A more perfectly party Speaker," said he, "one who would be more disposed to bend the rules of the House to meet the purposes of his own side in politics, never had pressed the soft and ample cushions of that gorgeous chair."[51]

There was little justification for this intemperate arraignment and for the conduct of the other fifty-six members[52] who co-operated with Prentiss in opposing the customary vote of thanks.

---

[51] *Cong. Globe*, 25 Cong., 3 sess., 251–252.
[52] The vote stood 94 to 57.

When forming his committees, Polk had simply followed precedent. Many Whigs bore testimony to the justness of his decisions. And yet, he could hardly complain because of this partisan attack, for he had himself, on a former occasion, quite as unjustly accused a Speaker of subserviency to "the throne."[53]

Polk's farewell address to the House, in response to the resolution of thanks just passed, did much to destroy the effect of the shafts which had been hurled at him, and to elevate him in the opinion of fairminded men of all parties. He did not descend to answer the charges made against him or to indulge in recrimination. Without boasting, he alluded to his record of "constant and laborious" service,[54] and to the peculiar difficulties which attach to the office of Speaker. All Speakers, said he, have borne testimony to the impossibility of giving entire satisfaction to all, but

it has been made my duty to decide more questions of parliamentary law and order many of them of a complex and difficult character, arising often in the midst of high excitement, in the course of our proceedings, than had been decided, it is believed, by all my predecessors, from the formation of this Government.

Ignoring the minority, he thanked the majority for the evidence of their approbation. With good-tempered adroitness, he belittled the effect of the negative vote by declaring that he regarded the resolution just passed "as the highest and most valued testimony I have ever received from this House," because, under the circumstances, it was not a mere and a meaningless formality.[55] Many who, for partisan reasons, had voted against the resolution, as soon as Congress had adjourned, hastened to assure the late Speaker of their personal good will.[56] Instead of discrediting

---

[53] See pp. 19–20.

[54] "I can, perhaps, say what few others, if any can—that I have not failed to attend the daily sittings of this House a single day since I have been a member of it [14 years], save on a single occasion, when prevented for a short time by indisposition."

[55] *Cong. Globe*, 25 Cong., 3 sess., 252–253.

[56] The Nashville *Union*, March · 22, 1839, quoted a letter from a person who had been present when Polk made his farewell address: "I

the Speaker, the minority had really made him an object of interest throughout the Union. Their conduct was generally condemned, while his dignified reply raised him in the estimation of all except the most zealous partisans.[57] His ability as a presiding officer was made still more apparent during the following session by contrasting him with his successor, R. M. T. Hunter, of Virginia. In the opinion of Cave Johnson, Hunter displayed "ignorance of rules and a want of energy & power to command"; he feared that the House had chosen a boy to do the business of a man.[58] J. W. Blackwell likewise reported that Hunter was too young for the position. "While you were Speaker," said he, "your friends praised, and your enemies abused you, but it is now admitted, on all sides, that Jas. K. Polk was the best presiding officer that we have had for many years, and some say— the best we ever had."[59]

At the close of the session Polk set out for Tennessee to engage in an active campaign for the governorship. After fourteen years of service in the House of Representatives, his party had assigned him duties in a new field of labor. Whatever his success in the new field might be, no one even dreamed that the retiring Speaker would next appear in Washington as President-elect.

---

never witnessed more enthusiasm than the Speaker's admirable reply to the vote elicited. Many of those who had voted in the negative expressed their admiration of it, and gave evident signs of shame and regret at the partisan course they had pursued. Even Mr. Graves, of Kentucky, declared to a friend at his elbow that the Speaker had done as well as any one could do under such circumstances, and stepping forward took manly leave of him—as also did most of the members, a few bitter and envious partisans excepted."

57 For example, the Worcester (Mass.) *Palladium*, an independent paper, said: "The disreputable conduct of the opposition members of Congress, towards the Speaker of the House, at the close of the session, makes that gentleman an object of peculiar interest, at the present moment, to the whole democratic party of the Union. An effort was made, as violent as it was uncourteous, to prevent the passage of the usual complimentary resolution to the Speaker on his retiring from the Chair. But it was an unavailing effort." Quoted by Nashville *Union*, April 8, 1839.

58 Johnson to Polk, Dec. 21, 1839, *Polk Papers*.

59 Blackwell to Polk, Dec. 30, 1839, *ibid.*

CHAPTER VIII

## POLK VERSUS CANNON, 1839

In May, 1838, shortly before he consented to become a candidate for the governorship of Tennessee, Polk was examined by a phrenologist, who, unless he had made a thorough study of his client beforehand, made some exceedingly shrewd *guesses*.[1] ''He is very quick of perception''; so reads the prepared statement,

when he enjoys, he enjoys remarkably well, and when he suffers, he suffers most intently. . . . His is a remarkably active mind, restless unless he has something of importance to do; cannot be idle for a moment, is by nature one of the most industrious of men; loves mental labour & hard study as he does daily food; . . . and is throughout a *positive* character.

The traits pointed out in another part of the statement are manifest throughout Polk's public career, but especially so during the four years of his Presidency: He

thinks well of himself; often asks advice, & does just as he pleases; is one of the firmest of men; slow in committing himself, but once committed, does all in his power to carry through his measures . . . has many acquaintances, few bosom friends . . . has an astonishing command of *facts* and can call to mind with great precision what occurred long ago.

To those who are familiar with Polk's career in national politics only, one part of the phrenologist's statement might seem very wide of the mark. In it, the phrenologist says that Polk would have succeeded on the stage, for he has ability in the use of pungent sarcasm and ridicule and ''could 'take off' the peculiarities of others if he would indulge this propensity.'' During the campaign which followed, Polk indulged this propensity to the full—especially against his opponent and Bailie Peyton—for ridicule and mimicry were among the chief weapons

---

[1] The phrenologist's name was O. S. Fowler, and the statement which he prepared bears the date of May 30, 1838 (*Polk Papers*).

used in assailing his adversaries. He is usually regarded as "a man who never smiled"; however this may have been, he was very successful in the art of amusing others.

There was rejoicing among the Democrats of Tennessee when, in September, 1838, Polk announced that he would enter the contest with Governor Newton Cannon for the highest office of his state. He received many letters in which the writers expressed their delight, promised support, and assured him of victory. It was the general opinion that he alone could restore the state to the Democratic party. It was, indeed, this belief that induced him to abandon his career in the national legislature. The unholy work of White and Bell must be undone; Old Hickory's state must be redeemed.

While he was still in Washington, presiding for the last time over the House of Representatives, Polk received many letters from Tennessee friends urging him to put the chief emphasis of his gubernatorial campaign on national issues and state internal improvements. It was pointed out that the Whigs would confine themselves almost exclusively to an attack upon the national administration and that the people of the state were much interested in internal development. The advice seems to have accorded with his own views. At any rate the topics suggested were the ones on which he placed the most emphasis.

As stated elsewhere, one of the most important events of Polk's campaign against Cannon was the advent of Jeremiah George Harris as editor of the Nashville *Union*. In response to the popular taste of the period, the press of the state had been notorious for extravagance of statement and personal abuse. It now entered upon a campaign of scurrility and abandon that has seldom been equaled; Mark Twain's employer could scarcely have made his editorials more "peppery and to the point."[2] Equipped with a style that was cutting without descending to mere ribaldry, and with a pen dipped in wormwood, Harris goaded his

---

[2] See Mark Twain, "Journalism in Tennessee," in *Sketches New and Old.*

opponents to a frenzy that was unprecedented. Lacking the ability to imitate his style, his enemies often resorted to coarse and vulgar abuse. No Whig editor in the state, except the inimitable Parson Brownlow, could cope with him in picturesque invective. Harris had a spread-eagle woodcut prepared, large enough to cover a considerable portion of the front page of his paper. As its appearance in the *Union* was always accompanied by news of Democratic victory, the Whigs expressed their contempt by calling it "Harris's buzzard."[3]

When Harris took charge of the *Union,* February 1, 1839, A. A. Hall, of the Nashville *Banner,* was already making capital of the charge made in Congress, by Wise and others, that Polk had "packed" the committees of the House. The new editor plunged at once into a vigorous defense of the Speaker and attributed the charges to jealousy of Polk's success and to a desire to injure him in Tennessee. When the House voted to select the Swartwout committee by ballot, the *Banner* exultingly heralded the event as proof positive that the House, having learned by experience that "Speaker Polk could not be trusted, proclaimed the fact to the world."[4]

Some of the other Whig papers were even more scurrilous than the *Banner.* For example, an article in the Knoxville *Register,* signed "Curtius," spoke of Polk as "lost to a sense of honesty, decency and integrity, laboring under insanity and disgrace, pliant tool, traitor, apostate and tory."[75] The Memphis *Enquirer* called him "a crouching sychophant" who lacked even

---

[3] It was said that a leading Whig, who had gone to the Murfreesborough post-office in quest of election news, saw through the window a package of "*Unions*" and exclaimed in disgust: "It's all over; there is Harris's infernal buzzard in the mail" (Phelan, *Hist. of Tenn.*, 381).

[4] "He has been tried by his peers and found wanting. A brand is upon him that no time can efface. He may cry 'Out d—d spot,' but it will abide with him for life" (Quoted in Nashville *Union,* February 8, 1839.) When criticizing a speech made by Dr. Duncan, candidate for Congress, the *Banner* called it "the roaring, staving, bellowing, howling Doctor's fanfaronade of bombast and nonsense" February 13, 1839.

[5] Quoted in *Union,* March 4, 1839.

the sense of shame.[6]   A friend had written to Polk that "your election is dovetailed into that of every candidate for Congress in the State.'"[7]   The Whigs apparently believed this, also, and were resolved at all hazard to defeat him.

In April, 1839, Polk formally opened his gubernatorial campaign by publishing a long and argumentative "Address to the People of Tennessee."[8]   The address deals almost entirely with national issues, the nature of the government, and the principles of the two great political parties.   It was pronounced by the *Banner*[9] to be "a poor enough concern"; but Phelan, with sounder judgment, has called it "the ablest political document which appeared in this State up to the time of the war.'"[10]   For the student of history, it is one of the most interesting documents ever penned by its author, for in it he has stated fully and with clearness the principles and doctrines which he considered to be essential to all just government.   It was evidently prepared with great care, and nowhere else does he give so full a statement of his views on so varied a list of subjects.

------

6 "Condemned and spit upon by a majority of the U. S. House of Representatives, in taking from him [Mr. Polk] the power of appointing committees, freely entrusted to all of his predecessors, but which he basely prostituted for the benefit of the party—of locofocoism—plainly told in language of thundering indignation that has been heard even to the shores of the seas, that he was no longer worthy of the confidence of Congress, like a crouching sychophant, instead of resigning his narrowed trust with shame, and disdaining tamely to see his integrity assailed by even those who exalted him, he submits, ignobly bears the rankling contumely, and in hope of political reward for 'self-sacrifice' upon the altar of loco-focoism, he still patiently ministers at its shrine reeking in corruption with a zeal that can only be inspired by a hope of reward.'' When quoting this, the *Union* replied in the same issue that "the raving of Mr. Prentiss, the ranting of Mr. Wise, and the management of Mr. Bell in reference to the appointment of the 'Swartwout Committee,' were all calculated for *effect* in Tennessee," and would be so regarded by the people (Nashville *Union*, March 4, 1839).

7 A. Balch to Polk, February 21, 1839, *Polk Papers*.

8 A copy in pamphlet form may be found in the *Polk Papers*, vol. 83. It is printed in full in the Nashville *Union*, April 10, 12, 15, 1839, as well as in other papers.

9 Nashville *Banner,* April 11, 1839.   On April 17 the *Banner* called it "an elaborate and ingenious production, but characterized by a want of manliness, candor and sincerity."

10 Phelan, *Hist. of Tenn.*, 381.

In stating his reasons for confining his address so largely to national questions, Polk asserted that the chief objections urged against him were based on the principles and policies which he had upheld as a member of Congress. He gave a historical summary[11] of the perennial contest between those who distrusted and ignored the will of the people and those who believed that government should carry into effect the popular will. The popular party, he said, had triumphed in the convention which drafted the Constitution, but Hamilton and his adherents soon procured by construction what they had failed to have embodied in the Constitution. Democracy triumphed under Jefferson, but under J. Q. Adams the

latitudinarian doctrines, with all the consolidating tendencies of the Hamilton school, as practiced under the administration of the elder Adams, were resuscitated and revived. It was publicly proclaimed that the wholesome restraints of the public will on the action of the servants of the people were to be disregarded, and that the 'Representative was not to be palsied by the will of his constituents.' It was declared by the Chief

---

11 "In the origin of the Government there were two parties. In the Convention that framed the Constitution one party distrusted the power and capacity of the people for self-government, and wished a strong central government. They admired the British Constitution—they were in favor of a President and Senate for life—they were for forming a strong government, far removed from the popular control; they wished to abstract from the power of the States—to restrict the right of suffrage, and to create other influences than the will of the people to control the action of their public functionaries. This party was not successful in the convention, and a constitution was formed which invested the new government with a few delegated and well defined powers, leaving all others to the States and the people, to exercise according to their sovereign will. The parties in the convention were the germ of the two great political divisions, which afterwards contended, and are still contending for the mastery in the Government.

"No sooner was the government put in operation under the Constitution, than the enemies of popular control over public authority, attempted by a latitudinous construction of the Constitution, to make the government in practice what they had in vain attempted to make it in principle and form. Alexander Hamilton, a professed monarchist in principle, and in the Convention the leading advocate of a strong central government, was the first Secretary of the Treasury, and immediately began, by strained and unwarranted constructions of the Constitution, to enlarge the power and influence of the Federal Government, with the view of diminishing the power of popular will over the administration of the Government." Jefferson himself could scarcely have penned a more telling indictment against the Federalists.

Magistrate to be ineffably stupid to suppose that the Representatives of the people were deprived of the power to advance the public weal, thereby substituting the unrestrained discretion of Congress and of the Federal Government for the specific grants of power conferred by a Constitution of limitations and restrictions.

Polk's recital of historical occurrences was accurate and well put; but it was begging the question to imply, as he did, that the framers of the Constitution had intended that representatives should divest themselves of all judgment and become mere automatons for registering the popular will. Custom and a desire for reëlection may prevent members of Congress from exercising their own judgment, but undoubtedly Adams rather than Polk reflected the views of those who drafted the Constitution.

It was thought by many politicians of both parties that Clay would be the candidate of the Whigs at the approaching Presidential election. Polk, therefore, devoted a considerable portion of his address to Clay and the policies which he advocated. The principal achievements of the Federalist administrations were, in Polk's opinion, the grasping of power by the general government and the creation of the money power. Their successors, the Whigs, likewise stood for these evils, and in addition, had adopted Clay's "miscalled 'American System' of high tariff and internal improvements, the result of which combination would oppress the poor and increase the evils of executive patronage.

The administration of Jackson he eulogized without stint. The adherents of White were told that they had supported the judge because he had been represented to be a better "Jackson man" than Van Buren, consequently there was no reason now why they should not return to the party of the people. It was untrue, said he, that Jackson had changed since his elevation to power; his detractors, not he, had deserted to the enemy. "I," continued Polk,

in common with the whole Republican party, am represented to you as one of these changelings. In what have I changed? I opposed Henry Clay on account of his odious Federal doctrines, and his coalition with

Mr. Adams, and I oppose him still. I opposed the high tariff policy, and I oppose it still. I opposed Internal Improvements by the General Government, and I oppose them still. I supported the removal of the deposits, and I have not changed my language or my opinions in relation to that great measure. In fine, what single point is there, involving the principles of the great Republican party, in which my course has not been uniform since 1825, when I was first honored with a seat in Congress, down to the present day?

From a man who had a reputation for concealing his views, this was certainly a most unequivocal declaration. Moreover, it was a true declaration, and it required courage to make it under the existing political conditions in Tennessee. Whether right or wrong, Polk had not swerved from his original political platform, although many of the policies for which he stood had become unpopular in his state. He may have broken with Judge White for personal as well as political reasons, but on national issues he had been consistent. He pinned his faith now, as he had always done, on government by the will of the majority; and however chimerical this may be in practice, his most private correspondence indicates that his belief in its practicability was sincere. Passing lightly over state issues, he asked for approval or condemnation on his record in national politics—a record which was being grossly misrepresented by the Whig papers of the state.[12]

At Murfreesborough, on April 11, 1839, Polk made his first speech of the campaign. Governor Cannon attended and was invited by Polk to speak first, on account of his age and office. This he declined to do, saying that, although he had not come prepared to speak, he might make a reply. Polk talked for two and a half hours, mainly on national issues and in commendation of the Jackson party. He said little on state issues, of which the *Banner* (April 15) ungenerously credited him with knowing "very little more than the man in the moon."

---

[12] "For months past I have been the unceasing and almost exclusive object of their calumnies and misrepresentation."

Cannon in reply said that *he* had never ''clung to the coat tail'' of General Jackson, and when ''danger approached, jumped into his pocket,'' but, instead, he had had to ''stem the buffetings of his wrath.'' Before the Creek war, according to his own story, Cannon was a member of a jury selected to try one Magnus on the charge of having murdered Patton Anderson, a personal friend of Jackson. When Cannon voted for acquittal, Jackson, pointing his finger at the young juror, exclaimed, ''I'll mark you, young man!'' Cannon insinuated, also, that, in fulfillment of this promise, Jackson had, during the Creek war, purposely exposed Cannon and a small detachment of troops to almost certain death, while the General himself remained in safety on the other side of the river. He was a ''tyrant by nature and education,'' and no one could be his follower·''who would not be his tool and his slave.''[13]

In a brief rejoinder Polk, according to the *Union* (April 12), made the ''roof ring'' with his ''power of ridicule.'' The *Banner,* on the other hand, reported that ''the locomotive candidate seemed to feel deeply that he had caught a *Tartar,*'' and that Governor Cannon ''triumphantly overthrew'' him.[14]

Polk's superiority, both in intellect and debating powers, was apparent from the beginning of the campaign. Cannon was slow and prosaic—lacking in force and personal magnetism. He was unable either to hold the attention or to arouse the sympathy of the multitude. He had until recently professed loyalty to Democratic doctrines, and he still seemed uncertain as to whether he had become a full-fledged Whig.[15] There was, on the contrary,

---

[13] Nashville *Rep. Banner,* April 16; Nashville *Union,* April 12, 1839.

[14] The *Banner* made much sport of Polk's ''grins and grimaces'' in imitation of Bailie Peyton and Henry Clay. ''James K. Polk, the narrow minded, superficial, little, grimacing politician attempting to expand his outward man, gesture and voice into something his hearers might take for *Henry Clay!*'' He tried, also, it said, to imitate Webster (*Banner,* April 13, 1839).

[15] In his reply to Polk, Cannon said: ''I believe I have always been a Democrat. Indeed, they used to call me an Ultra Democrat, a Radical.'' He claimed to be a Democrat still, but not in favor of Van Buren (*Banner,* April 16, 1839).

no uncertainty about Polk's views, and he knew how to state them most effectively.  He was, says Phelan,[16]

the first great ''stump speaker'' . . . always full of his subject, ready at retort, sophistical, quick to capture and turn the guns of the enemy against him, adroit in avoiding an issue whose result must be unfavorable, thoroughly equipped with forcible illustrations, humorous anecdotes, and a ridicule which ranged through all the changes from burlesque to wit.

With no pretensions to oratory, his strength lay in his ability to state the issues clearly and forcibly, and to argue these issues in language that was simple and convincing.

On April 13, the candidates met again at Lebanon.  On state issues they were in substantial agreement, and once more their time was occupied mainly with a discussion of national affairs. At the close of the debate Governor Cannon, pleading important state business, set out for Nashville.  Polk informed his wife that the Governor and himself got on ''very harmoniously,'' but there was little harmony in his relations with Bell.

Polk and Cannon had consumed the entire afternoon, and Bell, who was not expected to take part, took the stump at 5:30 in a ''rage of passion.''  He talked until sunset, and then announced that he would continue at the courthouse after supper. His first address, as reported, was most abusive in character.[17] Polk wrote home that even Bell's friends were disgusted by the speech, and that he had no difficulty, in his reply, in putting Bell in the wrong and winning tremendous applause.[18]

Governor Cannon resumed the debates, at McMinnville, on April 18, but shortly after he retired from the stump entirely. At McMinnville, having been taunted with indecision, he at last

---

[16] *Hist. of Tenn.,* 377.

[17] He said that Hopkins L. Turney, Representative from Tennessee, ''was not good enough for the Penitentiary—that Amos Lane was a scoundrel—that Dr. Duncan was a moral pestilence—that these were the tools which Col. Polk set forward to make speeches in Congress, instead of coming out and answering him [Bell] on the floor of Congress face to face'' (*Union,* April 17, 1839).

[18] Polk to Mrs. Polk, April 14, 1839, *Polk Papers.*

came out squarely for Clay, in the event of his nomination.[19] Because Polk had declared here and elsewhere that he and Cannon differed little in their views on state questions, the *Banner* called Polk a ''Government emissary'' and regarded it as extremely impudent in him to try to depose the Governor for his dislike of Van Buren.[20]

The people in those days took keen delight in political campaigns. They attended in large numbers, and no debate was long enough to be tedious if it were spiced with personal recrimination and with what passed for witty retorts. The popular ear in Tennessee of that day was not attuned to a very high grade of humor, while, in argument, pungent thrusts rather than logic won the sympathy of the audience. The festal side of a campaign was quite as important as the forensic, consequently political debates were usually held in open air, accompanied by a banquet or a barbecue. When Polk reached East Tennessee, the Whig section of the state, special pains were taken by the Democrats to give his journey the appearance of a triumphal procession.[21] Even though he could not hope to gain many votes in this section, the appearance of popularity in a Whig stronghold might aid him in other parts of the state.

---

[19] Nashville *Union*, April 22, 1839.

[20] ''Is it not a most impudent, unheard of request, then, on his part, to the people of Tennessee, that they should turn Governor Cannon out and put *him* in, all because the Governor is opposed to Mr. Van Buren's election? Is it not apparent that he is a Government emissary, traversing the State, county by county, with the sole view of revolutionizing it on the subject of national politics?'' (*Banner*, April 19, 1839). On May 22, the same paper called Polk a deserter from genuine republican doctrines, ''a political changeling—a weather cock, pointing ever in the direction from whence comes the breath of the President's nostrils—a devourer, eater-up of his own sentiments, formerly proclaimed in tones of self-gratification—a palace slave laborer for his master at Washington.''

[21] The *Tennessee Sentinel* thus described a Polk meeting at Jonesborough on May 17, 1839: ''As a means of enhancing the enjoyments of the day, suitable arrangements were made for a dinner, free to all of each party, without distinction, who might think proper to participate.'' After dinner there were toasts to Washington, Jackson, Van Buren, Polk, Amos Kendall, *et. al.*,—and one to ''*Newton Cannon*—the friend and supporter of Henry Clay for the next Presidency. Will the freemen of Tennessee be thus transfererd by *dictation* from the mouth of any *Cannon?* Cries of No! No!'' Quoted in Nashville *Union*, June 3, 1839.

The political contest was by no means confined to the stump and the platform. Wherever a group of people gathered, issues and candidates were freely discussed. Personal encounters not infrequently resulted[22] when arguments had failed to convince. Despite his surroundings, however, Polk always maintained his own dignity; although his language on the stump was often scathing and exasperating, he never descended to vulgarity or mere personal abuse.

Accuracy was not a desideratum in a political newspaper. That editor was most popular who could hurl grotesque epithets at his opponents and who always reported as well as prophesied victory for his own side. Harris of the *Union* fully measured up to the Democratic ideal,[23] and for this reason his paper wielded great political influence.

In June, A. A. Hall, of the *Banner,* caused consternation in Democratic ranks by quoting anti-slavery articles which had been written by Harris while he edited the New Bedford (Massachusetts) *Gazette.*[24] By befogging the issue and heaping abuse upon his accusers, Harris was quite successful in extricating himself from the difficulty. Nevertheless, the charge that Harris had been an abolitionist did Polk some injury in the canvass, for it was he who had been mainly responsible for bringing the editor to Nashville.[25] In order to divert attention from his own past record and to give new impetus to Democratic enthusiasm Harris

---

22 For example, Polk's brother-in-law, Dr. Rucker, is reported to have thrashed a ''bully'' whom the Whigs had brought to Murfreesborough to provoke a quarrel with him (John W. Childress to his sister, Mrs. Polk, May 27, 1839, *Polk Papers*).

23 For example, in reporting a debate between Bell and his opponent, Burton, the *Union* said that Bell abused Van Buren, eulogized Clay and called Polk ''the travelling missionary,'' but Burton ''literally dissected his opponent who has been schooled in the sophistries of partizanship, and laid the diseased limbs of Modern Whigism bare to the bone'' (May 27, 1839).

24 One of them, dated May 13, 1836, in opposing the annexation of Texas, called slavery ''the blackest, the foulest, blot on our national escutchen,'' and said that it would be ''the height of madness'' to extend it over more territory (*Banner,* June 11, 1839).

25 John W. Childress to Mrs. Polk, June 18, 1839, *Polk Papers.*

printed in the *Union* (June 24) the "Mecklenburg Declaration of Independence" and suggested its ratification on the Fourth of July. He dilated at length on the fact that Polk had been born in Mecklenburg county—a fact which proved that he had come from pure Democratic stock.

The Whigs hoped for good results from a speech made by Judge White in Knoxville, on the Fourth of July. He still professed adherence to Jeffersonian Republicanism, but denounced the Democrats, whose whole creed consisted in "always acting with the *same man,* or set of men." Far from being democrats they were, said he, "in reality *monarchists.*"[26] Harris was horrified because White had talked politics on the Fourth of July, but concluded from the "claptrap" which the judge had uttered that he must be in his "dotage."[27]

White's warning against monarchists did not produce the effect which the Whigs had anticipated, for Polk succeeded in winning back a considerable number of those who had supported the judge in 1836. Before the close of the campaign he received many letters telling of the good results which his canvass had achieved.[28]

Cannon was easily vanquished, and he retired from the stump, but Bell dogged Polk's footsteps, bringing into full play his great ability and oratorical powers. On July 17 he spoke at Nashville "from early candle-lighting until midnight" in an effort to defeat Polk in Middle Tennessee. He was, however, doomed to disappointment. On August 1 Polk was elected by a majority of three thousand votes, and Harris got out his "buzzard" to adorn the front page of the *Union* along with the election returns. The result of the campaign was justly regarded as a great

---

[26] Copied from Knoxville *Times* in Nashville *Banner,* July 18, 1839.

[27] Nashville *Union,* July 19, 1839.

[28] C. W. Hall, writing from Kingsport on July 12, told him that "one of my neighbors said the other day, 'Sir, I did not understand my political position, until I heard Col. Polk, and I then discovered most clearly, *that I was acting with men, who are opposed to my principles,* and I instantly resolved to quit their company'. . . . This is a common observation" (*Polk Papers*).

personal victory for Polk, inasmuch as the Whigs elected seven members of Congress and the Democrats only six.[29]   The Democrats elected a majority of the state legislature, which gave them the power to get rid of the Whig Senators by hampering them with obnoxious instructions.

Up to the very last the Whigs of the state seemed confident of victory.   They were reluctant to admit defeat even after the election had been held.   But the *Banner,* on August 9, mournfully informed its readers that owing to a lack of proper organization in Middle Tennessee[30] the ''Spoilsmen for a season will have the management of affairs in the State.''   Two days before this, prominent Whigs held a meeting in Nashville.   Resolutions were passed urging the organization of committees in every county for the purpose of retrieving the state.   They invited Clay to visit Tennessee, but he was unable at the time to accept the invitation.   Although the *Banner* from time to time reported enthusiastic Whig meetings, it was several weeks before there were signs of recovery from the shock of the recent defeat.

In their elation over Polk's election, the Democrats rather overrated its significance.   It has already been noted that they regarded the result as a personal victory for Polk over his enemies; but, in addition, they interpreted it to mean that Tennessee had returned, or at least was returning, to the party of Jackson and Van Buren.   Polk had been nominated for the avowed purpose of regaining the state for the national administration; he had made his canvass almost entirely on national issues; and Bell, as well as others, had opposed him on his record as an administration member of Congress.   As his friend Maclin said in a letter, more importance was attached to Polk's success than to the election of any other candidate.   There was, in his

---

[29] One of these was Cave Johnson.  Writing to Polk on August 11 he said that he had been elected by a majority of 1300 votes, and, as he had entered the race only on account of Polk and Grundy, he expected to retire from politics at the end of his term (*Polk Papers*).

[30] On August 13 the same paper attributed the result to bribery and illegal voting.

opinion, but one thing lacking to make the triumph complete—namely, the success of Burton over John Bell.[31]

To no one did the national effect of Polk's victory appear of greater importance than to General Jackson. As soon as the news reached him, he hastened to congratulate Polk and the country on his election and ''the return of old democratic Tennessee to the republican fold again.'' With customary hyperbole he predicted that ''it will be at least a century before she will permit herself to be again duped into her late false position by such jesuitical hypocrites & apostates as Bell, White & Co.''[32] Polk was doubtless well aware of the program that was to be carried into effect in the event of his election, and presumably he aided in formulating it; therefore Jackson did not allude to it in the letter just quoted. In a letter to Van Buren, however, the General outlined the party plans in characteristic fashion. As the Democrats have elected both governor and legislature, said he,

of course Mr. Foster[33] & his gagg law will not any more trouble the U. States Senate—Judge White must resign, or he will feel the weight of instructions & a Senator elected over his head—the precedent set by our last Legislature will justify this proceedure. My own opinion is, White will resign—Bell being disappointed in going into the Senate to fill White's vacancy, which was the price of his apostacy, if he is disappointed in getting into the Speaker's chair, will resign or *cut his throat* in despair & disappointment; and this catastrophy will end the existance of bluelight federalism in Tennessee.

For so great a triumph, he gave the principal credit to Colonel Polk and General Robert Armstrong.[34] As will appear in the

31 Sacfield Maclin to Polk, August 10, 1839, *Polk Papers*.

32 Jackson to Polk, August 13, 1839, *ibid.*

33 E. H. Foster was elected to the Senate when Grundy resigned.

34 Jackson to Van Buren, August 12, 1839, *Van Buren Papers*. ''I hope,'' wrote Richard Warner to Polk, September 29, ''we shall be able to adopt such measures as will compel Foster to give up the seat he and his friends usurped at the last session.'' The legislature should instruct the Senators to vote for the sub-treasury bill. If this does not bring ''poor old White'' to his senses, it should then be ascertained whether he is a Senator at all. (On account of ill health, White had tendered his resignation to Governor Cannon, but it had not been accepted.)

following chapter, the program here outlined, except the suicidal rôle assigned to Bell, was carried into successful operation.

When the election took place, the "old hero" was sojourning at Tyree Springs, in Sumner County. After it had been ascertained beyond question that the state had been redeemed, the leading Democrats of Middle Tennessee, including Polk, Attorney-General Grundy, Judge Campbell, and General Armstrong, reported, with their ladies, to that place in order to join with the General in celebrating the victory. Burdens of state as well as the infirmities of age were, for the time being, forgotten, and the company once more indulged in the frivolities of youth. Each morning, after breakfast, a mock court was held, of which Grundy was Chief Justice and General Jackson, Associate. From fines levied by this "court," provisions for the day were supplied—a proceeding which seems to have added much to the enjoyment of the company.[35]

Polk did not remain long within the jurisdiction of this improvised court. He soon returned to his home in Columbia to complete his plans for ousting the Whig Senators, and to prepare for his inauguration. Unlike many who offered him advice, Cave Johnson believed that the program of persecution would do the Democrats more harm than good, and therefore urged Polk to oppose it. "It is essential," he wrote,

to the existence of our party that every selfish consideration be laid aside & act in concert & no man can do so much to effect this as yourself. . . . It has struck me with some force, that *our friends* should go to work & do the business of the State without the slightest interference with Federal politics—let White and Foster take their course—go to Washington if they choose—if Foster adopts that course he is forever disgraced—toward the conclusion of the Session we can instruct.

He did not "wish our party to have the semblance of coercing either until it is absolutely necessary." He believed that Foster would resign even without instructions, but however that might be, "by all means let the necessity for interference be manifest

---

[35] Nelson, *Memorials of Sarah Childress Polk,* 60–63.

before it is done, rather let it be urged upon the Legislature by the people rather than upon the people by the Legislature.''[36] Johnson's advice may have been prompted by political sagacity rather than by a sense of justice, but whatever the motive his recommendations were good.

As will appear in the following chapter, other counsels prevailed, and the Democrats elected to make the most of their political power. Their choice gave them a temporary advantage, although eventually their unfair treatment of the Whig Senators helped to transfer votes from their own party to that of their opponents.

---

[36] Johnson to Polk, Clarksville, September 28. The year is not given. The letter has been put with the *Polk Papers* for 1838, but evidently it was written in 1839.

## CHAPTER IX

## GOVERNOR OF TENNESSEE

In accordance with an absurd custom, a governor of Tennessee, in the closing hours of his administration, enacted the solemn farce of submitting to the legislature a message in which he made elaborate recommendations for its consideration. This was done with a full knowledge that within a few days a new governor would be inaugurated and that he, in turn, would present entirely different recommendations.

On October 8, 1839, Governor Cannon submitted his final message to a legislature composed of thirteen Democrats to ten Whigs in the Senate, and forty-nine Democrats to thirty-three Whigs in the lower house. It is unnecessary to dwell on his suggestions concerning state affairs, for, needless to say, no heed was paid to them. For political reasons, however, the Democratic majority in the new legislature felt that his severe condemnation of the national administration merited both consideration and rebuke. Unanswered, the Governor's remarks might tend to influence the wavering, and a refutation would afford another opportunity to herald the glorious achievements of the "party of the people."

Among other things the retiring Governor had expressed a hope that "the country will ere long be delivered from the maladministration of the present rulers, with its pernicious train of experiments and spoliations." This part of his message was referred by the legislature to a "Committee on Federal Relations" which was created early in the session. The most active member of the committee was Samuel H. Laughlin, former editor of the Nashville *Union* and a personal friend of both Polk and

Jackson, and it was easy to foretell what the verdict would be. On January 29, 1840, Laughlin reported that his committee had been

wholly unable, from anything contained in said message, or in the past action of the Federal Government, executive, legislative or judicial, during the late or present administrations, which can, in the slightest degree, even by implication, afford the least warrant of authority for the imputations contained in that portion of said message.[1]

The verdict of the committee was approved by the legislature, and little attention was paid to a minority report which upheld the contentions of the former Governor. Laughlin's report served as a vindication of the national administration. In addition, it served as the basis for one of the instructions given to the federal Senators from Tennessee—the instruction to vote against the bill to prevent interference in elections by certain federal officers.

On October 14, 1839, Polk was inaugurated as governor of Tennessee. Among those present to witness the ceremony it gave Harris of the *Union* "great pleasure to notice ex-President Jackson, with health apparently improved." The inaugural address, according to the same writer, was "an effort of great happiness on the part of Gov. Polk." "It was," wrote Old Hickory, "a great address well suited to the occasion—there was a great contrast betwen his and Mr. Cannon's."[2]

On account of its supposed influence on national politics, more importance was attached to Polk's inauguration than is usually the case when a state executive is installed. Levi Woodbury voiced the sentiment of most Democrats when he wrote: "I have seldom known the result of any election to be more triumphant & gratifying over the whole Union than that of yours."[3]

---

[1] *Tenn. Sen. Jour.*, 1839–40, 7, 504.
[2] Jackson to Van Buren, Oct. 18, 1839, *Van Buren Papers.*
[3] Woodbury to Polk, October 20, 1839, *Polk Papers.*

The new Governor's first message was submitted to the legislature on October 22, and the subjects most emphasized in it were banks and internal improvements. He expressed the belief that there had been no necessity for the suspension of specie payments by the banks of Tennessee. On the assumption that they had suspended such payments simply because eastern banks had done so, he urged the enactment of measures which would compel resumption, for "like individual debtors, they should meet their liabilities honestly and promptly as long as they are able to pay." Banks often, said he, do their most profitable business during suspension, while the loss is borne by labor. He denied that the federal government had been responsible for derangement of the currency or that a national bank could have prevented it. The main cause of financial distress, he said, was speculation on borrowed capital. For remedy, therefore, he did not seek new legislation, but suggested something far more sensible—a remedy which in no degree depended on governmental action. "The only substantial and permanent relief," said the Governor,

is to be found in habits of economy and industry, and in the productive labor of our people. By the observance of these, another crop would more than liquidate our eastern debt. We must bring our expenses within our income. Our merchants and traders must cease to indulge in hazardous and wild speculations which they are unable to meet.

This was very sound advice, far too sound to be widely accepted in a period when most people believed that the government was able to dispense or withhold prosperity at will, regardless of their own reckless speculative ventures.

Another recommendation was that the legislature should, by law, prohibit the Bank of Tennessee from emitting notes under twenty dollars, because excessive issues of paper tended to drive out metal money, and in addition, to facilitate speculation.

Polk declared himself to be strongly in favor of internal improvements made by the state. He asked, however, that existing laws on that subject should be so modified as to prevent extravagance. For example, the legislature at the preceding session had enacted a law which required the state to subscribe for one-half of the capital stock of all railroads, macadamized turnpikes, graded turnpikes, and sanded turnpikes for which acts of incorporation "have heretofore been granted or for which acts of incorporation may be hereafter granted." Such a law had great possibilities for evil, and under it worthless enterprises had already been undertaken. Polk now urged that the law should be so modified that subscriptions in future must be limited to works of real improvement, and that a board of public works should be created to authorize and supervise such enterprises.[4]

On the whole the Governor's message was a creditable document, although it lacked the vigor and elaboration which usually characterized his written productions. It was evident that his interests were national rather than local. His recommendations were duly considered by the legislature, but even the members of that body seemed to be more interested in "doing practical politics" for the national party than in enacting laws for the good of the state. At any rate practical politics was given first place on their program.

It was well known to all that the main reason for making Polk the gubernatorial candidate was the belief that he alone could win the state back to Democratic allegiance. For this same reason he had consented to make the race. The question which soon presented itself was: What does he expect as his reward, if he succeeds? During the campaign the Whigs made the charge that Polk did not care for the governorship, and that his nomination had been simply a ruse to win Tennessee for Van Buren and the Vice-Presidency for himself at the approaching federal election. In such an event he would, of course, resign in the middle of his term. The charge was repelled by Polk's friends, but the probability of its truth was so great that many, especially in East

---

[4] *Tenn. Sen. Jour.*, 1839–40, 64–68.

Tennessee, declined to vote for him under the circumstances. He was urged[5] to make an emphatic denial of the charge, but he followed his usual policy of keeping silent. When, therefore, the state senate, within forty-eight hours after his inauguration, began to consider the question of nominating Polk for Vice-President, the *Banner* charged that this had been the sole purpose of making him governor, and that the people had been grossly deceived.[6]

The senate with little opposition passed a resolution nominating Van Buren and Polk, and on October 22, the same day on which it received the Governor's message, the house proceeded to consider this senate resolution. Two amendments were offered by the opposition—one to require the candidates to support a federal bank, another to strike out the name of Polk—but both were promptly rejected. After prolonged and animated debate the house, on November 4, concurred in the senate resolution and formally nominated the two candidates.[7] Until the question had been decided, the local newspapers kept up a war of words on the subject, each trying to surpass its rival in vulgar abuse, which doubtless pleased the readers but which made few converts in the legislature.[8]

In Washington the Democratic members of the Tennessee delegation in Congress were busily engaged in an effort to procure for Polk the second place on the national ticket. His principal competitor was the incumbent, Colonel Richard M. Johnson, of Kentucky. Johnson had the support of the conservative

---

[5] H. W. Anderson, of Brownsville, to Polk, September 10, 1839, *Polk Papers*.

[6] Nashville *Banner*, Oct. 19, 1839. One enthusiastic friend urged Polk not to leave the governorship for the Vice-Presidency: ''The plan that I had laid off was for you to be our Governor six years and then Senator Six and at the end of Benton's eight years make you President'' (Amos Kirkpatrick, of Meigsville, to Polk, Oct. 17, 1839, *Polk Papers*).

[7] *Tenn. House Jour.*, 1839–40, 68–69.

[8] To quote one sample of their ability in vivid description: The *Union*, on October 16, informed its readers that John B. Ashe, a state senator, ''came very near bursting his boiler and collapsing his flue on yesterday,'' in condemning the *Union*.

element of the party—of the class of people whose main rule of action is leaving well enough alone. But a portion of the party desired a more vigorous candidate, a man who would conduct a more energetic campaign, and a man who would be more acceptable to the southern states. These qualities were especially desired in the candidate for Vice-President in order to offset the want of them in Van Buren, their candidate for President.

The supporters of Polk fully realized that it would be difficult to procure for him the coveted nomination. They knew that there was little genuine enthusiasm for Johnson in any quarter, still they feared that he might be nominated by the national convention simply because that body would not know how to get rid of him. Their only hope seemed to lie either in preventing the calling of a national convention, or in preventing any nomination of a Vice-Presidential candidate if such a convention should be held. A letter outlining the situation was sent to Polk by six Democratic members of Congress from Tennessee.[9] It stated that a national convention had been recommended by New Hampshire, and that it now seemed to be a certainty. If so, it was their opinion that Johnson would probably be nominated, although New England, New York, Virginia, North Carolina and other states preferred Polk. Johnson was a "dead weight" on the party, they said, but it was hard to drop him. It was possible, they believed, that the convention might fail to nominate any one, and break up in confusion, but at all events Tennessee should be fully represented in the convention. In a separate letter (dated February 4) Brown tells Polk that Calhoun is for him on the ground of "your *position*, your *abilities* & your *principles*."

A few days after the receipt of the above-mentioned letter Polk informed Hubbard, a member of the House from New Hampshire,[10] that his position was "passive"—that he would accept

---

[9] The letter was dated at Washington, February 3, 1840, and was signed by Felix Grundy, A. McClellan, H. M. Watterson, H. L. Turney, C. Johnson, and A. V. Brown (*Polk Papers*).

[10] Polk to Hubbard, February 7, 1840, *Polk Papers.*

the nomination at the hands of his party, but would not seek it. Such at attitude was in line with his usual adherence to party unity. His passive attitude, however, seems to have been somewhat affected by his unanimous nomination by a Virginia convention. This nomination was made, it was said[11] at the instance of the friends of Calhoun. In response to Polk's letter, Hubbard strongly urged Polk to put aside all delicacy and run. Johnson, he said, was in favor of both tariff and internal improvements, and was unpopular with many in the party. For these reasons, said Hubbard, Democrats should oppose a national convention, and should nominate Polk in some other way; Virginia had done so, and why should other states not follow her example? Should the election eventually devolve upon the Senate, he was certain that Polk would be chosen.[12] In Washington, A. J. Donelson was using his influence to procure Polk's nomination. On March 4 he wrote that, although the South was unequivocally for Polk, yet he feared that the convention would choose Johnson instead.[13]

Polk was willing enough to run, but being a firm believer in party solidarity, he was reluctant to become the candidate of a portion of the party unless it should develop that the party as a whole could not agree upon a choice. Writing to Cave Johnson on March 27, he said that "up to now" he had maintained that he would not run unless nominated by the undivided party. But, said he, the refusal of Virginia and South Carolina to send delegates to the Baltimore convention had changed the situation by making unanimity in any case out of the question; consequently if the convention should fail to make a nomination, in other words, in the event of there being no party nominee, he might in that case consent to run.[14]

---

11 Theophilus Fisk to Polk, Richmond, February 21, 1840, *Polk Papers.* In reporting the news to Polk, Fisk added: "Wherever my paper, the Old Dominion, circulates, and it has a very wide one, the people will hear of no candidate but yourself."

12 Hubbard to Polk, February 23, 1840, *Polk Papers.*

13 Donelson to Polk, March 4, 1840, *ibid.*

14 *Polk Papers.* He wrote a similar letter to Hubbard on April 5, 1840.

Ready as ever to aid his friends, General Jackson used his influence in an attempt to procure Polk's nomination by the national convention. In a letter to Van Buren he said that

A man ought to be chosen that all the republicans in every state would cheerfully unite on, and if this is not done it will jeopardise your election—it ought to be a man whose popularity would strengthen you, not one that would be a dead weight upon your popularity.

Polk, in his opinion had double the popularity of Johnson, and his nomination by the party would insure victory. He was pained to learn from Major Donelson that many in Congress believed it advisable to make no nomination for the Vice-Presidency; "surely our friends have not taken a common sense view of the whole subject."[15]

Before leaving Tennessee, Laughlin and some of the other delegates to the Baltimore convention held a conference in Nashville with Polk, Jackson, and other political leaders. The General was firm in his belief that candidates ought to be nominated for both President and Vice-President, and that Van Buren and Polk should be the nominees. Polk, he repeated, would add strength to the ticket, while Colonel Johnson would be an encumbrance. On the other hand, Polk made it clear to the delegates that in no event would he run as a sectional candidate, as Judge White had done in 1836; should Johnson be nominated, he would earnestly support him. Should no nomination be made at Baltimore, and if within a reasonable time a sufficient number of states had not indicated a preference for himself, he would then take field in support of Colonel Johnson or any other candidate that seemed most likely to bring success to the party.[16]

Laughlin arrived in Washington on April 25, and three days later, after conferences with Tennesseans, he recorded in his diary that "all were now agreed that Gov. Polk could not be nominated—that Johnson could not without New York, and that

---

[15] Jackson to Van Buren, April 3, 1840, *Van Buren Papers*.

[16] S. H. Laughlin, "Diary," April 14, 15, *Tenn. Hist. Mag.*, March, 1916, 45–47.

the best way, if possible, was to make no nomination. This matter was in treaty between Mr. Grundy and Mr. Wright.'' On the day following, Laughlin reported to Polk that Benton and Buchanan were secretly in favor of Johnson and that ''such creatures as Walker and Sevier are only fit to do mischief,'' but that Calhoun was heartily in favor of Polk's nomination.[17] At a meeting held in Grundy's room on May 1 it was agreed that Polk's only hope lay in preventing any nomination by the convention, and some believed that a refusal by delegates to attend would be the most effective way of procuring the desired result.[18] This plan was not followed, however, and a few days later Laughlin wrote from Baltimore that the convention had nominated Van Buren but, by a vote of one hundred and thirty-two to ninety-nine, had declared it inexpedient to nominate a candidate for Vice-President.

After the convention had adjourned without naming a candidate for Vice-President, Polk prepared a statement in the form of a letter to Grundy and requested him to have it published in the Washington *Globe*.[19] It had been his wish, he said, that the Baltimore convention might nominate a candidate, but, as it had not done so, he still hoped that the opinions of the majority could in some way be ascertained. In that event he would cheerfully support the choice, but, as he had been nominated by some of the states, he would let the party decide whether to settle on one or more. He hoped that some one would be chosen by the electoral college. In answer, Grundy told him[20] that no doubt he would have won if there had been no convention, but as matters now

---

[17] S. H. Laughlin, ''Diary,'' April 28, 29, *op. cit.* Laughlin to Polk, April 29, 1840, *Polk Papers*. In his diary for May 4, Laughlin recorded that ''Mr. Buchanan from hostility to Gov. Polk's future prospects had allied himself to King, and by contrivance, their friends were trying first to effect a compromise with the friends of Johnson and Polk and thereby get King nominated upon the half-way house principle; but if they could not get this done, they united and were to unite with Johnson's friends and press for a nomination.''

[18] Laughlin to Polk, May 2, 1840, *Polk Papers*.

[19] Polk to Grundy, May 27, 1840, *ibid.*

[20] Grundy to Polk, June 1, 1840, *ibid.*

stood, he thought that Johnson would be elected. The Nashville *Union,* he said, had injured rather than aided Polk by calling on the states to declare their preference. As it would not look well to withdraw formally from the race, Grundy advised Polk simply to do nothing.

The contest between Polk and Johnson for second place on the Democratic ticket was more than a rivalry between the two men. Back of it was a party cleavage which four years later was to land Polk in the White House. Despite Jackson's loyalty to Van Buren, many of the General's best friends did not like the "little magician"; they supported him only from a sense of party duty. Still less did this wing of Democracy like Colonel Johnson, and, if they must support Van Buren, they wished at least to have a Vice-Presidential candidate for whom they could willingly vote. There seems to be no evidence that Polk himself had, up to this time, been opposed to Van Buren, nevertheless he was on very intimate terms with the insurgent faction of the party. This wing of the party was impelled mainly by a desire to promote southern interests, although a revolt against "old fogyism" was already becoming a political factor. Its adherents regarded Polk as sound on southern questions, while they had doubts in the case of both Van Buren and Johnson. Party cleavage had existed before Polk had been suggested for the Vice-Presidency, but the apparent hostility of the administration to his candidacy aided in widening it. Although the President himself seems to have expressed no preference, those who were in his confidence and who were supposed to voice his wishes were directly or indirectly supporting Colonel Johnson. Among them were Benton, Buchanan, Kendall, and Blair.[21] For a second time[22] Blair appeared reluctant to give aid to Polk when he was sorely in need of it. These instances alone furnish a very good reason

---

[21] Jackson's attitude toward the candidates had no connection with this party split. He favored Van Buren and Polk, and opposed Johnson, purely for personal reasons.

[22] The first time was when Polk was a candidate for Speaker of the House.

why Polk, when he became President, declined to adopt the *Globe* as his official organ.

Shortly after the Democratic convention had adjourned, Cave Johnson informed Polk[23] that a *Life of Van Buren and Johnson* had appeared and that he believed it had been published at the office of the *Globe*. Blair, he said, had declared himself to be impartial as to Colonel Johnson and Polk, but ''I have no faith in that establishment so far as your interests are concerned.'' For this reason he (Cave Johnson) and his friends were not eager to extend the circulation of Kendall's *''Extra Globes,''* which had been prepared especially for campaign purposes. On May 25, five of the Tennessee delegation[24] addressed a letter to Kendall himself. In it they stated that while they were anxious to advance the cause of the administration, they were unwilling to prejudice the cause of their favorite candidate, and therefore, ''before we undertake the circulation of the *Extra Globe,* we are desirous of being informed, whether the *Extra* will take any part, & if any what part, in the election of Vice President.'' Kendall gave a rather evasive reply[25] in which he stated that, while he thought well of their ''favorite candidate,'' he would attempt to promote the cause of the party by speaking well of any or all candidates as the occasion might require. With this reply, which was regarded as a virtual endorsement of Johnson, they had to be content, but the hostility to Kendall and Blair by no means abated. The element that supported Polk became more and more alienated from Van Buren and his intimates until, in 1844, they succeeded in preventing his nomination.

The other question of a purely political nature that engrossed the attention of the Tennessee legislature was that of forcing White and Foster out of the United States Senate by the use of humiliating instructions.

---

[23] Johnson to Polk, May 24, 1840, *Polk Papers*.

[24] Cave Johnson, A. V. Brown, H. L. Turney, A. McClellan, and H. M. Watterson.

[25] June 9, 1840. Both letters are in the *Polk Papers*.

In White's case another method was first attempted, for the judge was still popular in the state, and, if he could be eliminated without resorting to instructions, less odium would attach to his adversaries. In the fall of 1838 White had, on account of ill health, tendered his resignation to Governor Cannon. The Governor suspended action in the hope that White's health might improve. As it did improve sufficiently to enable him to make the journey to Washington, the resignation, at Cannon's request, was withdrawn without having been accepted.

Rumors of White's letter of resignation had found their way to Democratic ears and suggested the possibility of disposing of the judge by maintaining that by his own action his seat had become vacant. Accordingly, when the legislature convened in October, 1839, the senate by resolution asked Governor Cannon for copies of the correspondence which had passed between himself and White relative to the latter's resignation. Cannon replied that White's resignation had never been accepted and that his letter had been returned; all other correspondence had been personal, not official, and had not been preserved. Attorney-General Grundy wrote[26] from Washington urging that White's successor should be chosen without delay, and expressing the opinion that Foster would resign if instructed to vote for the sub-treasury bill. Such a program, if successful, would give the Democrats an opportunity to choose both Senators, one of whom was to be Grundy himself.

Notwithstanding Grundy's advice, the difficulty of proving that White's seat had become vacant seemed to be so great that, on October 25, Levin H. Coe introduced in the state senate a series of resolutions which instructed the Senators and requested the Representatives to carry out the wishes of the legislature on certain enumerated subjects.[27] While the resolutions were being

---

[26] Grundy to Polk, October 17, *Polk Papers.*

[27] (1) To vote against the chartering of a United States bank. (2) To vote for the sub-treasury. (3) To vote against any bill for the prevention of interference in elections by certain federal officers, as such a bill would

discussed by the legislature, Judge White wrote to one of the members of the lower house stating that he would resign rather than support the sub-treasury bill.[28]  His letter was read to the legislature, and soon afterwards that body, by a strict party vote, passed the resolutions.  General Jackson's program was thereby successfully carried into effect, and once more he had the satisfaction of humiliating the man who had dared to run for President against his wishes.  It was a contemptible transaction, and those who participated in it are deserving of nothing but condemnation.  It remained to be seen, of course, whether the Whig Senators would repudiate their instructions, but there was little doubt that White at least, would resign.

On his way to Washington, early in November, John Bell stopped at Knoxville to deliver a public address in which he scathingly denounced the administration and its supporters.  In response to a call from the audience, White addressed the same meeting in language which was reported to have been violently intemperate.[29]

While White was yet on his journey to Washington, Polk, in a letter to Van Buren, congratulated him on recent Democratic victories, and pointed out that they were a good omen for 1840.  "Judge White," said Polk, "forgetting the dignity of his station, as well as the former character of which he boasted, descended into the political arena, and became an active partisan and travelling electioneer."  He told Van Buren that the legislature

---

violate the Constitution of the United States. (4) To vote against distribution among the states of revenue derived from the sale of public lands— and for reducing the price of such lands. (5) To vote for a repeal of the duty on salt. (6) To support in good faith the leading measures of the present administration (*Tenn. Sen. Jour.*, 1839–40, 77–79; Scott, *Memoir of Hugh Lawson White*, 370).

[28] White to Jacobs, September 5, 1839 (Scott, *Memoir of Hugh Lawson White*, 371).

[29] Lewis P. Roberts to Polk, Nov. 11, 1839, *Polk Papers*.  Roberts doubtless exaggerated in reporting that White "characterized the whole of the V. B. party as gamblers and blacklegs" and accused Van Buren of pocketing the money which the people had lost from a derangement of currency.

had instructed the Senators to support the President's measures, and expressed the belief that Foster would resign and White obey the instructions. Grundy, he said, would be the best man to succeed Foster; he therefore urged the President to give up his Attorney-General for the good of the cause.[30]

Foster promptly resigned on November 15, thus leaving one seat in the Senate at the immediate disposal of the Democrats. Catron, who was holding court in Louisville, believed that White, too, would soon be forced to resign. Tennessee, he wrote, must be held loyal to the administration, and the best way of insuring this was to make Polk the candidate for Vice-President.[31]

The legislature by a party vote chose Grundy to fill Foster's unexpired term. As soon as the news reached Washington, however, one of his friends, H. C. Williams, pointed out to him that he was not eligible for the office.[32] The constitution required that a Senator, at the time of his election, must be a local resident, and it was thought that Grundy was not such a resident so long as he remained in the cabinet. He therefore resigned his seat in the Senate, and the technicality was obviated by his reëlection after his return to Tennessee.[33]

On receiving his instructions from the legislature, White decided that instead of resigning at once he would wait until some question had been presented which would compel him either to vote contrary to his principles or to violate his instructions. The Democrats, therefore, hastened to bring forward an obnoxious measure. On January 13, 1840, Silas Wright called up the sub-treasury bill and thereby forced the issue. White rose and explained to the Senate the embarrassment of his position, and then read the letter of resignation which he was about to send

---

[30] Polk to Van Buren, Nov. 11, 1839, *Van Buren Papers*.

[31] Catron to Polk, Nov. 19, (1839 ?), *Polk Papers*.

[32] Williams to Polk, Nov. 28, 1839, *"Most strictly confidential."* On December 1 Cave Johnson gave a similar opinion, and said that Grundy would go to Nashville to look after the matter *(Polk Papers)*.

[33] *Niles' Register*, Jan. 11, 1840.

to the Tennessee legislature.[34]  Grundy and others had expected from the persecuted Senator a bitter arraignment of the administration party.  They had come prepared to answer him, but Grundy himself admitted that White's letter to the legislature had been "drawn with some ability" and was too respectful to call for a reply.[35]

While no one questioned the legal right of a state to instruct its Senators, it was generally felt that the legislature had used its power for the unworthy purpose of punishing White and gaining a political advantage to which the Democrats were not entitled.  A dinner was given in the deposed Senator's honor at which all of the prominent Whigs were present.  His public career and his loyalty to principle were exalted in toasts and addresses made by Clay, Preston, and many others.[36]  It was his last public appearance.  An attack of pneumonia before his departure from Washington and the fatigue caused by the journey home greatly impaired his vitality, and his death occured on April 10, 1840.

White's resignation gave the choice of his successor to the Democratic majority in the legislature.  As the judge was from East Tennessee, custom required that his successor should be a resident of the same section of the state.  The legislature selected Alexander Anderson, a lawyer of fair ability but a man without national reputation.

As noted above, the principal recommendations made by Governor Polk in his message dealt with banks and internal improvements.  To these topics the legislature gave its attention when it was not too busily engaged with *practical politics*.  Like most banks in the Union those of Tennessee had suspended specie payments.  In response to the Governor's suggestion Yoakum, on October 28, 1839, presented a resolution which, if adopted, would

---

[34] Both explanation and letter are printed in Scott, *Memoir of Hugh Lawson White,* 375 ff.

[35] Grundy to Polk, Jan. 13, 1840, and other letters on the same subject in the *Polk Papers.*

[36] An account of this dinner is given in Scott, *Memoir of Hugh Lawson White,* 395 ff.

compel the Bank of Tennessee and its branches forthwith to resume and continue specie payments on all notes of and under ten dollars. Another resolution moved by Jennings, an opposition member, required the committee on banks to interrogate the president and directors of this bank as to whether financial accommodations were made on the basis of political sentiments. On November 11, Jennings presented a bill which embodied and made more explicit the ideas included in his resolution. The bill required the committee on banks to call on the Bank of Tennessee for the following items of information: (1) whether the choice of officers of the branch banks was influenced by politics; (2) whether contracts were so influenced; and (3) whether politics was considered in making loans. Another bill was proposed by Wheeler the purpose of which was to compel all banks of the state to resume specie payments within thirty days on penalty of forfeiture of their charters. On January 15, 1840, Jennings proposed an amendment to the state constitution the intent of which was to prevent the state in future from becoming the sole proprietor of, or a partner in, any bank, and from raising money on the credit of the state, except for defense.[37]

None of these proposals was enacted into law. The Democrats easily disposed of the political measures of their opponents, but, with the exception of a few minor remedial regulations, they were unable to carry their own. Toward the close of the session Laughlin submitted a report from the committee which had been appointed by the senate to investigate the banks. It stated that no evidence of politics in bank transactions had been discovered and that specie payments would, in the opinion of the banks, be resumed by July 1, 1840.[38] This belief, however, proved to be erroneous.

In response, also, to suggestions made in the Governor's message, the legislature undertook to modify existing laws on the

---

[37] *Tenn. Sen. Jour.*, 1839–40, 85–86, 109, 156–157, 407.
[38] *Ibid.*, Appendix.

subject of internal improvements. Yielding to a popular clamor for state aid, the legislature under Cannon's administration had made it obligatory for the state to become a partner in all improvement ventures regardless of the nature of the enterprise. Wholesale extravagance had been the result; nevertheless it was not an easy matter to eliminate the abuses without doing injury to those who, relying on continued support from the government, had invested capital in various projects.[39] The secretary of state reported to the senate that, under the act of 1836, $2,732,541⅔ had been subscribed by the state to improvement enterprises, and under the act of 1838, $889,500 had been subscribed for turnpikes and river improvements, $65,000 to the Louisville, Cincinnati, and Charleston Rail Road Company, and a similar amount to the Hiawassee Rail Road Company.[40]

In order to save the state in future from such ruinous expenditures, the legislature repealed all laws which had required the governor to subscribe for stock in improvement corporations. In the repealing act provision was made for the withdrawal, so far as possible, from partnerships already formed. By another act, passed on January 28, 1840, the legislature recalled $150,000 in state bonds which had been placed with banks to be sold and the proceeds invested in stocks of improvement companies. This legislation was substantially what the Governor had recommended, and, although there was no remedy for the waste that had already

---

[39] In responding to a vote of thanks at the close of the session, Speaker Coe, of the Senate, stated very clearly the difficulty which confronted the legislature: ''In 1836 and 1838 laws were passed for the encouragement of Internal Improvement and works of the most extensive character have been commenced, and are now in progress of erection. If we continued to advance under the law as we found it, many saw in it the germ of a disordered and bankrupt treasury, and a people loaded down with taxes, levied to pay the interest on an onerous State debt—whilst it was asserted by others, with much reason, that the State had voluntarily tendered the right hand of assistance to large bodies of our fellow citizens, and had invited enterprises, having for their object the cultivation and improvement of our common country; and under such circumstances the sudden withdrawal of all aid, would involve individuals in private ruin and consign public works to dilapidation'' (*ibid.*, 545–546).

[40] Reports of Luke Lea, secretary of state, Oct. 25 and Nov. 23, *Tenn. Sen. Jour.*, 1839–40, 74, 142.

occurred, so long as Polk remained in the governor's chair care was taken to restrict expenditures and to reduce the state debt.

During Polk's first year as governor of his state, the people of the nation were engaged in the whirlwind Presidential campaign of 1840—the first and most boisterous of its kind. In every state in the Union the contest was waged with unprecedented fury, and especially so in Tennessee. Reason and logical argument were cast to the winds, while noise and caricature became the order of the day. The ''stump speech'' played a less important part than usual; while both sides, but especially the Whigs, expended their energies in fantastic processions. The greater the din of deafening and discordant noises, the more spectacular or grotesque the banners and other devices designed to excite the emotions of the crowd, the more successful was the pageant considered.

For sentimental reasons, as well as for the importance of her electoral votes, the contest in Tennessee was regarded as of national significance. Failure to redeem ''Old Hickory's state'' was thought by Democratic politicians to be nothing short of disgrace, while the hope of thus humiliating their opponents spurred the Whigs to untiring effort. But the Whigs had the advantage from the outset. The rank and file of the Democrats did not share the feeling of the party leaders; they could not wax enthusiastic over Van Buren. In the Whig camp, on the contrary, there was unity.

In 1839, as soon as it became known that Polk had been elected, prominent Whigs held a convention in Nashville and arranged for the appointment of local committees throughout the state. These committees were effective engines of agitation, and the *Union* promptly denounced them as ''new and strange fermentations in the body politic to be put down by all lovers of peace and social order.''[41] Clay was invited to visit Tennessee by a delegation sent to Kentucky for that purpose by the Nashville

---

[41] Phelan, *Hist. of Tenn.*, 384.

convention, but, the sage of Ashland, pleading illness and pressure of private business, declined to make a definite promise to accept.[42]  It was expected, of course, that the legislature would instruct the Whig Senators and force their resignation, and the *Banner* was certain that such a course would be of great advantage to the Whigs in the Presidential campaign. This paper urged the Senators to remain in office until forced to resign.  In such an event their names were to head the Whig electoral ticket, and the state was to be "thoroughly and ably canvassed, in every county and every neighborhood and victory would be assured."[43]

The national convention of the Whig party met at Harrisburg, Pennsylvania, on December 4, 1839.  Due to prejudice against national conventions, the Whigs of Tennessee refused to send delegates, for it will be remembered that opposition to the convention which nominated Van Buren was a chief factor in the creation of the "White Whig" party.  As their hearts were set on Clay, they were disappointed, and at first somewhat discouraged, when Harrison received the nomination.  They soon rallied, however, and throughout the campaign their loyalty and energy were not surpassed by the Whigs of any other state.  Bell was their most eloquent speaker, although Foster, who canvassed the entire state, was more successful in winning votes.  In this campaign the Whigs appealed more to the eye than to the ear.  They relied more on banners and processions than on oratory or arguments.  "The fact is," wrote one of Polk's Democratic friends after the election, "the people like coonery and foolery better than good argument."[44]

The great event of the campaign was the Whig convention held in Nashville on August 17, 1840.  Delegations came from surrounding states, each joining in the spectacular procession

---

[42] *Niles' Register*, October 12, 1839.

[43] Nashville *Banner*, quoted in *Niles' Register*, September 7, 1839.

[44] Isaac Goladay to Polk, November 9, 1840, *Polk Papers*.

and each bearing aloft banners fantastically decorated and adorned with mottoes designed to win popular applause.[45] The procession wended its way to a grove in the outksirts of the city, where the multitude was entertained by speeches made by prominent Whigs of Tennessee and other states. Foster, who was chairman of the meeting, made the opening address, but the lion of the occasion was Clay himself, whose personal magnetism and oratorical flights electrified the audience, although his address was rather commonplace.

The Democrats were not so well organized as the Whigs and their speakers were decidedly inferior to those of their opponents. Their most effective debater, Polk, was prevented by his office from actively entering into the canvass, although he made a few speeches in favor of Van Buren, which led to his presentment as a "nuisance" by the grand jury of Sevier county,[46] and the Whig papers circulated the story that the Governor's grandfather had been a Tory during the Revolution.[47] Nicholson met Bell in debate; Cave Johnson, A. V. Brown, and H. L. Turney did their utmost to stem the Whig tide; Jackson wrote letters in which he lauded Van Buren, and denounced Harrison as a Federalist, but the people would not listen as of yore. On the eve of the election the Democrats tried to brand Harrison as an abolitionist. At the last moment, they distributed handbills on which they had printed a letter which Harrison was alleged to have written to Arthur Tappan declaring himself to be such. But the plot had been discovered, and the *Whig* was ready with Harrison's denial as soon as the handbills appeared.

Tennessee refused to be "redeemed"; the vote for Harrison was 60,391, while Van Buren polled but 48,289. It was a signal victory for the Whigs, and, unlike four years earlier, it could not be said that voters had supported the Whig candidate simply because he was a favorite son of the state. Undoubtedly one of

---

[45] The parade is described in some detail by Phelan, *Hist. of Tenn.*, 387 ff.

[46] *Ibid.*

[47] Edwin Polk to Polk, August 27, 1840, *Polk Papers.*

Polk's correspondents was right in saying[48] that many Democrats had refrained from voting because they "could not be rallied to Van Buren," and that the Democratic loss was much greater than the Whig gain. Still, any hopes built on such calculations were illusive, for in national politics the state was irretrievably lost to the Democrats.

Not realizing the real strength of the Whigs, the leading Democrats, almost before the smoke of battle had lifted, began to formulate plans for winning the next state election. First of all, Harrison and his administration must be vigorously assailed, regardless of the course he might pursue. The difficulty of finding anything of sufficient importance to attack caused them no little anxiety. A. O. P. Nicholson put the case frankly in a letter to Polk, written before it had been definitely ascertained that Harrison had been elected. The Democrats, he said, must

keep up a raking fire upon the whole of Harrison's inconsistent and imbecile history. It is unfortunate for us that Harrison's administration (if elected) will not be developed before our August elections, but still enough will probably have transpired to present available points of attack.[49]

And yet the politicians who uttered such sentiments claimed to be followers of Jefferson, one of whose cardinal principles was "absolute acquiescence in the decisions of the majority."[50]

Although the Democrats were hopeful and even confident, the Whig victory of 1840 made them realize that Polk's defeat in 1841 was within the realms of possibility. When, therefore, in December, 1840, it was reported in Washington that Grundy could not live, the Democratic members of Congress from Tennessee counselled together and decided that Polk ought to succeed him as Senator from his state. In a letter to Polk,[51] Hopkins L.

---

[48] Samuel P. Walker to Polk, November 4, 1840, *Polk Papers.*

[49] Nicholson to Polk, November 6, 1840, *Polk Papers.* Other letters to Polk also expressed regret that there would probably be little to attack.

[50] See Jefferson's first inaugural address.

[51] Turney to Polk, December 21, 1840. On the same day A. V. Brown wrote a letter of similar purport. Both in *Polk Papers.*

Turney pointed out to the Governor that his reëlection was doubtful and, even if such were not the case, he would stand a better chance of promotion if elected Senator. Both Cave Johnson and A. V. Brown, he said, concurred in this view. Before this letter had reached its destination, however, Polk had appointed Nicholson to succeed Grundy, whose death had occurred on the nineteenth of the month. So gratified was Nicholson by his appointment that, on his arrival in Washington, he saw visions of his benefactor's certain elevation to the Presidential chair. After telling the Governor of his popularity in Washington and of the anxiety for his reëlection, he added: "I shall be disappointed if your success in this contest does not lead on certainly to your elevation to the Presidency."[52]

While the politicians on either side were speculating on the probability of Harrison's calling an extra session of Congress, considerable excitement was caused in Nashville by the shooting of J. George Harris, editor of the *Union,* by Robert C. Foster, a son of the deposed Senator. Harris quickly recovered, but the affair furnished Democrats with something to denounce while they were awaiting further political developments.

In case Harrison, after his inauguration, should call Congress together in extra session, Tennessee would have no representation in the House[53] unless the Governor should see fit to call a special election. Anderson, who had been chosen to fill Foster's unexpired term, would cease to be Senator on March 4, and the official term of Nicholson, who was serving on the governor's appointment, would be automatically terminated should Polk decide to call an extra session of the legislature. Should no extra session be called, Nicholson would continue in office until the regular session which would open in October, 1841. As the probability of a called session of Congress increased, the Democrats differed as to whether it would be wiser to convene the

---

[52] Nicholson to Polk, Jan. 13, 1841, *ibid.*

[53] The terms of present members would expire on March 4 and a regular election would not be held until autumn.

legislature and attempt to elect two Senators, or to be contented with one Senator, Nicholson, leaving the other seat vacant.

When sounded on the subject, Polk expressed himself as opposed to convening the legislature. He gave, as his reasons, economy, and the fear that the Whigs would make political capital of such a procedure. On the other hand, Jackson, who had lost none of his political zeal, strongly favored an extra session in order that two Senators might be chosen and instructed as to how they should cast their votes. "If it can be done with propriety," he advised Governor Polk,

if there is a called session of congress, the Legislature should be convened to give us a full representation in the Senate; and to instruct our senators & request our representatives to vote against a high Tariff, a distribution of the Public Funds, against a national Bank of any kind, or deposits in the State banks, and against a repeal of the sub-treasury act, and, altho last not least, to pass a law to compell our Banks to resume specie payments or wind up.[54]

From Washington, Anderson urged the necessity of a full representation in the Senate.[55] Turney seconded this appeal and once more tried to induce the Governor to become a candidate. Polk, he said, could do much good in the Senate, for since Grundy's death there was no one able to cope with the Whigs. On this same subject Polk received what appears to be his first letter from Andrew Johnson.[56] In it Johnson advises the Governor to convene the legislature for the purpose of electing members of Congress whose terms, unless he is "rong," expire on the fourth of March.

While Nicholson was in Washington, still worrying for fear there would be little in the Harrison administration to assail,[57]

---

[54] Jackson to Polk, Feb. 8, 1841, *Polk Papers.*

[55] Anderson to Polk, Feb. 17, 1841, *ibid.*

[56] At least it is the first letter from Johnson in the Polk collection. It seems that Polk had written to Johnson, stating that either he or Blair must run for Congress. Johnson declined to become a candidate (Johnson to Polk, March 4, 1841, *Polk Papers*).

[57] "I do not calculate that we will be able to make any capital out of the Inaugural; but the Cabinet will be enough for our purposes, if we use

the much-reviled administration of Van Buren passed into history.[58]   Ignoring his critics, the "little magician" remained unperturbed and courteous to the end.   When his successor arrived in Washington, an invitation to dine was extended by Van Buren and accepted by Harrison, and the Nashville *Union* marvelled that Harrison could take "vermacilla soup from those horrible gold spoons!"[59]   The Whig newspapers never tired of contrasting the democratic simplicity and generous hospitality[60] of Harrison with the royalistic pomp and cold exclusiveness of Van Buren.   It was unkind of the Whigs thus to purloin from their opponents the very arguments—almost the exact phrases— which had done such effective service in winning popular support for General Jackson.   Such utter disregard for the proprietary rights of others fully justified J. George Harris in trying to render harmless the stolen implements of war.   Shortly after

---

it with skill.''   It is rumored, he said, ''that Webster will be Secretary of State; Granger, Post-Master-General; Ewing, Secretary of the Treasury; Bell, Secretary of War; Preston, Secretary of the Navy; and Crittenden Attorney-General.   What think you now of the Cabinet!   I think you may set it down as settled that we are to have an anti-war fed. for Secretary of State, an abolition fed. for Post-Master-General, a uniform fed. for the Treasury, a gag-bill Clay fed. for Atty. Gen., a gag-bill-no party-White Whig fed. for the War, and a Nullification fed. for the Navy.   Will not this open the eyes of Tennesseans!   If not, then may we surrender at discretion'' (Nicholson to Polk, Feb. 12, 1841, *Polk Papers*).

[58] ''Tomorrow night, at twelve o'clock,'' said the *Madisonian*, ''the administration of Martin Van Buren terminates.   That administration, accidental in its beginning, and unfortunate and profitless in its career, will then have gone, with all its powers, its prerogatives, its follies, its malign influence, and with whatever streak of virtue may have been possibly mingled in its texture, to control us, to agitate us, to injure us, no more. Four years it has lived, and its principal achievement has been the passage of the sub-Treasury, by trampling with contempt upon the broad seal of a sovereign State.   What good it has done, we are unable to point out. What harm it has accomplished, we may possibly conceive of, by considering the present condition of the Treasury, of our foreign relations, of our Navy, of the Army and the defences, of the Post Office, and of the public morals, and the condition of the people.   But we congratulate the country that it has at last come to an end.   It is gone'' (The *Madisonian*, March 3, 1841).

[59] *Union*, March 4, 1841.

[60] Under the heading ''Hospitality at the White House'' an article in the New Haven *Palladium* said:   ''He [Harrison] keeps his house open to all comers. . . .   The servants at the White House find more difficulty

his inauguration, the President had directed Webster to issue a most wholesome order stating that any interference in elections, state or federal, by federal officers, would be regarded as cause for removal. The plain farmer of the Whigs was promptly branded by Harris as a usurper of royal powers and a violator of the rights of states, for "the Autocrat of all the Russias never issued an *Ukase* more potent."[61] But before these unjust charges against the President had been put in type, the career of the "autocrat" had been cut short, and the same issue of the paper which contained them chronicled, also, the news of Harrison's death.

As Polk's campaign for reëlection began as soon as his competitor had been nominated on March 5, 1841, the incidents of the remainder of his gubernatorial term will be treated in the succeeding chapter, which deals primarily with that spirited political contest and with the transfer of Tennessee to the Whigs.

---

in adapting themselves to the change of Administration than any other officeholders. He breaks in on all the elegant aristocratic usages of the palace, and plays the mischief with that systematic courtly etiquette which with the Sub-Treasury constituted the two great radical reforms of the late President. He gets up at sunrise, like a plain farmer as he is, and wants his breakfast within an hour after, (the vulgar man!)—and eats with an appetite of a common day laborer. He gave one of his servants a regular 'blowing up' the other day, for leaving a visitor dripping wet and muddy in a cold 'ante-chamber,' because the President was at breakfast and could not be disturbed, and because the carpet would be injured by the muddy feet of one who came on foot! The President brought the visitor into the breakfast parlor, and insisted on making him comfortable at the fire at once. At all these things the *democracy* are much shocked, and look aghast at this desecration of the 'palace!' '' Quoted in Nashville *Banner,* April 5, 1841.

[61] Harris quoted from the *Evening Post:* "this document has added the last insult that can be given to a free and independent people, and will be held up to popular execration by every man who is not disposed to yield his neck to the yoke of party, or who is not a base and degraded slave. It is so insolent in spirit and dictation, breathes an air so vile and debasing, that it is difficult to speak of it without subjecting one's self to an unwonted excitement'' (Nashville *Union,* April 12, 1841).

## CHAPTER X

## DEFEATED BY JONES IN 1841

From the day of their defeat in 1839 the Whigs of Tennessee had been marshalling their forces for the next gubernatorial contest, and the great national victory of 1840 gave them reason to hope for success. It had also, by example, indicated the type of campaign that would be most likely to win that success. Cannon's main weakness as a candidate had been his inability to adjust himself to the guerrilla variety of campaign by which many a less brilliant politician had endeared himself to the people. Capable but painfully serious, Cannon was a shining mark for the shafts of wit and ridicule which Polk had hurled with unerring aim whenever they had met in joint discussion. On the contrary, Polk had demonstrated his adaptability to a degree that surprised his closest friends. Distinguished for his dignified and learned discussions in the national House of Representatives, Polk had, in 1839, discomfited his rival and won the people by a most skilful use of mimicry and sarcasm. The Whigs were therefore familiar with the campaign methods of the Governor as well as the predilections of the people, and the convention which assembled at Murfreesborough on March 5, 1841, displayed political wisdom by nominating the one man in the state who was thought to be capable of ''beating the governor at his own game.'' This man was Major James C. Jones,[1] a ''horny-handed'' farmer from Wilson County, who had represented his county in the legislature, served as a Presidential elector, and acquired a local reputation as an effective ''stump speaker.'' Tall and ungainly in appearance, Jones possessed many of those grotesque personal

---

[1] Jackson declined to call Jones, major, ''for he never was a corporal'' (Jackson to Polk, March 20, 1841, *Polk Papers*).

qualities which had made John Randolph famous. Even the sobriquet "Lean Jimmy," with which his admiring friends had christened him, served as a valuable asset in a contest so closely following the "great whirlwind campaign" of 1840. Realizing that, in knowledge and debating powers, he was no match for his adversary, Jones resorted to hectoring tactics and relied more on amusing than on convincing his audience. Nevertheless he was a man of considerable ability, and he displayed a fair knowledge of the political issues of the day. In spite of the picture drawn by Phelan and others, there was a serious side to the campaign of 1841. Jones did not devote all of his time to "coonery and foolery," but at times displayed alertness and skill as a debater.

As in 1839 the canvass dealt principally with national issues. In his "Address to the People," Polk stated that his views on national questions had been given in detail in his address of 1839, and that nothing had since occurred to alter them. He had, he said, been forced to begin the campaign early because of the untiring efforts of the Whigs to defeat him.[2]

Each side accused the other of being Federalists, and Harrison's "autocratic" order against interference in elections, and Van Buren's regal splendor, were offered as evidence to prove the opposing contentions. The death of Judge White nearly a year before did not prevent his name from being dragged into the contest. Jackson, in exhorting Polk to answer the "falsehoods" of Bell and Foster regarding Van Buren's extravagance in furnishing the executive mansion, provided him with a statement that it was Bell's disappointment at not being made a member of Jackson's cabinet, on White's recommendation, that had caused Bell to desert the party and to bring White out for

---

[2] "From the moment of my election in 1839, it had been manifestly an object of no minor importance with my leading political opponents in the State, to prostrate and destroy me. Their attacks were constant. Their presses kept up an incessant war upon me. No calumny or misrepresentation of my political opinions and course had been too gross to fill their columns" (Nashville *Union*, March 29, 1841).

the Presidency.[3]  A friend in Albany[4] furnished Polk with several letters written by Granger, the Postmaster-General which were to be used for the purpose of proving him to be an Abolitionist.  Jones and other Whigs tried to counteract the effect produced by these by asserting that Polk's grandfather had been a Tory.

Early in March Jones published a list of his speaking appointments.  He opened the campaign at Murfreesborough, where he boasted that he could tell a greater number of anecdotes than the Governor himself.[5]  He promptly accepted an invitation from Polk to meet in joint debate whenever possible,[6] and they met for the first time at Murfreesborough on the twenty-seventh of March.

Polk opened the discussion with a spirited attack, upon the Harrison administration.  He denounced Granger as an Abolitionist, and Webster as a Federalist who, in 1835, had been so unpatriotic as to declare that he would not support a certain bill to appropriate money for defense "though the *enemy* were battering down the walls of the Capitol."  Unfortunately for himself, Polk tried, as he had done in the canvass with Cannon, to weaken his opponent by making him an object of ridicule.  Among other shafts of sarcasm, he said that his friend Jones was a "promising young man," but "as for his being Governor, that's all a notion."[7]  As soon as Jones took the platform, he referred repeatedly to Polk as "my venerable competitor."  This he continued to do whenever they met in debate, much to the amusement of the audience, for Polk at that time was only forty-six years of age.

Before the candidates met again, Governor Polk issued a public statement in which he gave his reasons for not convening

---

[3] Jackson to Polk, March 20, 1841, *Polk Papers.*

[4] E. Crowell to Polk, March 19, 1841, *ibid.*

[5] Yoakum to Polk, March 15, 1841, *ibid.*

[6] Polk to Jones, March 15; Jones to Polk, March 18, 1841, *ibid.*

[7] Nashville *Union,* March 29, 1841.

the legislature in extra session so that Senators might be chosen in time for Harrison's called session of Congress. He had already called a special election for the purpose of choosing members of the House of Representatives. In declining to convene the legislature, Polk, as we have already noted, disregarded the wishes, not only of General Jackson, but of nearly all of the leading Democrats of the state. It was thoroughly characteristic of Polk to follow his own judgment rather than the wishes of his friends, even of "Old Hickory," and yet he was often charged with being a weak tool of General Jackson.

The main reasons assigned in his public statement for not convening the legislature were unnecessary expense and the impropriety of taking advantage of an accident to strengthen his own party in the federal Senate. The members elected to the legislature in 1839 had not, he said, been chosen with the selection of Senators in view, and "my opinion is that the frank, fair, and honest course, is to leave the choice open for the decision of the people at the next August election." Harrison, he said, had given him an opportunity to disregard the popular will, for it is

certain that if I had availed myself of them that the present General Assembly, if convened, would choose two Democratic Senators. If, however, the President under the influence and control of inflamed partisans, maddened with their late success . . . has committed a capital political blunder, it is no reason why I should commit one also.

He denounced the President for unnecessarily convening Congress, for, as there was plenty of money in the Treasury, the call must have been made for purely political reasons.[8]

---

8 "Large and extravagant promises which can never be redeemed had been made to the people, and it was doubtless deemed to be necessary to do something, or to *appear* to do something to keep up the public expectation, and thereby possibly to operate upon the elections which are to take place in States during the present year. . . . They probably fear to let the public mind sober down to a state of calm reflection, lest peradventure they may not succeed in their favorite measures of Federal policy, at the next regular session of Congress." Printed in Nashville *Union*, April 1, 1841.

Whether the Governor was influenced solely by a spirit of fairness, no one but himself could know, but, whatever his motives were, he received no thanks from the Whigs for his magnanimity. The *Banner* bitterly assailed him for impugning the motives of the President, and for praising himself. It pronounced his action hypocritical and declared that his forbearance had been due to a knowledge that the legislature would not dare to choose two Democrats in the face of the late election, and to fear that an attempt to make such a choice would injure his own prospects of reëlection.[9] At a debate held at Lebanon shortly after the publication of Polk's statement, Jones won applause by reminding the Governor that his solicitude for the popular will had not prevented him from appointing Nicholson Senator after the people had repudiated him (Nicholson) by refusing to make him a Presidential elector. The Whig paper of the town commended Polk's wit and added that "he makes as much of it with his face as with his tongue."[10] Most effective of all were his impersonations of Bailie Peyton, the chief feature of which was what the Whigs called "Polk's horrible grin."

The candidates visited the principal towns of the state. From the press notices, one would be led to believe that their time was occupied almost entirely with the relation of humorous anecdotes and the coining of witty remarks. Nevertheless, their printed speeches show that a serious discussion of political issues was by no means omitted. Polk, especially, displayed great power as a debater. He thoroughly understood the questions under

---

[9] Nashville *Banner*, April 5, 1841. The most abusive of all papers was Parson Brownlow's Jonesborough *Whig*. In an article addressed to Polk, the editor said that the Governor while "under the influence of *liquor* or opium, being *half drunk*" had denounced the *Whig* for criticising his ancestors who had been lying in the tomb for forty years. Brownlow reminded Polk that he had criticized both White and Harrison since their death, and then continued: "You canting, cringing hypocrite—you demagogue and time-serving politician, you advise mankind as to prudence and moderation!" Undated in *Polk Papers*.

[10] Lebanon *Chronicle*, quoted by Nashville *Banner*, April 5, 1841.

discussion, and few could excel him in clear and logical presentation. Had his opponent attempted to meet the Governor's arguments by a frank and fair discussion, he would have been easily vanquished, for his knowledge of political questions was superficial and limited. To Jones, however, ignorance of the subject was never a cause of embarrassment. By substituting bold assertion for knowledge, he was able to discuss any topic without hesitation, and, so far as his audience was concerned, he had disproved every contention of his adversary. It availed Polk little to demolish these assertions by clear presentation of historical data. Like Douglas in his debates with Lincoln, Jones would calmly reiterate his assertions, no matter how often they had been refuted, or else he would divert the attention of the audience by a humorous anecdote or by a dissertation on the beauties of coon fur. In either case the effect of Polk's argument was entirely lost, while his adversary succeeded in winning the vociferous applause of an uncritical audience. No wonder that a Democrat who heard their debate at Somerville exclaimed in disgust: ''Mr. Polk made an ass of himself, talking sense to a lot of d—d fools,'' and urged that the Governor ''ought to get a stick and crack Jones's skull, and end this tomfoolery!''[11]

One of Jones's most exasperating characteristics was his never-failing good humor. As he had declined to become embarrassed by the most complete demonstration of his ignorance, so, also, he refused to be angered by sarcasm or ridicule. At times Polk tried to crush his opponent by belittling his abilities and by holding him up to scorn. In reply, Jones would solicit the compassion of the hearers for his ''irascible but venerable competitor.'' Polk said that he had tried to discuss questions of state in a serious manner and that his opponent had wisely made jest of things which were beyond his comprehension. When he asserted that Jones was better suited to the circus ring than to the Governor's chair, Jones good-naturedly admitted that they

---

[11] Phelan, *Hist. of Tenn.*, 403.

would both do well in the ring—himself as a clown, and the Governor as "the little fellow that is dressed up in a red cap and jacket and who rides around on a poney."[12] The Governor wearied of the travesty, and would gladly have abandoned joint meetings, but, as they had been undertaken upon his own invitation, there was no way of breaking gracefully with his trifling antagonist.

The debates attracted attention in all parts of the state, and everywhere large audiences greeted the speakers. Much importance was attached to their meeting at Nashville, which was not only the capital, but the political headquarters of the state. Here, on May 19, they were greeted by a large and enthusiastic concourse of people, and each candidate according to agreement spoke for two and one-half hours. "Polk," as Phelan has well said, "made a speech that would have swept from the stump any man who had ever been Governor of Tennessee before him, and any man who was Governor after Jones until Andrew Johnson came forward."[13] It was a forceful and logical presentation of the issues, replete with historical data and spiced with humorous illustrations. Jones's address was a compound of sophistry and nonsense. Intead of answering Polk's arguments he constructed innumerable "men of straw" and then demolished them to the entire satisfaction of his audience. He misquoted and distorted everything that the Governor had said, after which he amused the crowd by poking fun at his opponent and by relating preposterous stories.[14] No man of Polk's training and dignity could cope with such politcal bushwhacking.

Had the people been really interested in political issues, Jones could not have commanded a hearing. But since 1840,

---

12 *Ibid.*, 402.　　　　13 *Ibid.*, 404.

14 The *Union* of May 24 thus described him: "Maj. Jones is a floater; amusing at times, but superficial as a bubble. He drifts along on the surface of today and plays with the uppermost passions and prejudices of his hearers; trifles with important matters and converts important matters into trifles. . . . In a word, he is quite possible as an electioneer for his party—good of the kind, but the quality is none of the best."

the Whigs had abandoned serious discussion and had staked everything on an appeal to the emotions. For this reason Polk's training and success were used to prejudice the people against him. Not only had his grandfather been a Tory, but the Governor himself was said to be an aristocrat, who, at heart, held the people in contempt. Ignorance, uncouth appearance, and slovenly dress were regarded as attributes of honest statesmanship, and Jones always emphasized the fact that he had followed the plow.[15] The Governor, however, deserved little sympathy on account of these misrepresentations, for with similar weapons he had aided in "putting down" the able and upright John Quincy Adams.

Up to the close of the canvass, no one could predict, with any degree of certainty, what the result would be. The Whigs did most of the shouting. They made extravagant claims, but many Democrats could not believe that a majority of the people would be willing to cast out a man of Polk's ability and reputation and put in his place a man whose sole claim to fame rested on a grotesque personal appearance and low-grade wit. The Democrats, however, had overrated the people's sense of propriety, and on that account were doomed to disappointment. At the election, which was held on August 5, Polk was defeated by a majority of over three thousand votes, but the *Union* congratulated the Democrats on their "signal TRIUMPH OF PRINCIPLE in sweeping away TEN THOUSAND of the last year's majority."[16] It was generally conceded, even by the Whigs, that no other man in the party could have polled so many votes, and instead of losing prestige, Polk was credited by his party with

---

[15] The Knoxville *Register* in contrasting the candidates said that Jones was "free, manly, undisguised, plain, and carrying conviction with every sentence." Polk was "hidden, dissembling, artful, shrinking and hypocritical in the extreme" Quoted in Nashville *Banner*, August 2, 1841.

[16] "Never," said Harris, the editor, "did Gov. Polk win for himself more laurels than he has won in this contest. The Democracy of the whole Union will appreciate his Herculean efforts at the expense of health to maintain the principles that he has uniformly supported, the principles of Jefferson and Jackson" (Nashville *Union*, August 12, 1841).

having won a great personal victory.  In a letter to Van Buren, General Jackson rejoiced in the reduction of the Whig majority and said that ''Gov. Polk deserves the thanks of the Democracy of the whole union, he fought the battle well and fought it alone, I may say.''  Strange to say, Jackson commended rather than criticized Polk for having disregarded his advice about convening the legislature.  He pointed out to Van Buren that, had the legislature been called, two Democratic Senators would have been elected, but ''the Governor threw aside policy, and adopted the real republican creed—that a majority have the right to rule.''[17]

In the legislature which was elected with Jones, the Whigs had a majority of three in the lower house.  In the senate the Democrats still had a majority of one.  But one of their number, Samuel Turney, was regarded as rather independent in politics, and, when the time came for him to take a definite stand with his colleagues, he proved to be weak and vacillating.  Nominally, however, the Democrats had a majority of one and thereby possessed the power to block any measure of the lower house that required their separate approval.  But on any question which required the joint vote of the two houses the Whigs, by virtue of their majority of three in the lower house, were in a position to outvote their opponents.

In Tennessee, politics had precedence over legislation.  Therefore the defeated party began at once to devise ways and means of preventing their opponents from filling the two vacant seats in the United States Senate.  The term for which Judge White had been elected, and which since his resignation had been filled by Alexander Anderson, had expired.  The other vacancy had been caused by the death of Senator Grundy, and had been filled temporarily by A. O. P. Nicholson, by virtue of the Governor's recess appointment.

Following the election, Polk received many letters, the main object of which was to congratulate him for having reduced the

---

[17] Jackson to Van Buren, Aug. 16, 1841, *Van Buren Papers.*

Whig majority. In these letters several of his friends expressed the opinion that the Democrats ought to demand the privilege of choosing one of the Senators, and that Polk himself should be the man. Among others, Hopkins L. Turney advised such a course. He assured Polk, also, that his brother, Samuel Turney, would vote with the Democrats.[18]

When plotting to force the Whigs to concede them one Senator, Democratic leaders tried to ease their conscience by asserting that in 1840 Whig members of the legislature had threatened, in the event of Polk's convening the legislature, to remain at home and thus prevent an election of Senators. It was further alleged that these threats had been made on the advice of Henry Clay.[19] It was said, also, that, during the recent campaign, when it was believed that the Democrats would elect a majority of the legislature, Jones had boasted that the Whig members would not permit the Democrats to hold an election for Senators.[20] Polk at first was noncommittal, but he soon made it known that he was not a candidate for the office. The reason which he gave for not permitting the use of his name was that he would not accept any office except one conferred upon him by a vote of the people.[21] With Polk out of the race, the politicians turned their attention to other candidates, but nothing could be done, of course, until the meeting of the legislature and the inauguration of a new governor.

---

18 Turney to Polk, Washington, Aug. 24, 1841 (*Polk Papers*). Laughlin, Huntsman, and others assured Polk that some of the Whigs had agreed to vote for him.

19 H. L. Turney to Polk, Jan. 2, 1842, *ibid.*

20 Alex. Anderson to Polk, Aug. 20, 1841, *ibid.* Anderson urged that the Democrats should now practice this plan upon those who had invented it.

21 Geo. W. Smith, of Memphis, advised Polk not to permit the use of his name for two reasons: (1) possibility of defeat and loss of prestige; (2) it would lend color to the Whig charge that he had never cared for the governorship, and had wished it only as a stepping-stone to a higher office. (Smith to Polk, Sept. 2, 1841, *ibid.*) Polk may have been influenced by considerations of this kind.

As soon as the legislature had convened, Polk, on October 7, submitted his final message as governor.[22]  It was a long document and filled with detailed information on various topics, but mainly on banks and internal improvements.  For a man who had only a week longer to serve, Polk was surprisingly free with advice and suggestions for the future.  He expressed satisfaction with the degree of prosperity which had been enjoyed by the people during the last two years, and he attributed it to corrective legislation and the consequent elimination of extravagant speculation.  He regretted that banks had not been compelled by law to resume specie payments, and once more recommended the enactment of such a law.  "There is," said he, "no sound principle of ethics or of public policy which should exempt Banks from the moral and legal obligations which rest upon individuals to pay their debts."  He pointed out that the bank note circulation amounted to about three million dollars and that the average rate of depreciation was eight and one-half per cent; this unnecessary burden was borne by the people, while the banks were prosperous—even paying dividends.  He reported that the law recently enacted which provided for "the reduction of the State debt" had enabled him to recall and to cancel fifteen hundred state bonds of one thousand dollars each.  The outstanding internal improvement bonds amounted to $1,816,916.66⅔, while, so far, only one company had paid a dividend to the state—the small sum of $1620.  The currency, he said, had been much improved by the law which prohibited the emission of notes under ten dollars; as a further remedy for financial ills, he recommended that commercial houses and improvement companies should be prevented by law from issuing checks designed to circulate as money.  The internal improvement board had, in his opinion, accomplished much good by requiring various companies to reduce their stock and to conduct their affairs in a more economical manner.  Among other things the retiring Governor

---

[22] *Tenn. Sen. Jour.*, 1841–42, 22–42.

recommended that improvements be made in hospitals for the insane, that sexes be segregated in penitentiaries, and that the governor be given power to commute the death penalty to life imprisonment.[23] His recommendations were salutary and sensible. Some of his suggestions indicated grave need for improvement in social conditions. .

One paragraph in the Governor's message is especially interesting, for in it Polk expressed his views on the slavery question, a subject which he usually avoided. He informed the legislature that he had, during the past year, received two communications from friends of negroes convened in London, on June 12 to 20, 1840, in which they had asked for the abolition of slavery and the slave trade. Viewing these communications ''as an impertinent and mischievous attempt on the part of foreigners to interfere with one of the domestic institutions of the State,'' he had declined to enter into any correspondence with this convention. Doubtless he was governed more by his belief in state rights than by an interest in the institution of slavery itself; still, he was ready to resent outside interference with the ''peculiar institution.''

On October 14 Polk delivered his valedictory, and on the same day James C. Jones was inaugurated as his successor.[24] While it is true that Polk's interests were national rather than local, yet the state was indebted to him for causing the enactment of beneficial laws. Under his leadership the state had been freed from a ruinous internal improvement policy, and he had done much to check currency inflation and to reduce the debt of the state. His reform measures were all in the line of sound statesmanship, and, if we may judge from the suggestions made in his final message, the people might have profited by continuing him in office.

---

[23] He could now pardon only.

[24] *Tenn. Sen. Jour.*, 1841–42, 78.

CHAPTER XI

POLK IN RETIREMENT

On October 14, 1841, James C. Jones became governor of
Tennessee, and on the nineteenth his first message was sent to
the legislature.[1]  His recommendations differed little from those
which had already been submitted by his predecessor,[2] and, also
like Polk, he attributed most of the distress of the people to their
own fault—to buying more than they could reasonably hope to
pay for.  In one respect only did Jones differ radically from the
former governor.  The crisis in the monetary affairs of the country, he said, had been produced by the destruction of the Bank
of the United States.  Such a statement was naturally to be expected, for some part of a Whig governor's message must needs
indicate the change of administration, and the bank was a subject of general interest.

As usual the legislature was far more interested in ''practical
politics'' than in the less sportive business of lawmaking.  The
paramount question was the election of United States Senators,
but first of all, the opinions of both legislators and constituents
must be molded so as to accord with those of the leaders.  The
Democrats were most active in the senate, for in this branch they
had, counting Samuel Turney, a majority of one.  The leaders
in the senate were Samuel H. Laughlin, former editor of the
*Union,* and Andrew Johnson, who, at the recent election, had
been promoted to the upper house.  Johnson had ability and
force, but Laughlin excelled him in political cunning and effec-
tiveness as a manipulator.  In the Polk-Bell contest, Johnson

---

[1] *Tenn. Sen. Jour.,* 1841–42, 116–125.

[2] Jones was accused of having *borrowed* from Polk's inaugural of 1839,
and to prove the claim the *Union* published the two addresses in parallel
columns (Laughlin, *Diary,* Oct. 21, 1843).

had supported the latter. Laughlin had ever been subservient and therefore enjoyed the entire confidence of Polk and other prominent Democrats.

On October 18, Laughlin, as chairman of the committee on federal relations, submitted a series of eight resolutions to which four more were added on the fifth of November.[3] The preamble recited the Virginia and Kentucky Resolutions of 1798 and declared that many of the laws enacted by Congress at the late extra session violated the spirit of the Constitution quite as much as did the laws against which those historic resolutions had protested. The first resolution reaffirmed those of 1798 and asserted that they were "universally true at all times and especially applicable to the present crisis and state of affairs." The succeeding seven resolutions condemned the convening of Congress by Harrison and, also, the various measures[4] proposed or enacted by the Whigs at that session. This indictment of the Whigs was intended to prepare public opinion for the items which were to follow—the four resolutions that were added on the fifth of November. The first of these, the ninth of the entire list, declared that the legislature had full power to instruct Senators chosen to represent the state in Congress, and that it was the duty of these officials to obey or resign. The second asserted that it was the duty of candidates for legislative offices to give explicit answers to queries made by citizens or members of the legislature concerning their views on public questions. The third affirmed the right of the people to instruct members of the legislature. The fourth formally instructed the Senators (not yet chosen) and requested the Representatives from Tennessee to conform their votes to the opinions expressed by the foregoing resolutions.

The last four resolutions displayed far more shrewdness than principle. On their face they contained nothing which any

---

[3] The resolutions may be found in *Tenn. Sen. Jour.* under the dates given.

[4] For example, the "bankrupt bill' and the tariff, distribution, and bank bills.

advocate of representative government could very well decline to support. But they were designed, as every one knew, for the purpose of harassing the Whig candidates with embarrassing interrogations and for rendering them ineligible should they decline to answer. By asserting the right of the people to instruct their representatives in the legislature, the Democrats hoped to hold in line their own members who might be inclined to follow their individual judgments. Their party had nothing to lose by obstructive tactics, and, by blocking their opponents at every turn, they might worry the Whigs into conceding one seat in the Senate.

Ephraim H. Foster and Spencer Jarnagin were selected as the Whig candidates and on November 16 the lower house sent to the senate a resolution urging the immediate election of two United States Senators lest delay "may lead to bargain, intrigue, and management, to the detriment of the public interest." As soon as the resolution was read in the senate, Andrew Johnson moved to amend by making it read that delay "may lead to bargain, intrigue, and management, to the great detriment of E. H. Foster and Spencer Jarnagin, and thereby promote and advance the public interest, by keeping them out of power for the next four and six years."[5] The Democratic majority in the senate soon came to be called "the immortal thirteen" and except for an occasional desertion by Samuel Turney they voted as a body on all questions of party politics.

The customary method of electing Senators in Tennessee was by a joint "convention" of the two houses. As the Whigs had a majority of three in the lower house and the Democrats a majority of but one in the senate, it was obvious that if the usual method were to be followed the Whigs would outnumber their rivals in the convention. The Democrats now made the discovery that the usual method was unconstitutional, for, as they alleged, the constitution of the state required that each house should vote

---

[5] Protests against the amendment were made, but it passed the senate by a vote of 13 to 12 (*Tenn. Sen. Jour.*, 1841–42, 227, 232–233).

separately for Senators. For their own purposes it was an important discovery; by no other method could they hope to prevent an election until the Whigs were ready to compromise on choosing one Senator from each party.

Up to November 22 the Democrats were confident of their ability to prevent an election unless the Whigs would yield to their terms. A few days before, Turney had introduced a resolution calling for an election by convention, but he had subsequently voted with the Democrats on the above-mentioned Johnson resolution. On the twenty-second, however, Turney caused consternation in Democratic ranks by announcing that he would call up and support his resolution in favor of a convention election.[6] According to William H. Polk, Turney had, for the last two weeks, "been shivering in the wind," due to the fact that the Whigs had "brought every influence to bear on him within the range of human ingenuity."[7] On November 22 Gardner moved to amend Turney's resolution by fixing the following Saturday as the date on which the Senate would vote *separately* for federal Senators. Turney accepted the amendment, but it was the younger Polk's opinion that, after one trial, Turney would revert to the convention plan. The Democrats offered another *compromise* resolution the purport of which was to declare elected Hopkins L. Turney and Thomas Brown, a Whig from East Tennessee. It was hoped that, having passed the senate, this resolution could be forced through the lower house.[8] On the twenty-third Gardner modified his amendment.

---

[6] "On Saturday last the '13' were safe against the world, and the Whigs considered themselves as beaten. Guess then, what our astonishment was, when coming into the Senate on Monday morning [November 22], Sam Turney announced that he had changed his mind, and would call up and vote for his own resolutions to bring on the Senatorial election at an early day on joint vote in Convention." Turney said that his change of mind was due to letters from his constituents (Laughlin to Polk, November 24, 1841, *Polk Papers*).

[7] W. H. Polk to J. K. Polk, November, 22, 1841, *ibid.*

[8] "My own impression is, that if the resolution passed the Senate, as now amended, declaring Turney and Brown the Senators elect—we *can force* it through the House, by lashing the doubtful men into a redemption of their former pledges . . . . can at least produce a tie" (*Idem*).

The legislature was now asked to choose one Senator from each party on the ground that the popular vote at the recent election had been nearly equally divided. Other modifications were suggested, but these, as well as Gardner's resolution, were rejected. The Democratic majority in the senate succeeded in passing a resolution which named Hopkins L. Turney as Grundy's successor, but, on December 1, the lower house refused to concur in its adoption. On the same day Speaker Samuel Turney joined the Whigs of the senate in making an agreement with the lower house to meet in joint convention on the second and third of December for the purpose of electing Senators. It was understood that each of those days would be devoted to filling one of the vacancies.

On December 2, therefore, Speaker Turney and the twelve Whigs proceeded, according to agreement, to the chamber of the lower house to join with that body in choosing one of the Senators. The other twelve Democratic senators declined to attend the election. When summoned by the doorkeeper, they sent written notice to their speaker (Turney) that they were in the senate chamber, ready for ''constitutional business.''[9] The joint convention, for want of a quorum, was forced to adjourn. On the morning of the third the lower house again notified the senate that it was ready to receive the senators and to proceed to the election of one of the federal Senators. It had already been arranged to hold the other election in the afternoon and for this reason Speaker Turney deemed it to be unnecessary to join the house in convention twice in one day, inasmuch as both elections could be held during the same half-day. He therefore voted with the Democrats in declining to attend the forenoon session of the convention. This vote so angered the Whig senators that they left the senate chamber in a body. By so doing they gave a distinct advantage to the Democrats, who now adjourned to the following day, thereby nullifying the original

---

[9] *Tenn. Sen. Jour.*, 1841–42, 280.

resolution which had designated December 2 and 3 as the days on which elections by *convention* should be held.

By seceding from the senate the Whigs had committed the tactical blunder of releasing Turney from his agreement. He now blamed them for the failure to elect Senators, and once more became one of the "immortal thirteen."[10]  Five of the twelve Democratic senators submitted a written statement of reasons why they had refused to participate in the proposed election. The proposed method of election, they asserted, would violate the Constitution of the United States, which vests the election of Senators in the legislature of the state—not in a convention.  It would violate, also, the state constitution, which says that Senators shall be chosen by the concurrent vote of the two houses *"sitting separately"*—not together.  Both statements were untrue, and besides, the convention method had been thoroughly established by custom, and up to this time its validity had never been questioned.  This new-born solicitude for constitutional limitations was simply a clever bit of pettifogging.

Before any attempt to elect Senators had been made, two interesting resolutions for dividing the state were offered in the senate.  The first was introduced by Andrew Johnson, on December 7, and provided that a joint committee of the two houses should be appointed to consider the expediency and the constitutionality of ceding East Tennessee to the United States so that it might be made an independent commonwealth and called the "State of Frankland."  The resolution directed Governor Jones to correspond with the governors of Georgia, North Carolina, and Virginia with a view to procuring portions of those states for inclusion within the limits of "Frankland."  On December 15, Gardner offered a similar resolution which provided for the

---

10 Turney's explanation, *ibid.*, 304–305. On December 13, J. Geo. Harris informed Polk by letter that there was no prospect of an election. "Thank God and the immortal thirteen Ephraim's [Foster] fiddle is broke. No more will its dulcet strains minister to the desponding faculties of faction" (*Polk Papers*).

creation of the state of "Jacksoniana." It was to include the "Western District" of Tennessee and portions of Kentucky and Mississippi.[11] The senate rejected Gardner's proposal by a vote of eleven to fourteen. Johnson's resolution passed the senate by a vote of seventeen to six (January 18), but after considerable discussion and many futile attempts to amend, this too was finally rejected by the lower house.

In accordance with the Laughlin resolutions,[12] Democratic members of the legislature had addressed queries to all senatorial candidates concerning their views on public questions. Foster and Jarnagin treated these queries with silent contempt. Hopkins L. Turney, the Democratic aspirant, gave satisfactory answers as a matter of course, and so, also, did Thomas Brown, a Whig of Roane County, East Tennessee. On December 20, Laughlin offered in the senate a resolution which differed little from the one previously submitted by Gardner. Whereas, in choosing Senators, the popular will should be consulted, so read the preamble, and, as the recent election had shown the people to be about equally divided in politics, and as neither party was able to choose Senators without the coöperation of the other, it was therefore resolved that Turney and Brown, having responded to all interrogatories, be declared the Senators to represent the state in the Senate of the United States. Turney was to fill the unexpired term of Grundy, and Brown was to have the full term of six years.[13] The resolution passed the senate but failed in the other house, and that body once more invited the senate to join them in an election by convention. The Whigs of both houses refused to coöperate with the Democrats in electing a

---

[11] *Tenn. Sen. Jour.*, 1841–42, 288, 345.

[12] Those which he had introduced on Nov. 5, relating to the interrogation of candidates for office. See above.

[13] *Tenn. Sen. Jour.*, 1841–42, 366–67. "Some of our friends here are of opinion—that after all our Senators should be elected—if the Whigs can be brought 'to elect one and one'" (A. V. Brown to Polk, Washington, Dec. 23, 1841, *Polk Papers*). This seems to indicate that the Democrats had counted more on preventing an election than on effecting a compromise.

comptroller and a treasurer unless the Democrats would agree to choose Senators by a joint vote. Of this refusal the Democrats tried to make political capital;[14] by exploiting it they endeavored to divert the attention of the people away from their own obstructive tactics.

Polk kept in close touch with the contest that was being waged at Nashville and from time to time gave directions to his political friends. He was one of the first to doubt the loyalty of his old friend A. O. P. Nicholson, and to suspect him of courting an alliance with Foster for the purpose of procuring their election to the Senate.[15] He was most severe in his denunciation of Nicholson and predicted that he would follow in the footsteps of John Bell.[16] Hearing that some of Bell's friends had made overtures offering to settle the senatorial deadlock by choosing Bell and some Democrat, Polk stated to Senator Maclin[17] that it would never do "to elect *Bell* by Democratic votes. It would not only be placing him in a position to do mischief but it would be rewarding his apostacy." He had heard also, he said, that similar overtures had been made by Foster's friends. "To no man in the State," he continued, "would it be more grating than to myself to be driven to the necessity of making a compromise by which he might obtain a seat in the Senate, and yet it is not

---

[14] "Our whole object is," wrote Wm. H. Polk, who was a member of the lower house, "to place them [the Whigs] in the position of refusing to elect State officers, necessary and essential to the proper administration of our State Government, because we prevent them from placing in the Senate men who stand *Mum*" (W. H. Polk to J. K. Polk, Jan. 6, 1842, *Polk Papers*).

[15] In answer to one of Polk's letters, J. P. Hardwick wrote from Nashville that "I have no doubt a great effort is being made to carry out an unholy alliance between F. & N." (Hardwick to Polk, Jan. 16, 1842, *ibid.*)

[16] "Every day convinces me more and more that he [N] is now travelling in the broad road—that John Bell travelled for several years before his apostacy—whilst he was making *loud professions* of his adhesion to our principles. We all know where *John Bell* now is, *and mark what I now say to you*, that five years, perhaps not one will pass—before he is where *Bell* now is, unless it shall be his personal interest shall make him *seem* otherwise. *I am not mistaken*" (Polk to State Senator Sackfield Maclin, Jan. 17, 1842, *Andrew Johnson Papers*, vol. 1).

[17] *Ibid.*

impossible that our *safety as a party* in the State might require such a sacrifice.''[18]  Should an agreement with Foster be made, Polk believed that the Democrat ought to be chosen from East Tennessee; but if any western Democrat was to be selected, it should be Hopkins L. Turney.  He preferred a Whig Senator to Nicholson, because he had ''more respect for an open opponent than a hypocritical friend.''[19]  Some of the ''immortal thirteen,'' however, were unwilling to accept any compromise which did not eliminate both Foster and Bell.

On February 7, the last day of the session, Laughlin, probably acting under instructions from Polk, offered a new resolution ''in the spirit of harmony, concession and compromise.''  This resolution authorized the Whig members of the legislature to choose a Senator from any of the three divisions of the state (east, middle or west), and provided that the Democrats should then select a Senator from one of the other divisions.  The resolution passed the senate by a strict party vote, but not until an amendment had been added which required that both Senators must be ''selected from men who have not been in public life for the last four years.''  Such a limitation had not been contemplated by either Laughlin or Polk, but some of the *thirteen* would accept nothing less.  The lower house would not, of course, agree to the resolution; all hope of compromise was at an end; and the legislature adjourned without having filled either vacancy.  On the same day the *thirteen* had the satisfaction of

---

[18] ''It would be a *bitter pill*,'' said Polk, ''to take Mr. F. even upon a compromise, and yet if nothing else can be done I have been brought very seriously to doubt, whether we had not better take him with *some good and true Democrat* than to have the State unrepresented in the Senate and thus raise up a perplexing troublesome issue of *Senators or no Senators* in the State, which may and probably will be the test question in our elections in 1843.  Before you can compromise at all with him or any other Whig— they must yield to *your mode of elections and agree to obey instructions.* If they will do this and agree to give us a Democratic Senator with him— my conviction is, that it is the course of safety to yield to it.''

[19] Polk to James Walker, Jan. 17, 1842, *Polk Papers.*  Whether well founded or not, the belief in Nicholson's disloyalty was quite general. H. L. Turney wrote from Washington to Polk, April 25, 1842: ''I think A. O. P. N. has put his foot in it.  Can it be possible that he can longer deceive the democra~y of Tennessee?''

rejecting for a second time a list of persons whom Governor Jones had nominated to be directors of the Bank of Tennessee, and as a result, the Democratic incumbents retained their positions.

In their game of obstruction the Democrats had won a decided victory—much greater than they had any reasonable hope to expect. Had any of the "immortal thirteen" failed them, everything would have been lost, and more than once Samuel Turney had threatened to desert to the enemy. By bad management, the Whigs had failed to take advantage of his willingness to coöperate with them, while the Democrats spared no effort to hold him in line. The tactics employed by the senate to attain its ends were as unscrupulous as they were successful. The aid given by Polk and Jackson was something of which neither man had reason to be proud, but politicians are seldom overscrupulous when party interests are at stake.

Just as the Democrats were rejoicing over their success in thwarting the Whigs, their own party suffered a real loss in the retirement of J. George Harris from the editorship of the *Union*.[20] He had taken charge of the paper when it was bankrupt and impotent, and under his management it had become one of the most influential papers in the state. His style was not always elegant nor his assertions true, but he was peculiarly fitted to perform the task to which he had been assigned. After his retirement the *Union* rapidly deteriorated, until Polk and his associates had to take its rehabilitation in hand during the campaign of 1843.

After the adjournment of the legislature, the thoughts of politicians turned to plans for the future. Although it was an open secret that Polk would, in 1843, again be the candidate for governor, both he and his friends were ever on the alert to promote his prospects for the Vice-Presidential nomination in 1844.

---

[20] In the issue of March 31 Harris announced that he was going to Europe for a few months and that the owners, Hogan and Heiss, would conduct the paper themselves.

The more apparent it became that Van Buren would again head the Democratic ticket, the more necessary it seemed to be to find a running mate that would be acceptable to the South and West. Maclin, of the Tennessee senate, voiced the general sentiment when he told Polk that ''Our friends intend to fight the battle' with you, and keep Van Buren as much out of sight as possible.'' In these two sections of the Union, influential leaders fully appreciated Polk's great services to the party and looked with favor upon his nomination for the Vice-Presidency, but, as Maclin frankly told him, it had been urged that he was not well known to the people in other parts of the country.[21]

Politicians of both parties attached much importance to Van Buren's visit to the Hermitage in the spring of 1842. Knowing Jackson's warm friendship for Polk, the Whigs expected and many Tennesseans hoped that the visit would result in a formal agreement between Van Buren and Polk. But, despite the efforts of Polk's friends in his behalf, the New Yorker remained noncommittal to the point of exasperation[22] and left Tennessee without having mentioned to Polk the subject of the Vice-Presidency.[23]

Although Van Buren declined to take any part in promoting Polk's candidacy or even to discuss it, and even though his indifferent attitude during his visit had still further alienated the supporters of Polk, yet both the Whigs and the Calhounites were

---

[21] Maclin to Polk, May 4, 1842, *Polk Papers*. Maclin had just returned from Mississippi, where he had been sounding Polk's praises and urging the people to call a convention for the purpose of nominating Van Buren and Polk.

[22] ''I am at a loss to know what to say to you, I can learn nothing. . . . Mr. Van Buren seems disposed to say nothing on the subject we spoke of when I last saw you. I made an effort through Donelson again this evening but it was all *Mum.* . . . It may be that he will say to you what he will not say to another person. The old Genl will *tell him before leaving the Hermitage,* to have a conversation with you'' (Gen. R. Armstrong to Polk, May 4, 1842, *Polk Papers*).

[23] Polk himself said in a letter that during Van Buren's visit neither had ''mentioned verbally or in writing'' the subject which the Whigs say brought him to Tennessee (Polk to Elmore, of South Carolina, June 13, 1842, *Polk Papers*).

certain that an agreement between the two candidates had been effected and that one of its objects was to crush Calhoun.[24]  Van Buren was not popular in Tennessee, and many Democrats felt that Polk's election would be more certain if some other than the New Yorker could be nominated for President.[25]  Cass was most frequently mentioned by those who held this belief.  Others were inclined to await developments.  Benton, like Van Buren, had declined to commit himself in Polk's favor, but his denunciation of Richard M. Johnson was regarded by Tennesseans in Washington as a hopeful sign.[26]  Realizing the general indifference toward Van Buren in southern states, friends of Calhoun began to entertain hopes that he would be nominated for the Presidency in 1844;[27] but, believing, as they did, that Polk was in agreement with Van Buren, they did not, it appears, seek assistance from his friends.  Then, too, the adherents of the great nullifier could hardly hope for the coöperation of a man who was thought to be under the dominating influence of General Jackson.

When the Tennessee legislature convened in the autumn of 1842, another futile attempt was made to fill the vacant seats in the federal Senate.  J. George Harris, who had returned to Nashville, reported to Polk that Bell's supporters had offered to make an agreement whereby Bell was to answer the queries which had

24 ''It is thought,'' wrote Dixon H. Lewis, ''Van has effected his purpose with Polk,'' while according to Gentry, of Tennessee, no one doubted that Van Buren and Polk would be the Democratic candidates (Lewis to Richard Crallé, May 31, and June 10, 1842, *Crallé Papers*).

25 ''I assure you, sir,'' wrote J. P. Hardwicke, ''there is a disinclination to take up Van Buren again.  I have taken some pains to arrive at this conclusion at our little caucuses'' (Hardwicke to Polk, Nov. 13, 1842, *Polk Papers*).

26 Cave Johnson to Polk, Jan. 29; H. L. Turney to Polk, Jan. 31, 1843, *Polk Papers.*

27 One of the hopeful was Duff Green.  He thought that, if the Van Burenites' plan of an early nominating convention could be thwarted, Calhoun would be nominated.  ''It has now narrowed down,'' he wrote, ''to a choice between Calhoun and Van Buren and the demonstrations are becoming more decided for Mr. Calhoun so that, in my opinion, the concentration in his favor will become so apparent as public opinion develops that the convention will indeed become obsolete'' (Green to Crallé, February 8, 1843, *Letters of Duff Green* in Library of Congress).

been ignored by Foster and Jarnagin.  Having done this, he was
to be elected as one of the Senators, and the Democrats were to
fill the other vacancy with a candidate of their own choice.
Harris was in favor of such an agreement if Polk would consent
to be the Democratic Senator; Foster would be killed, politically,
while Bell if properly instructed would be less powerful than at
present.[28]  Nothing, of course, resulted from the suggestion.
Polk had already declined to make any compromise with Bell,
and besides, the overtures of Bell's friends were probably made
without his knowledge.  During this session the Democrats made
little attempt to force a compromise, but simply contented themselves with blocking the Whigs from electing their candidates.
Their greatest fear seems to have been that Nicholson, by some
treacherous agreement with the Whigs, would attempt to promote his own selfish interests.[29]

Feeling that both his own and his party's interests could be
best served by defeating Governor Jones, Polk once more entered
the race.  The campaign was opened by a joint debate at Spring-
field, March 25, 1843.  Jones scathingly denounced the conduct
of the "immortal thirteen."  Polk retorted by charging that
Jones had originated the idea which they had put into practice.
The *Union*[30] published letters from Whigs who claimed to have
heard Jones boast that, in case the Democrats should have a bare
majority on joint ballot, the Whigs would prevent a choice of
Senators by refusing to participate in the election.  Throughout
the campaign the *Union* defended the thirteen for preventing
the election of men who refused to be bound by the wishes of
their constituents.  The refusal of the state senate to confirm
Jones's list of bank directors was purely for political reasons.
The truth was reprehensible enough, but on the stump Jones

---

[28] Harris to Polk, Dec. 11, 1842, *Polk Papers*.

[29] W. H. Polk to J. K. Polk, February 14, 1843, *Polk Papers*.  Andrew
Johnson, fearing that his known friendship for Nicholson might be mis-
interpreted, wrote to Polk that "you have always been my first choice for
anything" (Johnson to Polk, February 20, 1843, *ibid.*)

[30] March 31, 1843.

won applause by asserting that the Polk directors were corrupt and time-serving partisans who, for fear of exposure, did not dare to relinquish their offices.

In many respects the campaign was a repetition of that of 1841. There was, perhaps, more argument and less burlesque, although both candidates made use of anecdotes and sarcastic retorts. Polk was not unmindful of his own powers of wit. When writing to his wife of a debate held at Jackson with Milton Brown, he said that his opponent tried to turn the "occasion into a frolic . . . but I turned the laugh upon him & almost laughed him out of the Court House."[31]

In his "Letter to the People"[32] Polk, as usual, emphasized national issues such as the tariff, the national bank, and the general extravagance of the Whigs. Once more Tennessee was regarded as the pivotal state—the index to the approaching Presidential campaign. As it was practically certain that Clay would be the Whig candidate, much of Polk's time on the stump was devoted to Clay and his policies. Incensed by a revival of the old "bargain and corruption" charge of 1825, Clay challenged Polk to a discussion of this question at a time and place to be fixed by the Tennessean himself.[33] Apparently the challenge was not accepted.

Early in the campaign a group of persons in Memphis submitted to the two candidates a list of questions on political topics. Jones replied at once, and among other things expressed the following views. He favored a national bank, but was not fully satisfied with Clay's bill that had been vetoed by Tyler. He believed in a tariff for revenue, with incidental protection to home industries. In his opinion the legislature had full power to choose Senators in any manner which it saw fit. The last

---

[31] Polk to Mrs. Polk, April 4, 1843, *Polk Papers.*

[32] It bore the date of May 17, 1843, and was printed in the *Union,* May 23 and 26.

[33] Typewritten copy of a letter from Clay to Polk dated Ashland, May 20, 1843, *Polk Papers.*

answer did not harmonize very well with his condemnation of
the Democratic senate for insisting that each house should vote
separately.[34]

In answer to the same queries Polk stated that he believed
in the sub-treasury, and in metal money for the nation supplemented by a limited amount of paper issued by state banks.
He opposed direct taxes and endorsed tariff for revenue only.
Like Jones, he thought that the legislature possessed the right
to elect Senators in any manner agreeable to itself. He held,
on the other hand, that all candidates for office were under obligation, when called upon, to express their views before election
on all public questions. "The chief, if not the only value of the
right of suffrage," said he,

consists in the fact, that it may be exercised *understandingly* by the
constituent body. It is so, whether the immediate constituency consists
of the Legislature, as in the case of the election of United States Senators,
or of the people in their primary capacity, in the election of their Executive or Legislative agents. In either case the constituent has a right to
know the opinions of the candidate before he casts his vote.[35]

Except on the bank question the views expressed by the two
men were very much alike. Indeed, the paramount issue was:
Shall Tennessee be returned to the Democratic column in national
politics?

Throughout the campaign the Democrats were handicapped
by the weakness of their party press. Since Harris's resignation
the *Union* lacked both spirit and influence, and was rapidly drift-
ing into bankruptcy. On the other hand, the Whigs had several
vigorous papers, the most invincible of which was Brownlow's
Jonesborough *Whig*. Polk was condemned for the part he had
taken in the administrations of Jackson and Van Buren, and
again it was said that he sought the governorship merely as
a stepping-stone to the Vice-Presidency. Polk's "Tory"

---

[34] Jones's reply is dated April 24, 1843, and is printed in the Memphis
*American Eagle*, May 2, a copy of which is among the *Polk Papers*.

[35] The answer is dated May 15, and is printed in the *Union*, June 2, 1843.

grandfather was again held up to scorn, while a Chattanooga paper charged the Democratic candidate with being an aristocrat who had ''refused to eat with some wagoners who were stopping at the same tavern with him some years ago.''[36]

Although Polk made a thorough canvass and demonstrated his superiority over his rival, Jones was reëlected by a majority of nearly four thousand votes. This time the Whigs elected a majority of the legislature as well as the governor, and the power of the ''immortal thirteen'' had been broken. Polk attributed the victory of the Whigs to their success in drawing the attention of the people to local questions and away from great national issues. He was still confident that his party would carry the state in the federal election of 1844.[37]

Soon after the election the defeated candidate's friends once more turned their attention to procuring for him the Vice-Presidential nomination. They were interested of course in his personal advancement, and besides, they had hopes that, with their favorite on the ticket, Tennessee might be restored to the Democratic party. On September 5 the *Union,* in a series of editorials, urged his nomination and declared him to be ''one of the ablest men in the democratic party in the Southwest.'' In a letter to Van Buren, General Jackson expressed the belief that the former President would be nominated—and elected, also, if Polk were put on the ticket with him. Such a ticket, he said, would surely carry Tennessee; Polk would add strength to the party in all of the states, while Colonel Johnson would weaken it.[38]

The new legislature met on October 2, 1843. In the senate the Whigs had fourteen members, the Democrats, eleven; in the lower house the Whigs numbered forty, the Democrats, thirty-five. The two main political questions which confronted the

---

[36] Both articles and a denial are in the *Union,* June 27, 1843.

[37] Polk to Van Buren, August 8, 1843, *Van Buren Papers.*

[38] Jackson to Van Buren, September 22, 1843, *ibid.*

legislature were fixing a permanent location for the state capital, and the election of federal Senators. Although now in the minority, the Democrats planned to prevent the election of Foster and Jarnagin by supporting two other Whigs, A. R. Alexander, of West Tennessee, and Joseph L. Williams, of East Tennessee. Some of the Whigs, especially the Rutherford delegation, were eager to have the capital removed from Nashville to some more central location. The Democrats therefore concocted a scheme by which they hoped to procure a sufficient number of Whig votes to elect Alexander and Williams by offering to vote for the removal of the capital. Polk was then in Nashville and gave his support to the plan.[39] Their plotting was in vain. On October 7 both houses voted to retain the capital at Nashville, and on the seventeenth Foster and Jarnagin were elected Senators, the former to fill Grundy's unexpired term, the latter to succeed Anderson.[40]

Repeated defeats annoyed but did not discourage Democratic leaders. Harmony within their own ranks was the first desideratum, and Laughlin undertook the task of bringing Nicholson and his adherents back into the fold.[41] The task did not seem hopeless, for since the seats in the Senate had been filled by the Whigs there was no reason why Nicholson should not coöperate with his former associates. The "little magician" was the chief cause of embarrassment. Democrats, generally, were ready to support Polk, but from all parts of the state came reports of indifference or hostility to Van Buren.

Laughlin's "missionary" work was not confined to the Nicholson faction. As soon as the question of locating the capital had been settled, it was a foregone conclusion that Foster and Jarnagin would be elected. Freed from the responsibility of

---

[39] S. H. Laughlin, "Diary," October 1–4, 1843.

[40] *Ibid.*, Oct. 17. "*Jonakin* has gone home a Senator—and Ephe is running about, grinning and jumping like a pleased monkey—with just about the dignity of one, at best" (Laughlin to Polk, Oct. 20, 1843, *Polk Papers*).

[41] Laughlin to Polk, Oct. 12, 1843, *Polk Papers*.

manipulating the scheme to defeat this election, Laughlin could devote his entire energy to procuring for Polk the nomination for Vice-President. In letters to influential leaders and newspaper men, he almost demanded that Polk should be taken up by ''the press and the People.'' He proposed that the former Governor should be nominated by the state convention which was to meet in November, and that the Tennessee delegation should go to the national convention ''supporting his claims, and uncommitted as to Presidential candidate, but committed to abide its nomination.'' He told his correspondents that if Polk were put on the ticket with Van Buren or any other good Democrat the party would surely win, ''but without Polk's name we would be beaten and tied down in federal chains in Tennessee for the next six or ten years.''[42] His remark concerning the national convention seems to be the first indication of the plan, later adopted, to nominate Polk, and to remain noncommittal as to the Presidential candidate. The determination to make no nomination for President was strengthened, no doubt, by a letter written from New York by Harvey M. Watterson to A. O. P. Nicholson. Van Buren was Watterson's own choice, but, fearing that his favorite could not be elected, he did not believe it wise to nominate him. Cass, in his opinion, was the most *available* candidate. He said that ''the Van Buren party intend to give Polk the *go by* as to a nomination for the Vice Presidency,'' and that Johnson would be nominated by the national convention.[43] On October 18, two days after the receipt of Watterson's letter, Laughlin conversed with A. V. Brown. Brown advised serving notice on the New Yorkers that the Tennesseans would support Van Buren if his adherents would agree to support Polk; otherwise they would go for Cass. To this Laughlin and Armstrong assented, and Donelson was selected to state their views to Silas Wright and other friends of Van Buren.[44] Probably this threat

---

[42] S. H. Laughlin, ''Diary,'' Oct. 9, 1843.

[43] *Ibid.*, October 16, 1843.

[44] *Ibid.*, October 18, 1843.

was not carried into effect. At any rate Polk later disclaimed any knowledge of a project to drop Van Buren for Cass.[45]  In January, 1844, he asked Heiss to place Van Buren's name along with his own at the head of the political columns of the *Union*,[46] but, for the time being, the editor refused to comply.

The State convention met at Nashville on November 23, 1843. Polk was nominated for Vice-President by a unanimous vote, but no one was named for the Presidency.  The convention simply agreed to support whatever candidate the Baltimore convention might see fit to nominate.  The reason assigned for not nominating Van Buren, as stated to him in letters from both Polk and Jackson,[47] was a fear that the Cass supporters might resist such action, and that a breach in the party would result.

On hearing from Cave Johnson and A. V. Brown that Van Buren was stronger in Washington than Cass and that he would, in all probability, be nominated at Baltimore, Polk advised the editors of the *Union* to come out for the ex-President.[48]  His real feeling toward Van Buren is not easy to determine, but from his silence rather than his words, one always gets the impression that his support of the New Yorker was based, as in this case, on expediency instead of admiration for the man.  It was quite natural that this should have been so, for Van Buren had more than once shown indifference when Polk needed his aid.

Realizing that the party had suffered from the want of a vigorous newspaper, Polk turned his attention to rehabilitating the Nashville *Union*.  Since its purchase by Hogan and Heiss, it had been edited by the senior partner.  He had never been a forceful writer, and of late his health had become so impaired that the paper was practically without an editor.  With the consent of the owners, Polk asked Laughlin to take charge of the

---

[45] Polk to Cave Johnson, March 18, 1844, ''Polk-Johnson Letters.''

[46] Polk to Heiss, Jan. 21, 1844, ''Heiss Papers.''

[47] Jackson to Van Buren, Nov. 29; Polk to Van Buren, Nov. 30, 1843, *Van Buren Papers*.

[48] Polk to Heiss, Dec. 21, 1843, ''Heiss Papers.''

paper and promised him financial support from the party. Fearing, however, that he might jeopardize his chances of being elected to Congress (from his home district), Laughlin at first declined to accept the position.[49]  His subsequent acceptance and his editorial services to his party will be considered in the following chapter.

------

[49] Polk to Heiss, Dec. 21, 1843, ''Heiss Papers.''  Laughlin to Polk, Dec. 7; Heiss to Polk, Dec. 19, 1843, *Polk Papers.*

CHAPTER XII

## SELECTION OF CANDIDATES, 1844

The campaign of 1844 may be said to have opened with the new year. From early in January announcements from prospective candidates, declarations of principles, and notices of nominations made by local bodies, began to occupy leading places in the columns of the party journals. There was little doubt that Clay would be chosen to head the Whig ticket, although, in response to an inquiry from friends, Webster announced his willingness to accept a nomination at the hands of the Whig convention. Tyler had been read out of the Whig party, and, since the Democrats had not shown a disposition to adopt him as their own, it seemed likely that he would enter the contest as an independent candidate. Van Buren's nomination by the Baltimore convention was fully expected by all parties not so much because any considerable portion of his party wanted him, as because there seemed to be no one who had a better claim. He had been left by General Jackson as a legacy to the party, the position he had occupied gave him prestige, and, as Dixon H. Lewis remarked, he had the advantage of *"being considered the candidate of the party."*[1] These influences combined would insure him the nomination unless something should happen before the meeting of the convention to change indifference into active hostility. For some time, of course, there had been active hostility in certain quarters, but this came generally from those who were promoting the interests of some other still more unpopular candidate, such as Calhoun or Tyler, consequently there was little danger from that source. Unless something should occur to cast doubts on

---

[1] Lewis to Crallé, June 10, 1842, *Crallé Papers.*

his orthodoxy or his personal fitness, Van Buren was reasonably certain of the nomination, but unfortunately for him, that something did occur—the unexpected turn in the Texas question. Before the appearance of this firebrand, friends of other aspirants were exerting every effort to weaken his hold on the party and to strengthen that of their favorites. The most active were the supporters of Calhoun and Cass; some were ready to join with the followers of Tyler; and a few, like W. C. Rives,[2] announced that, as Van Buren's nomination seemed assured, they would vote for Henry Clay.

Early in the year, when Van Buren's nomination seemed to be a foregone conclusion, the main topic of discussion in Democratic ranks was the choice for the second place on the ticket. The persons most frequently mentioned were Colonel Richard M. Johnson, of Kentucky, and James K. Polk, of Tennessee. As in Van Buren's case, many were ready to support Colonel Johnson simply because they did not see how the party could drop him gracefully.[3] The Van Burenites favored Johnson, but for this very reason his nomination was vigorously opposed, especially in the South and Southwest. It was felt by many that if Van Buren must be accepted, the Vice-President should be a man more agreeable to the southern wing of the party. For some time the Tennessee Democrats had been urging Polk's claims to this office, and since his second defeat by Jones they were still more determined to procure for him the nomination.

Ardently desiring this office, Polk began as early as the fall of 1843 to ask his friends to use their influence with politicians of other states. In a letter to Donelson he expressed the belief that Van Buren would be made the candidate for President, and if so, ''the candidate for the Vice Presidency must come from the West,—and from a slave-holding state.'' He hoped that the

---

[2] His letter, dated January 1, is printed in *Nat. Intell.*, Jan. 12, 1844.

[3] It was rare to see a person, wrote Cave Johnson, who did not prefer Polk. The main trouble was getting rid of ''Old Dick'' (Johnson to Polk, Jan. 31, 1844, *Polk Papers*).

press and party leaders would come out early for Van Buren and himself, at least before R. M. Johnson had yielded his "pretensions for the Presidency" and had become his competitor for the second place. Even this early he expressed distrust for the Washington *Globe.*

I do not understand *Blair's* course. . . . . I do not think he is inclined to do me justice. Why I know not, unless it be that he has strong attachments for *Col. Johnson,* and looks to his restoration with *Mr. Van Buren.*

The attitude of Ohio and Mississippi, he said in another letter, would go far to settle the question, therefore Donelson and other Tennessee friends should send letters to prominent politicians in those states.[4]

Early in January, 1844, Laughlin and others procured from General Jackson letters to political leaders in various states. These letters were used in an effort to induce state conventions to declare their preference for Polk.[5] A letter signed "Amicus" that appeared in the *Globe* and advocated the nomination of William R. King, of Alabama, gave Cave Johnson and A. V. Brown an opportunity to sound Polk's praises and to urge his nomination. In an article signed "A Tennessee Democrat," they pointed out that King, voluntarily, and Van Buren, under instructions, had voted for the United States Bank, and that it would never do to have two candidates who had endorsed that discredited institution. But, they asked, who does not remember in Jackson's battle against the bank "the unterrified ability displayed by Governor Polk on these trying occasions?" The very fact that Tennessee was a doubtful state was an additional reason for nominating Polk.[6] To a friend in Tennessee Johnson wrote that old-line politicians such as Buchanan, Calhoun, Benton, and Blair were doing their utmost to ruin Polk's prospects, and other

---

[4] Polk to Donelson, Oct. 19, Dec. 20, 1843, "Polk-Donelson Letters." The Ohio politicians mentioned were Allen, Tappan, Medary, Dawson, and Medill.

[5] Letters of W. H. Polk and Laughlin to Polk (*Polk Papers*).

[6] Washington *Globe,* Jan. 15, 1844. Johnson to Polk, Jan. 13, 21, 31, 1844, *Polk Papers.*

letters told Polk that these men feared him as another rival for the Presidency.[7]

In general, conservatives evinced a preference for either King or Colonel Johnson,[8] but the more aggressive element favored Polk. The Mississippi state convention at its Jackson Day (January 8) celebration drank toasts to Polk and nominated him for Vice-President,[9] and in many other states there was growing sentiment in his favor. The attention of the country had recently been called to the state of Tennessee by the introduction in Congress of a bill to reimburse General Jackson for the thousand dollar fine imposed upon him at New Orleans in 1815. William H. Polk moved in the Tennessee legislature to instruct the Senators and request the Representatives from that state to vote for the bill. Although such an action was only to be expected from any Tennessee Democrat, it is not unlikely that Polk had considered the probable effect on his brother's candidacy.[10]

The private correspondence of this early part of 1844 is very interesting in view of the assertion made later that an anti-Van Buren plot had been hatched in Tennessee by the intimate associates of Polk. · The letters show conclusively that instead of opposing the ex-President's nomination the leading politicians were trying hard to bring it about. On the other hand, the rank and file of the Democracy of the state cared little for Van Buren and feared that he would be a ''dead weight'' upon the party. Even Hogan and Heiss, the proprietors of the *Union,* at first declined to place his name at the head of their political column,

---

[7] Levin H. Coe to Polk, Jan. 27, 1844, *ibid.*

[8] In a letter to the editor of the *Globe,* dated January 28, Johnson stated that he had, at various places, been nominated—sometimes for President, sometimes for Vice-President. He would accept either, he said, if ratified by the national convention, but in any event he would support the regular nominees.

[9] Nashville *Union,* Jan. 23, 1844.

[10] When Polk's resolution reached the senate, a Whig member moved that the preamble should be changed to read that the ''question is now brought before the American people not with a view to relieve Gen. Jackson . . . but alone for political effect'' (Nashville *Union,* Jan. 25, 1844).

although Polk had requested them to do so.[11]  Urged by Laughlin as well as by Polk, the editors finally, though reluctantly, consented.  His name appeared for the first time on February 8, 1844, and the editors stated frankly that

in placing Mr. Van Buren's name at the head of our paper, subject to the action of the National Convention, we assume no new position either in reference to our views or the preferences of the great body of the democracy in Tennessee.

They would support, they said, the nominee of the convention, whoever he might be.[12]  On March 12, after much urging by Polk, Laughlin assumed the editorship not only of the *Union* but of the *Star Spangled Banner,* a weekly campaign journal which was to be published from the same office.[13]  The tone of the *Union* now became more favorable to Van Buren, and there seemed to be little doubt that he would be nominated at Baltimore.

Up to the time that Van Buren's Texas letter was published, there was no indication that influential Tennesseans had any intention of opposing his nomination.  Cave Johnson, who, with R. J. Walker, was charged later with having instigated the plan to defeat him at Baltimore, was a hearty supporter of the ex-President.  In a letter written from Washington he told of a movement in that city to nominate Cass.  This movement, he believed should be vigorously opposed, for "in my opinion *your only chance* for the position we wish" depends upon the nomination of Van Buren.[14]  At a large meeting held at Nashville on March 15, 1844, to celebrate the anniversary of Jackson's

----

[11] "Tell the General," said Polk in a letter to Donelson, December 20, 1843, "that I had an interview with both Editors of the Union, when I was at Nashville and both agreed to take decided and bold ground for *Van Buren* in their paper.  If they do not do so, in their next paper, I will write to them and urge it upon them.  The paper here has done so" ("Polk-Donelson Letters").

[12] Nashville *Union,* Feb. 8.  Polk to Heiss, Jan. 21 "Heiss Papers"; Laughlin to Polk, Feb. 4, *Polk Papers.*

[13] Polk's letters to Heiss advising the employment of Laughlin are in the "Heiss Papers."  Various letters of Polk and Laughlin on the subject are in the *Polk Papers.*

[14] Johnson to Polk, March 6, 1844, *Polk Papers.*

birth and the remission of his fine by Congress,[15] efforts were made to create enthusiasm for both Van Buren and Polk. While at Nashville Polk answered Johnson's letter and fully concurred in the views he had expressed. A few days later he wrote again on the same subject and said that ''the movement which you say is on hand—to profess publicly to support Mr. Van Buren, with a secret intention to attempt to nominate Genl Cass in the Convention,—can receive no countenance.'' If there is any movement in Tennessee, said he, to couple his name with that of Cass to the prejudice of Van Buren, he is not aware of it, and if discovered, he will not permit it.

It is now settled that the preference of a large majority of the party is for *Mr. Van Buren,* and the whole party should yield to his nomination and make it unanimous. Such men as *Duff Green,* and the discontented in our ranks may attempt to produce confusion by resisting the popular choice of the party, but their movements can receive no countenance or support from me.[16]

Immediately following the Nashville meeting Laughlin sounded the trumpet more vigorously than ever for Van Buren and Polk, and insisted that four-fifths of the Democrats in Congress were in favor of the ex-President's nomination. Although a friend of General Cass, Laughlin deplored the agitation in his behalf. Cass himself, said he, ''has frowned upon the design.'' Those who had come out for Cass had, in Laughlin's opinion, done so for the purpose of dividing the party, and most prominent among them was Duff Green, ''a renegade deserter.''[17]

On March 20, the day before the appearance of Laughlin's editorial, Polk had declined an unofficial offer of a place in the cabinet of John Tyler. Abel P. Upshur, Secretary of State, and Thomas W. Gilmer, Secretary of the Navy, had been killed in the *Princeton* disaster of February 28, leaving two vacancies in

---

[15] Laughlin submitted a resolution which declared that revenge had led Judge Hall to impose the fine. Polk seconded the resolution and made a speech on political questions (*Union,* March 19, 1844).

[16] Polk to Johnson, March 18, 1844 (''Polk-Johnson Letters'').

[17] Nashville *Union,* March 21, 1844.

the cabinet.  Calhoun had been selected to succeed Upshur,[18] but John Y. Mason, who had been invited to take Gilmer's place declined, at first, to accept the offer.  At this juncture Theophilus Fisk, former editor of the *Old Dominion* and a friend of the President, sent a letter to Polk asking whether he would accept the navy portfolio "without any pledge, shackle, or trammel being asked of you, other than is already guaranteed by your exalted character and standing."[19]  Mason, however, changed his mind,[20] and by accepting the appointment left no vacancy to be filled.

Without knowledge of the offer made to Mason, or of his accceptance, Polk had already written to Fisk, stating that he would not accept a place in the cabinet.  In a letter to Cave Johnson, which was intended also for the eye of Silas Wright, Polk gave a twofold reason for declining a cabinet position.  In the first place, it would seem like withdrawing from the race for Vice-President, and this he had no intention of doing.  Again, Tyler's administration was supposed to be hostile to Van Buren; consequently, if he accepted, he would be placed in a false position, for he was heartily in favor of Van Buren.  This, in effect, was a notice to the Van Burenites that he was still in the race for Vice-President and that, as he was loyal to their candidate, he expected their support in return.  He also called attention to Laughlin's editorial in the *Union* against the attempted movement for Cass.  In another passage of the letter he not only declared his own views on the Texas question, but he intimated, also, that he took it for granted that Van Buren would not oppose annexation.  Speaking of Calhoun's call to the Department of State, he said:

---

[18] For the circumstances of Calhoun's selection, see Schouler, *Hist. of U. S.,* IV, 455.

[19] Fisk to Polk, March 9, 1844, *Polk Papers.*  Fisk said that the idea was his own, but he told Cave Johnson that he was acting by authority of the President (Johnson to Polk, March 10, *ibid.*).

[20] Much to the surprise of both Tyler and Fisk—so said the latter in a letter to Polk, March 13 (*ibid.*).

I think it probable that he will see that it is his interest to co-operate thoroughly with the Democratic party, so heartily for *Mr. Van Buren,* harmonize his friends at the South, and make a great effort upon the Texas and Oregon questions.[21]

At the time that Polk declined to accept a place in Tyler's cabinet, the Texas question was fast approaching its critical stage. Since Polk was soon to become closely identified with this important question, it seems necessary to give a brief summary of its history up to this point and to ascertain, if possible, whether he or his friends had any part in bringing it forward.

The idea of annexing Texas was not new; but since the failure of the first attempt, during Jackson's administration, no party had made annexation an active political issue. That it was made an issue in the campaign of 1844 was due, according to Benton,[22] to the machinations of Calhoun, who hoped by this means to prevent the nomination of Van Buren and the election of Henry Clay. The first move in this direction was made in the winter of 1842–43. At that time a letter, written by Thomas W. Gilmer but inspired by Calhoun, was printed in a Baltimore paper. It advocated the immediate annexation of Texas in order to forestall the designs of Great Britain. The letter, said Benton, was ''a clap of thunder in a clear sky,'' for no one was aware of any such design. Webster left the Department of State in May, 1843, and after the brief term of Legare, was succeeded on June 24 by Abel Upshur, of Virginia. Upshur was a friend of Calhoun and interested in the annexation of Texas. It was probably due to the influence of Upshur and Gilmer that Tyler first became interested in annexation, but before long the President had determined to use it for his own purposes. In his third annual message, which was sent to Congress early in December, 1843,

---

[21] In another letter of the same date which was intended for Brown and Johnson only, Polk made still more explicit the purpose of the first letter, for he pointed out that Wright, if he would, could certainly prevent R. M. Johnson from being nominated (Polk to Johnson, March 21, 1844, ''Polk-Johnson Letters'').

[22] Benton, *Thirty Years' View,* II, 581 ff.

Tyler alluded to the dangers that might result from continued war between Texas and Mexico, and hinted pointedly at possible annexation.

At this stage of the question Aaron V. Brown, an intimate friend of Polk, became a leading factor in the annexation program.  Whether or not he was consciously lending his aid to the Tyler-Calhoun project is not easy to determine.  In a conversation with Benton on the first day of the session, Brown spoke of annexation as ''an impending and probable event,'' and he was rebuked by the Senator who said that it was *''on the part of some, an intrigue for the presidency and a plot to dissolve the Union—on the part of others, a Texas scrip and land speculation.''*[23]  In a ''confidential'' letter to Polk, Brown alluded to Tyler's message and added: *''But this is not all.* I have reason to suppose it will soon be followed up with some definite and precise proposition—some think a treaty.''  The Whigs, said he, think that Tyler has brought the question up as a firebrand between North and South in order to gain support for himself, and that nothing will come of it; but however this may be, it is Brown's opinion that neither Whigs nor Democrats of the South and West should commit themselves against annexation.[24]

This was not the first time that Brown had shown an interest in the Texas question.  In January, 1843, he had sent to Jackson a copy of the *Madisonian* containing Gilmer's letter and had received in reply the famous letter of February 12 in which the General urged the necessity of immediate annexation.  Jackson's letter was not made public until a year later, about three months after Tyler had submitted his message on the subject of Texas.  The procurement and the publication of Jackson's letter have been declared by Benton to be links in the chain of events which had been forged by Calhoun and his fellow-conspirators for the purpose of making Texas the leading political issue and Calhoun the candidate, although he does not say that Brown was fully

---

23 *Ibid.*, 583.
24 Brown to Polk, Dec. 9, 1843, *Polk Papers*.

aware of the part he was playing.[25]  He has intimated, also, that the letter was purposely dated 1844 instead of 1843; but Brown's own letter—published at the same time—explained the circumstances under which it had been procured and stated explicitly that it had been in his possession for a "long time."[26]  However, Benton's interest in Van Buren's nomination and his opposition to annexation seem to have led him to associate events which in reality were not related; on the other hand, Brown's own desire for Texas is sufficient to explain his soliciting the opinion of General Jackson on the subject.

If Brown was a conscious participant in any conspiracy to undermine Van Buren, it is quite evident that his bosom friends, Polk and Cave Johnson, were not aware of the fact.  Although Johnson looked with favor on the acquisition of Texas, he was averse to having it made an issue for campaign purposes.  At the time that Polk's name was mentioned in connection with Tyler's cabinet, Johnson stated his opinions very explicitly in a letter to Polk:

> I fear some secret movements are making here so as to bring up the Texas question here prominently before the Convention meets & to make it operate if practicable agt Van in the Convention & agt Clay in the election—if it can be brought up fairly & properly & with a reasonable prospect of getting it I should have no objection, but if it is designed merely as a political question to operate in the ensuing canvass then I shall deplore it.  An effort no doubt will be made to unite the destinies of Oregon & Texas so as to unite the South & West—may you not be identified with these movements if in the cabinet? & if unsuccessful what follows?[27]

The friends of Calhoun confidently expected that their leader would profit from the emergence of the Texas question.  Fearing that "being considered a candidate" would, if left unchallenged, procure for Van Buren the coveted nomination, they began at an early date to seek support for their favorite.[28]  Due to their

---

<sup></sup>

25 Benton, *Thirty Years' View*, II, 584.

26 The letters of both Jackson and Brown were published in various newspapers—among others, the Nashville *Union* of April 2, 1844.

27 Johnson to Polk, March 10, 1844, *Polk Papers*.

28 Dixon H. Lewis to Richard Crallé, June 10, 1842, *Crallé Papers*.

efforts the time for holding the national convention was postponed from December, 1843, to a later date, in order that they
might have a longer time to educate public opinion; for even
before Jackson's Texas letter was written, they were confident
that Calhoun would be nominated.[29]

During the summer of 1843 the administration had become
convinced that Great Britain was about to interfere in Texan
affairs and effect, if possible, the abolition of slavery there.  Duff
Green was in England gathering information, and his communications were supplemented by reports which came from Texan
representatives in London.[30]  In December, as we have already
noted, Tyler called the attention of Congress to the dangers of
foreign interference in Texas, and soon afterwards he began to
formulate plans of annexation.  The supporters of Calhoun co-
operated with the President, and there seemed to be no doubt
in their minds that their patron, and not Tyler, would reap the
political reward.  Their hopes of success mounted high when
Calhoun was called to take charge of the Department of State.
Like the President they were interested in annexation *per se;*
in addition, they fully appreciated its importance as a campaign
issue.  "It is the greatest question of the *Age*," wrote Dixon H.
Lewis, and he rejoiced that Calhoun was in a position "to direct
its force & control its fury."[31]  Three days after Lewis had made

---

[29] In a letter written from Washington, February 8, 1843, Duff Green
told Crallé that although the Van Buren faction wanted an early convention, he hoped that it could be delayed until June.  "It has now,"
said he, "narrowed down to a choice between Calhoun & Van Buren and
the demonstrations are becoming more and more decided for Mr. Calhoun
so that, in my opinion, the concentration in his favor will become so
apparent as public opinion developes that the convention will indeed
become obsolete" (Letters of Duff Green, Library of Congress; Benton,
*Thirty Years' View*, II, 585).

[30] Smith, *Annexation of Texas*, chap. vi.

[31] "Every thing depends on the Texas question, which is an element
of Power so much stronger than Clay, V Buren & their conventions that
it unsettles all calculations as to the future course of men & parties.  It
is the greatest question of the *Age* & I predict will agitate the country
more than all the other public questions ever have.  Public opinion will
boil & effervesce . . . more like a volcano than a cider Barrell—but at

this assertion Jackson's Texas letter appeared in the Richmond *Enquirer*. No doubt it fitted into the Calhoun program, yet it is not at all certain that this was Brown's motive in having the letter published. Surely General Jackson did not write it for any such purpose.[32]

The emergence of the Texas question was not welcomed by Henry Clay. Early in December, 1843, he stated his opinions on the subject in a letter to John J. Crittenden.[33] There were, he said, already a sufficient number of issues without "adding freak ones" of this character, and he did not think it right to allow John Tyler to make capital out of this exciting topic. In his opinion, annexation, either by treaty or by conquest, was entirely out of the question; however, unless Tyler should present some definite project of annexation he did not feel called upon to make public expression of his views. In the following March, when it was rumored that the President was negotiating with Texas, Clay—with his usual faith in his own ability both to shape and to direct political issues—still felt confident that he could stem the tide of Texas agitation.[34]

last will settle down with *unanimity* for annexation in the South & West & a large majority in the North. It will in the meantime *unite* the *hitherto divided South,* while it will make Abolition & Treason synonymous & thus destroy it in the North.

"The beauty of the thing is, that Providence rather than Tyler has put Calhoun at the head of this great question, to direct its force & control its fury. It is understood by letters from him that he accepts.

"P. S. It is understood the preliminaries of the Treaty have already been arranged & only awaits the special minister who is daily expected." (Lewis to Crallé, March 19, 1844, Crallé Papers). Alexander H. Stephens believed that "the dissolution of the present Confederacy" lay "near Mr. Calhoun's heart" (Stephens to James Thomas, May 17, 1844, *Rep. Am. Hist. Assn.,* 1911, II, 58).

[32] Benton says that Blair declined to publish the letter in the *Globe* (*Thirty Years' View,* II, 587). Later, however, it was printed in that paper, along with Brown's letter explaining his reasons for publishing it.

[33] Clay to Crittenden, December 5, 1843, *Crittenden Papers.*

[34] Writing from Savannah, he said: "I think I can treat the question in a manner very different from any treatment which I have yet seen of it, and so as to reconcile all our friends, and many others to the views which I entertain. Of one thing you may be certain, that there is no such anxiety for the annexation here at the South as you might have been disposed to imagine" (Clay to Crittenden, March 24, 1844, *Crittenden Papers*).

The time was fast approaching when candidates must take a definite stand either for or against annexation. Despite the desire of some of them to eliminate this topic from the issues of the campaign, every day brought the subject more into prominence. Calhoun's position was already well known, for in his letter accepting the cabinet portfolio he had come out strongly in favor of annexation. Clay would probably be nominated by his party no matter what position he might choose to take with respect to the all absorbing topic. Of greater importance, therefore, was the stand to be taken by Van Buren; for on this would depend, in all probability, his success or failure in the nominating convention.

On March 27, 1844, W. H. Hammet, a member of Congress from Mississippi and an ''unpledged delegate to the Baltimore convention,'' addressed a letter to Van Buren asking for his views on the annexation of Texas. In writing this letter Hammet was evidently coöperating with the most loyal friends of Van Buren, and not, as Benton has intimated, with the supporters of Calhoun.[35] After taking ample time for consideration Van Buren on April 20, drafted his reply and sent it to his most intimate friend, Silas Wright. When it reached Wright on the evening of the 26th, it was read to a number of Van Buren's friends, including Fairfield, King, and Benton. They approved it and decided that it should be published immediately in the *Globe*. This course was decided upon before Hammet had even seen the letter.[36] The ex-President began his letter by asserting his belief that the United States had the constitutional right to annex Texas. He then gave a history of the quesion and of his own attempt to purchase it while Secretary of State under Jackson.

---

[35] Benton, *Thirty Years' View*, II, 587.

[36] Wright to Van Buren, Washington, April 29, 1844, *Van Buren Papers.* ''Hammet was frightened,'' said Wright, ''and it was with some difficulty that we induced him to our proposition for publication, before he had read it; but he behaved well and himself and the Major remained at the Globe office until about midnight, to examine the proof.''

But, said he, as conditions are now, annexation would in all probability bring on a war with Mexico, and

could we hope to stand perfectly justified in the eyes of mankind for entering into it; more especially if its commencement is to be preceded by the appropriation to our own uses of the territory, the sovereignty of which is in dispute betwen two nations, one of which we are to join in the struggle?

He thought not, for "we have a character among the nations of the earth to maintain." He did not believe that there was danger of foreign interference in Texas or that nothing but immediate action could prevent Texas from being lost to the United States.[37]

On the very day that Van Buren penned his answer to Hammet, Cave Johnson sent him a letter from Washington.[38] He informed the ex-President that within two days the Texas treaty would be sent to the Senate, and, from all appearances, would be the controlling factor in the next Presidential election. For this reason he and other friends hoped that Van Buren would favor annexation, because "they hope such a position will not injure you in the North, whilst it must overwhelm Mr. Clay in the South if he hesitates or equivocates." In order to forestall intrigues to prevent his nomination, Johnson urged him to make his position known at the earliest possible date.[39] Johnson's warning, to be sure, came too late; on the other hand, it seems

---

[37] The letter was published in the Washington *Globe*, April 28, 1844.

[38] Whether Johnson had any knowledge of Hammet's letter to Van Buren, I am unable to say. If he had, Van Buren's long delay in answering probably induced him to write.

[39] "In the event of your being favorable to the treaty, I entreat you to take the earliest opportunity of giving your views—we have intrigues on hand here if practicable, to supersede you in the Baltimore Convention—and this question is one of the means used to arouse some of the Western & S Western members agt you—from a supposition that you are hostile to it—the delay of the Globe in coming out—your delay and the opinion of some of the N. Y. Democrats—all are urged & I fear with some effect among the members." Already, said he, some are expressing fears of Van Buren's "availability" and are talking of other candidates, such as Stewart, Dodge, and Cass. He is gratified to learn that Nicholson, who had headed the Cass movement in Tennessee, now says that Van Buren is the only man who can carry that state. Such, also, is the opinion of Governor Polk (Johnson to Van Buren, April 20, 1844, *Van Buren Papers*).

to show that he was sincerely desirous of Van Buren's nomination until the New Yorker had taken a position which would, in all probability, render his election impossible. The sincerity of Johnson's regret when Van Buren's opposition to annexation became known is expressed in a letter to Polk. ''Many of us are in rather low spirits today—his course gives great advantage to the discontents over us and they will make the most they can out of it.''[40] Two days later he reported that the excitement over Van Buren's letter was not abating, and that the friends of Texas had called a meeting at the capitol over which R. J. Walker had presided. They wanted another candidate—some were looking to Cass, others to Calhoun.[41]

Clay, who was then on a canvassing tour, reached Wahington in the latter part of April. While there his letter on the Texas question, dated at Raleigh on April 17, was given to the *National Intelligencer* for publication. He was decidedly opposed to annexation, because it would surely result in a war with Mexico. Even if Mexico should agree, he believed that it would be inexpedient to admit Texas into the Union.[42] Knowing that Van Buren, whom he supposed would be his opponent, did not favor annexation, Clay had not the ''smallest apprehension'' in stating his position.[43]

Inquiries were not limited to candidates for the Presidency. Late in March a nonpartisan, anti-Texas meeting assembled in Cincinnati and a committee of five, including Salmon P. Chase, drafted a letter to Polk asking his views on annexation. When the letter reached Columbia, Polk was on his farm in Mississippi,

---

[40] ''A serious & powerful effort,'' he continued, ''will be made to get a new nomination in which I think most of my democratic colleagues will unite, from the little I can learn. The discontents aré moving heaven and earth & will never stop until the Convention is over if they do so then.'' At present, he said, the desertion is toward Cass, but he does not believe that Cass will get the nomination (Johnson to Polk, April 28, 1844, *Polk Papers*).

[41] Johnson to Polk, April 30, 1844, *ibid.*

[42] *Nat. Intell.*, April 27, 1844.

[43] Clay to Crittenden, April 21, 1844, *Crittenden Papers.*

but as soon as he had reached home his reply to the committee was prepared without hesitation. It bore the date of April 23 and advocated unequivocally "immediate re-annexation."[44] Like Jackson in his letter to Brown, Polk emphasized the point that our original title to Texas had been valid beyond question and that the territory had unwisely been ceded to Spain. He conveniently ignored the fact that the cession had been made by those who possessed the constitutional authority to make it. And however unwise such an action may have been, it is difficult to see the bearing of this lack of wisdom on our subsequent right to re-annex the lost territory. On account of the danger that Texas might become a British colony, Polk maintained that all European countries should be excluded from both Texas and Oregon. "Let Texas be re-annexed," said he,

and the authority and laws of the United States be established and maintained within her limits, as also the Oregon Territory, and let the fixed policy of our government be not to permit Great Britain or any other foreign power to plant a colony or hold dominion over any portion of the people or territory of either.[45]

These remarks on colonization are not without interest, for they are a forerunner of what was later called the "Polk Doctrine."

Polk's letter was written only three days after that of Van Buren and of course without knowledge of its contents. Indeed, as late as May 4, after he had read Clay's anti-Texas letter, he expressed the hope and the belief that Van Buren would "now take ground for annexation."[46] The views which he expressed coincided with those held generally by Democrats in Tennessee. On the very day that Van Buren penned his indictment against annexation, an enthusiastic meeting of Democrats at Nashville

---

44 "I have no hesitation in declaring that I am in favor of the immediate re-annexation of Texas to the territory and government of the United States. I entertain no doubt as to the power or the expediency of the re-annexation."

45 MS, dated Columbia, April 23, 1844, *Polk Papers*. Printed in Washington *Globe*, May 6, 1844.

46 Polk to Johnson, May 4, 1844, "Polk Johnson Letters."

passed resolutions in favor of it by a unanimous vote.[47]   It is not
surprising, therefore, that Van Buren's letter had a ''prostrating
and cooling effect'' upon his supporters in that state or that many
who had stuck to him from a sense of duty should now feel relieved from further obligation.[48]   Individuals could express their
sentiments very freely to one another, but Laughlin, who for some
time had been sounding Van Buren's praises, was now in somewhat of a quandary.   As editor of the party organ, he must of
course make some comment.   On May 9, therefore, he pointed
out in an editorial that, while Clay's objections to annexation
were permanent, those of Van Buren were temporary—objections only until certain obstacles had been removed.   Laughlin
himself advocated immediate annexation, regardless of consequences; still, if a majority of Democrats should decide to wait,
he was ready to acquiesce.   This left the way open for continued
support of Van Buren.   Since taking charge of the *Union,*
Laughlin had been bitter in his assaults upon Clay.   The Whig
candidate had perjured himself by challenging Randolph to fight
a duel; he was guilty of Cilly's death, because he had written
the challenge for Graves; but neither crime was surprising in a
man who had ''defrauded Gen. Jackson out of the Presidency,
for an office worth $6000 per annum.''[49]

Before his treaty with Texas had been consummated, Tyler
seems to have given up hope that he might be nominated by the
Democrats.   His official organ indignantly denied the assertion
made by the *Globe* that he was knocking for admission to the
Baltimore convention; on the contrary, ''the friends of the Veto-
Administration intend having a Convention which will represent the Republican party more truly than Mr. Van Buren's

---

[47] Nashville *Union,* April 23, 1844.

[48] ''Indeed it has given a pretext for doing that which they have had
in their minds to do—to declare against V. B., and a considerable portion
of them will never be reconciled to him'' (Nicholson to Heiss, May 8, 1844,
''Heiss Papers'').

[49] Nashville *Union,* March 30, 1844.

Convention, and the nominee will be elected."[50]   Still, the President was ready to welcome assistance from any quarter, for in May his friend Fisk sounded Cave Johnson concerning Jackson's opinion of his administration, and at the same time Polk was being considered for the War Department or the British mission.[51]

Cass was the last of the aspirants to declare himself on the Texas question.  In response to a letter from Hannegan, he, too, came out for immediate annexation.[52]

On May 1, four days after Clay's Texas letter had appeared in print, the Whig convention assembled at Baltimore.  One day sufficed for nominating the candidates and adopting a platform. Without a dissenting voice, Clay was chosen for the first place, and on the third ballot, Frelinghuysen, of New Jersey, was selected as his running mate.  The platform was drawn to suit the candidate.  It avoided the Texas and bank questions and emphasized tariff, currency, distribution, and usurpation by the Executive.  With one omission—the bank question—Clay took his stand on the traditional Whig policies, and appealed to the people to sustain him.

While the Whigs rallied with enthusiasm to the standard of their chief, harmony within Democratic circles was rendered impossible by the appearance of the "lone star" on the political horizon.  The party which had long been distinguished for its effective discipline and its unity of action now appeared to be hopelessly divided on the eve of battle.  Even the great "chief" at the Hermitage seemed to be uncertain as to the proper plan of campaign.  His commands were ambiguous, for they resulted from conflicting emotions; he longed to see his old friend Van Buren nominated, but his desire for Texas was still stronger. Although few had a definite idea as to the best means of restoring harmony, as the time for the Baltimore convention approached

---

[50] *Madisonian,* April 3, 1844.

[51] Johnson to Polk, May 8, 1844, *Polk Papers.*

[52] His letter was dated at Detroit on May 10.  There is a copy in *Niles' Register,* May 25, 1844.

the conviction that Van Buren could not be elected became very widespread. The Virginia Democratic central committee, by resolution, released the delegates of that state from the obligation to obey their instructions, and delegates of other states announced publicly that they would not vote for Van Buren.[53]

Before the appearance of his Texas letter Van Buren had been accepted generally as the candidate; not because he enjoyed a wide popularity, but because a small minority urgently advocated his nomination and the rest of the party, being more indifferent than hostile, simply acquiesced, since they had no substitute to offer. After the publication of his Texas letter, his downfall was brought about by much the same process that had procured his elevation to party leadership. The few who were violently opposed to his nomination had little difficulty in convincing others, and especially the friends of Texas, that he could not possibly be elected. Those who had supported him from a sense of duty only, now had no hesitancy in transferring their allegiance to another candidate who would be more likely to win. Amos Kendall emphasized this point in a letter written to Van Buren. He told him frankly that he had no good news, and that unless some one else could be nominated at Baltimore the southern delegates would put up a third candidate. Kendall did not believe that the pro-Texas feeling was due to any organized movement, but rather to the "continued ding-dong sung in their ears" by a few of the most interested. Van Buren's letters, he said, had appeared at the worst possible time; the guns were being trained on Clay, and Van Buren appeared just in time to get the shot.[54]  Cave Johnson reported the political situation as apparently hopeless. Benton and the New Yorkers seemed to

---

[53] Many such details are given in *Niles' Reg.*, LXVI, 162–163.

[54] Kendall to Van Buren, May 13, 1844, *Van Buren Papers*. Hendrick B. Wright, of Pennsylvania, believed that Van Buren could not be nominated—and if nominated, could not be elected, and Wm. R. King, writing from New York, reported it to be generally admitted that the ex-President could not be elected (Wright to Buchanan, May 13; King to Buchanan, May 14, 1844, *Buchanan Papers*).

be determined not to yield; Calhoun and his supporters were equally uncompromising, while each faction claimed a majority of the convention. ''I see no hope,'' said Johnson, ''unless some man can be found disconnected with both these fragments of the democratic party & who will yield to the annexation of Texas.''[55] Polk, the man to whom this letter was written, fulfilled these requirements; and before the letter had reached its destination, his *availability* had already been discussed at the Hermitage.

The correspondence which passed between Democratic leaders in Tennessee about the middle of May shows an absence of definite plans for the future. On May 10 Donelson[56] summoned Polk to Nashville to consult with General Jackson and others in the hope that they might find some means of preventing a split in the party over the annexation question. ''I feel deeply mortified,'' said he,

that our wise men should differ so much; and particularly that a measure of such vast consequences should have been kept so long in the dark and precipitated with so much haste.

Donelson was fully aware that Jackson's indorsement of annexation would aid Tyler and Calhoun; and, apparently, although his letter is not very clear, he did not approve making Texas a leading issue.[57] Polk accepted the invitation and reached Nashville on the twelfth. On the following day he and General Armstrong repaired to the Hermitage. They were met on the road by Donelson, who was taking to Nashville for publication in the *Union* Jackson's well-known letter which appeared a few days later under date of May 13th. In it, Jackson insisted that Texas must be annexed.

---

[55] Johnson to Polk, May 12, 1844, *Polk Papers*.

[56] Gen. Armstrong and other politicians wrote, also.

[57] ''I am particularly anxious that the ground occupied by the Genl. should be thoroughly understood by you. What he may now say if not modified by disclosures recently made will produce important results. If the Texas question is urged as it doubtless will be by Tyler & Calhoun, and Genl. Jackson gives the weight of his name to sustain their views, making it a leading question in the South, the sooner we know it the better. Come and talk over the matter with the Genl. and our friends generally'' (Donelson to Polk, May 10, 1844, *Polk Papers*).

When reporting the interview to Cave Johnson,[58] Polk said that

He [Jackson] speaks most affectionately of *Mr. Van Buren,* but is compelled to separate from him upon this great question, and says both he and *Mr. Benton* have by their letters cut their own throats politically. He has no idea that *Mr. V. B.* can be nominated or if nominated that he can receive any Southern support.

Jackson said that the Baltimore convention must select some other candidate and that he should be from the Southwest; and Polk's letter hinted that the General had suggested that Polk himself ought to be placed at the head of the ticket. Polk asserted that he aspired to the second place only, but that his friends might use his name as they might see fit; in any event the party should unite on some "*one* candidate" and he must be in favor of annexation. "I have stood by *Mr. V. B.,*" he continued, "and will stand by him as long as there is hope, but I now despair of his election—even if he be nominated." In another letter written on the following day,[59] Polk was more explicit concerning Jackson's desire to substitute his name for that of Van Buren. The General remarked, said he, that writing the anti-Texas letter was the only vital error over committed by Van Buren; nevertheless, it would be fatal to his election.

He thinks the candidate for the Presidency should be an annexation man and reside in the Southwest, and he openly expresses (what I assure you I had never for a moment contemplated) the opinion that I would be the most available man; taking the Vice-Presidential candidate from the North. This I do not expect to be effected.

Polk thought it was more probable that some northern man would be nominated for first place, and himself for the second. If Van Buren should be withdrawn, his friends would doubtless control both nominations, therefore great pains should be taken to conciliate them. Nothing, said Polk, could prevent Clay's election except the harmonious selection of a candidate at Baltimore. In offering suggestions for bringing about such harmony

---

[58] Polk to Johnson, May 13, 1844, "Polk-Johnson Letters."

[59] Polk to Johnson, May 14, 1844, *ibid.*

he displayed that shrewedness and attention to detail which made him one of the most astute politicians of his time.[60]   Along with this went another letter to Johnson, marked ''Highly Confidential.''[61]   Johnson was authorized to show the first letter to Silas Wright, and we are not left in doubt as to the reason.

*Mr. Wright's* declaration to you, in the conversation which you detail in your letter of the 8th that I was ''the only man he thought the Northern Democrats would support if Van Buren was set aside, because I was known to be firm and *true* to the cause,'' is precisely the opinion which *Genl J.* expressed to me when I saw him two days ago.   The General had previously expressed the same thing to others.

He once more asserted that he had aspired to the second office only and had been loyal to Van Buren; but since the secret attack on the ex-President '' 'Fortune is in a frolic,' and . . . there is no telling what may happen.''   He recommended General Pillow to Johnson as a shrewd and reliable colleague in carrying out all plans.

In Jackson's letter of May 13 to the Nashville *Union,* in which he commented on Van Buren's Texas letter, the General said his old friend evidently was unaware that conditions had changed since he had been President.   No difference of opinion could change his confidence in Van Buren, but as to Texas, ''Let us

---

[60] ''I have but little hope that union or harmony can be restored among the members, but I have hope that the Delegates *'fresh from the people'*— who are not members of Congress—and have not been so much excited can be brought together.   Let a strong appeal be made to the Delegates as fast as they come in, *to take the matter into their own hands, to control and overrule their leaders at Washington, who have already produced such distraction, and thus save the party.*   The Delegates from a distance can alone do this.   I suggest as a practical plan to bring them to act,—to get one Delegate from each State who may be in attendance to meet in a room at Brown's hotel or somewhere else, and consult together to see if they cannot hit upon a plan to save the party.   If you will quietly and without announcing to the public what you are at, undertake this with energy and prosecute it with vigor, the plan is feasible and I think will succeed.   If the preliminary meeting of a Delegate from each State can agree upon *the* man, then let each one see the other Delegates from his own State, and report at an adjourned meeting the result.   This is the only way to secure efficient action when the Convention meets.''   The essential features of this plan were followed, and resulted in success.

[61] Polk to Johnson, May 17 [14], 1844, ''Polk-Johnson Letters.''

take it now and lock the door against future danger.''[62]  His complimentary remarks about Van Buren were much like an epitaph for a departed friend.  When he penned them he felt certain that his former protégé was doomed.  In a letter written on the following day he told Benjamin F. Butler that nothing could restore Van Buren except indorsement of annexation, for ''you might as well, it appears to me, attempt to turn the current of the Miss[iss]ippi as to turn the democracy from the annexation of Texas to the United States.''[63]

Texas must be annexed, and Van Buren must be dropped.  So much, at least, was settled; and if Polk could be substituted, so much the better.  The *Union* now began to prepare its readers for the change.  Laughlin had been chosen as a delegate to the Baltimore convention, and Heiss took charge during his absence.  On May 14, Heiss announced that Van Buren's name had been placed at the head of the political column because he was thought to be the choice of the Democracy.  It would be left there until some action had been taken by the convention, although the editor disagreed with his weak position on the Texas question.  On the 18th, Heiss declared further support of the New Yorker to be hopeless, and by the 23rd he was ready to hazard some ''guesses'' regarding the nomination.  The first was that Van Buren would come out for Texas or withdraw.  The second was that one from a suggested list would be selected as the candidate.  Heading the list was the name of Governor Polk,[64] but since Laughlin was a member of the pre-convention conference held at Nashville,

---

[62] This letter was dated May 13, and published in the Nashville *Union*, May 16, 1844.

[63] ''Clay's letter had prostrated him with the Whiggs in the South & West, and nine tenths of our population had decided in favour of Mr. V. Buren & annexation of Texas—when this, illfated letter made its appearance and fell upon the democracy like a thunderbolt'' (Jackson to Butler, May 14, 1844, *Van Buren Papers*. A full copy, also, in *Am. Hist. Rev.*, July, 1906, 833–834).  The letter was carried to Butler by Donelson.  Both men were delegates to the Baltimore convention.

[64] The others suggested were Calhoun, Cass, Stewart, Tyler, and Buchanan.

the ''guess'' regarding Polk required no great powers of divination.[65]  On May 28, Heiss made another significant statement in the *Union:*

We do not believe Mr. Van Buren will receive one vote from the Tennessee delegation.  If he does, that delegate who votes knowingly against the wishes of his constituents, will be marked, hereafter, as a man unworthy of their confidence.

Nearly all the delegates to the Democratic convention gathered in Washington on their way to Baltimore.  For what transpired there, we must rely mainly on letters written by Gideon Pillow.[66] Pillow and Laughlin reached Washington on May 21 and began a campaign of interviewing delegates to ascertain their views. Pillow represented Cave Johnson as being rather apathetic and without hope of success.  It is true that Johnson was inclined to see the dark side; but he was a shrewd politician and a personal acquaintance of most of the delegates, and it is probable that he exerted fully as much influence as either Pillow or Laughlin.[67]

Pillow reported the party to be hopelessly divided.  The insurgents declared that they would not attend the convention unless the two-thirds rule were agreed upon, and that they would not support Van Buren in any event.  The Van Burenites were equally insistent on a majority rule.[68]  The pro-Texas Democrats

---

[65] On June 4 the *National Intelligencer* quoted the guesses made by Heiss and remarked that the ''inference is irresistible'' that the arrangement for dropping Van Buren and bringing Polk forward was made in the neighborhood of Nashville.

[66] Pillow was both conceited and unprincipled; still, if allowance be made for his exaggeration of his own importance, his account is probably authentic.  His letters to Polk are among the *Polk Papers.*  Copies edited by Professor Reeves are accessible in the *Am. Hist. Rev.*, July, 1906, 835ff.

[67] In his letter of May 24, Pillow said: ''I saw your letter to C— J— and noted its suggestions.''  Evidently he refers to the letter to Cave Johnson, May 14, 1844.  See above.

[68] In a letter written from Washington to Van Buren, May 26, Wright said that the Texas men were plotting to defeat him by means of the two-thirds rule.  New Hampshire men were told, said he, that Woodbury would get the nomination in case Van Buren should be set aside; the Pennsylvanians were told the same with respect to Buchanan, and the Tennesseans with respect to Polk, *Van Buren Papers.*

tried to commit Polk's friends against Van Buren, but all except a few of the Tennessee delegates maintained a discreet silence on this subject. Two of them, Anderson and Jones, were bitterly opposed to the New Yorker and would not coöperate with their colleagues. Even Andrew Johnson was ready to sacrifice Polk in order to get rid of Van Buren. Pillow was satisfied that two-thirds of the delegates favored Polk for Vice-President; many expressed a preference for him as the candidate for President. No agreements were reached before leaving Washington, yet Pillow was quite certain that Van Buren would be forced to withdraw, and, if so, that his friends would never support Cass. On the other hand, he thought it probable that they would be willing to support Polk. If Polk should be brought forward, it must be done by the North, because it would never do for southerners to suggest his name.

The Democratic convention assembled in Baltimore on May 27, 1844. A large majority of the delegates had been instructed to vote for Van Buren by state conventions which had been held before the publication of his anti-Texas letter—in fact, before Texas had been seriously considered as a political issue. But Tyler and Calhoun had precipitated the question, and many who were bitter opponents of both of them were nevertheless in favor of annexation. Because Van Buren had taken his stand against annexation, many held that their instructions were no longer binding, for the conditions under which they had been framed had changed completely, and Van Buren no longer represented the will of the people. In a few cases, as in Virginia, steps were taken to annul the instructions. Some of the delegates from other states openly repudiated their instructions, and others went to Baltimore prepared to vote for Van Buren on the early ballots and then to use their own judgments. Benton, Welles, and other adherents of the ex-President have asserted that there was wholesale intriguing against their favorite. No doubt there was, but the widespread defection which preceded the convention was not wholly due to intrigue.

The convention selected as its chairman Hendrick B. Wright, of Pennsylvania, and as its secretary William F. Ritchie, whose father was editor of the Richmond *Enquirer*. The friends of Van Buren desired a majority nomination, but his opponents succeeded in adopting the two-thirds rule, which had been used on former occasions. The Van Burenites complained that the rule was now adopted for the purpose of defeating their favorite, but, although the charge was true, the majority merely followed the usual practice of Democratic conventions. In asking for a new rule the New Yorkers were requesting a personal favor for their candidate, which, under the circumstances, they had no right to expect. Van Buren himself had not been overscrupulous about accepting a nomination at the hands of Jackson's "made to order" convention. He had small reason to complain because the advantage was now with his opponents. On the first ballot he received a majority of the votes, but not the necessary two-thirds. In succeeding ballots his vote steadily decreased. After the seventh ballot had been taken, J. L. Miller, of Ohio, moved, by resolution, to declare Van Buren the party nominee, on the ground that he had, on the first ballot, carried a majority of the convention. Hickman, of Pennsylvania, caused much laughter by moving that General Jackson be nominated for President by a unanimous vote. Both motions were ruled to be out of order, and the convention adjourned for the day without having selected a candidate.

The evening of May 28, the second day of the convention, was a momentous one for Polk; and Pillow and George Bancroft are in substantial agreement as to what happened, except that each claims first honors in the transactions which took place. In a letter to Polk, in which he chronicled the events of the day, Pillow said: "I have within the last few minutes received a proposition from a leading Delegate of Pennsylvania and of Massachusetts to bring your name before the Convention for President." Pillow explained to them that if done at all this must be done by the North. "There is, I think a strong probability of your name ultimately coming up for President. I do not think it prudent to move in *that* matter now. I want the North to bring you forward as a *Compromise* of all interests."[69] The delegate from Massachusetts was evidently George Bancroft, for, in a letter to Polk, Bancroft said that after the convention had adjourned on the second day "it flashed on my mind, that it would be alone safe to rally on you."[70] Carrol and Hubbard, of the New Hampshire delegation, heartily agreed, and likewise Governor Morton, of Massachusetts.

I then went to your faithful friends Gen. Pillow and Donelson. They informed me that if we of N. E. would lead off, they would follow with Mississippi and Alabama. . . . Certain of this, I repaired with Gen. Donelson and Pillow to the house where were the delegates of Ohio and New York, and I spent the time till midnight in arguing with them.

Medary, of Ohio, was agreeable, and assured Bancroft that Ohio would go for Polk in preference to Cass. Kemble, of New York, also agreed to support Polk.

On the morning of the third day, May 29, Tibbatts, of Kentucky, withdrew the name of Richard M. Johnson and, as Pillow reported to Polk, "we brought your name before the Convention for the Presidency."[71] On the first ballot of the day, the eighth of the session, Polk received forty-four votes.[72] As soon as the

---

[69] Pillow to Polk, May 28, 1884 (*Am. Hist. Rev.*, July, 1906, 841).

[70] Bancroft to Polk, July 6, 1844 (Howe, *Life and Letters of George Bancroft*, I, 253). Years afterward Bancroft wrote a still more detailed account of his activities during that evening. He stated explicitly that "Polk owed his nomination by the Democratic Convention to me," and that "I was the one who of my own mind and choice, first, on the adjournment of the nominating convention, for the day, resolved to secure the nomination for Polk" (Bancroft to I. G. Harris, *Bancroft Papers*, Lenox Library; cited by Reeves in *Am. Hist. Rev.*, July, 1906, 841). Perhaps, without realizing it, Bancroft was inspired by Pillow and Laughlin to suggest Polk's nomination.

[71] Cave Johnson told Polk that John Kettlewell, of Baltimore, was "the man who first started your name in the Baltimore Convention" (Johnson to Polk, Jan. 11, 1845, *Polk Papers*).

[72] In his letter of the 29th to Polk Pillow said 42 votes, but the Baltimore *Sun* reported the vote as follows: Van Buren, 104; Cass, 114; Polk, 44; Buchanan, 2; and Calhoun, 2. Polk received 6 from N. H., 7 from Mass., 2 from Pa., 1 from Md., 9 from Ala., 6 from La., and the 13 votes of Tennessee.

result had been announced, Frazer, of Pennsylvania, stated that he had at first voted for Van Buren because he had been instructed to do so, and then for Buchanan as the favorite son of his state; but seeing that neither could be nominated, he had cast his vote for ''James K. Polk, the bosom friend of Gen. Jackson, and a pure, whole-hogged democrat, the known enemy of banks and distribution.'' His remarks were greeted with applause and several warm friends of Van Buren now announced that for similar reasons they were ready to unite upon Polk. Governor Hubbard, of New Hampshire, and General Howard, of Maryland, pleaded for Polk and harmony, and Medary pledged the vote of Ohio.[73] Roane took the Virginia delegation out for consultation and returned to announce that its vote would be transferred from Cass to Polk.[74] The ninth ballot had not proceeded far before it became evident that it would be the last. The Polk list became so large that Butler withdrew the name of Van Buren, and many who had supported other favorites now transferred their votes to the Tennessean. In this way his vote was made unanimous, and although South Carolina was not represented officially, Elmore and Pickens were present and pledged the support of their state to the new candidate. Silas Wright, of New York, a warm friend of Van Buren, was nominated for Vice-President; he declined the honor, and George M. Dallas was chosen in his stead.[75] A series of resolutions was adopted, one of which declared in favor of ''the re-occupation of Oregon and the re-annexation of Texas at the earliest practicable period.'' The committee on resolutions had considered the ''one term'' pledge which had been referred to it by the convention, but reported against such a restriction on the ground that it would

---

[73] Speaking of Bancroft's influence, Laughlin told Polk that ''he and old Morton'' were mainly responsible for wheeling the ''Yankee States'' into line (Laughlin to Polk, May 31, 1844, *Polk Papers*).

[74] Bancroft to Polk (Howe, *op. cit.*, I, 254).

[75] The above details, unless otherwise noted, have been taken from the report of the convention published in the Baltimore *Sun*, May 28–30, and *Niles' Register*, June 1, 1844.

be inconsistent to take such action after so many had been instructed to support Van Buren for a second term.

When notifying Polk of his nomination, Pillow[76] was inclined to take all the credit for bringing it about. To be sure, he very modestly said that "I had good help in some *true-men* in the North," but that he "got no help" from "our home people." On the other hand, Bancroft has made it clear that Donelson took a leading part in procuring votes for Polk, and it is unlikely that two such veteran politicians as Laughlin and Cave Johnson were entirely inactive. It appears that the knowledge of Jackson's preference for Polk was by no means confined to Tennesseans,[77] and it would be interesting to know in what degree this fact had a bearing on the ultimate choice of the convention.

From the above account it will be seen that Polk's nomination resulted from a combination of influences originally distinct. Seeing no hope of their own election, both Tyler and Calhoun were ready, for two reasons, to lend their support to the new candidate. In the first place, he believed as they did on the Texas question; in the second, so long as the office was beyond their own reach, they would rather see it go to a new man than to one of the competitors who had so roundly abused them. In the long run the Van Burenites were, for similar reasons, constrained to acquiesce in Polk's nomination and to contribute their support to his campaign. The Calhoun faction and the insurgent element led by R. J. Walker were enemies in other respects, but they agreed on annexation and therefore combined successfully to prevent the nomination of Van Buren. There is plenty of evidence that the Van Burenites had no love for Polk,

---

[76] His letter bore the date May 30, but obviously it was written on the 29th (*Am. Hist. Rev.*, July, 1906, 842).

[77] J. B. Jones, writing from Baltimore to his paper, the *Madisonian*, May 29, said: "It is true I hear it whispered about the streets, that the nomination of Mr. Polk was agreed upon at the Hermitage, Mr. B. F. Butler, in behalf of Mr. Van Buren and the *Globe*, concurring" (*Madisonian*, May 30, 1844).

yet their feeling toward him was indifference rather than hostility.  Though they were not strong enough to nominate their favorite, they could at least veto the nomination of an objectionable rival like Cass, and, within certain limits, could determine the choice of the candidate.  To Polk they had no specific objection; consequently, if all factions would agree to accept him, his nomination would be less objectionable than that of Cass or Buchanan.  Therefore they made a virtue of necessity and reluctantly transferred from Van Buren to Polk.  They claimed afterwards that they had been responsible for Polk's nomination, and this was true in the sense that they could have prevented it; still, under the circumstances, Polk had small reason to feel under obligation to men who, after all, had acquiesced in his nomination merely as a choice of evils.

Even before the appearance of his anti-Texas letter, Van Burean had little real popularity outside of a small circle of friends.  After its publication, his defeat at the polls being inevitable, his nomination would have meant party suicide.  This fact should have been obvious to his most ardent supporters, and yet they chose to regard his defeat at Baltimore as the result of a series of political intrigues.  They did not, of course, have all the information which is now accessible, consequently the motives of many of their contemporaries were misjudged.  Benton's version of Van Buren's downfall has already been noted; still more elaborate and equally erroneous is the version of Gideon Welles.

In a history of the contest which he prepared but never published,[78] Welles, like Benton, attributed the shelving of Van Buren to a many-sided intrigue in which Calhoun, originally, was the chief actor.[79]  In a "last desperate struggle for the

---

[78] MS article, "A Review of the Political History of the United States and Presidential Contests" (*Welles Papers*, Library of Congress).

[79] "If Mr. Calhoun was insatiable in his ambition, he was also fertile in his schemes to promote it.  They were often visionary and startling, so much so as to forfeit rather than beget general confidence, yet to those

presidency'' he brought forward the Texas question, and, when he entered Tyler's cabinet, he believed that the President would assist him. His main object, up to this time, according to Welles, was to make Van Buren's nomination impossible. But Tyler appropriated the Texas question and resolved to stand for reëlection; and while many Democrats were ready to espouse annexation, they would not rally to the standard of Calhoun. In other words, he had succeeded in weakening Van Buren, but had failed in the attempt to attract support for himself. Robert J. Walker, said Welles, was interested in the annexation of Texas because it offered an opportunity for land-scrip speculation. Working through Mason, Tyler's Secretary of the Navy, Walker had convinced the Richmond politicians that the surest means of defeating the aspirations of Calhoun was the nomination of some other pro-Texas Democrat. The preference of the Virginians, said Welles, was Levi Woodbury, but on arriving at Baltimore they found that New England would not support him.

Up to this point, with some modification as to Walker's motives, Welles's account is apparently accurate, but his statements concerning the promotion of Polk's interests are erroneous in detail and give an unfair impression of the attitude of the Tennessee politicians.

Although Calhoun had announced before the meeting of the convention that he would not permit his name to be presented, Welles believed that he still had hopes of being nominated and that they had been blasted by the nomination of Polk. After asserting that Polk was ''brought forward'' by the friends of Van Buren who, under the circumstances, would not support any of the other competitors, Welles then proceeds to tell how the Tennesseans under the leadership of Cave Johnson and Gideon

with whom he was intimate, or who were within the circle of his influence, there was a charm in his plans that was to the adventurous inviting. There were always some one or more prominent points in his intrigues that enlisted ardent supporters, and on these points he concentrated the energies of an intellect of unusual power, and pursued his object with an intensity that had no limits.''

Pillow had, for some time before the meeting of the convention, been playing a "deep and subtle game" to procure Polk's nomination. They "concealed their purpose from Genl Jackson who would give no countenance to the movement"[!]; they "fastened themselves on Wright and Benton as friends and partisans of Van Buren, which they were except in the contingency of securing Polk's nomination," betrayed their confidence and secretly intrigued against Van Buren.[80]

Many of the items in Welles's statement may be true enough, but in one of the main clauses the terms are inverted. He contends that the Tennesseans were ready to support Van Buren *unless* they could nominate Polk; whereas, they desired to nominate Polk *because* Van Buren's nomination, or his election at any rate, was no longer possible. Their efforts in Polk's behalf were made not only with Jackson's knowledge, but at his instigation. Under the circumstances, neither he nor they considered these efforts to be a betrayal of Van Buren. Surely Jackson had made it clear to both Van Buren and Butler, as well as to Benton, that he favored the nomination of some pro-Texas candidate. So successful, however, were the Tennessee delegates in their deception, according to Welles, that the friends of Van Buren "had no conception of the duplicity in that quarter" until all was over, and then they were forced to support the party nominee. The "reserve" of Wright and the "indignant resentment" of Benton were caused by the discovery of this "treachery." The New York Democrats worked loyally for the ticket, and "few knew what doubt & repugnance their strongest men entertained for the candidate"[!]

The New Yorkers were chagrined by the defeat of their favorite, and not knowing all the facts, it was natural for them to suspect the motives of those who had profited by their defeat.

---

[80] Welles admits that for two years the Tennesseans had been loyal to Van Buren while others were intriguing against him. He states that New Yorkers desired to associate Polk on the ticket with the ex-President, instead of R. M. Johnson. This is extremely improbable.

It was rumored at Baltimore that Polk's nomination had been agreed upon at the Hermitage, and Whig papers made assertions to this effect.[81]  In stating to Polk his reasons for declining the Vice-Presidential nomination, Wright said that the people of New York believed that there had been intrigue against Van Buren in the convention and that votes for Polk could be procured in the state only by asserting that the candidate had had nothing to do with the intrigue.[82]  Doubtless Wright shared the belief of his associates; but even if all of the charges against the insurgent element had been true, Van Buren's rejection had been brought about not so much by *intrigue* as by the application of the Democratic doctrine of majority rule.  To be sure, he received the votes of a majority of the convention, but the delegates had been selected before his views on Texas had become known; and although there is no means of ascertaining with certainty the desire of Democratic voters as a whole, there is ample reason for believing that a large majority of them did not prefer Van Buren after the publication of his anti-Texas letter.  From the first, Calhoun Democrats had been openly hostile, and those led by Walker, whom Welles had called the "chief engine" of the convention, made no attempt to conceal their unalterable opposition to Van Buren.  It is not easy to see why their efforts to defeat his nomination should be termed an *intrigue* any more than the efforts of his supporters to procure it.  Even "Old Hickory" did not hesitate to say that no anti-Texas man could possibly win, and surely he could not be accused of *plotting* against his old friend and protégé.  Naturally Polk's immediate friends did not confide

---

[81] "There is one circumstance, and only one," said the Nashville *Union* (June 11, 1844) in denying these charges, "which could impress any honest mind with the belief that General Jackson controlled the nomination—that circumstance is this: *the work is so well done, that to an honest mind, it looks reasonable that, it might have been done by old Hickory!*"

[82] Wright to Polk, June 2, 1844, *Polk Papers*. It has been said, continued Wright, that Van Buren was set aside because of his anti-Texas letter.  Better leave it so.  Had he (Wright), who held the same views, accepted the nomination on an annexation ticket, the people would have concluded that Van Buren had been dropped for some other reason.

their secret hopes to Wright or to Benton, and the realization of
these hopes was contingent on the defeat of Van Buren's nomination; but if this amounted to deception, it should be remembered that the ex-President's doom was sealed by the vote of 148
to 118 in favor of the two-thirds rule, and even if the Tennessee
delegates had joined with the minority, such action would not
have altered the result. Van Buren had always been indifferent
when Polk stood in need of assistance, consequently there was no
valid reason why the Tennesseans should continue to follow the
ex-President in his pursuit of a forlorn hope. On the first seven
ballots they voted for Cass, after which they transferred to Polk.

Irrespective of intrigues in his behalf, the selection of Polk
as the compromise candidate was quite natural, if not inevitable.
Apparently, a majority at least had come to Baltimore prepared
to support him for the second place. He was the only aspirant
who was not also a candidate for the Presidency, and for that
reason, objectionable to the different factions. The Van Burenites
would not support any of their hero's rivals, with the possible
exception of Colonel Johnson; and the other factions would never
consent to make Johnson the Presidential candidate. Some new
man must be selected; and of these, who had a better claim than
Polk's? As a member of Congress he had done valiant party
service, and had proved himself to be a man of ability and discretion. The statements made by Welles[83] that he "was destitute of
personal popularity" and especially that he had "no qualities to
recommend him" are gross exaggerations. Welles himself had
expressed a different opinion in 1844.[84] Even Horace Greely,
although he spoke disparagingly of Polk during the campaign,
had, in 1839, called him "one of the ablest men and most powerful

---

[83] Welles, *loc. cit.*

[84] In a letter written to Van Buren, Nov. 13, 1844, he asked whether
Polk would have sufficient energy and discernment to make the administration his own, and added that "my own belief is, that he will prove
himself worthy of being the choice of the democracy, after it could not
have its first choice" (*Van Buren Papers*).

speakers in the south west.''[85] General Jackson aptly summarized
Polk's qualifications for office when he wrote that

his capacity for business [is] great—and to extraordinary powers of labor,
both mental and physical, he unites that tact and judgment which are
requisite to the successful direction of such an office as that of Chief
Magistrate of a free people.[86]

Joseph Storey was ''thunderstruck'' by the selection made at
Baltimore; Governor Letcher exclaimed ''Polk! Great God, what
a nomination!'';[87] and the Whig journals predicted an easy victory. But the Democrats, in the public press and in private correspondence, gave abundant evidence of both satisfaction and
relief because a party crisis had been averted. Of course, due
allowance must be made for partisan zeal, and for a self-seeking
desire to stand well with the nominee. No doubt many professed
a friendship which they did not feel, and, in the hope of reward,
claimed to have been influential in procuring the nomination.[88]
Still, he was scarcely less *popular* than any of the other aspirants,
and as the campaign proceeded it came to be recognized generally
that the convention had chosen the leader who would be most
likely to win.

The *Spectator,* which was supposed to voice the sentiments
of Calhoun, while expressing surprise that Polk had been selected,
nevertheless approved the choice which had been made.[89]   Its

----

[85] *Biographical Annual,* 1841, p. 52. When quoting this the Washington
*Globe,* July 12, 1844, called attention to the fact that Clay lived in the
southwest.

[86] Letter dated June 24. Quoted by Nashville *Union,* Aug. 13, 1844.

[87] Story to McLean, Aug. 16, 1844, *McLean Papers.* Letcher to Buchanan, July 7, 1844, *Buchanan Papers.*

[88] ''If you were here,'' wrote Pillow, ''you would imagine yourself
the most popular man in the world, and you would be sure you *never had*
an enemy in the convention. You cannot know how much pains they take
to give in to me *their adhesion* to you, and to impress me with the *great
merit* of their *conduct.*'' ''Never,'' said Benton, ''was such a multitude
seen claiming the merit of Polk's nomination, and demanding the reward,
for having done what had been done before they heard of it'' (Pillow to
Polk, May 30 (29?), 1844, *Polk Papers;* Benton, *Thirty Years' View,* II,
594).

[89] *Spectator,* May 29, 1844.

editor, John Heart, announced his intention to publish a weekly journal, to be called ''Young Hickory'' in honor of Polk. Tyler was nominated by a convention of his own, but his letter of acceptance intimated that he might cease to be a candidate if Texas should be annexed by treaty or otherwise.[90]  Polk entered the canvass, therefore, supported by an apparently united Democracy, and with some prospect of eventual assistance from those who had recently unfurled to the breeze the banner of ''Tyler and Texas.''

[90] *Nat. Intell.*, May 31, 1844.  Several years later he hinted that his main object had been to force the Democrats to stand firmly for Texas (Tyler to Wise, Tyler, *Letters and Times of the Tylers*, II, 317).

CHAPTER XIII

## CAMPAIGN OF 1844

"Who is James K. Polk?" Such was the derisive query raised by the Whigs as soon as the result of the Democratic convention had been announced.[1] It was an effective campaign cry. More than argument could have done it attached to Polk the stigma of mediocrity and obscurity, and, to some extent at least, it appears to have influenced the opinion of later generations. But as it turned out this very cry recoiled as a boomerang upon those who hurled it, for this "obscure" person was soon to be known as the vanquisher of their own renowned "Prince Hal."

Justly or unjustly, both in 1844 and since that time, Clay has enjoyed the reputation of being a great man. On the other hand, Polk's opponents have rated him as a man possessed of scarcely second-class ability—a man whom accident alone had placed in an exalted position. Even his friends have usually been rather apologetic—not insisting that he was really a great man, but that he was more able than he has been represented to be by his adversaries.

The Whigs entered the campaign full of confidence in their standard bearer and delighted that the Democratic party had made the "blunder" of passing over a man of ability like Van Buren, and had as the *National Intelligencer* put it, *"let itself down"* to Polk. The Demcrats, on the contrary, while they rallied loyally to the ticket, were manifestly full of misgivings because one of the *prominent* men of the party had not been selected to

---

[1] Writing from Columbia, S. C., to Crittenden, Wm. C. Preston said: "The democrats here cry hurra for Polk in the street and come round to ask me who the devil he is" (undated letter in the *Crittenden Papers,* vol. 9).

enter the contest with Clay. Some of the newspapers, while admitting that Polk was not of the first rank, argued that great men and democracy were incompatible.

And yet, what is a great man, and by what standard is he measured? In his long career in the political field, Clay had been an opportunist, and, to a considerable degree, an adventurer. He had mounted one hobby after another in the hope of political advancement. There was little consistency in his record, for the panacea which he advocated on any particular occasion might differ radically in principle from the one offered only a year or two before. Many of the policies championed by Clay were visionary and impracticable, and few of them would now be considered sound. Furthermore, if greatness is to be rated by success, Clay's claim to it was not very well founded; for although he frequently succeeded in upsetting the plans of others, he was seldom successful in inaugurating his own most cherished policies. His greatest strength lay in his power of persuasion, and his greatest achievements were in compromising the divergent views of others and in procuring the adoption of measures after the compromise had been agreed upon.

Polk early adopted the fundamentals of the Jeffersonian creed. A conservative by nature, he was wary of experiments and shaped his course in accordance with the principles of the party which had been founded by his patron. His record, therefore, was consistent, and he could seldom be accused of trimming his sails to catch the varying winds of popular opinion. He was not a creator of issues, but his judgment on those which were presented was far sounder, as a rule, than that of his great opponent. With no pretense to oratory, he was an effective and convincing debater, while his thorough knowledge on public questions was conceded even by his foes. When he was nominated for the Presidency, he could point to a career of almost uniform successes, and as President few have had a more definite program to carry out or have succeeded so well in accomplishing their purposes. But in spite of all this Clay was conceded a place in the first rank of statesmen, while many, even of Polk's supporters, did not claim for their candidate more than second-rate ability. The *Democratic Review*,[2] although it denounced the methods by which Clay had achieved his fame, did not deny that in the popular mind Clay was rated higher than Polk, so it made the best of the situation by saying that ''our opponents are welcome to all their pride in their chief as a 'great man'—we are content with ours as a good one, and great enough for all practical purposes.''

At the time that the two men were nominated, it was natural enough that Clay should be heralded as the superior of his rival. It was a period that was dominated by great personalities, and spectacular qualities were regarded as essential attributes of greatness. The influence wielded by Clay, Webster, and Calhoun, resulted more from the eloquence of their delivery than from the soundness of their arguments. Even the tempestuous and generally illogical conduct of President Jackson was easily mistaken for statesmanship.

Polk was not possessed of spectacular qualities, and he never tried to cultivate them. He was by nature secretive, even sly,[3] and the degree of his influence in shaping public policies was known only to his intimate friends. In all of those qualities which are thought to make men *illustrious*, Polk suffered by comparison with his rival; but, as the *Review* pointed out, a Democratic candidate might succeed without possessing them, however essential they might be for the Whig.

In no other campaign has Democracy and Whiggery so definitely contested for victory; in no other campaign have the

---

[2] Article on ''First and Second Rate Men,'' August, 1844.

[3] For example, he made a practice of sending his Nashville correspondence under an extra cover, addressed to General Armstrong, so that his opponents, through the Whig postmaster, might not learn its final destination.

candidates so clearly represented the principles and policies of their respective parties.[4]

Polk was the first "dark horse" ever nominated for President by a political party, but while his name had not been previously associated with that office, it is not true that he was *unknown* or that his nomination was entirely accidental. The Baltimore convention did not simply make a grab in the dark, with the hope that either Providence or Fate would save the party from disaster. The man who, as chairman of the Committee of Ways and Means, had borne the brunt of the war against the Bank was unknown to neither party; a Speaker who was so thoroughly hated that his opponents had wished to deny him the customary vote of thanks could not have been so soon forgotten—least of all by the Whigs. He had never filled any of the great executive offices, but he had been intrusted by his party, during a most critical period, with the two most responsible positions in the lower house of Congress. No faction of his party doubted his ability, but like John Quincy Adams, his personal following was small. For personal reasons, many in the party may have preferred another candidate, but, if a certain newspaper story is to be credited, Clay, at least, recognized that the wisest choice had been made.[5]

---

[4] "The two candidates indeed, with a felicity of adaptation and correspondence, which is no mere accident, may be said in a remarkable manner to represent, respectively, the spirit and character of the two great parties by whom they have been chosen. . . . Mr. Clay is truly the living embodiment and incarnation of his party. Eloquent, showy, versatile, adroit, imperious, . . . the first Whig in America. A second-rate man in point of eloquence, intellectual force, and eminence of rank, would never have answered—could never have been adopted—as the head of such a party. We concede them this credit. They are naturally fond of splendor and strength—large and sweeping action—bold and brilliant energy and enterprise. Such is precisely the character their instinct has ever tended and striven to impress upon the government." Thus abbreviated, this characterization of Clay and his party is by no means an inaccurate description, and it is quite as true that Polk would "have been perfectly satisfactory to us for the presidency, even if he possessed in a far less degree than he has already amply proved, the further addition of the latter qualification [intellectual eminence], for the high office to which he is about to be called" (*Dem. Rev.*, August, 1844).

[5] "When the news of the democratic nomination reached Ashland, young Clay, who was impatiently waiting its announcement at the office,

Apparently the Democrats of all sections received the news of the nominations with genuine satisfaction—only in the Van Buren camp were there signs of resentment and reluctant support. They had not looked with favor on Polk's claim to the Vice-Presidency, and now he had beaten their patron in the race for first place. One of Catron's letters throws some interesting light on the attitude of political leaders toward Polk. It indicates also that, aside from the Texas question, Polk had profited by a desire on the part of the younger Democrats to get rid of the older leaders, by whom they had "been treated as boys." Together with others to be cited presently, this letter seems to make it plain that Polk's desire for a new party organ did not result from any bargain with Calhoun, but from a real distrust of the *Globe,* which of course was the organ of Van Buren.[6]

Polk's nomination was a victory for the annexationists, and it was also a victory for the younger element of the party. All factions were in duty bound to support the ticket, but it was evident from the first that "old fogies" must give way to those

---

hastened with the news to his father, who remained at home. 'Well, my son, who is nominated?' 'Guess, father.' 'Why Matty, of course.' 'No, father; guess again.' 'Cass?' 'No.' 'Buchanan?' 'No.' 'Then who the devil have they nominated?' 'James K. Polk,' said the son. The old man started from his seat, and rushing across the room, with disappointed hopes painted on his countenance, exclaimed, 'Beat again, by G-d' '' (N. Y. *Plebeian,* copied in the Washington *Globe,* Oct. 29, 1844).

[6] ''Mr. Van B.,'' said Catron, ''was out of luck—we again have it. Had the Dem. Con. met a month sooner, we w'd have been ruined in the west & South for ten years. Clay is out fully—many of the undermen are out, on annexation—and we have the strength added of a *rejection* of our V. P. on the precise ground, drawing in all the Calhoun strength— a vast, & controlling power, in the South. Among the leaders, you have many jealousies to quiet; they feared to see you on any ticket as vice, for fear you would set up for chief, after the first success. My position has let me into the deepest recesses of these things. I traversed the city night after night, last winter, encountering and *pledging* myself to the contrary of this opinion: But, sir, I made no converts, as I then believed. Buchanan was for Johnson—Benton for King; the Van B. men for either, sooner than yourself'' [Both Calhoun and Tyler friendly to Polk]. ''The coarse brutality of the Globe, was loathed last winter, by a large majority of our party.'' . . . ''Your strength lies mainly as I think in this; you are of the present generation—the old leaders are thrown off; to do this has been an ardent wish by nineteen in twenty of our party in the House

who were abreast of the times. Old in years, but young in spirit, Jackson gave his enthusiastic support to both platform and candidates;[7] nevertheless, even his wishes went unheeded in cases where he desired to restore any of the "old guard" to power.

Within a few days after Polk's nomination, his Tennessee friends in Washington began to formulate plans, not only for the campaign, but for his course as President of the United States. The most active—not to say presumptuous—of all was A. V. Brown, who did not hesitate to draft a list of instructions for the guidance of the candidate. First of all Polk was told that he *must,* in his letter of acceptance, commit himself to a one-term policy.[8] The Democratic platform had said nothing on this point, but it was evidently thought necessary to checkmate the Whigs, whose platform had limited their candidate to a single term. Besides, as Brown seems very clearly to intimate, other "deserving Democrats"[9] with high aspirations might be expected to support the campaign with more enthusiasm if they could be assured that the way would be open for them at the end of four

---

R. for two sessions—but they would not do it, as they believed—not as I believed. They are now gone" (Catron to Polk, June 8, [1844], *Polk Papers*).

[7] "Although I regret losing Mr. V. B. and the cause, yet I rejoice that the Convention have made choice of those worthy Democrats, Polk and Dallas. They are the strongest and best selection that could have been made" (Jackson to Gen. Planché, June 14, 1844, *Polk Papers*. Same to W. G. Reeves *et al.*, June 5, 1844, Wash. *Globe*, June 28, 1844). Polk doubted that the Planché (often spelled Plauche) letter was intended for publication, and thought it imprudent in Planché to publish it. He feared the cry of "dictation" (Polk to Donelson, July 11, 1844, "Polk-Donelson Letters").

[8] "In your acceptance you must some way or other express yourself in favor of the one term system. This is important—I might say all important—you will know exactly *how* it will be highly useful. The thing is right *per se* & under all the circumstances I think you ought not to *hesitate* to do it" (Brown to Polk, May 30, 1844, *Polk Papers*).

[9] Laughlin, although not without some doubt as to the wisdom of such a declaration, thought that "perhaps all in all it may be best—and will be making assurance doubly sure, and put us on an equality with the Whigs on that question" (Laughlin to Polk, May 31, 1844, *Polk Papers*).

years. Although Brown's suggestion may have been entirely superfluous, the one-term pledge found a place in Polk's letter of acceptance.[10]

The next instruction was for Polk to prepare data on his life and career for Brown to turn over to Bancroft, Kendall, or some other person who would incorporate it into a biography.[11] Another thing to be considered, said Brown, was whether the *Globe* was to be continued as "the Polk organ"; and while he was not yet certain that it should not be so continued, it is apparent that the discarding of that paper was already being discussed.[12]

Cave Johnson, as well as Brown and Catron, distrusted the *Globe*,[13] but he by no means believed in courting the favor of or permitting the domination by the southern wing of the party. On June 1 he wrote to Polk that the party was more united than at any time since the election of Jackson, but he pointed out that danger might result from the fact that the South had been zealous in procuring Polk's nomination. The *Globe,* he said, is noncommittal, and is already expressing doubts of Democratic success— a new paper of unquestioned loyalty is very much needed. Two weeks later he wrote that matters are growing worse and must soon come to a head. "The struggle now is by a few Southern men to appropriate *you* & the nomination to their exclusive benefit whilst the northern Democrats are determined to yield no such

[10] In 1835 Polk had, on the floor of the House, advocated a single term for all Presidents (*Cong. Globe*, 23 Cong., 2 sess., part 2, 292).

[11] Brown had asked Laughlin to write the biography and it was he in turn who had suggested Bancroft (Laughlin to Polk, May 31, 1844, *Polk Papers*).

[12] "Much is said here by *some* as to continuing the Globe as the Polk organ—this we will manage with sound discretion. The Globe will change its tone & perhaps take back much that it has said & go in *warmly* if not heartily—if so—well. But we will not commit ourselves to it *after* the election."

[13] "Benton & the Globe falls in but not with so good a grace as we expected" (Johnson to Polk, May 31, 1844, *Polk Papers*). He referred to an editorial of the 29th in which Blair had said that the nomination of Polk would at first be received with disappointment by those who had stood for favorites, but that a little reflection would convince all that it was for the best.

thing.'' Johnson had called a caucus in the hope of compromising differences, but the northern men became alarmed for fear the Calhoun members would get control; and Johnson decided that the best thing he could do was to prevent *anything* from being done.

> I have been to see S. W. Jr. [Silas Wright] hoping to have it controled in some way & ended—he is furious and I think determined to push C[alhoun] and his clique to the wall or finish—in this battle. The object *of both* will be to make us take sides—the Northern know, that you have always been with them, whilst the South think that the question & the position of Genl J[ackson] will take you with them—how both are to be kept I cannot see—already we have much secret talk of upsetting the Globe—turning Benton overboard &c. I was disgusted to day, even Reuben Whitney talked of turning Benton out of the Democratic church. I am sick of this state of things & see no means of avoiding the explosion & most anxious to leave here.[14]

Johnson's fears increased rather than abated, for a few days later he expressed a belief that the combined obstinacy of Benton and the South Carolinians would lead to a southern movement that might imperil not only the Democratic party but the Union itself.[15] It seems very evident that Johnson had entered into no

---

[14] Johnson to Polk, June 13, 1844, *Polk Papers.*

[15] He has seen, he said, many prominent Democrats and all are pleased with the nominations, but ''the only difficulty I fear arises from the course of T. H. Benton, when connected with the movements of S. C. The latter uses *immediate annexation* for the purpose of uniting the South and killing T. H. B. & will if practicable *identify you* & Genl J. with all their future movements—fears are entertained in the North, that this *may be so*—& if any incident takes place to confirm the suspicion, our cause is jeoparded. I have given every assurance to S. W. Jr. & a few others that you could not be induced to separate yourself from the Northern Democracy—instanced your former course, in the case of White &c &c and also thought it impossible that Genl J. should lend himself to any such purpose. The only danger of the latter taking any step to favor the Southern movement they think will arise, from some letter from him, that will seem to favor the movement without sufficiently weighing the consequences.

''Can not you see him & have a free conversation as to the Southern movement & put him on his guard?'' Johnson fears that there will be a southern convention called to meet at Nashville, and advises that this should be forestalled by an earlier meeting to which Wright and other northern men should be invited. ''I have the most serious apprehensions from the Southern movement not only to our cause but the country. Mason & Dickson's line now divides the Methodist church & will soon

agreement with southern delegates to procure Polk's nomination, and it is equally clear that he had no desire to see the party brought under southern domination. He desired harmony, to be sure, and support from all factions, but harmony that would leave Polk indebted to neither section—free and unhampered in shaping his own course. Polk's replies show that he fully agreed with the views expressed by Johnson. He promptly warned General Jackson and took other steps to forestall a sectional convention; ''no countenance must be given to any attempt should it be made.''[16]  A few days later he asked Donelson to prepare an article on this subject for the Nashville *Union*.  ''The idea,'' said he, ''of a Southern convention or a sectional meeting at Nashville or elsewhere *must not for a moment be entertained.''*  He did not believe it to be necessary to allude specifically to disunion sentiments in South Carolina, but

> Let the article strongly enforce the leading idea, that a meeting of the masses from all sections of the Union is what is intended, and let every thing giving it the appearance of a sectional or Southern affair be expressly negatived.  This would have the effect of allaying the fears of the North, by satisfying them that we in Tennessee gave no countenance to the suggestion for a Southern Convention upon the Texas or any other subject.[17]

While Johnson was warning Polk against the southern wing of the party, Catron was exhorting him not to listen to those who insisted that the salvation of Democracy depended upon the restoration to office of the old guard that had been ousted by Harrison, ''cabinet & all,'' leaving no place for the rank and file whose money and talents would be responsible for the victory. ''You who fought in the very van,'' said Catron,

---

divide the other churches.  This movement will tend to divide political parties by it.  The Texas question brings into the contest the fanaticism of the North with increased fervor.  Our only safety for the country & our cause depends upon the Southern Democracy maintaining the position we have hitherto occupied—firm & consistent friends of the Northern Democracy—yielding much for conciliation & harmony'' (Johnson to Polk, Louisville, June 21, 1844, *Polk Papers*).

[16] Polk to Johnson, June 21 [?], 1844, July 1, 1844, ''Polk-Johnson Letters,'' *Tenn. Hist. Mag.*, Sept., 1915, 245–246).

[17] Polk to Donelson, June 26, 1844, ''Polk-Donelson Letters.''

and who the worthy old gentlemen thought last winter, had died in the *ditch*, have been brought out alive, not by their consent, nor help, but [by] those who look to chances for themselves. ''Treason & Traitor,'' ''rotten to the core,''—have been the gentle epithets that have greeted every move tending to wrench the power, as a party, from the old clique. Mr. Van Buren thought this public opinion, if Col. Benton let him think at all, which I doubt.[18]

Like Johnson, Catron warned Polk against unnecessarily expressing his views, and, as he had ''a soul to be *saved*,'' he should avoid answering letters of the Sherrod Williams type.[19]

Benton had written a letter in which he had exonerated Polk and Dallas from any part in the ''intrigue which had nullified the choice of the people,''[20] but on June 13 he openly accused A. V. Brown of having ''vicariously'' procured from Jackson the letter in favor of annexing Texas.[21] While General Jackson was charitable enough to attribute Benton's outbursts to insanity, caused by the Princeton disaster,[22] others knew that he was simply expressing what Van Burenites generally were thinking; and, although the appearance of harmony prevailed during the campaign, mutual distrust was manifest in private correspondence,[23] and a break was almost inevitable as soon as the election had been held.

In general, the Democratic press of all sections and factions rallied to the support of the candidates without reservation or

---

[18] Catron to Polk, June 10, [1844], *Polk Papers*.

[19] In 1836 Williams had catechised Van Buren, Harrison, and White as to their opinions on certain campaign isues. See Shepard, *Martin Van Buren*, 264.

[20] Dated June 3. *Nat. Intell.*, July 1, 1844; Benton, *Thirty Years' View*, II, 595.

[21] ''A card,'' printed in the Wash. *Globe*, June 13, 1844.

[22] ''Gen. Jackson was a good deal excited at Benton's course—said 'he shall hear from *me* soon'; and asserts that ever since the explosion of the big gun Benton has not been in his right mind. I think so too'' (J. Geo. Harris to Bancroft, June 25, 1844, *Polk Papers*).

[23] For example, Sacfield Maclin, of Tennessee, wrote from Little Rock, Arkansas, to Polk, on June 14, that ''Colo Benton and the Globe for the last eighteen months have done our party more damage than all the Whig papers in the Union. I have no doubt, and our friends here believe with me, that if Colo Benton thought he could hold his place in the affections of the Democratic party, and go against you, he would do so with all his energy'' (*Polk Papers*).

qualification. Most enthusiastic and influential of all, perhaps, was the Richmond *Enquirer*,[24] but Calhoun's Washington organ was hardly less effusive in its praise.[25]

Cass bore his defeat with better grace than any of the other aspirants. At a ratification meeting held in Detroit he commended the action of the Baltimore convention and promised his support. He spoke of Polk as a man who would follow in the footsteps of Washington, Jefferson, Madison, and Jackson, a statement which caused the Charleston *Courier* to remark that Polk, in order to do this, would have to "walk all sorts of ways."[26] He took an active part in the campaign[27] and spent his energies freely in preaching the Texas gospel in a northern latitude.

Polk's letter accepting the nomination bore the date of June 12, 1844. In it the most significant phrase, aside from approval of the Baltimore platform, was that

I deem the present to be a proper occasion to declare, that if the nomination made by the convention shall be confirmed by the people, I shall enter upon the discharge of the high and solemn duties of the office with the settled purpose of not being a candidate for reëlection.

This self-denying declaration resulted evidently, as we have noted, from an effort to checkmate the Whigs and a desire to

---

[24] "Mr. Polk's nomination has been received at Baltimore, at Washington, and at Richmond, with enthusiasm. It heals all divisions, unites our party with bands of iron. It thwarts every hope the Whigs had indulged of discord and divisions. It blasts the election of Mr. Clay, and saves our country from the sceptre of the dictator. Mr. Polk is true to all our republican principles, and he is the friend of Texas." Quoted by Nashville *Union*, June 11, 1844.

[25] "The great mass of the people wantd a man pure in morals, sound in political principles, *and in favor of the immediate annexation of Texas,* and such they have in James K. Polk. He is a consistent and sound politician, of the Jeffersonian Democratic school; talented, firm and discreet" (Washington *Spectator*, May 29, 1844).

[26] Quoted in *Nat. Intell.*, June 24, 1844.

[27] Geo. N. Sanders to Polk, July 12; Austin E. Wing to Polk, Aug. 2, 1844, *Polk Papers*.

harmonize factional discords in Democratic ranks. ''I said nothing to commit the party upon the *one term* principle,'' he told Cave Johnson, ''but expressed simply my own determination.''[28]

The pro-Texas Democrats may be said to have included three fairly well defined groups. The first was made up of the followers of Calhoun whose interest centered mainly in promoting his advancement. The second comprised those who were not friends of Calhoun, but who were interested primarily in wresting the control of the party from the hands of the older leaders. They saw in the Texas question a possible means of accomplishing this purpose; and, in addition, annexation would enlist southern sympathies and place the party reins in southern hands. Some of them were accused, and perhaps not unjustly, of being influenced by prospective profits from Texas land scrip. The third group was composed of men like Cave Johnson, and apparently Polk, who favored annexation but who, at the same time, did not desire southern domination. They wished above all things to harmonize differences which were threatening to disrupt the party, if not the Union itself. The second group was most active in the nominating convention, and Robert J. Walker, of Mississippi, was its reputed head. Catron and A. V. Brown were close friends of Polk but, unlike Cave Johnson, they had strong leanings toward the southern groups. Walker had long been interested in Texas. During Jackson's administration he had worked hard for the recognition of the new republic. In February, 1844, he had written a long letter in which many reasons were assigned why Texas should be annexed.[29] It was alleged by his opponents that he was influenced by the hope of profit from land speculations, but undoubtedly this personal motive was greatly exaggerated.

---

[28] Polk to Johnson, June 21 [?], 1844, ''Polk-Johnson Letters,'' *Tenn. Hist. Mag.*, Sept., 1915, 245.

[29] For an excellent summary, see Smith, *Annexation of Texas*, 140–144.

The annexation of Texas was not the only question on which the Democrats of 1844 were unable to agree. For a time considerable anxiety was felt for fear that Polk's well-known views on tariff might cost him votes in northern states, particularly in Pennsylvania. The discussion of Polk's views on this subject was precipitated by the so-called Irvin-Hardin correspondence. Shortly after Polk's nomination James Irvin, of Pennsylvania, had addressed a letter to John J. Hardin, of Illinois,[30] asking about the candidate's opinions on tariff. Hardin replied that Polk was a believer in free trade. As soon as Polk read the letters in the papers, he asserted that, although the second letter had been signed by Hardin, it must have been written by Milton Brown, a member of Congress from Tennessee. He asked that the "trick" be exposed.[31]

Walker undertook to instruct the nominee as to the stand he should take on this perplexing subject, and also as to the proper treatment of Democrats who had left the party in 1840. He suggested that Polk should make it known that he would welcome "all Jacksonian Democrats." On the tariff he was to declare for a revenue basis, adjusted in such a manner as to give "incidental aid" and a "reasonable profit" to every branch of domestic industries. He urged especially that the word *aid* should be used instead of *protection.*[32] But before Walker's letter had left Washington, Polk had already announced his views on the tariff in a letter to J. K. Kane, of Philadelphia. When he penned his "Kane letter," Polk had not of course read Walker's suggestions, but their ideas were practically identical and even the phraseology of their letters was very much the same. More straightforward than Walker, however, and less southern in his leanings, Polk did not sugar-coat incidental protection by calling

---

[30] Both men were members of Congress. Their letters, dated May 30, 1844, are printed in *Niles' Reg.*, LXVI, 234.

[31] Polk to Johnson, June 8, 1844, "Polk-Johnson Letters."

[32] Walker to Polk, June 18, 1844, *Polk Papers.*

it an "aid."[33]  It was said at the time that Polk in drafting his letter made a definite attempt to face both ways—that his emphasis on incidental protection was for the North, while the substance was for the South.  But if the tariff Democrats were in any sense deluded it must have resulted from a meaning which they had read into the letter, for, as Polk had pointed out in the letter itself, his present views were to be found in his own record, the record of his party, and the declarations that had been adopted at the Baltimore convention.  In such a statement there was nothing equivocal—nothing to which a protectionist had reason to pin his hopes.  "On all great questions," wrote General Jackson in a letter commending Polk, "from the Panama mission to the present day, he has been consistent, orthodox, and true to the standards of old-fashioned Jeffersonian democracy";[34] and the Kane letter promised no departure from such a course.  To an intimate friend Polk wrote that his letter had been sent to Kane

with a request that he would show it to *Mr. Dallas* and *Mr. Horn,* and if in their judgment, it was absolutely necessary, they were at liberty to publish it, but not otherwise.  It was but a re-declaration of the opinions upon which I have acted on that subject; it was carefully prepared and upon its doctrines I am ready to stand.[35]

---

[33] "I am," said Polk, "in favor of a tariff for revenue, such a one as will yield a sufficient amount to the Treasury to defray the expenses of the Government economically administered.  In adjusting the details of a revenue tariff, I have heretofore sanctioned such moderate discriminating duties, as would produce the amount of revenue needed, and at the same time afford reasonable incidental protection to our home industries.  I am opposed to a tariff for protection *merely,* and not for revenue."  [Cites his votes on tariff bills.]  "In my judgment, it is the duty of the Government, to extend as far as it may be practicable to do so, by its revenue laws & all other means within its power, fair and just protection to all the great interests of the whole Union, embracing agriculture, commerce and navigation" (Polk to Hon. J. K. Kane, June 19, 1844; copy of original in *Polk Papers;* printed copies in newspapers).

[34] Jackson to M. M. Jones, Utica, N. Y., June 25, 1844, Wash. *Globe,* July 20, 1844.

[35] Polk to Johnson, June 21 [?], 1844, "Polk-Johnson Letters."

Shortly after the adjournment of the Democratic convention the Senate took a vote on Tyler's treaty of annexation. Instead of the two-thirds in its favor which the President had promised the Texan diplomats, more than two-thirds (35 to 16) voted to reject it. Many who were not averse to annexation voted against the treaty, for they resented the manner of its negotiation and despised the renegade President and his Secretary of State. Tyler's friends tried to cast the blame for ill feeling on Calhoun and his Pakenham correspondence, while Calhoun regretted that the question had been brought forward under such a weak administration.[36] In the Senate, Benton now introduced a bill of his own for annexing Texas whenever Mexico should be ready to acquiesce, while McDuffie presented a joint resolution which would require simply a majority vote of both houses of Congress. Both failed, and without taking further action Congress adjourned on June 17, to await the result of the pending campaign.

When, on May 1, Clay was nominated at Baltimore, all signs seemed to augur success for the Whigs. The party was united and the choice of the candidate was unanimous. Tyler's annexation treaty had caused some annoyance to be sure, but by his "masterly" Raleigh letter Clay was thought to have made his own position unassailable. Besides, it did not appear that Texas would be an important issue, for Van Buren, whose nomination by the Democrats seemed a foregone conclusion, had also taken a stand against immediate annexation. Although Van Buren's nomination was fully expected, it was known that many Democrats had set their hearts on procuring Texas, consequently division and weakness appeared to be the inevitable result.

At first it did not seem that Polk's nomination had solved the difficulties which had confronted the Democrats, for despite the professions of harmony it was well known that Benton, Van

---

[36] Schouler, *Hist. of the U. S.*, IV, 470.

Buren, and their followers were dissatisfied with, if not indeed hostile to, their party. Tyler had been nominated on an annexation ticket, barring any accessions from Democrats who with him had deserted to the Whigs in 1840. His official organ even insisted that Polk should decline the nomination in favor of the man who had been responsible for bringing the Texas question forward.[37]

The Democrats had trouble in plenty, but the Whig program was likewise going awry. Van Buren had not been nominated as they had expected, and Clay's Raleigh letter, instead of settling the Texas question, bid fair to cost him many northern votes. In August, 1843, the Liberty party had nominated James G. Birney, of Michigan, on an anti-slavery ticket, and, after the publication of Clay's letter, many who under ordinary circumstances would have voted for him now announced their intention to support the Liberty candidate. Although Clay was a slaveholder and did not oppose the annexation of Texas with the consent of Mexico, still the Whigs had, originally, no reason to believe that the Liberty Party would be more hostile to him than to the Democratic candidate, who was likewise a slaveholder and, in addition, an advocate of immediate annexation. Nevertheless the unexpected happened, for on the stump Birney avowed a preference for Polk, arguing that Clay's superior ability, coupled with his equivocal attitude, made him the more dangerous and objectionable of the two.[38]

The Raleigh letter was denounced even more bitterly in the South, and, as will appear later, it was defection in this quarter which caused the candidate most alarm. No wonder that a leading Whig declared the Texas question to be ''an enigma and

---

[37] ''Mr. Polk is too wise a man to suffer the Blairs and Kendalls to set him up as a mark for the shafts of the Whigs . . . to enter the contest, with Mr. Tyler already in the field, and with the certainty of an overwhelming defeat awaiting him'' (The *Madisonian*, June 1, 1844).

[38] Schouler, *Hist. of the U. S.*, IV, 475; Smith, *Annex. of Tex.*, 306, 308.

a puzzle to the most astute,''[39] for the most ardent advocates of annexation would lose, economically, by its consummation, while the opponents of annexation, for the sake of *principle,* were indirectly aiding Polk.

After Congress had adjourned, all parties were free to devote their energies to the campaign. The Democrats fully realized that the contest would be close, that defection must be prevented, and new recruits gained. Benton and the *Globe* must be whipped into line, and if possible, Tyler must be made to withdraw in favor of Polk. No one was in a better position than Old Hickory to perform this valuable service, and no one was more ready to undertake the difficult task. Jackson was much excited by Benton's heated reply to McDuffie while discussing his own annexation bill, and still more so by the report that his old friend had solicited the coöperation of John Quincy Adams.[40] His irritation was increased because Benton had not been convinced by a letter he had sent him stating that the Union could not be preserved except by annexing Texas and extending the laws of the United States over Oregon. He was certain that Benton had induced Van Buren to declare against annexation. He called Blair's attention to Polk's one-term pledge, and prophesied that Van Buren would succeed Polk if he should take the proper course. ''My dear friend,'' he pleaded with Blair, ''permit not Col. Benton to have controle over your

---

[39] Chas. A. Davis to Crittenden, New York, June 5, 1844, *Crittenden Papers.* It was a curious fact, said Davis, that on two important questions party considerations had made people in the South and West blind to their own interests; they had crushed the bank and thereby driven much needed capital back to the North and East, and were now clamoring for Texas, although the other sections would profit more by its annexation.

[40] Jackson to Blair (*confidential*), June 25, 1844, *Jackson Papers.* ''The last Washington papers give an account of the very irrated reply of Col. Benton to Mr. McDuffie on Benton's annexation Bill in the Senate after which Col. Benton seized J. Q. Adams by the hand & said 'we are both old men, we must now unite & save the constitution'—do my dear Mr. Blair inform me if this can be true—if it is, I want no better proof of his derangement, & it political[ly] prostrates him.''

editorial column, as he will ruin y^r paper. If he will, he must pursue his eratic course, which has, & will political[ly] destroy him if not already done.'' Blair assured Jackson that Benton was zealous in the cause of Polk and Dallas, but that he distrusted Calhoun and opposed his program of Texas with or without the Union. These views were shared by Blair himself. Jackson wrote again to Blair on July 12, criticizing Benton's attitude and urging Blair to attend the ratification meeting to be held at Nashville on the fifteenth of August.[41]

Before Jackson had received his reply from Blair he expressed his opinion of Benton in a letter to Polk.[42] Benton's hatred of Calhoun and his jealousy of the growing popularity of Tyler, said Jackson, had deranged him, but

you will perceive I have estopped Benton or any others from believing that you or I could countenance nullification or disunion. Every letter I get gives us joyfull news—You will get 20 states at least & your one term [pledge] will get you 22.

He told Polk that, while it was quite unnecessary for Cave Johnson to put him on his guard lest he should inadvertently give aid to the nullifiers, still every Democrat should ''put his face against any meeting of *disunion,* or nullification—we must & will have Texas, with & in our *glorious Union.* The Federal Union must be preserved—A. J.''[43]

---

[41] Blair to Jackson, July 7; Jackson to Blair, July 12, 1844, *Jackson Papers.* The ''Texas, with or without the Union,'' program mentioned by Benton was an attempt made in South Carolina, while Tyler's treaty was before the Senate, to call a southern convention and annex Texas to the southern states if it should be rejected by the federal government. See Benton, *Thirty Years' View,* II, 616.

[42] Jackson to Polk, June 29, 1844, *Polk Papers.* ''In my reply to Col. Benton's first letter to me in which he adverted to my toast,—'The Federal Union must be preserved,' amongst other things, I said to him, *The Federal Union must be preserved,* and to do this effectually & permanently—Texas must be reunited to the United States—the laws of the Union extended forthwith over the Oragon, which would place this Federal Union on as permanent basses as the Rocky mountains, and preserve our glorious Union, & our Republican system as long as time lasted.''

[43] *Ibid.*

Johnson was still much concerned for fear that something
might be said or done at the Nashville meeting which might
be construed as an approval of the South Carolina program of
"annexation or a dissolution of the Union." Doubtless he exaggerated both the strength and the determination of the disunion
element. So far as the success of the campaign was concerned,
much more was to be feared from the attitude of Benton, whose
irascible temper could not be held in check. He did not hesitate
to discuss, even with Whigs,[44] the "villany" of the Baltimore
convention, and no plea for harmony could induce him to abate
his attacks on those who had been responsible for reviving the
Texas question. To be sure he had, in a public declaration
exonerated Polk and Dallas from participation in the "intrigue,"
but in a speech made at St. Louis he said that the Texas question
had been "exploded" only forty days before the Baltimore
convention—"just time enough for candidates to be interrogated,
and for the novices to amend their answers."[45] Polk was evidently the novice whom he had in mind.

As the campaign progressed Polk came more and more to
distrust both Benton and Blair. "Since the nominations," he
said in a letter to Donelson,

none can fail to have observed the *coldness* or indifference of the Globe.
After *Blair's* professions made confidentially to you, I had expected that
he would come zealously into the support of the nominations, and not
throw cold water upon them.

After quoting a letter in which Dallas spoke of this hostility,
Polk suggested that Donelson and Jackson should urge Blair
to alter the tone of his paper.[46]

---

[44] Letcher to Buchanan, July 19, 1844, *Buchanan Papers*.

[45] Speech printed in Wash. *Globe,* Nov. 6, 1844. Yoakum, of Tennessee,
in calling Polk's attention to this speech says that he has "no doubt but
Col. Benton has injured us 100,000 votes"! (Yoakum to Polk, Nov. 22,
1844, *Polk Papers*).

[46] Polk to Donelson, July 22, 1844, "Polk-Donelson Letters."

Toward the end of June certain overtures made by close friends of President Tyler gave hope that he might yet withdraw from the race. J. B. Jones, the editor of the *Madisonian*, approached A. V. Brown and others with a suggestion that J. George Harris should be brought to Washington to assist in editing that paper. Harris was an intimate friend of both Polk and Jackson, and had made the Nashville *Union* an effective party organ. Harris suggested to Polk that a new paper might be started with which the *Madisonian* (Tyler) and the *Spectator* (Calhoun) might soon be merged. A new paper, in his opinion, would be more likely to succeed because of prejudices against those already in existence. General Armstrong, like Harris, thought favorably of the plan to merge these papers, and believed that after the election even the *Globe* might be joined with the rest. Both Johnson and Brown, however, were opposed to this plan, and especially to putting Harris in charge of the *Madisonian*.[47]

Early in July R. J. Walker, who had from the first urged a friendly attitude toward the deserters of 1840, called on Tyler in order to ascertain his views. The President told Walker that he would withdraw at once were it not for the fact that his friends felt hurt by the abuse heaped upon them by the *Globe* and other papers. There were, he said, about 150,000 of his friends who had voted for Whigs in 1840; he would withdraw and his friends would support Polk and Dallas, provided that assurance be given that they would be welcomed by the Democratic party as brethren and equals. "Now I think," said Walker when reporting the conversation to Polk, "that the importance of this union & co-operation cannot be overrated"; therefore he suggested that Polk and Jackson might write letters to political friends, speaking kindly of Tyler and his followers.[48]

---

[47] Harris to Polk, June 27, 29; Johnson to Polk, June 28; Armstrong to Polk, June 30, 1844, *Polk Papers*.

[48] Walker to Polk, July 10, 1844, *ibid.*

After reading Walker's letter Polk sent it to the Hermitage by Gideon Pillow. In a letter of his own, sent by the same messenger, he told Jackson that, however desirable the object sought by Walker might be, he would not write any letter or make any promises. He would like of course to see a reunion of "all the old Jackson Democrats of '28 & '32," but he would neither write a letter to Tyler nor "make any pledges to any one—except as it regards my public principles, in advance of election." He suggested, however, that if the attacks of the *Globe* were responsible for Tyler's continuing in the race and thereby jeopardizing the result in certain states, something should be done to induce Blair to cease abusing the President. He told Jackson that he was the only one who could influence Blair, but as to the wisdom of exercising such influence Jackson must judge for himself.[49]

Jackson was disgusted with Walker's "want of common sense" in suggesting that he and Polk should write letters in commendation of the President. Such letters, he told Polk, would "damn you & destroy your election," for the Whigs would at once charge "bargain & intrigue."[50] Although not yet ready to ask favors from John Tyler, he was quite willing to remove, if possible, the cause of the President's injured feelings. On that very same day he dispatched a letter to Blair in which he condemned Benton's conduct, urged the importance of annexation, and ordered Blair to "support the cause of Polk & Dallas, & let Tiler alone—leave Calhoun to himself we in the South & West will attend to the Federal Union, it must be preserved."[51] Indeed, on the same day, he authorized Major Lewis to express to the President his (Jackson's) wish for the success of the

---

[49] Polk to Jackson, July 23, 1844, *Jackson Papers*. See also Polk to Donelson, same date, "Polk-Donelson Letters." In this he doubted the propriety of Jackson's writing a letter for publication; still, he seemed anxious that the general should write a private letter "which might reach the President's eye."

[50] Jackson to Polk, July 26, 1844, *Polk Papers*.

[51] Jackson to Blair, July 26, 1844, *Jackson Papers*.

administration and the assurance that Tyler's friends would be received as brethren into the Democratic fold.[52]

From various quarters pressure was brought to bear upon Tyler, and appeals to his vanity were not wanting. Ritchie, of the Richmond *Enquirer,* who was called the "king of the Democratic press," warmly urged the President to withdraw, while Democratic electors agreed to support Tyler in case it should develop that he was stronger than Polk. The Democratic general committee of New York, on August 6, drafted resolutions lauding the President and asking his support;[53] and on August 1 Jackson sent another letter to Major Lewis in which he argued that Tyler ought to withdraw, for if he did not, it would be said

---

[52] Jackson to Lewis, July 26, 1844 (Tyler, *Letters and Times of the Tylers,* III, 143–146). The letter read in part: "You know I have a great desire that Mr. Tyler should close his term with credit to himself. It is certain he can not now be elected, and he has now a fair field by withdrawing, to add great and lasting popularity to himself by the act, and free himself from the imputation that his exertions to re-annex Texas were to make himself President, and show that his energy in this case was from imperious public duty, to prevent a country so important to the defence, safety and great interest of our whole Union from falling into the hands of England, our most implacable enemy. On Mr. Tyler's withdrawal from the canvass every true American will say, Amen to his patriotism in the case of Texas.

"Several of Mr. Tyler's friends yesterday visited me, and wished me to cause it to be known to him their wishes, as his withdrawal at once would unite all the Democrats into one family without distinction. This would render our victory easy and certain by bringing Mr. Tyler's friends in to the support of Polk and Dallas, received as brethren by them and their friends, all former differences forgotten and cordially united once more in sustaining the Democratic candidate.

". . . It is impossible now that Mr. Tyler should be elected, and if he does not withdraw he will be charged with conniving with the Clay Whigs to defeat the Democratic nominees. *Although this would be untrue,* yet really it would have that affect and would do Mr. Tyler much injury. I told Mr. Tyler's friends I could not write to him on such a subject, but that I had such confidence in his good sense and patriotism, that I was sure he would withdraw in due time, as I believe him to be a good Democrat, and that he would do nothing to promote Clay or injure Democracy. If you think it prudent, you can make these suggestions to Mr. Tyler. I think he would receive them kindly, be his determination what it may. His proper dignified course is a magnanamous withdrawal, with such reasons as his good sense may suggest for the occasion. These hints flow from a real regard for Mr. Tyler and a sincere wish that he may retire with much credit.''

[53] Tyler, *Letters and Times of the Tylers,* II, 337–339.

that he had adopted the annexation program merely to obtain
a reëlection and that he was remaining in the field in order to
defeat Polk.  Tyler soon informed Jackson that this letter had
determined him to retire,[54] and on August 20 his letter of withdrawal appeared in the *Madisonian*.  His present action, he said,
had resulted from changed conditions.  The people had vindicated him by driving from power those who had tried to crush
him; the Democrats had adopted his policies, and he no longer
felt compelled to run.  On the next day this paper stated that
its sole object all the time had been to defeat Henry Clay, and,
as the principles of Polk and Tyler were identical, it would
henceforth support the Democratic candidates.[55]  Two years
later Tyler wrote that he had accepted the nomination ''for the
sole purpose of controlling events . . . . for the public good''
and, having accomplished his purpose, he withdrew.[56]

The *Spectator,* also, gave Polk and Dallas its enthusiastic
support, and Calhoun predicted that the results would ''equal
the defeat of 1828.''[57]  Doubtless he indulged hopes that he, in
the event of Polk's election, would be the guiding spirit of the
administration.

During the summer considerable anxiety was caused by the
fear that British and French influence might induce Houston
to agree to some arrangement with Mexico.  Major Lewis was
authorized by Calhoun to communicate ''confidentially'' to
General Jackson that the State Department was in possession
of reliable information that these nations had offered to acknowledge the independence of Texas without any pledge of abolition,

---

[54] Smith, *Annexation of Texas*, 310.

[55] The *Madisonian* (Aug. 24) even supplied an election pun: ''Change—
It is James *Knox* Polk now, it will be Polk knocks Clay, about election
time.''

[56] Tyler, *Letters and Times of the Tylers*, II, 341.

[57] Alex. Anderson to Polk, Aug. 22, 1844, *Polk Papers.*  ''We should
have carried North Carolina,'' said Anderson, ''but for the course and
speeches of that arch Traitor Benton—so say our letters from North
Carolina.''  Anderson was a strong adherent of Calhoun.

provided that Texas would agree to remain an independent nation. Similar information was given to Polk by Calhoun's friend, Alexander Anderson. Before he had seen these letters, however, Jackson had written to Houston "as strong a letter as he [I] could dictate," exhorting him not to yield to the wishes of foreign nations.[58]

While politicians were emphasizing the foreign menace, the *Democratic Review* was trying to win votes in northern states by maintaining that the area of slavery would be restricted by acquiring Texas, for slaves would be drawn to the new fields, leaving the border states to the Yankees.[59] Some of the slavery advocates, too, believed that such would be the result, and for this reason violently opposed annexation.[60]

There was some defection from their own ranks and there was fear that annexation might be defeated by an act of Texas itself, but the Democrats as a party never wavered from their position in favor of annexation. They had, therefore, the advantage of a consistent program. Clay, on the other hand, in order to retain his hold on both North and South, adopted a shifty course and modified his views from time to time, as the occasion seemed to demand. In his Raleigh letter of April 17 he had definitely opposed immediate annexation, but he soon discovered that such a stand had made him unpopular in the South and West. To retrieve his fortunes in those sections he wrote to Stephen F. Miller, on July 1, his first "Alabama letter." "Personally," said he, "I could have no objection to the annexation of Texas; but certainly I would be unwilling to see the existing Union dissolved or seriously jeoparded for the sake of

---

[58] Lewis to Jackson, July 19, 1844, *Jackson Papers*. Jackson to Polk, July 23, 1844, *Polk Papers*. See also, Polk to Donelson, July 22, 1844, "Polk-Donelson Letters."

[59] *Dem. Rev.*, July, 1844.

[60] Letter of Waddy Thompson to editors of *National Intelligencer*, printed in that paper, July 6, 1844.

[61] Printed in *Nat. Intell.*, Aug. 8, 1844.

acquiring Texas.''[61]   As this was not strong enough to win votes in the South, he wrote again on the twenty-seventh that if annexation might be accomplished ''without national dishonor, without war, with the general consent of the States of the Union, and upon fair and reasonable terms, I should be glad to see it.''[62] Both Democrats and Abolitionists seized upon the last phrase and widely advertised the fact that ''Clay would be glad to see it.''   Other letters followed in an attempt to show that he had not changed his original views, but the more he explained the more he became the target of denunciation and ridicule.   The papers made much sport of his ''six manifestoes,'' while Jackson charged that Clay by his letters had made a ''perfect devill'' of himself.[63]

Although this was a campaign in which party principles were clearly defined and important questions involved, nevertheless the personal element was not wanting.   The Whig ignorance even of Polk's identity was soon replaced by a minute knowledge not only of his own shortcomings but of those of his ancestors.   It devolved, therefore, upon the candidate's friends in Tennessee to enlighten the public on his past record and to defend his reputation against the slanders of his opponents.   As soon as the news of his nomination had reached Nashville a mass meeting was called to celebrate the event.   Speeches were made by prominent Democrats, and A. O. P. Nicholson ridiculed the Whig cry of ''Who is Polk?''   Arrangements were made for another meeting in July to be composed of delegates from all parts of the state.[64]   Biographical materials had already been forwarded to George Bancroft under the frank of General Jackson.   But as Bancroft, according to Harris, was ''somewhat sensitive on the

---

[62] Fourth Alabama letter, in which former letters are quoted (*Nat. Intell.*, Oct. 1, 1844).   The letter of July 27 is printed in *Niles' Reg.*, LXVI, 439.

[63] Schouler, *Hist. of U. S.*, IV, 477.   Smith, *Annex. of Texas*, 309.

[64] Nashville *Union*, June 8, 11, 1844.

point of *authorship*," and declined, it was decided that editorials in the *Union* would do quite as well as a biography.[65]

Some of the Whig papers charged Polk with being a duelist, while others said he was a cringing coward who had feared to fight Wise. The first allegation was refuted in letters written to the *Globe* by Cave Johnson and A. V. Brown, and the second, by the publication of an old letter of Jackson's in which he had expressed approval of Speaker Polk for having treated Wise with contempt.[66] For the purpose of injuring Polk in the North, the Whigs circulated widely the "Roorback" canard the gist of which was that a gang of slaves branded with the initials "J. K. P," had been seen on their way to southern markets.[67]

Polk was most annoyed by the revival of the story that his grandfather, Colonel Ezekiel Polk, had been a Tory during the Revolution. The Washington *Globe* and various northern papers repelled the charge, and the Nashville *Union* printed many letters and affidavits from persons who had certain knowledge that the elder Polk had been a Revolutionary officer; it published, also, a copy of his commission dated June 18, 1775. Under Polk's direction this material was printed in pamphlet form under the title of "A Vindication of Colonel Ezekiel Polk," and General Armstrong was instructed to send copies to prominent Democrats all over the United States.[68] To these Whig campaign stories the Democratic press retorted in kind. Clay's use of profane language was emphasized and he was called a drunkard, a duelist, a gambler, and a perjurer.[69]

---

[65] J. Geo. Harris to Polk, June 25, July 17, 19, 1844, *Polk Papers*. Doubtless Bancroft's sensitiveness on authorship resulted from his experience as campaign biographer of Van Buren.

[66] Wash. *Globe*, June 13, 19, 1844.

[67] See *Niles' Reg.*, LXVII, 73.

[68] *Union*, Sept. 11. Polk to Heiss, Sept. 13; Polk to Armstrong, Sept. 16, 1844, "Heiss Papers," *Tenn. Hist. Mag.*, June, 1916.

[69] The perjury consisted in the alleged violation of his oath of office by challenging John Randolph to fight a duel for words spoken in debate during the campaign. Henly, of Indiana, said on the floor of the House

Naturally Polk was especially desirous of carrying his own state, and his energy and skill as a machine politician are manifested in many ways. Realizing, as usual, the importance of a spirited party press, he induced Heiss to make J. George Harris joint editor with Laughlin of the Nashville *Union*. ''The Union,'' he wrote, ''should be made in Tennessee what Medary's Statesman is in Ohio, and what the Union itself was in 1839. It is looked to from all parts of the Union and must be a *great paper* during this canvass.'' In another letter he urged that ''fire and spirit and power should be thrown into it'' in order to counteract the Whig falsehoods and misrepresentations.[70]

On July 13 a dinner was given in Polk's home town, Columbia, in honor of delegates to the late nominating convention, Presidential electors, and members of Congress from Tennessee. To Cave Johnson was assigned the duty of inducing prominent Democrats to be present in order to counteract the effect of a Whig rally held at the same place.[71] Early in the campaign arrangements had been made for a great mass meeting to be held at Nashville on the fifteenth of August. Both Polk and Johnson were anxious that the northern states should be well represented at this meeting so that it could not be said that it was a gathering of disunionists. Once more it fell to Johnson to send the invitations and to urge the importance of a large and representative attendance.[72]

On the appointed day the multitudes assembled, and Nashville, according to the *Union*, ''was from sunrise to sunset as

---

that ''the standard of Henry Clay should consist of his armorial bearings, which ought to be a pistol, a pack of cards, and a brandy-bottle'' (Adams, *Memoirs*, XII, 45).

[70] Polk to Heiss, July 31, Aug. 21, 1844; Heiss to Polk, Aug. 3, 1844, *Polk Papers*.

[71] Polk to Johnson, July 1, July 6, 1844, ''Polk-Johnson Letters.''

[72] Johnson to Polk, June 21, 1844, *Polk Papers*. Polk to Johnson, July 16, 1844, ''Polk-Johnson Letters.'' Among those invited were Wright, Cass, Buchanan, Woodbury, Hubbard of New Hampshire, and Duncan and Medary, of Ohio.

a *Military* Camp.''[73]  In the evening the Honorable Thomas F. Marshall, of Kentucky, addressed ''thousands'' in front of the courthouse on the annexation of Texas.  On the second day, August 16, the throng gathered at Camp Hickory where by noon, ''the great grove at the Camp, fifty acres in extent, was as full as it could hold,'' and there ''were two miles of table on which the *Great Dinner* was served.''  Speaking followed the dinner, and Cave Johnson, as presiding officer, made the opening address.  We have already noted his solicitude lest a disunion character might be attributed to this meeting, and he now embraced the opportunity

in the presence of this great assembly, to give a direct contradiction to the false charge of disunion, and a wish to dissolve the Union, which had been propagated by the whig press of this and other states, against those concerned in calling and getting up the present meeting.

The number in attendance was so great that speakers addressed crowds simultaneously in various parts of the grove; each speaker, following Johnson's lead, repelled the charge of disunion.  General Case was the principal orator of the day; among the others were Gansevoort Melville;[74] Governor Clay, of Alabama; Colonel Terry, speaker of the house from the same state; and J. B. Bowlin, a member of Congress from Missouri.  Letters were received from leading Democrats of both sections, regretting their inability to be present and expressing hearty coöperation.[75] Among these was Judge Douglas, but within a few days he was in Tennessee stumping the state for Polk and Dallas.[76]

---

[73] Nashville *Union*, Aug. 17, 1844.  Also *Niles' Reg.*, LXVII, 3–4.  ''On every road to the city was to be seen approaching companies, battalions and regiments, mounted and on foot, with their bands of music, their banners and their mottoes, on their way to this great encampment of the sovereign people.''

[74] A Tammany Hall leader.

[75] The same number of the *Union* contains copies of letters from Franklin Pierce, Silas Wright, Levi Woodbury, James Buchanan, Stephen A. Douglas, Geo. McDuffie, Robt. J. Walker, R. M. Johnson, *et al.*

[76] Polk to Johnson, Aug. 20, 22, 26, 1844, ''Polk-Johnson Letters.''

Despite the absence of so many of the party leaders the Democratic meeting was regarded as highly successful, but in glittering pageantry and boisterous enthusiasm it was far excelled by the "Great Whig Convention" which, on August 21, likewise essembled in the city of Nashville and was, to quote Phelan, "the finest of the kind ever held in the Southwest."[77] While the chief feature of the meeting was the display of gorgeous battalions and expensive campaign banners, there were soul-stirring addresses by prominent Whig orators. The great speech of the meeting was made by Sergeant S. Prentiss, of Mississippi, who was regarded by many as the peer of either Webster or Clay. On this occasion Prentiss surpassed even his own brilliant record, for to partisan considerations was added a personal hatred for the Democratic candidate whose casting vote had once deprived him of a seat in the House of Representatives.[78]

The enthusiasm caused by the Whig meeting spurred the Democrats to a still more vigorous effort to win the election in Tennessee. Custom did not permit Polk to mount the platform in his own behalf, but from his home at Columbia he directed the campaign, even to the minutest details. He planned itineraries, assigned speakers, and even arranged for barbecues.[79] Local orators were assisted by prominent politicians from other states. This list included Douglas, of Illinois, Pickens, of South Carolina, Melville, of New York, and Clay, Terry, and McClung, of Alabama. Of local men the most notable were the veteran campaigners, Nicholson, Brown, and Cave Johnson. Johnson was much broken in health, but so highly did Polk value his services that he goaded him to an active part in the campaign.[80]

---

[77] Phelan, *Hist. of Tenn.*, 419.

[78] See above, p. 120.

[79] Various letters of Polk to Johnson, Aug.-Oct., "Polk-Johnson Letters."

[80] *Ibid.* On Oct. 14 he told Johnson that "all our energies are necessary to keep the State safe, as I believe she now is. The least relaxation at the close of the canvass might loose her."

Near the close of the canvass Polk was confident of carrying the state by a "handsome majority," but, instead, he lost it by the small margin of one hundred and thirteen votes.

In southern states the Whigs had little hope of success in opposing the Democratic annexation program, nevertheless strenuous efforts were made to prevent defection from their own ranks because of this annoying issue. The indomitable Prentiss labored to show that Polk was not entitled to profit from the revival of this question,[81] and in a speech at Natchez he referred to Polk as a "blighted burr, that had fallen from the mane of the war-horse of the Hermitage." In an attempt to counteract the work of Prentiss and others, and to win Whig votes in the South, Senator Walker, of Mississippi, wrote a most inflammatory pamphlet entitled "The South in Danger"[82] in which he argued that as Whigs and Abolitionists had joined hands in the North, therefore all parties in the South should unite in the interest of annexation. The pamphlet probably did little good in the South, and many Democrats were fearful that it might do serious damage in the North.[93]

In Ohio the contest bid fair to be close, and, after Clay's repudiation of the utterances of his relative, Cassius M. Clay,[84] leading Democrats had hopes that many Whigs would desert him and vote for Birney.[85] But the result of the state elections made

---

[81] "If ever I join the Mormons," he wrote in August to the editor of the Vicksburg *Whig,* "I shall attach myself to Joe Smith, the founder of the sect, and not to one of his rival disciples, and should I ever turn Locofoco on the question of *the immediate annexation of Texas,* I will support *John Tyler, not James K. Polk''* (*Memoir of S. S. Prentiss,* II, 316).

[82] This pamphlet was issued by the Democratic Association of Washington, D. C., Sept. 25, 1844. Copy in Library of Congress.

[83] For example, William E. Cramer, editor of the Albany *Argus,* informed Polk that New York could never be won on the program outlined by Walker, while Ohio and other states would surely be lost (Cramer to Polk, Oct. 4, 1844, *Polk Papers*).

[84] C. M. Clay had represented Henry Clay as opposed to slavery. The latter in a letter contradicted the former's statements.

[85] Gansevoort Melville to Polk, Oct. 3; Cass to Polk, Oct. 4, 1844, *Polk Papers.* Both wrote from Cleveland and expressed the opinion that the Democrats would carry the state.

it evident that Clay's letter had not produced any defection,[86] while Walker's ill-advised pamphlet added strength to the Whigs.[87]  The so-called "Garland forgery" transferred many votes from Birney to Clay, and may possibly have brought victory to Clay in Ohio.[88]

Pennsylvania was normally Democratic, yet there were misgivings lest the strong sentiment in favor of tariff might jeopardize Polk's success in that state.  His "Kane letter" had been generally accepted as satisfactory, but the Whigs represented him to be an unqualified free-trader.  The *Pennsylvanian* refuted this charge and, on October 15, published extracts from his speeches to prove that he had always favored incidental protection.  As noted above, Polk, in his letter to Kane, did not pretend to favor tariff except that which might be necessary for revenue, but by means of construction Pennsylvanians were able to hold voters in line by representing him to be in favor of tariff. "We have succeeded," wrote the oily-tongued Simon Cameron, "in fixing the belief that you 'are as good a tariff man as Clay,'" and he added significantly that no man known to be opposed to protective tariff could possibly carry the state.[89]  Polk did not of course take pains to undeceive his supporters in Pennsylvania; on the other hand, he did not, in any of his public utterances, commit himself to tariff for protective purposes.  However, Cameron's ruse met with success, and Polk's strength in Pennsylvania greatly exasperated the Whigs.[90]

---

[86] H. C. Williams wrote from Washington that "the letter repudiating C. M. Clay has had no effect in the northern states, while it satisfies the Southern Whigs.  The Whig papers will not publish it."  Democrats, he said, have to oppose all "fag end" parties, and Greely is now trying to stir up the Irish (Williams to Polk, Oct. 14, 1844, *Polk Papers*).

[87] Armstrong to Polk, Nov. 5, [1844], *Polk Papers.*

[88] See Birney, *James G. Birney and his Times*, 355.

[89] Cameron to Polk, Oct. 18, 1844, *Polk Papers.*

[90] Governor Letcher, of Kentucky, scoffed at the idea of Polk being in favor of tariff, and he tried to persuade Buchanan to refrain from advocating his election.  "Polk," said Letcher, "has no more chance to be elected than if he were dead and *buried*, and d—nd, as he will be in due time" (Letcher to Buchanan, Aug. 3, 1844, *Buchanan Papers*).

"Native Americanism" was said to have cost the Democrats votes in Pennsylvania. Catholics, as a rule, affiliated with that party, and the Whigs made political capital out of the fact that Shunk, the Democratic candidate for governor, had been induced to march in a Catholic parade.[91]

It was alleged that the Whigs used money freely in Pennsylvania,[92] and that they were guilty of practicing frauds,[93] but it is unlikely that the Whigs were the sole transgressors in these respects.

New York was regarded as the pivotal state. There thirty-six electoral votes were to be won or lost, and the result seemed to be highly problematical. In this state various extraneous elements helped to complicate the political situation. Both "Native Americans" and Abolitionists commanded a considerable number of votes in the state, but it was by no means certain just how these votes would be cast. At the beginning of the campaign it was feared that the followers of Van Buren might not rally with enthusiasm to the party standard, and besides, there was lack of harmony in Democratic state politics with respect to policies and candidates. In order to carry the state it was necessary to hold the Van Burenites in line, and since the Baltimore convention many of them had been silently nursing their resentment. Governor William C. Bouck wrote that a number of Wright's friends had tried to get up a secret intrigue to procure Polk's defeat, but that Wright had been nominated for governor and his adherents brought into harmony.[94] Van Buren told Jackson that Wright had accepted the nomination reluctantly and not until

91 J. Miller to Polk, Oct. 12; J. M. Porter to Polk, Oct. 12, 1844, *Polk Papers;* also, newspapers.

92 For example, Kane informed Polk that $20,000 had been subscribed at the office of John Sergeant, of Philadelphia. Sergeant's nephew, Wm. B. Reed, had by mistake sent a letter regarding this money to some Democrat (Kane to Polk, Oct. 24, 1844, *Polk Papers*).

93 Henry Horn, for example, wrote that desponding letters had been sent to his friends with his forged signature attached (Horn to Polk, Oct. 31, 1844, *Polk Papers*).

94 Bouck to Polk, Sept. 7, 1844, *Polk Papers*.

he had been told that it was the only means of saving New York,[95] but the supporters of Bouck felt that he had been unceremoniously sacrificed to satisfy the ambitions of Wright and his friends.[96]  Some of the extreme anti-Texas leaders in New York supported the candidates, but repudiated the annexation plank in the platform.[97]  This was the policy of the New York *Evening Post.*

According to William E. Cramer, of the Albany *Argus,* the Democrats in New York "were on a volcano" until Clay repudiated the statements of Cassius M. Clay and changed his position on the Texan question.  The Abolitionists, he said, held the balance of power and would poll from fifteen thousand to twenty thousand votes.  "Before Mr. C's fatal letter they were hesitating whether they should not vote for him," but "this puts an impassable gulf between them."[98]  On the other hand, in predicting victory for Polk and Dallas in New York, Wright reported that "Never have I witnessed an equal degree of enthusiasm among our democracy, not even in the days of Genl Jackson, nor have I, at any time, known greater harmony, activity or confidence."[99]  Late in October another letter from Cramer stated that the Whigs were putting forth every effort to form coalitions with "Native Americans," Abolitionists, and Anti-renters, and that they were confident of winning the election.  Prospect of success, he said, had brought them much campaign money from manufacturers who desired high tariff.[100]

---

[95] Jackson to Polk, Sept. 26, 1844, *ibid.*

[96] In a letter to Polk, Sept. 11, Marcy stated that Bouck had made a satisfactory governor, and that Wright had been nominated for political reasons; while an anonymous letter, Sept. 14, said that Bouck had been set aside without reason, and that the action might cause Polk to lose the state.

[97] See the signed statement of Bryant and others in *Niles' Reg.,* LXVI, 371.

[98] Cramer to Polk, Sept. 17, 1844, *Polk Papers.*

[99] Wright to Buchanan, Sept. 23, 1844, *Buchanan Papers.*

[100] "The report is that the Bostonians promised $100,000 provided they could receive ample assurance that it would secure New York for Mr. Clay!!" (Cramer to Polk, Oct. 22, 1844, *Polk Papers*).

Still other factors complicated the political situation in New York. The Abolitionists who had formerly voted the Whig ticket were appalled when Birney came out in favor of free trade and opposed to distributing among the states the proceeds derived from the sale of public lands, and it was feared in Tammany circles that his announcement might cause them to vote for Clay.[101] In order to win votes for their national ticket the Whigs withdrew some of their candidates for Congress and the state legislature in favor of the "Native American" candidates.[102] It availed them little, however, for Polk and Dallas carried the state.[103]

It appears that the Democrats, also, withdrew some of their candidates in favor of "Native Americans,"[104] and in the process of rapid naturalization they outrivaled their opponents. "Tammany Hall," wrote Melville, "is a perfect jam from 8 A. M. till after midnight. Naturalization going on among our friends to an immense extent. On Saturday 260—all Democrats—rec'd their papers."[105] Charges of wholesale frauds were made by both parties,[106] but it may be doubted that such frauds materially affected the election results.

The Texas question was of course the paramount issue of the campaign, although it was not, apparently, the chief factor in winning the election for Polk. Many contemporaries believed that Clay's defeat was not caused by the emergence of this question,

---

[101] Melville to Polk, Oct. 26, 1844, *Polk Papers.*

[102] Alex. Jones to Polk, New York City, Oct. 30, Nov. 6, 1844, *ibid.*

[103] Jones told Polk in a letter dated November 21, that some of the Whigs had been so confident of winning that they had bet all of their money, and even their homes. One had lost $38,000; another, $40,000. One Whig's wife lost her mind because of his losses (*Polk Papers*).

[104] John P. Heiss to Polk, Nov. 3, 1844, *Polk Papers.*

[105] Melville to Medary, Nov. 4, 1844, *ibid.*

[106] A correspondent from New London, Conn., informed Polk that in Connecticut, Massachusetts, and Rhode Island "the *lords of the spindle* compelled the degraded operators to vote their will, and thus obtained large majorities for your opponent" (Dr. Charles Douglas to Polk, Nov. 22, 1844, *Polk Papers*). For a useful summary of press opinions on frauds, see Smith, *Annexation of Texas,* 316 ff.

and this belief is held by Justin H. Smith,[107] who has recently made a thorough examination of conflicting opinions and carefully weighed their value. The *Democratic Review* evidently stated the truth when it said on the eve of the election that neither party had won or lost many votes on account of the Texas issue, and that "the issue is between the principles of the two parties more than ever before."[108] If Polk owed his success in the election to the Texas issue, it was due to the fact that it brought him the support of President Tyler and his followers. While we can not be sure that Tyler would have remained in the field if the Democrats had not espoused annexation, certainty that they would continue his Texas program at least furnished him with a plausible excuse for retiring from the canvass.[109]

Polk received 170 electoral votes; Clay only 105. In the North, Polk carried the great states of New York and Pennsylvania, while New Hampshire, also, contributed her six votes. Much to their delight the Whigs carried not only Polk's own state, Tennessee, but even the very precincts of both Jackson and Polk.[110] The Tennessee Democrats were keenly disappointed, of course, because they had failed to win the election in their candidate's own state; but their disappointment soon gave way to rejoicing over the general party victory. On receiving the news that New York had gone Democratic, Jackson sent the letter on to Polk with a marginal note, " 'who is J. K. polk,' will be no more asked by the coons—A. J."[111]

---

[107] Smith, *Annexation of Texas*, 317.

[108] "One Last Word before the Election" (*Dem. Rev.*, Oct., 1844). It thanked heaven that Polk was not a "military chieftain" and had never even killed an Indian; also, that "there is no peculiar eminent 'popularity' attaching to him, of a character personal to himself, and distinct from his simple position as the representative of the general principles and policy of the party whose candidate he is."

[109] See correspondence, including his letter of withdrawal, in Tyler, *Letters and Times of the Tylers*, II, 338 ff.

[110] Nashville *Banner*, Nov. 11, 1844. The *Union* on the 14th retorted that these precincts had been carried by non-resident Whigs who had gone there and voted illegally.

[111] Written on a letter from A. C. Flagg to Jackson, Nov. 7, 1844, *Polk Papers*. The "coons," of course, were the Whigs. The name had been attached to them during the "log-cabin" campaign of 1840.

Polk received the news of his election some hours before it was known to the people of either Columbia or Nashville. The New York mail arrived at Nashville at nine o'clock in the evening, and on the outside of the package the postmaster at Cincinnati had written a note stating that Polk had been elected. This attracted the attention of General Robert Armstrong, postmaster at Nashville and one of Polk's most intimate friends. Without giving out the news, Armstrong sent a messenger to Columbia with a note for Polk. At dawn he read the glad tidings which the note contained, but he said nothing about it to his neighbors and friends. For the next twenty-four hours he went about his work, and calmly received expressions of sympathy on his defeat.[112] Sphinx-like silence was a rôle that Polk dearly loved to play, and an opportunity to do so on this occasion no doubt added much to the gratification caused by the information contained in the note.

When the result of the election at last became known there was great rejoicing in Democratic ranks. On the other hand, desperado admirers of Clay, both in Tennessee and Kentucky, threatened Polk's life, and friends warned him to "take some thought of *where* you go & eat & drink."[113] No violence, however, was attempted, and apprehensions were forgotten in the din of exuberant celebrations. At Nashville Polk was given an elaborate reception. A. O. P. Nicholson made the principal address, and there was general rejoicing because the "Young Hickory" was soon to grasp the helm that had been so firmly guided by the "Old Hickory."[114]

Some of the Democratic factions had little love for Polk, but all could agree with the *Democratic Review* in thanking God for the defeat of Henry Clay. "Had he succeeded," said the *Review,* "it would have stamped him, his ideas and his character upon the future history of our government, with a fatal depth and extent of mischief never perhaps to be again effaced."[115]

---

[112] Nelson, *Memorials of Sarah Childress Polk,* 76–77.

[113] A. V. Brown to Polk, Nov. 13, 1844. Also Gen. John A. McCalla, Lexington, Ky., Nov. 22, 1844; both in *Polk Papers.*

[114] Nashville *Union,* Nov. 30, 1844.     [115] *Dem. Rev.,* Nov., 1844.

## CHAPTER XIV

## PRESIDENT-ELECT

Various individuals and factions claimed the credit for Polk's nomination and election, and as soon as the result of the balloting had become known their claims to recognition were presented. While in one sense it was true that the successful candidate owed his elevation to a number of discordant elements within the party, in another sense he was under no obligation to any of them. With the exception perhaps of the younger element the several groups within the party had united on Polk, not from choice but necessity, and not until each had found it impossible to procure the nomination of its particular favorite. The circumstances under which he had been nominated—the very fact that he had not been generally considered for the first place—relieved the President-elect from the necessity of making pledges to any one. Although Polk himself fully appreciated this fact and resolved to make the most of it, others did not and the ''jockeying for position'' at once began.

One of the first to congratulate Polk on his victory was James Buchanan. The Senator from Pennsylvania was usually numbered with the *old* leaders, but his plea, oddly enough, was for the recognition of young men in the distribution of offices. ''The old office holders generally,'' said he, ''have had their day & ought to be content. Had Mr. Van Buren been our candidate, worthy as he is, this feeling which everywhere pervaded the Democratic ranks, would have made his defeat as signal as it was in 1840.'' Even Polk, he added, would have run better in Philadelphia had it not been rumored that he would distribute the patronage among the ''old hunkers.''[1] Such a letter from Robert

---

[1] Buchanan to Polk, Nov. 4, 1844, *Polk Papers*.

J. Walker would not have been surprising, but Buchanan's solicitude for the younger men was significantly of recent origin.

Tyler's withdrawal from the canvass occasioned speculation as to the recognition which his friends would receive from the Democratic party, and during the campaign Polk received many letters which were designed to pledge him in advance. The candidate discreetly refrained from committing himself, although his supporters may have given assurance that the followers of the President would not be proscribed. Special importance was attached to a letter written by Jackson to Major Lewis[2] in which the General said that Tyler's friends would be received as brethren. Then, too, Walker, as chairman of the national Democratic committee, had made promises to influential adherents of the President. Nevertheless the Tylerites were apparently unwilling to run any risks, and soon after Polk's election they were charged by prominent Democrats with having concocted a scheme whereby they hoped to intrench themselves in office. One part of this scheme, according to H. C. Williams, was to procure the resignation of Whigs so that President Tyler might fill the offices with eleventh-hour Democrats whom it would be embarrassing for Polk to remove.[3] Probably such reports exaggerated the facts, especially as to Whig resignations, but it is certain that the Tyler faction believed themselves to be entitled to a share of Democratic patronage. In plaintive note, John Y. Mason, Tyler's Secretary of the Navy, expressed a willingness to remain in the cabinet. He had, he told Polk, from a sense of duty resigned a judgeship so that he might take charge of the Navy Department, and had felt ''very unhappy'' since Tyler had become a candidate. Jackson, whom he had consulted, had advised him to remain in the cabinet because Tyler would soon withdraw. He would resign of course on March 3 *unless Polk should*

---

[2] Dated July 6, 1844. See Tyler, *Life and Times of the Tylers*, III, 143 ff.

[3] H. C. Williams, Washington, Nov. 15; Henry Simpson, Philadelphia, Nov. 21, 1844, *Polk Papers*.

*desire otherwise,* therefore he desired a "frank statement" of
Polk's intentions.  Mason had been a college mate of Polk and
they had since been warm personal friends, but with habitual
caution the President-elect replied that he would leave all such
matters to be settled after his arrival in Washington.[4]

Directly and indirectly Polk received much unsolicited advice
on the subject of patronage, and especially on the selection of
his cabinet.  Through General Armstrong, H. C. Williams
warned him that rival factions were already planning for the
succession of their respective favorites, therefore he should discountenance all of them.[5]  As usual, Judge Catron was free with
his fatherly advice.  He had been told by Governor Letcher, of
Kentucky, that the Whigs confidently believed Polk to be under
pledges to Calhoun; and that because Calhoun's friends and
those of Van Buren and Benton could never work in harmony, discord and disaster would beset the new administration.
Catron assured Letcher that Polk had made no pledges to any
wing of the party, but despite the truth of his statement, the
rumors regarding Calhoun continued to circulate.  Since Polk
had been elected without making promises, Catron's advice was
that he should "go to Washington *entirely* unpledged, down to
a post office."  The cold shoulder, he said, might at first give
offense; but no matter, for "you are under no pressure of
obligation to your party, other than to administer the government through the agency of men of undoubted strength and
worth of character, *from head to foot.*"[6]  John Blair, of

---

[4] Mason to Polk, Nov. 16; Polk to Mason, Dec. 6, 1844, *ibid.*

[5] Williams to Armstrong, Nov. 26, 1844, *ibid.*

[6] Catron to Polk, Nov. 23, 1844, *Polk Papers.*  Catron, like others, had
his own individual preferences, but he continued to urge Polk to make
his own selections.  Both Johnson and Brown wrote on December 14 that
Catron had suggested Buchanan, Wright, and Cass for the State,
Treasury, and War Departments, respectively.  "Of one thing I am absolutely certain," wrote Catron to Polk on February 4, "that you must
begin as *absolute* master of your will, if this be possible, in framing your
cabinet.  Strength it must have, and men in it that will work in harmony:
This done and you are perfectly safe, regardless of fretting for a brief
space.  The *old* dare not, as the young will overthrow them—and the
young, set up no claim to such assumptions" (*Polk Papers*).

Tennessee, offered a happy solution for sectional discord—patronage in plenty for the North and principles for the South.[7]

Warnings and advice, however well meant, were entirely superfluous, for Polk felt himself to be fully capable of formulating his own plans. He could not prevent gossip and speculation, but he declared emphatically to Cave Johnson that he was "under no pledges or commitments to any of the cliques (if such exist) mentioned by the newspapers." The policy which he had chosen to follow relieved him in a great measure from consulting the wishes of discordant factions, and his success in executing it proved the wisdom of his choice. "My object," he told Cave Johnson,

will be to do my duty to the country, and I do not intend if I can avoid it, that my counsels shall be distracted by the supposed or not conflicting interests of those cliques. Another thing I will say—that I will if I can have a united and harmonious set of cabinet counsellors, who will have the existing administration and the good of the country more at heart than the question who shall succeed me, and that in any event I intend to be *myself* President of the U. S.[8]

No one can follow his career for the next four years without being convinced that he held the executive reins firmly in his own hands.

Selecting a cabinet from men of ability who would subordinate their own personal interests to those of the administration and of the country required an unusual degree of independence. The desired coöperation could not be obtained without the elimination of recognized leaders of factions; and such a course would inevitably subject the administration to attacks from all who had been disappointed.

The claims of the Tylerites might be ignored with impunity, but what to do with Calhoun was a more embarrassing question.

---

[7] "North of Mason & Dickson's line should be *plied* with patronage as principles more congenial to the South must of necessity be established & carried out whatever your personal predelections" may be (Blair to Polk, Dec. 2, 1844, *Polk Papers*).

[8] Polk to Johnson, Dec. 21, 1844, "Polk-Johnson Letters."

Although Calhoun denied emphatically that there had ever been any understanding between Polk and himself,[9] apparently he was not without hope that he would be invited to remain at the helm in the Department of State. Late in November one of his intimate friends, General James Hamilton, sounded Polk on the subject and dwelt on the desirability of having Calhoun continued in charge of the Texas and Oregon questions. For a southern member of the cabinet, said he, the entire South, from the Potomac to Louisiana, would prefer Calhoun.[10]

The difficulties which might result from any attempt to harmonize factions were set forth in a letter from Cave Johnson. He said that it was understood in Washington that Calhoun and other members of Tyler's cabinet desired to remain. It was also the general opinion that should Calhoun be retained Benton and his friends would oppose Polk's administration, while, on the other hand, the southern element would be hostile unless Calhoun should be continued in office. Calhoun, said Johnson, is the choice of southern men for Secretary of State, while many from the North want Silas Wright; and Benton is reported to have declared that should Polk retain any of the Tyler cabinet he would open fire on the "rotten eggs."[11] General Jackson's advice to Polk was the exclusion from his cabinet of "all aspirants to the presidency, or vice"; and the General was so confident that his advice would be followed that he assured Blair that neither Calhoun nor any other aspirant would be appointed. In another letter to Polk, Jackson urged that Calhoun must not be retained, because other members of the cabinet could not get along with him: "England is the place for him there to combat with my Lord Aberdeen, the abolition question." The entire cabinet,

---

[9] "Nothing has ever passed between Mr. Polk and myself, directly or indirectly, on the subject. I neither know his views nor he mine on the subject" (Calhoun to J. A. Stuart, Oct. 21, 1844, *Rep. of Am. Hist.*, 1899, II, 626).

[10] Hamilton to Polk, Nov. 29, 1844, *Polk Papers*.

[11] Johnson to Polk, Dec. 1, 6, 1844, *ibid.*

said he, ought to be composed of new men.[12]  Writing late in December, Cave Johnson said that the friends of Benton and Calhoun feared each other's influence with Polk, consequently the breach between the wings of the party was widening.  Especially did the northerners fear that Polk would be brought under the influence of Calhoun.  In a similar strain A. V. Brown wrote that all elements were working to induce Polk not to retain Calhoun.  There was, he said, scarcely less opposition to Cass; while Benton and Wright opposed Buchanan on account of the stand he had taken at Baltimore in favor of the two-thirds rule.[13]

While others were doing their utmost to prevent his retention, Calhoun himself was telling his friends that there was much speculation concerning the cabinet and not a little intriguing in various quarters.  He reported himself to be ''perfectly passive'' and ''indifferent.''  Whether he would remain or not, if invited, would depend on the ''probable course of the administration.''[14] His supporters, however, were both active and hopeful.  Some of them were sanguine enough to believe that Calhoun would be able to build up such a strong party following that Polk would not dare to remove him.[15]  Hearing that Gideon Pillow had remarked that Polk's chief difficulty was ''how to get rid of Calhoun,'' even Duff Green felt constrained to warn the President-elect of the dangers which would result from sacrificing Calhoun in order to conciliate Benton and Wright.  ''I make no pretense of friendship for you,'' he told Polk very frankly; but as a

---

12 Jackson to Polk, Dec. 13, 16, *Polk Papers;* Jackson to Blair, Dec. 14, 1844, *Jackson Papers.*

13 Johnson to Polk, Dec. 26; Brown to Polk, Dec. 29, 1844, *Polk Papers.*

14 Calhoun to his son-in-law, Thos. G. Clemson, Dec. 13, 1844, *Rep. Am. Assn.*, 1899, II, 633.  Dr. Gwin, who was supposed to be voicing Calhoun's views, suggested to A. V. Brown the following cabinet: Calhoun, Sec. of State; Walker, Sec. of Treasury; Woodbury, Sec. of War; Reed, of Pa., Atty. Gen.; Flagg, P-M Gen.; Mason, Sec. of Navy.  Van Buren was suggested as minister to England (Brown to Polk, Jan. 5, 1845, *Polk Papers*).

15 C. A. Davis, New York, to Crittenden, Dec. 17, 1844, *Crittenden Papers.*

friend of the South, he urged Calhoun's retention.[16]  Calhoun himself continued to remain *passive* until February 26, when, in a personal interview, Polk informed him that there was to be an entirely new cabinet and offered to send him as minister to England.  On the day following he sent Polk his resignation and assured him that there was neither dissatisfaction nor abatement of kind feelings on his own part.[17]

New England began at an early date to solicit a place in the cabinet.  In New Hampshire, Hubbard and Woodbury were mentioned, but her congressional delegation preferred Pierce.[18] Bancroft was suggested as the New England member, but he informed Polk that he would prefer a foreign mission.[19]  Maine was especially insistent in her claims for recognition, and Polk received numerous letters from politicians of that state.  In several of them Governor Fairfield was suggested as Secretary of the Navy, and Nathan Weston as Attorney General.

The greatest rivalry, however, aside from the solicitation in Calhoun's behalf, was that between New York on the one side, and Pennsylvania and the West on the other.  In Pennsylvania Buchanan and Dallas were the recognized heads of two rival factions, each of which was desirous of gaining a strategic position in the new administration.  In order to accomplish his purpose, Dallas recommended that Robert J. Walker, of Mississippi, be made Secretary of State.[20]  Dallas and Walker were connected by family ties as well as by political sympathies.  In addition, Walker had the support of the aggressive forces in the southwestern states.  Richard Rush urged the claims of Buchanan.

---

[16] Green to Polk, Jan. 20, 1845, *Polk Papers.*  On January 1, Memucan Hunt wrote from Galveston that leading public men in Texas wished Calhoun to be retained and Donelson to be made Secretary of the Treasury.

[17] Calhoun to Polk, Feb. 27, 1845, *Polk Papers.*  Same to Clemson, March 11, 1845, *Rep. Am. Hist. Assn.,* 1899, II, 647.

[18] John P. Hale to Pierce, Dec. 3, 1844, *Pierce Papers.*

[19] Lewis Josselyn, of Boston, to J. Geo. Harris, Dec. 4, 1844; Bancroft to Polk, Jan. 1, 1845, *Polk Papers.*

[20] Dallas to Polk, Dec. 15, 1844, *ibid.*

The latter had also received the formal endorsement of the Pennsylvania electoral college, but Dallas informed Polk that this action had been procured by the intrigue of a man who wished to be made collector of the port of Philadelphia. Dallas once more recommended Walker, dwelling on his command of foreign languages and upon the fact that he would be especially acceptable to the Texans.[21]

The rejection of Van Buren at Baltimore made it desirable that the powerful state of New York should be placated if possible. Polk very naturally, therefore, turned his thoughts in that direction, and his offer of the Treasury Department to Silas Wright was the first tender of a cabinet position to any one. Wright promptly declined the offer. The reason, as stated in his letter, was that he had pledged himself to serve as governor, if elected, and should he fail to do so it would be said that his nomination had been a trick to enable him to procure a cabinet position. When expressing regret because Wright had felt constrained to decline, Polk stated that while he had not yet decided upon a person for any of the cabinet positions, he intended to select either the Secretary of State or the Secretary of the Treasury from the state of New York. He asked Wright freely to suggest a man for either position.[22] In his reply Wright recommended Benjamin F. Butler for the State Department and Azariah C. Flagg for the Treasury. Lest Polk might think that he would have accepted the State portfolio, he assured the President-elect that he did not feel qualified to fill that office. Had he been at liberty to fill any such position he would have accepted the Treasury appointment.

In a letter dated January 4, 1845, Polk assured Van Buren that his nomination at Baltimore had been unsought and unexpected. He prevaricated to the degree of stating that: ''Until

---

[21] Rush to Polk, Dec. 27, 1844; Dallas to Polk, Jan. 10, 1845, *ibid.*

[22] Polk to Wright, Dec. 7; Wright to Polk, Dec. 20, 1844; Polk to Wright, Jan. 4, 1845, *ibid.*

the moment it was made, it was very far from my thoughts, that any state of circumstances could arise, which could lead to such a result.'' He thanked the ex-President for his ''powerful support'' and requested his advice as to suitable members of the cabinet. Wright, he said, was the only selection he had made without consulting anyone, but as  that offer had been declined, he would like to have Van Buren suggest persons for either the State or Treasury Departments.[23] In reply, Van Buren stated that Polk had acted just as he would have done in offering the Treasury portfolio to Wright, and that Wright's refusal to accept was due entirely to the political situation in New York. He knew of no one so well qualified to take charge of foreign affairs as Benjamin F. Butler, and he believed either Flagg or Cambreleng to be suitable for the Treasury Department. A month later he told Polk that Donelson would be a good man to have near him. He had desired to have Donelson in his own cabinet, but had feared that modesty would prevent him from accepting.[24] Jackson believed that Wright's refusal to accept a cabinet position had been due to the fear that Calhoun would be retained. He advised Polk to deliberate well and to make no final decisions until he had reached Washington. He believed Mason and Wilkins to be worthy men, but ''surely you will do well to select an entire cabinett fresh from the people as your own, & leave Mr. Tylers out to be provided for, if thought worthy otherwise.''[25]

Before making another tender of a cabinet office Polk prepared a form of invitation to be used in future cases. Its purpose was to make clear to those who might receive it that a cabinet position was not to be used, during the next four years, as a stepping-stone to the Presidency, and that each member

---

[23] Polk to Van Buren, Jan. 4, 1845, *Van Buren Papers*. Also, copy in *Polk Papers*.

[24] Van Buren to Polk, Jan. 18, 1845, *Polk Papers* and *Van B. Papers;* Van Buren to Polk, Feb. 21, *Polk Papers*.

[25] Jackson to Polk, Jan. 10, 1845, *Polk Papers*.

must devote his whole time to the duties of his office.[26]  Although he was not a military man, Polk possessed at least one attribute of a true soldier.  As a private in the ranks of his party he was ever ready to submit without complaint to the judgment of the leaders; and now, as party chieftain, he required from others a similar respect for authority.  Jackson, who knew Polk thoroughly, assured Blair that ''He will have no caball about him, his heads of Departments must be a unit.  *This is my opinion of the man,* and I think you will, when you know the men be pleased with his selection.''[27]

On January 28, 1845, Polk left his home at Columbia and set out for Washington.  The fact that he was going to fill the highest office of his country did not for a moment overcome his habitual caution nor prevent him from giving thoughtful attention to minute details.  He had written to Cave Johnson and other friends and asked them to procure rooms for him at Coleman's hotel, but the rates must be reasonable and the bargain made in advance.[28]

When he arrived in Washington in the middle of February the President-elect had not, with the exception of Buchanan, definitely decided upon any member of his cabinet.[29]  Early in

---

[26] See *infra*, p. 325.

[27] Jackson to Blair, Jan. 21, 1845, *Jackson Papers*.  There were, of course, those who held a radically different opinion.  ''Polk,'' wrote Prentiss, ''was elected by a union of factions.  He has neither honesty nor capacity to be the president even of his party—he will become at once the tool of those factions'' (Prentiss to Crittenden, Dec. 22, 1844, *Crittenden Papers*).  J. K. Paulding, also, considered Polk weak and unable to cope with the situation, ''whether he selects a northern, a southern, or a mixed cabinet.''  ''He is by no means a great man—nor scarcely one of extraordinary mediocrity; and if the truth must be told, I admire Mrs. Polk much more than I do the colonel (Paulding to Van Buren, Jan. 19, 1845, *Van Buren Papers*).

[28] ''You know I have no money to spend unnecessarily,—and to avoid being subjected to an extravagant or enormous charge, it is necessary that a *distinct bargain* shall be made in advance'' (Polk to Johnson, Dec. 21, 1844, ''Polk-Johnson Letters'').

[29] According to Gideon Welles, he had also settled upon Bancroft for the Treasury and Walker for Attorney General, before leaving Tennessee (MS ''Rev. of Pol. Hist. of U. S. and Pres. Contests,'' *Welles Papers*).

the winter, at a meeting held at the Hermitage, Buchanan had been discussed as a possible premier for the cabinet, but then it was believed that his appointment would cause too much jealously on the part of Benton, Calhoun, Cass, and Wright.[30] However, on his arrival in Washington, Polk immediately invited Buchanan to take charge of the State Department, and the tender was promptly accepted.[31]

Having thus provided for Pennsylvania, Polk addressed another letter to Van Buren. When he last wrote, he said, he intended to look to New York for either a Secretary of State or a Secretary of War. Subsequently he had decided to call a citizen of another state to the Department of State, but was still desirous that a citizen of New York should take charge of the Treasury. Such had been his intention when he came to Washington. On his arrival, however, he found that the South had already united on a distinguished individual from that section and that Indiana as well as other western states favored the same person.

I was not satisfied that it was proper to appoint him to that Post—but became convinced—that if I did not—great and extensive dissatisfaction would prevail—unless I could find some individual in some part of the Union who would be unexceptionable to them & also to the North.

Believing that Bancroft would fulfil these conditions, ''my present determination therefore is to call him to that [Treasury] Department.'' He was inclined, he said, to retain Mason in charge of the Navy, and would be glad to have either Butler or Marcy as his Secretary of War.[32] Evidently the distinguished individual mentioned in the letter was Robert J. Walker, of Mississippi. Writing early in January, A. V. Brown told Polk

---

[30] J. P. Brawles to Buchanan, Dec. 20, 1844, *Buchanan Papers*. Brawles was told this by A. V. Brown, who had been present when Polk discussed cabinet appointments with Jackson.

[31] Polk's letter was dated at Washington on Feb. 17 (*Buchanan Papers*) and Buchanan replied on Feb. 18 (*Polk Papers*).

[32] Polk to Van Buren, Feb. 22, 1845, *Van Buren Papers*.

that Joseph A. Wright, Representative from Indiana, had reported that his own section as well as the Northwest wished Walker to be made Secretary of the Treasury so that he might have the appointment of land agents and other western officials. If, said he, Silas Wright should be given the office, he would use it to his own advantage and to the prejudice of Cass. From Cave Johnson, also, came the information that the ''Cass men'' all preferred Walker, and he gave the same reasons for their preference.[33]

Polk did not yield immediately to the importunities of Walker's friends; instead he held to his original plan of making Bancroft Secretary of the Treasury and Walker Attorney General. He even drafted a letter in which he invited Walker to accept the latter position, but probably it was never sent.[34] On February 25, without awaiting a reply from Van Buren, he offered the War portfolio to Benjamin F. Butler. Butler promptly declined because of ''domestic and prudential considerations,'' although he would have made the *sacrifice* if he had been tendered either the State or the Treasury Department.[35]

Van Buren deliberated well before answering Polk's letter of February 22; but on March 1, he drafted a reply and sent it to Washington by his son, Smith Van Buren. In it he said that the ''honest portion'' of the New York Democracy were excited by a rumor that Woodbury was to be made Secretary of the Treasury, and that New York was to be passed over entirely. He did not say, but seemed to assume, that Butler would reconsider his refusal of the War portfolio.[36] Polk appears to have felt

---

[33] Brown to Polk, Jan. 9; Johnson to Polk, Jan. 11, 1845, *Polk Papers*.

[34] Copy, dated Feb. 19, 1845, *ibid.*

[35] Butler to Polk, Feb. 27, 1845, *Polk Papers*. Mrs. Butler wrote to Van Buren that she was responsible for her husband's refusing the War portfolio; that she had promised that if he were offered the State Department she would not object, but this promise did not apply to other departments. Her reason was that she did not like to live in Washington (Mrs. Butler to Van Buren, Feb. 27, 1845, *Van Buren Papers*).

[36] Van Buren to Polk, Albany, March 1, 1845, *Polk Papers*.

that Butler's prompt refusal and Van Buren's delay had absolved him from further obligation to that wing of the party, for, on March 1, he informed Van Buren that, as Flagg did not have a *national* reputation, he had decided to make Marcy Secretary of War. He hoped that this appointment would be satisfactory to New York. The rumor that Bancroft was to be made Secretary of the Treasury had ''brought down upon me'' the delegations from New Hampshire and Maine, and many—on account of the patronage he dispenses—were demanding the appointment of a southern man to that office.[37]

When Smith Van Buren arrived in Washington with the letter from his father he was chagrined to learn that Polk had already appointed Marcy. ''Well,'' he reported to the ex-President,

the letter which you rec'd dated last night from the illustrious cabinet-maker of our day has advised you of the fate of my mission; and unless the excuses & explanations were more skilfully done in writing than in conversation, you will have seen through the flimsy pretexts—the contradictory & evasive & trimming character of the business, at least so far as New York is concerned.

Polk, he said, had declined to receive him for half an hour, in order to give himself and A. V. Brown time to ''concoct'' an answer. Polk wished that he might have seen Van Buren's letter a day earlier, but the matter had now been decided. ''The Treasury arrangement [Walker's appointment] you perceive tells the whole story for New York. The only chance now is that your letter may upset the whole concern, & start anew the business tomorrow.'' In a letter written on the following day he said that when he read his father's letter to Polk, the latter, instead of feeling crestfallen, had the ''impudence'' to say that he felt relieved. ''I denounced Marcy to him in good round terms'' and

---

[37] Polk to Van Buren, March 1, 1845, *Van Buren Papers.* Evidently Marcy had been expecting an offer, for on Feb. 24 he wrote to Dickinson about ''my appointment as a member of the cabinet.'' This must have been speculation, because on the day following (25th) Polk offered the War portfolio to Butler.

said that he was simply an office seeker in whom honest Democrats had no faith. Polk replied that he had never heard these things before and was "thunderstruck," although "Dix has told him the same thing over and over again."[38]

Instead of beginning anew with his cabinet making, Polk dispatched another letter to Van Buren. If he had committed an error, he said, it had been unintentional; and it pained him to think that Van Buren might think he had acted unkindly to him or his friends. He had acted, he said under no outside influence; he had followed his own judgment, and harbored no unkind feeling toward either Van Buren or Wright.[39] Nevertheless, Smith Van Buren had formed quite a different opinion. "The soundest judges here," he wrote, "think P. came here all right—but has been be-deviled since he arrived. To a large extent this is of course evident, but·not wholly so."[40]

It is scarcely to be wondered at that Polk should have dissembled during the days just preceding his inauguration. He was beset on every hand by conflicting demands, all of which he was expected to satisfy. That he strove to harmonize factional discord so far as his own self-respect would permit, there is no reason to doubt. He tried to deal fairly with each faction, but to accept the dictation of none. If the Van Burenites suffered disappointment they had only themselves to blame, for Polk had given them more consideration than he had ever received from them. He had tendered cabinet positions to two of their number,

---

[38] Smith Van Buren to his father, March 2, 3, 1845, *Van Buren Papers.* Tilden and O'Sullivan, who bore letters from Butler to Polk, were, on the other hand, thoroughly captivated by the President-elect. The latter reported that Polk seemed like "one of us" and evinced great admiration for both Wright and Van Buren. "He certainly entirely won the hearts of both of us, and has effectually dissipated whatever slight degree of anxiety may have rested in our minds in regard to the Adm'n" (O'Sullivan to Van Buren, Washington, March 1, 1845, *Van Buren Papers*).

[39] Polk to Van Buren, March 3, 1845, *Polk Papers.*

[40] Smith Van Buren to his father, March 4, 1845, *Van Buren Papers.* "Armstrong," said he, "so far as I can observe, is the only honest man about him. He [Armstrong] is sick & very much affected by our affairs. He doubtless sees the approaching storm from Nashville."

and he had kept Van Buren fully informed regarding his plans.
He had even told the ex-President of his intention to appoint
Marcy unless Butler should accept the place offered to him. Van
Buren had delayed in answering his letter, and it was unreasonable to expect Polk to wait indefinitely when inauguration day
was already at hand. Surely Polk had the right to make his own
choice for the office of Secretary of State, and it was cool effront-
ery on Butler's part to intimate that the position should have
been bestowed upon himself.

Walker's assignment to the Treasury evidently was contrary
to Polk's own wishes, yet he felt constrained to make this concession to the western element after his own choice, Bancroft,
was found to be unpopular even in New England states. A new
adjustment became necessary, therefore Mason was made
Attorney General so that Bancroft might be assigned to the Navy.
Mason's retention in the cabinet was due to personal friendship,
and not to a desire to placate Tyler and his friends. Tyler had,
in January, bestowed a diplomatic appointment upon William H.
Polk, but the latter declined to accept it in order to free his
brother from any obligation to the retiring President.[41] In fact,
Tyler was much displeased by the ingratitude of his successor,
and, in 1846, wrote that Polk seemed to be "avenging the supposed wrongs to Mr. Van Buren."[42] Marcy's acceptance of the
War portfolio[43] completed the cabinet, for Cave Johnson had
accepted the appointment as Postmaster General shortly after
Polk's arrival in Washington.[44] Although many persons had
suggested Donelson as the Tennessee member, Polk evidently
preferred Johnson, and Jackson assured Polk that Donelson

[41] Cave Johnson to Polk, Jan. 8; J. L. O'Sullivan to Polk, Jan. 20,
1845, *Polk Papers*.

[42] Tyler to Alex. Gardner, July 11, 1846 (Tyler, *Letters and Times of
the Tylers*, II, 342).

[43] Welles says that "Gen. [William O.] Butler of Kentucky accompanied the President-elect to the seat of government in expectation of the
appointment [War Dept.] then tendered him" (MS "Rev. of Pol. Hist.,
etc."). I have seen nothing else to indicate that such an offer was made.

[44] Johnson to Polk, Feb. 26, 1845, *Polk Papers*.

would be satisfied with a foreign mission. Jackson had made it clear to Donelson, he said, that he was the one who had suggested a diplomatic appointment in preference to any other.[45] Johnson thoroughly deserved a place in Polk's cabinet, for no one had stood by him so loyally or had rendered more efficient service during his entire political career. Polk was by nature secretive and self-reliant, but to Johnson more than to any other person he disclosed his plans and his aspirations. Johnson had never failed him in the hour of need, and, both in Washington and in Tennessee, had done much to aid his political advancement. As a statesman, Johnson was conservative and rather narrow; but he was a crafty and capable politician, and a recognized leader in the House.

In selecting his cabinet, as in distributing the patronage, Polk had to steer between Scylla and Charybdis. When he tried to be fair to all wings of the party, he was charged with weakness; while independent actions were attributed to vanity and conceit, or characterized as downright treachery to his benefactors. It was freely predicted that leading cabinet members would dominate the President and reduce him to a mere figurehead, yet, from the beginning, Polk was master of the situation.

Scarcely less difficult than the selection of a cabinet was the choice of a party ''organ'' which would give ungrudging support to the new administration. Historians have indulged in no small amount of conjecture as to Polk's reasons for discarding Blair and the *Globe* despite General Jackson's vigorous protests. His action is usually said to have been the consummation of a preëlection bargain to obtain votes. Sometimes Tyler is made the other party to the contract, sometimes Calhoun; and in an attempt to make out a strong case, some have asserted that Blair's head on a platter had been offered to each of them in return for his political support. Usually their information has been derived

---

[45] Jackson to Polk, Jan. 10, Feb. 15, 1845, *ibid.* On account of Donelson's delicate health, Jackson asked that he might be sent as full minister to Spain, Brazil, or Mexico.

from Benton, and accepted without question. But even von Holst, who had no difficulty in believing the Tyler story, balks at the absurdity of a bargain between Polk and Calhoun.[46] For very good reasons both Tyler and Calhoun despised the editor of the *Globe,* and both supported the nominees of the Democratic party, but such a coincidence does not imply any bargain between them and the Democratic candidates. Calhoun's letter to Stuart concerning the prospective cabinet[47] seems to indicate that he had no knowledge of Polk's plans for the future, and Tyler has specifically and emphatically denied that he and Polk had ever entered into an agreement by which Tyler's withdrawal from the canvass was made contingent on Polk's promise not to make the *Globe* his official organ. As Tyler very aptly remarked, "Blair was already dead," and it only remained for Mr. Polk to chant his requiem.[48]

It is unnecessary to seek some mysterious intrigue or pre-election pact in order to find Polk's motive for establishing a new paper in Washington. The obvious reason for establishing the *Union* was his desire to have an organ at the capital which would give his administration its undivided and loyal support. He had always believed Blair to be hostile or indifferent to his political advancement when he had been a candidate for Speaker, and when he had sought the Vice-Presidential nomination. Both Polk and his friends believed that the *Globe* had supported the nominees of the Baltimore convention with great reluctance and that its editor was now, and would continue to be, under the absolute domination of Senator Benton. This belief is the best of reasons for Polk's refusal to make the *Globe* his official newspaper. Walker and others were hostile to Blair and undoubtedly

---

[46] von Holst, *History of the United States,* III, 7–8.

[47] See above, p. 288, note 9.

[48] Tyler to Ritchie, Jan. 9, 1851; same to John S. Cunningham, May 8, 1856 (Tyler, *Letters and Times of the Tylers,* II, 409 ff., 415). In the second letter, Tyler said that the "conspiracy to supplant the *Globe,* by substituting Mr. Ritchie or anybody else as the editorial mouth-piece of Mr. Polk, is the sheerest invention that ever was conceived of."

desired his elimination. Their feelings may have strengthened Polk's determination to look elsewhere for an editor, but there is no reason for believing that they caused it. Polk's Tennessee friends wrote freely concerning the advisability of establishing a new paper, but in his correspondence there is no letter from Walker on this subject.[49]

Polk's feelings toward Blair are manifested in a letter written to Cave Johnson on January 21, 1844. "Amicus" had published in the *Globe* an article which urged the claims of W. R. King to the Vice-Presidency. In reply, S. H. Laughlin and H. L. Turney prepared an article in Polk's behalf and sent it to Blair for publication. "Blair," said Polk, "surely cannot do me the injustice to exclude it from his columns"; if so, he instructed Johnson to have it published in pamphlet form. After alluding to his nomination by the Mississippi state convention, Polk wondered whether Blair would suppress this news "or stick it in an obscure corner as he did the Tennessee and Arkansas nominations?"[50] Such remarks indicate that he did not, even at that time, regard Blair as his friend.

Immediately after Polk had been nominated at Baltimore, A. V. Brown reported from Washington that "much is said here by *some* as to continuing the Globe as the Polk organ—this we will manage with sound discretion. The Globe will change its *tone* & perhaps take back much that it has said & go in *warmly* if not heartily—if so—well—But we will not commit ourselves to it *after* the election.''[51] The last remark might seem to indicate that Blair's fate *after election* had already been determined, but this is disproved by letters written later in the campaign. Cave Johnson, who was hostile to Calhoun and averse to the Tylerites, wrote that the *Globe* was noncommittal and that a new paper was

---

[49] Although Ambler assigns to Walker the chief rôle in the overthrow of Blair, he admits his inability to produce any tangible evidence (Ambler, *Thomas Ritchie*, 252).

[50] Polk to Johnson, Jan. 21, 1844, ''Polk-Johnson Letters.''

[51] Brown to Polk, May 30, 1844, *Polk Papers*.

needed; but two weeks later, when he had come to believe that the southerners were trying to ''appropriate'' Polk, he spoke with disgust of the ''secret talk of upsetting the Globe [and] turning Benton overboard.''[52]   Judge Catron vehemently denounced the *Globe* and declared that its ''coarse brutality'' was loathed by a large majority of the party.[53]

Late in June, J. B. Jones, editor of the *Madisonian,* invited J. George Harris to become joint editor of that paper.  Harris and General Armstrong looked with favor upon the offer and believed that all three Washington papers—*Madisonian, Spectator* and *Globe*—might be merged into one.  However, A. V. Brown, who had come from Washington recently, did not approve such an arrangement.[54]  It was not yet a question of an *administration organ,* for there was no certainty that Polk would be elected, but many of Polk's friends felt that Blair's support of the ticket was merely perfunctory and that a more vigorous journal was needed. This feeling was not caused entirely by what appeared or did not appear in the columns of the *Globe*.  The campaign leaders believed Blair to be under the thumb of Benton, and the latter was vociferously denouncing the ''intrigue'' which had deprived Van Buren of the nomination and, also, the annexation program. Despite the need of a reliable party organ there seemed to be no satisfactory solution of the difficulty, therefore the matter was dropped until after the election.

The correspondence does not disclose who it was that first suggested inviting Ritchie to come to Washington, but Brown rather than Walker seems to have been the prime mover.  In a letter written to Polk, soon after the election, Brown said that Walker ''entertains the same opinion with us'' as to the importance of procuring Blair's half of the *Globe* for Ritchie.  Blair would not be approached, he said, until Cave Johnson had gone

---

[52] Johnson to Polk, June 1 [1844?, year not given], June 13, 1844, *Polk Papers*.

[53] Catron to Polk, June 8, [1844], *ibid.*

[54] Harris to Polk, June 27, 29; Armstrong to Polk, June 30, 1844, *ibid.*

to Richmond to sound Ritchie on the subject. "If that dont take—then B & Rives must sink into mere *proprietors,* with *an able & competent* Editor having *absolute* controul of the political character of the paper."[55]  Cave Johnson, also, had become convinced that Blair must go.  Some of the politicians, said he, fear that the *Globe* will be dominated by Benton and they will therefore oppose giving it the public printing; "I see no chance of a reconciliation with them if F. P. Blair is retained."  A few days later he reported that "the Globe is regarded as Benton's organ by the friends of C[alhoun] & will oppose him to the uttermost & will in connection with the Whigs defeat him & therefore B[rown] & myself have been sounding, to learn the prospect of getting Ritchie . . . . T. H. B[enton] has a great dislike to Ritchie & I expect will be greatly provoked, if he learns any such movement."[56]  This letter shows a desire to prevent opposition from the Calhoun faction, but it indicates, also, that there had been no preëlection understanding.  Had there been any such understanding Johnson would have been one of the first to learn of it.

As soon as General Jackson heard of the scheme to supplant the *Globe* he took immediate steps to thwart it.  Assuming that Polk knew nothing about the matter, Jackson warned him that an intrigue was being concocted in Washington which might divide the party and wreck his administration.  Some, he said, wished to substitute the *Madisonian* for the *Globe;* others wanted to make Ritchie editor of the *Globe*.  He urged Polk to discountenance such maneuvers for

the first would blow you sky high & destroy the Republican party— The second would be an insult to the Editor of the Globe & seperate him from you, whose administration he is determined to support— Keep Blairs Globe the administration paper, and William B. Lewis, to ferret out & make known to you all the plotts & intrigues Hatching against your administration and you are safe.

---

[55] Brown to Polk, Dec. 5, 1844, *ibid.*
[56] Johnson to Polk, Dec. 6, 12, 1844, *ibid.*

These men had been such a source of strength to Jackson himself that very naturally he desired his friend Polk to have the benefit of their services. But battling for Old Hickory was one thing, and loyal support of the man who had profited by the *intrigue* against Van Buren was quite another. Polk well knew that both men had always been ready to throw obstacles in his way, and he had no reason to believe that their feeling toward him had undergone any change.

Jackson may have been wrong in his belief that Blair and Lewis would labor for the glory of Polk's administration, but another part of his letter showed that he understood Ritchie's weaknesses better than did those who were so anxious to bring him to Washington. "Ritchie is a good Editor," he told Polk, "but a very unsafe one— He goes off at half bent, & does great injury before he can be set right."[57] Before many months had elapsed, Polk realized fully the accuracy of the General's statement.

On the following day, Jackson informed Blair of the scheme to merge the *Spectator* and the *Madisonian* into a Polk organ. He attributed this scheme to Calhoun. Believing that his word was still law, he told Blair that "I am sure polk when he hears of it will feel as indignant at the plott as I do."[58] In Washington the "plott" had already been discovered, and Cave Johnson (on account of his known intimacy with Polk) feared to go to Richmond for the purpose of negotiating with Ritchie. The premature discovery greatly annoyed Johnson, and he complained that "even old J. Q. A[dams] asked when we were going to Richmond."[59] Brown, who facetiously called himself "the President elect ad interim," was somewhat disconcerted by Johnson's timidity. He even suspected that his colleague did not desire to

---

[57] Jackson to Polk, Dec. 13, 1844, *ibid.*

[58] Jackson to Blair, Dec. 14, 1844, *Jackson Papers.*

[59] Johnson to Polk, Dec. 14, 1844, *Polk Papers.*

get rid of Blair.[60]  General Bayly, of the Virginia delegation, and a personal friend of Ritchie, now undertook to negotiate by letter with the veteran editor of the *Enquirer*.  "If my road is blocked there," said Brown, "I shall then go for sinking Blair & Rives into *Proprietors* only & putting the political controul (absolute) into the hands of a new Editor & that man Burke would not be a bad one."  Brown believed that Blair would not oppose the change "if he sees that Benton means to be antagonistic to your administration as many of his *Western* friends think likely enough.  He shews no *mitigation* of his opposition & nothing but instructions plain & powerful can subdue him."[61]  Here again is a statement of the main reason for wanting a new party organ— not pledges to Tyler or to Calhoun, but distrust of Blair and a fear that he would be controlled by Benton, who was considered to be an enemy of the incoming administration.  Another indication that Polk had made no bargain with the Tylerites is the sentiment voiced in a letter written by J. B. Jones, editor of the *Madisonian*.  The plan contemplated was, in his opinion, the only sensible one, for he believed that discord would surely result from the employment of any of the Washington editors. "When," said he, "Col. Polk shall convince all parties that he is in his own hands—that he will be the *President,* and not a partisan of any aspirant, there will be no door left open for the ingress of factious schemes."[62]

---

[60] "He feared some newspaper squibs at him & *I feared* he was rather indifferent about any matter that was against the Globe Benton & Co but perhaps I was wrong."

[61] Brown to Polk, Dec. 23, 1844, *Polk Papers*.

[62] Party factions can not "object to the [new] paper because its conductor entertains no special partiality for any one of the aspirants to the succession.  But if *I* were to conduct the paper it would be said that Mr. Polk had thrown himself into the hands of the Tyler men—if the editor of the Globe, into the hands of Col. Benton—and if the Constitution [successor to the *Spectator*], into the hands of Mr. Calhoun" (Jones to ——, Dec. 23, 1844).  Apparently this was written to J. Geo. Harris, for it was inclosed in his letter to Polk, Jan. 4, 1845, *Polk Papers*.

At first Ritchie did not take kindly to the plan which had been arranged for him, and, in a letter to Bayly, he declined the invitation. He was not able, he said, to purchase the *Globe,* and rival Democratic papers would do the party more harm than good.[63] After reading Ritchie's letter, Brown concluded that "If Benton goes right on Texas & Calhoun is not in the Cabinet there would be no insuperable difficulty with the Globe—but you would find it hard to keep in order."[64] Edmund Burke was once more considered, but his former affiliations with Calhoun were urged against his selection.[65] A few days of reflection seem to have convinced Brown that neither Benton nor Blair could be kept in order, for he presented for Polk's consideration an entirely new solution of the difficulty. He offered to purchase Blair's share of the *Globe* and to continue the paper under the firm name of Brown and Rives. Brown was to have exclusive control, and, with Kendall's help, to edit the journal in the interest of the administration.[66] His new scheme, like the others, came to naught, and no arrangement had been made when Polk reached Washington. Apparently the President-elect gave no encouragement to the editor of the *Globe,* for Smith Van Buren reported to his father that "Blair says—'Where am I to go?' "[67]

Polk's own opinions concerning a party journal were expressed in very definite terms before he left Tennessee. In a letter to Cave Johnson, he said:

As to the *press* which may be regarded as the Government organ, one thing is settled in my mind. It must have no connection with, nor be under the influence or control of any clique or portion of the party which is making war upon any other portion of the party—with a view to the succession and

---

[63] His letter, dated Dec. 28, is printed in full in Ambler, *Thomas Ritchie,* 247–249.

[64] Brown to Polk, Jan. 1, 1843 [1845], *Polk Papers.*

[65] Cave Johnson to Polk, Jan. 2, 1844, *ibid.*

[66] Brown to Polk, Jan. 5, 1845, *ibid.* He told Polk that if this plan did not work out he might consent to run for governor of Tennessee, although he would rather "rent a brick yard" than go through that campaign!

[67] March 2, 1845, *Van Buren Papers.*

not with a view to the success of my administration. I think the view you take of it proper and of the proposed arrangement the best that can be made. I hope it may be effected.[68]

Apparently Polk felt that he was regarded as a sort of *chargé d' affaires* who was to keep things running while the great men contended for the prize. He had no intention of playing such a rôle, and his determination to make the administration his own and to have a paper which would promote its interests was both characteristic of the man and an exhibition of sound sense.[69] Even von Holst, who has found little in Polk's career to commend, obsolves him from the charge of subserviency to factional leaders. He says,

Obedience to party commands, was certainly one of the principal articles of his political creed. But if politicians had expected that they were now going to have the mastery, because he was willing to play the part of a manikin, they were greatly mistaken in the man.[70]

As to patronage in general the President-elect maintained a discreet silence. There was much speculation concerning future rewards and punishments, but all had to wait until the new President had canvassed the situation and was ready to act. Although General Jackson made no exception to his rule of attempting to provide for his friends, he did not find Polk as accommodating as Van Buren had been. His solicitation for the welfare of Blair and Lewis has already been noted, and Polk had scarcely been elected before Jackson consulted Amos Kendall in order to ascertain the position which would be most acceptable to the star member of his "kitchen cabinet." Kendall selected the Spanish mission and his wishes were forthwith reported to

---

[68] Polk to Johnson, Dec. 21, 1844, "Polk-Johnson Letters." The "proposed arrangement" evidently refers to the attempt to procure Ritchie.

[69] A rumor that Laughlin was going to Washington to edit the *Madisonian* caused General Jackson much needless worry. He warned Polk to keep clear of Tyler influence, for, if he did not, he would be in as bad a position as Tyler himself (Jackson to Polk, Feb. 28, 1845, *Polk Papers*).

[70] von Holst, *History of the United States*, III, 21–22.

the President-elect.  Jackson assured Polk that ''there can be no delicacy in recalling Erwin [Washington Irving]—he is only fit to write a Book & scarcely that, and has become a good Whigg.''[71]

Congress had already consented to annex Texas before Polk became President of the United States.  Nevertheless, since one of the principal planks in the platform on which he had been elected related to this subject, and since he had been an indirect, if not a direct, participant in this important transaction, it is necessary to give a brief outline of the progress of events during the period between the rejection of Tyler's treaty and the passage of the joint resolution of annexation.

Tyler's annexation treaty was rejected by the Senate on June 8, 1844.  Calhoun, we are told,[72] disheartened by this action, was ready to abandon all further attempts at annexation.  His dejection was so great that Tyler thought of requesting his resignation, but he soon recovered his spirits and his old-time vigor.  Since the treaty method had failed, nothing could be done without the coöperation of Congress.  During the summer, a rumor to the effect that Tyler was about to convene Congress in extra session caused the Democratic candidate no little anxiety, and he appealed to Jackson as the only man who could dissuade the President from committing such a political error.  A month later Jackson assured him that Congress would not be convened, although it is not clear whether Jackson was instrumental in preventing such a course.[73]  At any rate no call for an extra session was issued, and no further action could be undertaken until winter; but the death of T. A. Howard, the American *chargé* in Texas, gave Tyler an opportunity to strengthen his position by assigning A. J. Donelson to the vacant post.  When notifying

---

[71] Kendall to Jackson, Dec. 2; Jackson to Polk, Dec. 13, 1844, *Polk Papers.*

[72] Tyler, *Letters and Times of the Tylers,* II, 331.

[73] Polk to Donelson, Aug. 27, 1844, ''Polk-Donelson Letters.''  Jackson to Polk, Sept. 26, 1844, *Polk Papers.*

Jackson of Donelson's appointment the President expressed the belief that the selection of ''a member of your family . . . . will have a controuling influence with Gen^l Houstin and incline him . . . . to pause ere he declares against annexation.'' He declared his determination to proceed with his Texas program, and to protect that country from the threatened aggressions of Mexico. Jackson informed Polk of the President's plans and remarked that ''This is the true energetic course.''[74]

On December 3, 1844, Tyler submitted to Congress his last annual message. In it he called attention to the threatening Mexican manifestoes that had resulted from the treaty which the United States had negotiated with Texas. Mexico, he said, had no cause for complaint; on the contrary, the measure ''should have been regarded by her as highly beneficial.'' The treaty, said he, had been rejected by the American Senate on the ground that the question had not been submitted to the people, but popular approval had since been expressed at the recent election. Such being the case, he urged Congress to annex Texas by joint resolution.[75] He followed this up with another message on December 18, and along with it submitted a collection of correspondence. He called attention to the abusive character of this correspondence and to the barbarous measures which were threatened by Mexico. Especially did he resent Mexico's criticism of southern states, and he declared with emphasis that annexation was not a sectional question.[76] His statement that ''the subject of annexation addresses itself, most fortunately, to every portion of the Union'' was, to say the least, an exaggeration; still, since the election had been decided, there were many indications of a change in public opinion, and the question was becoming more *national* every day. Could the subject, when it was presented originally, have been divested of its factional and its sectional

---

[74] Tyler to Jackson, Sept. 17, 1844, *Jackson Papers.* Jackson to Polk, Sept. 26, 1844, *Polk Papers.*

[75] Richardson, *Messages,* IV, 341–345.

[76] *Ibid.,* 353–356.

concomitants, doubtless there would have been little opposition to annexation. Now that the election was over, those who had really wished to see Texas admitted into the Union no longer had the same incentive to oppose annexation for mere factional reasons. They might still cavil over ways and means, yet the prospect of eventual compromise was perceptibly brightening.[77] There was no certainty, however, that the friends of Texas would be able to effect annexation during the present session, for those who had been defeated at Baltimore still harbored a bitter resentment. Late in December, Calhoun believed that the House would take favorable action, but that annexation would be defeated in the Senate. ''The real opposition is from the Benton V. Buren party'' who would join with the Whigs against Texas; still he was not without hope that ''publick opinion will force them to give up their opposition. Its effects are already apparent.''[78] It was at this time that Calhoun was ready to make the ''sacrifice'' of accepting a place in Polk's cabinet, if the probable course of the administration should appear to be satisfactory.

While Calhoun denounced Benton and Van Buren for their obstructive tactics, others believed that the South Carolinian himself had sounded the knell of the Texas treaty. A long article on ''Abolitionists'' which appeared in the January number of the *Democratic Review* held him responsible, in the main, for the widespread hostility to annexation. Although himself in favor of annexation, the writer flayed Calhoun for the position he had assumed regarding the slavery side of the question. In the writer's opinion, the fanatical demands of the Abolitionists and the ''gag rule'' of Congress were equally to be deplored; but the climax of absurdity had been reached when Calhoun, in his letters to Pakenham and King, had represented the United States as

---

[77] See press comments, Smith, *Annexation of Texas,* 323 ff.

[78] Calhoun to Clemson, Dec. 27; same to Hunter, Dec. 29, 1844, *Rep. Am. Hist. Assn.,* 1899, II, 634–636.

desiring Texas in order to protect slavery. In his effort to nationalize slavery, he had also nationalized abolition. Other critics of Calhoun expressed similar sentiments. Since the opposition had been aimed, for the most part, at the negotiators of the treaty and their methods, acquiescence in annexation was made easier when it became practically certain that Calhoun as well as Tyler would soon depart from the scene of action.

Soon after Congress had convened in December various plans of annexation were offered in each house, some to admit Texas as a state, others to acquire it as a territory. In the House, after several projects had met with serious objections, Milton Brown, one of Polk's Whig antagonists from Tennessee, offered a resolution which, after certain alterations, was eventually adopted by the House. Brown's resolution provided that the territory rightfully belonging to Texas should be admitted as a state. The federal government was to undertake the adjustment of the boundaries of the new state, but was not to assume her debt or take over her public lands. Slavery was prohibted in all territory north of 36° 30′; south of that line the people were to decide the question for themselves.

In the early days of the session, McDuffie once more presented the joint resolution of annexation which had failed to pass in the spring. It voiced the sentiments of the Tyler administration and was, in substance, a restatement of the rejected treaty. As such, it was unacceptable to the Senator from Missouri, and Cave Johnson reported to Polk that "the great battle between Mr. T. H. B. [enton] & Mr. C. [alhoun] has commenced." Apparently the main reason for presenting the resolution in this particular form was the desire to embarrass the Van Burenites by compelling them either to accept a measure which they had denounced or to incur the odium of opposing annexation after they had endorsed the Baltimore platform. Such, at least, was the opinion of Cave Johnson:

The friends of T. H. B.—— Silas Wright, who took general ground before the people for annexation but against the Treaty are to be forced to take that Treaty or appear before the people as hostile to Texas. Mr. C. thinks that he has got the advantage of T. H. B. on this issue & intends to drive him home upon it. The N. Y. democrats will go en-mass ag't the treaty & I have no idea, that the friends of C—— will take any thing but the Treaty.[79]

On the day following the appearance of McDuffie's resolution, Benton met the issue by reintroducing his own bill which had failed at the close of the last session, with a modification for making the territory half slave and half free. Since this bill could not by any possibility get but a few votes, Johnson considered Benton's conduct to be "outrageous." He asked the Senator to coöperate in offering a joint resolution which would assert the determination of the United States to defend Texas against all assaults, leaving the question of annexation to Polk's administration. Benton declined to accept this resolution, and continued to rage against his opponents.[80] Late in December Johnson thought that the hostility between the two factions was increasing; each feared that the other would influence the incoming President.[81] Benton blustered, of course, for, under the circumstances, he could hardly do otherwise. Since the election, however, he must have known that he was championing an unpopular cause. There was also a future ahead, and his course had alienated a large majority of his party—even many of his lifelong friends. In addition, the legislature of Missouri had, by resolution, requested members of Congress from that state to support annexation.[82] This made it clear that his conduct did not meet with approval at home; on the other hand, such a request made it easier for him to modify his attitude on the subject. About the same time a letter from Donelson told him "that his course is injuring his friends and his country, and that I hoped he would

---

[79] Johnson to Polk, Dec. 12, 1844, *Polk Papers.*
[80] *Idem,* and Johnson to Polk, Dec. 14, *Polk Papers.*
[81] Johnson to Polk, Dec. 26, 1844, *Polk Papers.*
[82] Meigs, *Life of Thomas Hart Benton,* 351.

be willing to modify his position.''[83]  No doubt all of these manifestations of displeasure had their influence in determining Benton to retreat, provided he could do so in good order.  His avenue of escape was by way of a new bill, and this he introduced on February 5, 1845.  No mention was made in the new measure of obtaining the consent of Mexico.  It provided for the admission of a state of suitable size and boundaries, said state to be formed out of the territory of the republic; the remainder of Texas was to be a territory of the United States.  The measure was to become effective as soon as an agreement had been reached by the governments of the two nations concerned.  His plan would delay, but not necessarily defeat, annexation, although defeat is evidently what its author desired.  His bill and the House resolution seemed hopelessly irreconcilable until R. J. Walker, a few days later, offered as an amendment a combination of the two methods, and Haywood proposed to leave the choice between them to the President of the United States.  To this modification Walker readily agreed.[84]  Calhoun, according to a statement made later, believed that Benton's bill would have defeated annexation, and he was scarcely less opposed to the combination measure.[85]  He used his ''best efforts'' to defeat both, but was unsuccessful in the second instance.  Many counseled delay, but at the evening session of February 27, 1845, the Senate was ready to vote on Walker's combination amendment.  Before the vote had been taken, however, Archer, of the Committee on Foreign Relations, offered a substitute bill.  This proposed a transfer of the territory of Texas, with the assent of the people thereof, to the United States.  The vote on the substitute resulted in a tie, and it looked for a time as if annexation were doomed.  Nevertheless, relief was already at hand.  When the vote on the Walker

---

[83] Donelson to Calhoun, New Orleans, Dec. 26, 1844, *Rep. Am. Hist. Assn.*, 1899, II, 1012.

[84] Smith, *Annexation of Texas,* 343.  Smith gives an exhaustive account of the various proposals offered in each house (*idem,* chap. xvi).

[85] Calhoun to Donelson, May 23, 1845, *Rep. Am. Hist. Assn.,* 1899, II, 658.

amendment was taken in Committee of the Whole, Johnson, a Whig from Louisiana who had voted for the Archer bill, now swung to the Democrats and made the vote twenty-seven to twenty-five. According to Judge Catron, Johnson had difficulty in supporting the joint resolution on constitutional grounds, but, after consulting Catron, finally agreed to do so.[86] As soon as the committee had reported the measure to the Senate, Miller, of New Jersey, offered Benton's original bill as a substitute. Benton said from his seat that he would vote against this substitute, and when asked if he would destroy his own child, he replied, "I'll kill it stone dead." The substitute failed, and Walker's amendment passed the Senate by a vote of twenty-seven to twenty-five, Johnson again aligning himself with the Democrats.[87] The amended resolution was transmitted to the House for approval, and although it met with strenuous opposition there was never any doubt of its passage. This measure was given precedence over other matters; the Speaker, by his rulings, prevented filibustering; and, in Committee of the Whole, the debate was limited to five minutes. Milton Brown, the author of the House resolution, tried to "kill his own child," but the measure as amended by Walker passed by a vote of one hundred thirty-two to seventy-six.[88]

The President-elect had been in Washington since February 13, but whether and to what extent his influence was effective at this time is very difficult to determine. Before Polk had left Tennessee, Cave Johnson assured Calhoun that the incoming President and his friends desired to have Texas annexed during

------

[86] "The amendment offered by Mr. Senator Walker," continued Catron, "was rather sudden; it left the slave line at 36° 30′ N. open. To this Gov. Johnson had most decided objections; it threw Mr. Senator Foster the other way, and endangered the measure." Johnson, said the judge, voted for the measure because he had confidence in Polk, and because he believed that 36° 30′ would be definitely fixed as the northern boundary of slavery (Catron to Buchanan, March 15, 1845, *Buchanan Papers*).

[87] *Cong. Globe,* 28 Cong., 2 sess., 362; Smith, *Annexation of Texas,* 344-345.

[88] *Cong. Globe* (Feb. 28), 28 Cong., 2 sess., 372.

the present session, and Donelson informed Calhoun that both Jackson and himself hoped for immediate action by the existing Congress.[89] While at Coleman's hotel awaiting his inauguration the President-elect, according to his own account,[90] freely expressed the wish that annexation in some form might be effected before the adjournment of Congress. Should Congress fail to take definite action, he feared that Texas would be forever lost to the Union. He did not, he said, have time to examine the different measures proposed, but thought that any measure would be better than none. That he desired to have this vexed question settled before his inauguration, we may very well believe. Indeed, it was said that he offered rewards and threatened punishments for the purpose of influencing votes. Such charges rested on no tangible evidence and doubtless, for the most part, were unfounded, although it is quite probable that he may have let it be known that the disloyal need not look to him for favors. Always ready to ''play the game'' himself, he was a firm believer in party discipline.

Later, a more serious charge was brought against Polk in this connection—a charge of base deception instead of party discipline. In a letter printed in the New York *Evening Post,* July 28, 1848, Senator Tappan, of Ohio, asserted that, in February, 1845, Polk had personally assured Senator Haywood that, should the joint resolution pass, he would choose the Benton alternative and negotiate under it. In a letter to Tappan, F. P. Blair averred that he, also, had discussed the matter with Polk, and that the President-elect had promised to choose the Benton plan of negotiating a treaty with Texas. It was charged, therefore, that at least five Senators had voted for the joint resolution because they had been deceived by Polk.[91] Polk denied all recollection of any

---

[89] Johnson to Polk, Dec. 9, 1844, *Polk Papers.* Donelson to Calhoun, Dec. 26, 1844, *Rep. Am. Hist. Assn.,* 1899, II, 1012.

[90] Polk, *Diary,* IV, 41.

[91] The essential parts of both letters may be found in Benton, *Thirty Years' View,* II, 636–637.

conversation on the subject with either Blair or Haywood, and called attention to the fact that no complaint of violated pledges had been made at the time. In addition, he pointed out that in August, 1846, Blair had expressed to him a warm approval of the principal measures of his administration.[92] The members of Polk's cabinet disclaimed all knowledge of such a pledge, and even the fine-meshed dragnet of Justin H. Smith has failed to find any evidence to substantiate the charges made by Tappan and Blair. On the contrary, Smith offers some valuable suggestions as to why it is highly improbable that the President elect made pledges to any one.[93] Polk had committed himself to *immediate* annexation; and even if he had been as unprincipled as his enemies alleged, it seems incredible that so crafty a politician should have made so stupid a blunder. Besides, Polk was a man who seldom disclosed his intentions until he was ready to act, and, as Cave Johnson said in his letter, it was extremely unlikely that he would do so to Blair. It is significant, also, that, as soon as Texas had approved annexation, Polk wrote a letter to Haywood in which he commented on the wisdom of choosing the House resolution and expressed the belief that Texas would have been lost if the Benton alternative had been selected. "It was not," wrote the President, "until after I entered upon my duties that I had an opportunity—deliberately to consider the

---

[92] Polk, *Diary*, II, 84.

[93] Smith, *Annexation of Texas*, 347–350. In answer to Polk's request for a statement on the subject, Cave Johnson (Oct. 6, 1848) said that he conversed with the President-elect while the joint resolution was before Congress. Polk said that he hoped one of the alternatives would pass, but expressed no preference. After the measure had passed, he expressed no preference until the cabinet had met. Walker (Oct. 6) said that when the measures were before Congress, Blair came to him and, after saying that the House resolution could not pass, asked him to vote for the Benton bill. Walker refused. Blair stated that Texas would prefer Benton's bill. Walker then said that he would combine the two and let Texas take her choice. After consulting Benton, Blair said that they would support the combined resolution, if the choice were left to the President instead of Texas. Walker agreed, and so it passed. Polk expressed no preference—the cabinet was divided. Bancroft's letter of Oct. 13, Buchanan's of Nov. 9, Mason's of Nov. 12, and Marcy's of Nov. 20 all stated that Polk had not expressed any preference. All letters are in the *Polk Papers*.

two propositions—and select between them. I acted upon my own best judgment and the result has proved that I was right.''[94] It is inconceivable that he could write thus to a man to whom he had given a pledge to select the Benton method of annexation.

When the provision was added to the joint resolution which gave the choice of alternatives to the President, it was intended of course to give this selection to Polk. Nevertheless, it was suggested during the debate that Tyler and Calhoun might make the selection, but McDuffie, who was a close friend of both men, declared in the Senate that they would not have the ''audacity'' to do such a thing. When, therefore, the House passed the measure on February 28, it was fully understood that the choice would rest with President Polk. But the resolution gave this choice to the ''President of the United States,'' and for three days more that office was occupied by ''Captain'' Tyler. Despite McDuffie's assurances Tyler possessed the necessary *audacity,* for he immediately took steps both to make the selection and to carry it into effect. In 1848 he prepared a statement which gives his version of the transaction and explains his reasons for forestalling his successor. As soon as Tyler had approved the resolution, on March 1, Calhoun, the Secretary of State, remarked that the President now had the power to make his selection. Tyler replied that he had no doubt of his power, but that he had some doubt as to the propriety of exercising it. The danger of delay, urged Calhoun, was sufficient to overrule all feelings of delicacy regarding Polk. Next day, at a cabinet meeting, all agreed that Tyler ought to select the House resolution and act at once. He decided to do so and requested Calhoun to call upon Polk, after the meeting, ''and explain to him the reasons'' for immediate action. Calhoun complied with the request, and reported that ''Mr. Polk declined to express any opinion or to make any suggestion in reference to the subject.'' On the third instructions were dispatched to A. J. Donelson, whom Tyler had recently

---

[94] Polk to Haywood, Aug. 9, 1845, *Polk Papers.*

appointed to be *chargé d'affaires* at the capital of Texas.[95]   When Polk became President he still had the option of reversing Tyler's action[96] and recalling the messenger or of acquiescing in the choice made by his predecessor.   Since he chose the latter alternative there was little delay in carrying out the mandate of the Baltimore platform.   The progress of annexation under his administration will be considered in another chapter.

[95] See statement, Tyler, *Letters and Times of the Tylers*, II, 364–365. At a later time Tyler was angered by Calhoun's assertion in the Senate that *he* had selected the House resolution. *"If he selected*, then Texas is not legitimately a State of the Union, for Congress gave the power *to the President* to select, and not to *the Secretary of State.*"   He referred to Calhoun as "the great 'I am,' " and to Benton as "the most raving political maniac I ever knew" Tyler to Gardiner, March 11, 1847, *ibid.*, 420).

[96] There was a difference of opinion regarding this.   Walker, and perhaps other members of the cabinet, believed that Polk had no power to reverse Tyler's action.   See Polk, *Diary*, IV, 44.

## CHAPTER XV

## ADMINISTRATION AND PATRONAGE

On March 4, 1845, an unusually large "concourse of people" congregated in Washington to witness the inauguration of President Polk. The "arrangements were admirable"[1] and, in true American fashion, men who had bitterly assailed each other in the press and on the platform now joined in doing honor to the new chief executive. Climatic conditions proved to be the only disturbing element. Rain began to descend in torrents as the procession wended its way to the capitol where, according to the picturesque description given by John Quincy Adams, the new executive delivered his inaugural address to "a large assemblage of umbrellas." "At night," said the same writer, "there were two balls: one at Carusi's Hall, at ten dollars a ticket, of all parties; the other of pure Democrats, at five dollars a ticket, at the National Theatre. Mr. Polk attended both, but supped with the true-blue five-dollar Democracy."[2]

Not yet fifty years old, Polk enjoyed the distinction of reaching the highest executive office at an earlier age than any of his predecessors—a fact which he did not fail to note in his inaugural address. This address was in the main a reiteration of Jeffersonian principles and of his own oft-expressed opinions. Strong emphasis was laid on the value of the Union; "no treason to mankind since the organization of society would be equal in atrocity to that of him who would lift his hand to destroy it." On the other hand, he frowned upon the "schemes and agitations" which aimed at the "destruction of domestic institutions

---

[1] *Niles' Reg.*, LXVIII, 1.

[2] Adams, *Memoirs*, XII, 179. He added that "my family and myself received invitations to both, but attended neither."

existing in other sections,'' and urged the necessity of preserving the compromises of the Constitution.

If the compromises of the Constitution be preserved, if sectional jealousies and heart-burnings be discountenanced, if our laws be just and the Government be practically administered strictly within the limits of power prescribed to it, we may discard all apprehensions for the safety of the Union.

Having thus expressed his disapproval of both abolition and disunion, he again declared himself to be in favor of a tariff for revenue, but not for ''protection merely.'' He congratulated the country on the passage of the joint resolution to annex Texas, and he pronounced our title to Oregon to be ''clear and unquestionable.'' Experience, he said, had disproved the old belief that a federal system could not operate over a large area, and like a true expansionist expressed the opinion that as the system ''shall be extended the bonds of our Union, so far from being weakened, will become stronger.''

The reference to Texas must have been inserted shortly before the address was delivered, but certain letters written by A. V. Brown indicate that the first draft of the inaugural was written early in December and sent to Washington for criticism and approval by Polk's political friends. The Brown letters are too enigmatical to throw much light on the subject, but as Polk had many times before expressed practically all of the views contained in his address, there was no reason for believing that it was not substantially his own product.[3]

---

[3] On December 14, 1844, Brown wrote from Washington to Polk: ''I received yours of the 7th Inst. *our* friend called yesterday & informed me that he would be ready in a few days & I shall loose no time after examination to forward it to you.''

On December 23 he wrote: ''You must not be impatient—Our friend has been sick a few days—has sent me for examination about *half* to be returned with my comments & then the whole to be finished & polish'd— say all by the first January or sooner. So far it is a happy conception for instance in allusion to the Union.

'' 'If this be not enough, if that freedom of thought word and action given by his Creator to fallen man & left by human institutions as free as they were given, are not sufficient to lead him into the paths of liberty

Among the rejoicing Democrats none felt more sincere satisfaction in the defeat of Henry Clay or expressed a more ardent wish for the success of the new administration than did the ''old hero'' at the Hermitage. In a letter written two days after the inauguration he told Polk that

I have the pleasure to congratulate my country on your now being, really, president of the United States, and I put up my prayers to the great Jehova, that he may conduct you thro' your administration with honor to yourself, and benefit to our Glorious Union.

Success could be attained only by ''continuing to take principle for your guide, and public good for your end, steering clear of the intrigues & machinations of political clickes.''[4] If the General had any misgivings regarding Polk's independence, they must have been removed by the receipt of a letter from Judge Catron—a letter written before his own had reached Washington. ''Our friend,'' wrote the judge, ''is very prudent, and *eminently* firm, regardless of consequences. He came here to be—THE

---

& peace, whither shall he turn? Has the *sword* proved to be a safer and surer instrument of reform than enlightened reason? Does he expect to find among the ruins of this Union a happier abode for our swarming millions, than they now have under its lofty arch & among its beautiful columns? No, my countrymen never, until like the blind Israelite in the Temple of the Philistines, we find ourselves in chains and dispair, shall we be justified in thrusting those pillars from their base; for whenever we do, we shall like him be crushed by their fall.'

''It will be surely ready in time & finished with a polish suitable to the occasion. I shall enclose it to you under an envelope to our friend J. H. Thomas but securely sealed so that he shall [not] be aware of its contents.'' (Compare the part quoted by Brown with Polk's inaugural. See *Messages*, IV, 376. *Query:* Was Brown quoting from Polk's original draft, or was this paragraph written in Washington and remodeled by Polk?)

On December 26 Brown wrote: ''In a few days now I shall hear from our friend K again & be ready to meet your wishes. The Major is here on yesterday we went up to see the President. He is acting very friendly but I shall encourage the idea of his remaining here but a short time or the letter writers will be speculating on the purpose of his visit &c.'' (*Polk Papers*).

Probably ''K'' means John Kane, of Philadelphia, but the identity of ''our friend'' and ''the Major'' is difficult to conjecture. Major Lewis was not a close friend of either Brown or Polk, and Major Donelson was then in New Orleans.

[4] Jackson to Polk, March 6, 1845, *Polk Papers*.

PRESIDENT—which at this date is as undisputed as that you was
THE GENL at N. Orleans.''[5]

On March 5 the new President submitted to the Senate his
list of cabinet officials. James Buchanan, the Secretary of State,
had long been a leader in Pennsylvania politics and for many
years a Senator from that state. His selection was a concession
to that wing of the party which believed in a moderate protective
tariff, and his subsequent opposition to the tariff of 1846 caused
the President no little annoyance. He was a man of more than
average ability, but he possessed certain traits which made him
the source of constant irritation to the President. With a timidity which caused him to quail before responsibility he combined
an obstinacy and a petulance which manifested themselves in
obstructive tactics and petty insolence. After four years of intimate association Polk concluded that ''Mr. Buchanan is an able
man, but is in small matters without judgment and sometimes
acts like an old maid.''[6] He was the only member of the cabinet
whom the President found it necessary to discipline, and he was
the only one whom Polk believed that he could not fully trust.
Robert J. Walker, the Secretary of the Treasury, was a man of
ability and industry. He was cordially hated by the Whigs and
was disliked and distrusted by many Democrats. Originally selected for the office of Attorney General, he was called to the
Treasury Department in order to placate the Cass-Dallas element
of the party. He was the only member to whom General Jackson
offered objections,[7] but Polk had full confidence in both his integrity and his ability. As Secretary of War, William L. Marcy

---

[5] Catron to Jackson, March [1845], *Jackson Papers.*

[6] Polk, *Diary*, IV, 355.

[7] ''*I say to you, in the most confidential manner*, that I regret that you
put Mr. R. J. Walker over the Treasury. He has talents, I believe honest,
but surrounded by so many broken speculators, and being greatly himself
incumbered with debt, that any of the other Departments would have been
better, & I fear, you will find my forebodings turn out too true, and added
to this, under the rose, he is looking to the vice presidency'' (Jackson to
Polk, May 2, 1845, *Polk Papers*).

displayed both ability and tact. He was a leader of that wing of the party in New York which opposed Van Buren, and his appointment greatly imbittered the friends of the ex-President; otherwise his appointment added strength to the administration. George Bancroft, the Secretary of the Navy, had had little experience in practical affairs. His appointment seems to have been a makeshift, and he was soon given a diplomatic position, for which he had originally expressed a preference. His most notable achievement as a cabinet officer was his success in procuring the establishment of the naval academy at Annapolis. John Y. Mason, a college mate of the President, was made Attorney General. He had served as Secretary of the Navy in Tyler's cabinet and was again put in charge of that department when Bancroft was made minister to England. Cave Johnson, the Postmaster General, had for many years been Polk's closest political friend. Although he was not considered to be a brilliant statesman, his good judgment and methodical habits well fitted him for the office assigned to him. He was a democrat *par excellence,* and when a member of Congress he was best known as an enemy of extravagant appropriations. His friends gave him the sobriquet of ''watch-dog of the Treasury''; some called him the ''scourge of private claimants,'' and Adams once referred to him as the ''retrenchment monsoon.''[8]

The appointment of an entirely new[9] cabinet caused general surprise and considerable press comment. None except his intimate friends realized that Polk was a man of unusual determination, and that he was resolved to be President in fact as well as in name. The belief that he would be a mere figurehead—a pliable instrument in the hands of able politicians—had become

---

[8] Adams, *Memoirs,* XI, 223.

[9] Mason, of course, had been a member of Tyler's cabinet, but not in the position assigned to him by Polk. ''An entire new Cabinet, at the accession of a new President without a reverse of politics, is a novelty under the present constitution. Rumors of it have been in circulation for some weeks, which I did not believe'' (*ibid.,* XII, 180).

so firmly fixed in the public mind that the most convincing evidence to the contrary had little weight. Although it is now well known that Polk dominated his cabinet to a greater degree than most chief executives, so keen an observer as Gideon Welles could at the time write:

In none of his [Polk's] Cabinet, I am sorry to say, have I any confidence. Yet this cabinet appears to me to have more influence and higher authority than any other I have ever known. The Cabinet is a sort of council of appointments, and the President is chairman of this council, instead of being President of the United States. It is, as I wrote our friend Niles, a sort of joint Stock Company in which the President is, by no means the principal partner. *Yet several of them have been at particular pains to tell me that the President has his own way—does as he has a mind to—makes his own appointments &c.* There is not, however, a man in the cabinet, except Johnson, who does not believe himself the superior of the President in abilities & qualifications as a statesman.[10]

Writing in 1860, Claiborne says that Polk's cabinet was "one of the ablest ever assembled around any executive," but that the President himself "can only be regarded as a man of mediocrity."[11] Both statements are exaggerations. Although each member of the cabinet performed well the duties of his office, none except Buchanan, Walker, and Marcy can be included among statesmen of the first rank. On the other hand, an executive who could formulate important and far-reaching policies, and successfully carry them out despite strenuous opposition, could not have been "a man of mediocrity." To say that the President ranked below the members of his cabinet is only to add praise to his executive ability, for, as a recent writer has well said: "In the Cabinet Council Polk was the unmistakable guide and master."[12] Welles had been correctly informed. Undoubtedly the President had "his own way."

---

[10] Welles to Van Buren, April 29, 1845, *Van Buren Papers*. The italics are mine.

[11] Claiborne, *Life and Correspondence of John A. Quitman*, I, 229–231.

[12] Learned, *Some Aspects of the Cabinet Meeting*, 128.

Polk's control over his cabinet was not the result of accident or of incidental circumstances, for, with his usual forethought, he had planned to be ''guide and master.'' Before leaving his home in Tennessee he prepared the draft of a letter a revised copy of which was sent to each prospective member of his cabinet. After calling attention to the ''principles and policy'' which he expected to carry out it was made very clear that he desired only such advisers as would ''cordially co-operate'' in effecting his purposes. Each member would be expected to give his time and ability in promoting the success of the present administration; whenever he should feel that he could no longer do so, he would be expected to retire. Should these restrictions prove acceptable, the person addressed was invited to become a member of the cabinet. The following is a copy of this interesting document:

Sir:

The principles and policy which will be observed and maintained during my administration, are embodied in the Resolutions adopted by the Democratic National Convention of Delegates, assembled at Baltimore in May last, and in my Inaugural address this day delivered to my Fellow Citizens.—

In making up my Cabinet I desire to select gentlemen who agree with me in opinion, and who will cordially co-operate with me in carrying out these principles and policy.

In my official action I will myself take no part,—between gentlemen of the Democratic party, who may become aspirants or candidates—to succeed me in the Presidential office, and shall desire that no member of my Cabinet shall do so. Individual preferences it is not expected or desired to limit or restrain.—It is official interference by the dispensation of public patronage or otherwise that I desire to guard against.—Should any member of my Cabinet become a candidate or an aspirant to the Presidency or Vice Presidency, of the United States,—it will be expected upon the happening of such an event, that he will retire from the Cabinet.—

I disapprove the practice which has sometimes prevailed of Cabinet officers absenting themselves for long periods of time from the seat of Government, and leaving the management of their Departments to Chief Clerks—or less responsible persons.—I expect myself to remain constantly at Washington—unless it may be an occasional necessary absence,—and then for a short time,—It is by conforming to this rule,—that the President and his Cabinet can have any assurances that abuses will be prevented—and that the subordinate executive officers connected with them respectively,—will faithfully perform their duty.—

If Sir: you concur with me in these opinions and views, I shall be pleased to have your assistance as a member of my Cabinet; and now tender you the office of            and invite you to take charge of the Department.—

I shall be pleased to receive your answer at your earliest convenience.

I am with great respect

Your Ob't S'v't.[13]

To every item of the program outlined in this letter the President rigidly adhered. He had "his own way" despite the incredulity of Gideon Welles. Catron's above-quoted remark, and not the opinion expressed by Welles, is a true statement of Polk's position as chief executive. Even Welles at a later date, although he continued to underrate the President's ability, was forced to admit that "he had courage and determination and shrank from no labor or responsibility."[14] Claiborne has called Polk a "political martinet":[15] he was likewise something of an executive martinet, but no member of his cabinet except Buchanan seems to have questioned his right to dictate the administrative policy of the government. Quite frequently the Secretary of State tried to substitute his own policies for those of the President, but invariably he was forced to submit to the will of his superior. On several occasions Polk was on the point of dismissing him from the cabinet for violating his pledge to put aside Presidential aspirations.

On questions of importance the President sought freely the advice of his cabinet, members of Congress and private individuals; very often the advice given led to modifications in matters of detail, but, except in very rare instances, the main essentials of his policies were carried into effect as originally planned by

---

[13] On the back is written: "Rough Draft of Letter. To be revised corrected. Jan. 15, 1845" (*Polk Papers*). The revised copy which was sent to Buchanan is printed in his *Works*, VI, 110.

[14] MS "Review of Pol. Hist. of U. S. etc.," *Welles Papers*.

[15] Claiborne, *op. cit.*, 228.

himself.  His habit of considering carefully the problems involved before they were presented for discussion left little of importance for his advisers to suggest.  He felt keenly the individual responsibility of his office; it followed, therefore, that his own, and not the opinions of others, should dictate the policies to be pursued.

The President yielded his convictions neither easily nor for petty reasons. Politics influenced him.  But he seldom forgot principles even though he had to sacrifice the friendship and influence of men as powerful as Senator Benton of Missouri and to some extent the assistance of Buchanan.[16]

Polk was not indulging in idle flourish when he told prospective cabinet members that he would ''remain constantly at Washington,'' for during his entire term he was absent from the capital not more than six weeks.[17]  Being a strict sabbatarian he abstained from Sunday labor except in cases of absolute necessity. The other six days of each week were devoted to unremitting toil, and frequently his labors extended far into the night.  Near the middle of his official term he noted in his diary:

It is two years ago this day since I left my residence at Columbia, Tennessee, to enter on my duties as President of the U. S.  Since that time I have performed great labour and incurred vast responsibilities. In truth, though I occupy a very high position, I am the hardest working man in this country.

A few weeks later he wrote:

This afternoon I took a ride on horseback.  It is the first time I have mounted a horse for over six months.  I have an excellent saddle-horse, and have been much in the habit of taking exercise on horseback all my life, but have been so incessantly engaged in the onerous and responsible duties of my office for many months past that I have had no time to take such exercise.[18]

---

[16] Learned, *op. cit.*, 124.

[17] *Ibid.*, 120.

[18] Polk, *Diary,* II, 360, 456.  A year and a half later his story is the same:  ''Since my return early in July, 1847, from my Northern tour, I have not been more than two or three miles from my office, and during the whole period (13 months) my labours, responsibilities, and anxieties have been very great'' (*ibid.,* IV, 85–86).

The office of President is never a sinecure, yet why, it may be asked, did Polk find it necessary to expend his energies more lavishly than other chief executives. The answer is that he felt under obligation to make himself familiar with all branches of executive government. He alone must bear the responsibility for efficient administration, consequently he alone must direct the affairs of the various departments. Supervision on so vast a scale meant a sacrifice of time and energy, but he had the satisfaction of believing that he had not sacrificed them in vain. We are not left in doubt regarding his feeling of self-reliance, for on September 23, 1848, he observed:

I have not had my full Cabinet together in council since the adjournment of Congress on the 14th of August last. I have conducted the Government without their aid. Indeed, I have become so familiar with the duties and workings of the Government, not only upon general principles, but in most of its intimate details, that I find but little difficulty in doing this. I have made myself acquainted with the duties of the subordinate officers, and have probably given more attention to details than any of my predecessors. It is only occasi[on]ally that a great measure or a new question arises, upon which I desire the aid and advice of my Cabinet. At each meeting of the Cabinet I learn from each member what is being done in his particular Department, and especially if any question of doubt or difficulty has arisen. I have never called for any written opinions from my Cabinet, preferring to take their opinions, after discussion, in Cabinet & in the presence of each other. In this way harmony of opinion is more likely to exist.[19]

Still another passage from his diary may be cited as indicative of his industry and of solicitude lest some duty might go unperformed:

No President who performs his duty faithfully and conscientiously can have any leisure. If he entrusts the details and small matters to subordinates constant errors will occur. I prefer to supervise the whole operations of the Government myself rather than entrust the public business to subordinates and this makes my duties very great.[20]

Although the excerpts just quoted were written during the last year of his administration, Polk's painstaking supervision

---

[19] Polk, *Diary*, IV, 130–131.
[20] *Ibid.*, 261.

of the "whole operations" of the government began as soon as
he had entered upon the duties of his office. His searching examination of all documents presented for his signature and his
ability to detect errors caused considerable newspaper comment.[21]
His thorough knowledge of affairs enabled him to win a wager
from the astute Buchanan in an argument concerning proper
diplomatic usage.[22]

The introduction of systematic methods in the handling of
department affairs added greatly to the efficiency of the administration. On questions of policy Polk preferred oral discussions
to written opinions from his cabinet, but each member was required to report regularly on all matters relating to his department. In a circular dated April 11, 1845, he asked the head of
each department to furnish him with a monthly report concerning the work of the various bureaus and clerks under his jurisdiction. The tendency of bureau chiefs to favor large expenditures made it necessary for each cabinet officer to "give vigilant
attention" to all estimates, and to pare them down whenever
possible.[23] Such reports, supplemented by discussions at regular
meetings of the cabinet, enabled the President to understand
thoroughly the operations of all departments.

As a rule the cabinet met regularly on Tuesdays and Satur-
days of each week, and there were frequent special meetings on
other days. Frequency of meeting afforded ample opportunity
for the consideration of administrative policies. Apparently the
President never attempted to interfere with a free expression of
opinions, yet by adroitly directing the discussions he was able to

---

[21] For example: "The President is devoted to his official tasks. He
signs nothing without the strictest examination, and has frequently, to
the confusion of clerks, detected serious errors in the papers sent for his
signature" (New York *Evening Post*, May 3, 1845; quoted by the Washington *Union*, May 8).

[22] Polk, *Diary*, III, 97–99. The bet was made in a jesting mood and
the President declined to accept his basket of champagne. "I record this
incident," said he, "for the purpose of showing how necessary it is for
me to give my vigilant attention even to the forms & details of my [sub-
ordinates'] duties."

[23] Polk, *Diary*, I, 48, and *passim*.

"have his own way" without causing offense. That his method of dealing with his cabinet resulted in both harmony and unity of purpose is corroborated by the testimony of Buchanan, the most discordant member. "However various our views might have been and often were upon any particular subject when entering the cabinet council," he wrote, in advising Pierce to follow Polk's example, "after mutual consultation and free discussion we never failed to agree at last, except on a few questions, and on these the world never knew that we had differed." More surprising, perhaps, is his praise of the President for having personally directed diplomatic relations. "Mr. Polk," said he, "was a wise man, and after deliberation he had determined that all important questions with foreign nations should be settled in Washington, under his own immediate supervision."[24] Another proof of the President's ability to gain and to retain the good will of his cabinet is contained in a letter written by Bancroft in 1887 after he had made an exhaustive examination of the *Polk Papers:*

His character shines out in them just as the man he was, prudent, far-sighted, bold, excelling any democrat of his day in undeviatingly correct exposition of democratic principles; and, in short, as I think, judging of him as I knew him, and judging of him by the results of his administration, one of the very foremost of our public men and one of the very best and most honest and most successful Presidents the country ever had.[25]

In a letter written during the following year Bancroft again sounded the praises of his former chief and gave the reasons for the success of his administration:

His administration, viewed from the standpoint of results, was perhaps the greatest in our national history, certainly one of the greatest. He succeeded because he insisted on being its centre, and in overruling and guiding all his secretaries to act so as to produce unity and harmony. Those who study his administration will acknowledge how sincere and successful were his efforts, as did those who were contemporary with him.[26]

---

[24] Curtis, *Life of James Buchanan,* II, 72, 76.

[25] Bancroft to J. Geo. Harris, Aug. 30, 1887 (Howe, *Life and Letters of George Bancroft,* I, 294).

[26] Bancroft to J. G. Wilson, March 8, 1888 (Wilson, *The Presidents of the United States,* 230).

With a deep sense of personal integrity and a desire to avoid everything which might impair his absolute independence, Polk declined to accept presents of more than nominal value. Shortly after his inauguration Thomas Lloyd sent him a valuable saddle-horse, but he promptly gave orders that it should be returned to the donor. Another admirer who sent a consignment of wine and other delicacies for the President's table was instructed to send a bill or to take the articles away. It soon became known that he would accept nothing of greater value than a book or a cane. The same rule applied to presents for Mrs. Polk.[27] The same scrupulous regard for propriety is shown in his refusal to invest in government securities a certain sum of money belonging to his nephew and ward, Marshall T. Polk.[28] His public policies were denounced in unmeasured terms, and his political honesty was frequently impugned, but even his enemies credited him with personal integrity and purity of character. His own personal affairs were characterized by simplicity and frugality. This fact has already been noted in the care with which he guarded against exorbitant charges at the time of his inauguration.[29] On the other hand, his generosity is shown by loans and gifts to friends whenever he believed the recipients to be deserving.[30] The improvident beggar was unceremoniously dismissed, for Polk had no sympathy for the man who believes that the world owes him a living.

One of the first purely political questions which required the new President's attention was the establishment of a newspaper which would serve as the "organ" of the administration. We

---

[27] Letters among *Polk Papers;* also, Nelson, *Memorials of Sarah Childress Polk,* 89.

[28] Polk, *Diary,* III, 15–17.

[29] See above, p. 293, note 28. He was, according to a remark in the *Diary,* his "own barbour" (*Diary,* III, 9).

[30] For example, when the news came that Colonel Yell had fallen in the battle of Buena Vista the President wrote: "His eldest son, and perhaps his only son, is now at College at Georgetown, and as my impression is that Col. Yell died poor, I will in that event educate the boy, and shall take great interest in him" (*Diary,* II, 451–452).

have seen that the subject had already been discussed, but nothing definite had been accomplished when Polk entered upon the duties of his office. The refusal of Ritchie to leave Richmond determined the President to procure, if possible, the services of Donelson, for in no case would he consent to make Blair the administration editor. On March 17 he told Jackson in a ''confidential'' letter that

There is at present no paper here which sustains my administration for its own sake. The Globe it is manifest does not look to the success or the glory of my administration so much as it does to the interests and views of certain prominent men of the party who are looking to succeed me in 1848. The arrangement which above all others I prefer would be that, the owners of the Globe would agree to place it in the hands of a new Editor,—still retaining the proprietorship of the paper if they choose. You may rely upon it, that without such an arrangement, the Democratic party who elected me cannot be kept united three months. If *Maj^r Donelson* would take charge of the Editorial Department—all the sections of the party would be at once reunited and satisfied.

Donelson and Ritchie, he said, were the only ones whom he would permit to edit his government organ.[31]

Within the next two weeks the President ''had full and free conversation with Mr. Blair and in good feeling frankly told him, that it was impossible for the whole party ever to be united in support of the administration whilst the Globe was regarded as the official organ,'' and that he must have a new paper. In sending this information to Donelson on March 28 Polk said that within the last forty-eight hours the whole matter had ''been brought almost to a head.'' Ritchie had been in Washington and Blair had agreed to sell the *Globe* and retire, leaving Ritchie and Donelson to take charge as joint editors. Blair had made but one stipulation, that the arrangement should be delayed until he could consult Van Buren and Jackson; ''he says positively that if *Gen^l Jackson* assents, he will at once sell and retire.'' After repeating the reasons, already given to Jackson, why he

---

[31] Polk to Jackson, March 17, 1845, *Jackson Papers*.

could not employ the *Globe* and expressing the hope that the arrangement then pending might be effected, he added that ''if it should fail I am still deeply convinced that it will be indispensable to have a new paper and I have so informed *Mr. Blair.*''[32]

After some further negotiation Blair and Rives consented to dispose of the *Globe* and retire. The purchasers were Thomas Ritchie, of the Richmond *Enquirer,* and John P. Heiss, of Tennessee, formerly editor of the Nashville *Union.* A new paper called the Washington *Union* succeeded the *Globe* with Ritchie as its chief editor and Heiss as its business manager. The daily edition of the new ''Polk organ'' made its début on May 1, 1845, and a semi-weekly followed four days later. Among the noteworthy features of the initial numbers were a eulogy on the late editors of the *Globe,* and the first installment of ''Mrs. Caudle's Curtain Lectures,'' copied from the London *Punch.* The humor of the lectures may have been the more apparent to ingenuous readers.

General Jackson was quite as unsuccessful in his attempt to make Major William B. Lewis the ''ferret'' of the Polk administration as in his effort to have Blair retained as editor of the ''organ.'' Lewis had for some time held the office of second auditor of the treasury, and, as he was considered to be a still more treacherous politician than Blair, the new President summarily dismissed him. In a letter to Polk, Lewis stated that he had learned from a private source that

you have intimated that my removal from office was rendered necessary, because the position I occupied was dangerous to the Government, in as much as it would enable me to impart information to a foreign power to the disadvantage of my own country.

He hoped that the report was unfounded but desired to know whether Polk had made such a remark. As the President made no reply to this or to other letters on the same subject, Lewis

---

[32] Polk to Donelson, March 28, 1845, ''Polk-Donelson Letters.''

left for his home in Tennessee and published the correspondence in a Nashville paper.[33]  Polk's reasons for declining to make explanations are given in a letter to a friend in Tennessee:

As to Maj. Lewis I shall of course enter into no controversy with him. What he desires most is to make himself conspicuous by such a controversy. His course since his removal from office proves his unworthiness of which I had full & ample proof before I dismissed him. . . . [Had Jackson known the reasons he would have approved.][34]

The enforced retirement of Blair and the dismissal of Lewis have been given special notice because many have cited them as evidence to convict Polk of ingratitude and disloyalty to General Jackson—the man to whom, it was said, he owed his own political advancement.  There is little consistency in some of the criticisms relating to this matter.  The man whom the critics denounced for being bold enough to ignore the wishes of ''Old Hickory'' was, by the same men, said to be weak and temporizing.  Such critics commended Jackson for discarding his old friend Van Buren on account of the Texan question; but they condemned Polk for dismissing his own detractors and obstacles to party success because these detractors happened to be friends of the General.[35]  Jackson himself, when replying to Lewis's complaints, pointed out that the President had the right to fill offices with men in whom *he,* and not others, had confidence.[36]

Although General Jackson was undoubtedly disappointed because his two most intimate friends had been dismissed, their removal does not seem to have impaired his friendship for the President or his desire for the success of the administration. The last letter which the General ever penned was written to

---

[33] The originals are among the *Polk Papers*.  Printed copies may be found in *Niles' Reg.*, LXVIII, 277.

[34] Polk to A. O. P. Nicholson, July 28, 1845, *Polk Papers*.  In a letter to Polk, July 19, J. Geo. Harris expressed the belief that both Blair and Lewis had plotted against Polk.

[35] Claiborne, for example, reflects these contrary opinions of Polk.  See *Life and Correspondence of John A. Quitman*, I, 228–229.

[36] Jackson to Lewis, April 10, 1845 (*Niles' Reg.*, LXVIII, 277).

Polk on June 6, 1845. It expressed not only personal friendship for the President, but warned him that certain rumored acts of Secretary Walker and land speculators might ''blow you & your administration sky high.'' The letter was characteristic of the writer and exhibited his well-known traits—solicitude for his friend and protégé, a wish to supervise public affairs, and a patriotic desire to serve his country, even though his methods were not always of the best. ''Here, my son,'' he said, as he handed it to Andrew Jackson Jr., ''read this letter, I want you to be a witness to the fact that I have warned the government against the disaster with which it is threatened—and have done my duty.'' The letter was mislaid under some papers and not found until October and it was feared it had been stolen. The high value set upon it by the President, as well as his feeling toward the writer, is stated in a letter in which Polk asked that a search be made to recover it:

I shall prize the letter as above all price as being the last ever written by the greatest man of the age in which he lived—a man whose confidence and friendship I was so happy as to have enjoyed from my youth to the latest.[37]

On the question of ousting Whigs from office in order to make room for Democrats, Polk's own views accorded with those of his party,[38] and when making appointments, except a few military positions, political orthodoxy was a *sine qua non*. Despite the importunities of Buchanan, he refused to appoint John

[37] Jackson to Polk, June 6; J. Geo. Harris to Polk, June 28; Polk to Nicholson, June 28, 1845, *Polk Papers*. Andrew Jackson, Jr., approved what the President had done and when writing, on October 10, to explain how Jackson's last letter had been mislaid said: ''*Our old friend Majr Lewis* has completely killed himself here & I expect else where by his imprudent publications—he is now very sick of it, and well he may be'' (*Polk Papers*).

[38] In 1846 an officer who had been notified that he would be removed protested that, although he had once been a Federalist, he had been a Democrat for many years. ''Although not the only reason for making the change proper,'' the President observed, ''I have no doubt he is a Whig in all his feelings, and that his patronage is bestowed exclusively on members of that party, as far as he thinks he can do so with safety to himself'' (*Diary*, II, 113–114).

M. Read to a place on the Supreme Bench, because that distinguished jurist had once been a Federalist. His remarks in this connection on the perdurance of original ideas showed his political sagacity, for Read later deserted the party and became a Republican:

Mr. Read, I learned, was until within 10 or 12 years ago a leading Federalist, and a Representative of that party in the Legislature. Although he has since that time acted with the Democratic party, I have no confidence in the orthodoxy of his political opinions or constitutional doctrines, and was therefore unwilling to appoint him to a station for life, where he would almost certainly [have] relapsed into his old Federal Doctrines & been latitudinarian in his doctrines. I have never known an instance of a Federalist who had after arriving at the age of 30 professed to change his opinions, who was to be relied on in his constitutional opinions. All of them who have been appointed to the Supreme Court Bench, after having secured a place for life became very soon broadly Federal and latitudinarian in all their decisions involving questions of Constitutional power. Gen'l Jackson had been most unfortunate in his appointments to that Bench in this respect. I resolved to appoint no man who was not an original Democrat & strict constructionist, and who would be less likely to relapse into the Broad Federal doctrines of Judge Marshall & Judge Story.[39]

Even Benton's son-in-law, William Carey Jones, was denied an office because he had once edited a Federalist paper in New Orleans. Like Jackson, Polk seemed to take it for granted that honesty, except in very rare cases, was not to be found among the Whigs, and his naïve remarks about the exceptions which he discovered are very amusing. Senator Mangrum, for example, "though a Whig, is a gentleman, and fair & manly in his opposition to my administration." Senator Crittenden, also, "though differing with me in politics is an honorable gentleman."[40] He does not, however, seem to have found a Whig honorable enough to hold an appointive office. Still, though he declined to place Whigs in appointive offices, he did not, on the other hand, dismiss them for partisan considerations merely. In his diary he

_____________

[39] Polk, *Diary,* I, 137–138.
[40] *Ibid.,* III, 381, II, 349.

has noted the gratitude of those whom he had retained in office, despite their political opinions:

Many Whigs whom I retained in office were among those who called. Though many removals & new appointments to fill vacancies have been made by me, my administration has not been proscriptive, and the Whigs who were faithful & good officers, whom I have retained in their places, seem to appreciate my liberality towards them and many of them have called to express their gratitude & to take leave of me.[41]

The independence displayed in dropping Blair and Lewis was characteristic of the policy which Polk endeavored to employ in all matters of patronage. He was soon to discover, however, that the dispenser of offices is by no means a free agent, and that "political considerations" must be taken into account.

Although many at the time alleged that the President had made preëlection pledges to the Tyler and Calhoun factions, there is now no reason for doubting Polk's oft-repeated assertions that he was "under no pledges or commitments"[42] to any of the political cliques. Even so, their wishes could not be wholly disregarded with impunity. Hostile elements within the party had united for the purpose of winning the election, and each was ready to claim its share of the "spoils." Having no assured "administration majority" in Congress, the success of his own program must depend upon his ability to enlist the support of several discordant factions. His effort to deal fairly with all of them resulted in general criticism, for each laid claim to all important offices and resented all favors accorded to its rivals. To have allied himself with any one of these factions would have resulted in disaster; the refusal to do so was attributed to timidity and a temporizing disposition.

It has been noted in the preceding chapter that there were three rather well-defined groups within the Democratic party. The first comprised the followers of Van Buren and Benton; the

---

[41] Polk, *Diary*, March 2, 1849, IV, 360.

[42] For example, Polk to Cave Johnson, Dec. 21, 1844, "Polk-Johnson Letters."

second, the adherents of Calhoun; and the third, that element
in the South and West which accepted the leadership of Walker
and Cass.[43]   Until the appearance of Van Buren's anti-Texas
letter nothing had occurred to disturb the harmony which long
existed between the Van Burenites and Jackson's followers in
Tennessee, consequently Polk had been identified with the first
group even though his claim to the Vice-Presidency had met with
no cordial response.

Due, no doubt, to this affiliation and to a desire to assuage
the disappointment caused by the dropping of Van Buren by the
Baltimore convention, Polk turned first to New York when making up his list of cabinet appointments.   Wright, as we have
already seen, was invited to take charge of the Treasury Department; and when this invitation was declined, Butler, on the advice
of Van Buren, was tendered the War portfolio.   Rebuffed a
second time, Polk ceased his efforts to placate the Van Burenites,
and appointed their rival, Marcy, to be Secretary of War.   For
the sake of harmony within the party he had done all that any
self-respecting man in his position could have been expected to
do, and if the friends of the ex-President did not receive their
proper share of the ''loaves and fishes,'' the blame rested entirely
upon their own shoulders.   The President's offer, a few months
later, to send Van Buren as minister to England was likewise
declined, and the attitude of the ex-President and his adherents
continued to be one either of sullen reserve or of secret opposition
to the administration.   When Polk reached New York on his northern tour in July, 1847, Van Buren sent him a verbal invitation
to call.   Believing the invitation to be a mere ''formal courtesy''
impelled by public opinion, the President promptly declined to
accept it.   ''The truth is,'' is the comment in his diary, ''Mr.
Van Buren became offended with me at the beginning of my administration because I chose to exercise my own judgment in the

---

[43] With characteristic pungency J. Q. Adams divided Democracy into
two parts: ''Southern Democracy, which is slavery, and Western Democracy, which is knavery'' (*Memoirs*, XII, 11).

selection of my own Cabinet, and would not be controlled by him and suffer him to select it for me.''[44]

Although the President could not consent to retain Calhoun in his cabinet, he was prepared at the outset to deal fairly with that wing of the party. The British mission was offered first to Calhoun himself, and after his refusal, to his friends, Elmore and Pickins. But this faction, like the Van Burenites, declined to accept anything because their chief had not been permitted to control the administration.

The Treasury Department with the patronage incident to the office was assigned to Walker as a clear concession to the South and West. The selection of Greer, a friend of Dallas, for the Supreme Bench was likewise a recognition of the claims of this wing of the party. Apparently Cass did not seek an appointive office, but preferred to remain in the Senate.

When selecting federal officers the President did not, of course, overlook his own personal friends. First of all, Cave Johnson was made Postmaster General, and Donelson, after being considered as possible editor of the *Union,* was, on his return from Texas, sent as minister to Berlin. J. George Harris, whose vitriolic pen and exasperating ''buzzard'' had made the Nashville *Union* so effective a party journal, was made purser in the navy. The loyal but dissolute Laughlin was appointed to be recorder of the general land office as a reward for his services as editor of the Nashville *Union* and for his support of Polk in the Baltimore convention. The President's old friend and former law

---

[44] Polk, *Diary,* III, 74. Polk had received information from many sources concerning the hostility of the Albany regency. For example, Buchanan, who visited Albany in the fall of 1846, reported that, while Governor Wright himself was friendly, Cambreleng and others avoided him. A month later George Bancroft, who had always been a warm friend of Van Buren, after a similar visit informed Polk that New York politicians were hostile to the administration and that Van Buren evinced no desire to renew friendly relations with the President. Although Bancroft had originally suggested the tender to Van Buren of the British mission, he now advised that no further attempt be made to placate the ex-President (Buchanan to Polk, Sept. 5, 1846; Bancroft to Polk, Oct. 4, 1846, *Polk Papers.* Van Buren's correspondents freely criticized the President, *Van Buren Papers, passim*).

partner, Gideon Pillow, who claimed to be mainly responsible for Polk's nomination at Baltimore, was, when the war broke out, made a brigadier-general of volunteers. Even John O. Bradford, whom a Whig bishop had excommunicated for editing the Nashville *Union*, was now rewarded by a pursership in the navy. Most questionable of all, however, in point of propriety, was the appointment of the President's own brother, William H. Polk, to be *chargé d'affaires* at Naples.

Having pointed out that the President, in an effort to promote harmony, assigned to the several factions some of the most desirable appointive positions, and that friendship rather than merit dictated the selection of certain minor officials, we may now consider his general policy in dealing with the public patronage. The patronage incident to the office of chief executive is a source of great power, and for this reason the popular belief seems to be that it is also a source of great pleasure. The corollary is doubtful in any case and certainly is erroneous when applied to Polk, for his administration had not proceeded far before he came to regard patronage and office-seekers as a veritable nightmare.

Polk was a man of very positive ideas, and one of those ideas was that public office is an opportunity for public service. Although in the finesse of practical politics he was no more scrupulous than his fellows, he never regarded any position held by himself as a sinecure and he believed that offices should not be so regarded by others. The keynote of his policy was foreshadowed in the circular letter, already quoted, that was sent to prospective members of his cabinet. He would aid no aspirant for the Presidential nomination in 1848 and he would not permit his subordinates to use their offices for such a purpose; his and their energies must be devoted to the "principles and policy" of the existing administration. Determined to devote his whole time to the public service, he required that cabinet members should do likewise; intrusting of important business to chief clerks was not to be tolerated.

In theory, therefore, the President believed office to be an opportunity for present service and not a reward for acts already performed. And if we except the few instances already noted where appointments were made either for personal reasons or in an effort to promote harmony it may be said that Polk, at the beginning of his administration, sincerely endeavored to carry his theory into practice. The more important appointments received his own personal attention, and, in order that he might conserve his time for affairs of state, the selection of minor officials was turned over to his cabinet.[45] The *Union,* soon after its establishment, repelled in an editorial assertions made by politicians that Polk would have to dispense patronage in accordance with the wishes of the various candidates for the Presidency. On the contrary, said the editor, the President, in making his appointments, will take no thought of whether the person is a Van Buren man, a Calhoun man, a Cass man or a Buchanan man. His thought will be simply: ''Is the man honest and capable?'' Two months later the following editorial appeared:

Mr. Polk has avowed and acted, and will continue to act, upon the settled determination not to permit the course of his administration to interfere with, or influence, the selection of a candidate of the democratic party to succeed him. That important duty he will leave to be performed by the people, unbiased and uninfluenced by his official action. Can any portion of the democracy object to this course?[46]

---

45 Commenting on this policy, *Niles' Register* said: ''The course adopted by President Polk, on taking hold of the helm of state, in relation to the importunities for office which had grown out of an erroneous course admitted by some of his immediate predecessors, seems to have given satisfaction to every body except those who were in full cry for office. We allude to his having announced semi-officially that personal attendance at the seat of government, and personal importunities for office would operate *against* the applicant;—that the papers designed to urge claims for appointment, must be submitted in the first place to the presiding officer of the department to which the office belonged, and must be by him deliberated upon and presented in due form, together with those of all other applicants for the same office, by the chief of the department to the president, for *his* deliberate judgment—with the whole subject before him.

This announcement occasioned a general *scatterfication.* Washington city immediately lost a large proportion of its transient crowd. It is to be hoped the position will be adhered to in its genuine spirit, and with due decision'' (*Niles' Reg.,* LXVIII, 51, March 29, 1845).

46 Washington *Union,* May 13, July 14, 1845.

Despite the soundness of the President's position, it was already apparent that not only "any portion" but *every* portion of the party was displeased. A few days before the appearance of the latter editorial he had told Silas Wright that dispensing of patronage was his greatest source of annoyance. Concerning the general policy of the administration, said he, there seems to be no complaint, but much dissatisfaction about offices; "I sincerely wish I had no office to bestow."[47]  Could he have seen contemporary private correspondence his wish undoubtedly would have been still more emphatic. For example, old line Democrats complained because room had not been made for them by the ousting of all "Federalists," and because Polk and Walker were too busy to see their fellow-citizens. One of them in reporting to Van Buren this sad state of affairs remarked that one "never had to call twice" to obtain an interview with either Jackson or Van Buren.[48] Enraged because he had not fared so well as certain other Tennesseans, Andrew Johnson pronounced Polk's appointments to be the "most *damnable*" ever made by any President,[49] and this fact he attributed to duplicity and the want of moral courage. Nevertheless, it required greater courage to resist importunities than to gratify them, and dissatisfaction from so many sources is but evidence that an attempt was being made to divorce patronage from factional politics, even though that attempt was destined to prove unsuccessful.

We are not left in doubt concerning the President's own opinions on the subject of patronage, for in making daily entries in his diary he seldom neglected to express his loathing for the

---

[47] Polk to Wright, July 8, 1845, *Polk Papers*.

[48] John P. Sheldon to Van Buren, Oct. 30, 1845, *Van Buren Papers*.

[49] "Take Polk's appointments all and all and they are the most *damnable* set that were ever made by any president since the government was organized, out of Tennessee as well as in it. He has a set of interested *parasites* about him who flatter him till he does not know himself. He seems to be acting on the principle of hanging one old friend for the purpose of making two new ones" (Johnson to ——? [someone in Tennessee], July 22, 1846, *Johnson Papers*).

office-seeker. He had the utmost contempt for those whose
"patriotism" consisted solely of a willingness to draw a salary
from the government; he regarded them not merely as an in-
cubus but as a serious public menace. The personal boredom
caused by listening to their tales became almost intolerable, but
Polk was even more exasperated because they prevented him
from devoting his time to important governmental affairs.

At the beginning of his administration Polk tried to follow
the program announced in the *Union* of making his appointments
on the basis of honesty and merit. He attempted also, as we
have seen, to conserve his own time by delegating to his cabinet
the lesser appointments. But for "practical" reasons he was
constrained to modify this salutary program. In the first place
his predecessors had made themselves accessible to the public and
it was difficult for any President, particularly a Democratic
President, suddenly to reverse the precedent. In the second
place he had several important measures which could be carried
into effect only by the coöperation of Congress, and he soon discovered that such coöperation could not be procured by ignoring
the claim of members to their "share" of the patronage. Regardless of his own wishes, therefore, he was forced to give audience to individual office-seekers, and to make many appointments
on the recommendation of members of Congress. In order to
give a complete history of his patronage tribulations it would be
necessary to reproduce his entire diary; some selected passages
may serve to illustrate the annoyance experienced not only by
Polk but by every chief executive.

Once the horde had been admitted to his presence the President, being a very courteous man, found it difficult to get rid of
them. A few months' experience, however, taught him that "the
only way to treat them is to be decided & stern." In February,
1846, Washington was infested with an unusually large number
of persons "who are so patriotic as to desire to serve their country

by getting into fat offices.''[50]   On the anniversary of his inauguration he wrote in his diary:

> I am ready to exclaim will the pressure for office never cease!  It is
> one year to-day since I entered on the duties of my office, and still the
> pressure for office has not abated.  I most sincerely wish that I had no
> offices to bestow.  If I had not it would add much to the happiness and
> comfort of my position.  As it is, I have no offices to bestow without
> turning out better men than a large majority of those who seek their
> places.[51]

The inconvenience of possessing a courteous disposition is illustrated by an entry made on June 4, 1846:

> When there are no vacancies it is exceedingly distressing to be com-
> pelled to hear an office [seeker] for an hour tell his story and set forth his
> merits and claims.  It is a great and useless consumption of my time, and
> yet I do not see how I am to avoid it without being rude or insulting,
> which it is not in my nature to be.[52]

There were times, however, when politeness ceased to be a
virtue, especially after the same individual had called repeatedly
''on the patriotic business of seeking office.''   After a trying
experience with ''old customers,'' he observed on August 17,
1846:

> I concluded that it was useless to be annoyed by them any longer, and
> I was more than usually stern and summary with them.  I said no! this
> morning with a free will and a good grace.  The truth is that the persons
> who called to-day, with but few exceptions, were a set of loafers without
> merit.  They had been frequently here before, and I find as long as I treat
> them civilly I shall never get clear of them.[53]

If, as the Whigs would have it, Polk needlessly precipitated
the war with Mexico, he suffered ample punishment in the form
of renewed scramble for office.  Congressmen now not only sought
places for their constituents, but many of them desired military
positions for themselves.  For the sake of harmony the President

---

[50] Polk, *Diary*, I, 158 (Jan. 9, 1846); *ibid.*, 255.

[51] *Ibid.*, 261.

[52] *Ibid.*, 446–447.

[53] Polk, *Diary*, II, 85.  See also *ibid.*, 105–106.

was ready to suffer much inconvenience, but when it came to a matter of principle he was unyielding. The *Diary* for June 22, 1846, notes that

The passion for office among members of Congress is very great, if not absolutely disreputable, and greatly embarrasses the operations of the Government. They create offices by their own votes and then seek to fill them themselves. I shall refuse to appoint them, though it be at the almost certain hazard of incurring their displeasure. I shall do so because their appointment would be most corrupting in its tendency. I am aware that by refusing their applications I may reduce my administration to a minority in both Houses of Congress, but if such be the result I shall have the high satisfaction of having discharged my duty in resisting the selfishness of members of Congress, who are willing to abandon their duty to their constituents and provide places for themselves. I will not countenance such selfishness, but will do my duty, and rely on the country for an honest support of my administration.

By December 16, 1846, the unscrupulous methods resorted to by members of Congress in their efforts to procure offices for their clients had become so appalling that Polk began ''to distrust the disinterestedness and honesty of all mankind.'' Complaints and disaffection over petty offices gave him more trouble than did great national policies. ''There is,'' he confided to his diary, ''more selfishness and less principle among members of Congress, as well as others, than I had any conception [of] before I became President of the U. S.''[54] Every day added new evidence of congressional depravity, and he was ''disgusted with the trickery and treachery'' exhibited in recommendations for office.[55] The way in which patronage had become a menace to both political parties and to the country is set forth in the entry for January 7, 1847:

The passion for office and the number of unworthy persons who seek to live on the public is increasing beyond former example, and I now predict that no President of the U. S. of either party will ever again be re-elected. The reason is that the patronage of the Government will destroy the popularity of any President, however well he may administer

---

[54] *Ibid.*, 278–279.

[55] *Ibid.*, 296.

the Government. The office seekers have become so numerous that they hold the balance of power between the two great parties of the country. In every appointment which the President makes he disappoints half a dozen or more applicants and their friends, who actuated by selfish and sordid motives, will prefer any other candidate in the next election, while the person appointed attributes the appointment to his own superior merit and does not even feel obliged by it. The number of office seekers has become so large that they probably hold the balance of power between the two great parties in the country, and if disappointed in getting place under one administration they will readily unite themselves with the party and candidate of the opposite politics, so as to increase their chances for place. Another great difficulty in making appointments which the President encounters is that he cannot tell upon what recommendations to rely. Members of Congress and men of high station in the country sign papers of recommendation, either from interested personal motives or without meaning what they say, and thus the President is often imposed on, and induced to make bad appointments. When he does so the whole responsibility falls on himself, while those who have signed papers of recommendation and misled him, take special care never to avow the agency they have had in the matter, or to assume any part of the responsibility. I have had some remarkable instances of this during my administration. One or two of them I think worthy to be recalled as illustrations of many others. In the recess of Congress shortly after the commencement of my administration I made an appointment upon the letter of recommendation of a senator. I sent the nomination to the Senate at the last session & it was rejected, and, as I learned, at the instance of the same Senator who had made the recommendation. A few days afterwards the Senator called to recommend another person for the same office. I said to him, well, you rejected the man I nominated; O yes, he replied, he was without character & wholly unqualified. I then asked him if he knew upon whose recommendation I had appointed him, to which he replied that he did not. I then handed him his own letter & told him that that was the recommendation upon which I had appointed him. He appeared confused and replied, Well, we are obliged to recommend our constituents when they apply to us. The Senator was Mr. Atcheson of Missouri, and the person appointed & rejected was Mr. Hedges as Surveyor of the port of St. Louis.[56]

A week after the above had been written the begging for office had become "not only disgusting, but almost beyond endurance."

---

[56] *Ibid.*, 313–315. Polk crossed out the last sentence, but undoubtedly Atchison was the Senator in question. Members of Congress frequently signed enthusiastic recommendations for applicants and then sent private letters which requested Polk to pay no heed to the recommendation. The applicant of course blamed Polk when the appointment was not made. See *ibid.*, 278, note.

"I keep my temper," wrote the President, "or rather suppress the indignation which I feel at the sordid and selfish views of the people who continually annoy me about place." The rule which he had adopted under which no member of Congress was to be appointed to office, except diplomatic and high military positions, had already caused twenty disappointed applicants to oppose the measures of the administration.; nevertheless he was determined to persist in applying the rule, regardless of consequences. "If God grants me length of days and health," he wrote in desperation, "I will, after the expiration of my term, give a history of the selfish and corrupt considerations which influence the course of public men, as a legacy to posterity. I shall never be profited by it, but those who come after me may be."[57] More than a year later he again expressed his determination to write an exposé of office-seeking,[58] and it is very probable that he would have done so had his death not occurred a few months after his retirement. It would have been an interesting volume, for he possessed both the data and the disposition to do the subject full justice.

The phrenologist who examined Polk in 1839 stated, among other things, that "when he suffers, he suffers most intently." No one who has followed the President's almost daily denunciations of place-hunters will be inclined to deny the truth of this statement. "I was doomed this morning," is the diary entry for February 18, 1847, "to pass through another pressure of importunate office seekers. I am ready to exclaim God deliver me from dispensing the patronage of the Government."[59] His suffering was made the more intense by his efforts to conceal it. His habit

---

[57] Polk, *Diary*, II, 328–330.

[58] Polk, *Diary*, III, 419. "If a kind Providence permits me length of days and health, I will, after I retire from the Presidential office, write the secret and hitherto unknown history of the Government in this respect. It requires great patience & self command to repress the loathing I feel towards a hungry crowd of unworthy office-hunters who often crowd my office."

[59] Polk, *Diary*, II, 382.

of reticence and a desire to preserve his dignity led him, for the most part, to endure the agony in silence; to his diary alone did he communicate his real opinions. "It is enough," he wrote on one occasion, "to exhaust the patience and destroy the good temper of any man on earth, to bear the daily boring which I have to endure. I keep, however, in a good humor as far as it is possible to do so."[60] It was this same passive exterior which led many to believe that he did not have positive opinions on other subjects.

The severest of weather was no deterrent to the procession of the office-seeking "patriots," for "neither ice nor fire" could stop them. Polk "pushed them off and fought them with both hands like a man fighting fire," but "it has all been in vain."[61] He felt the need of "one of Colt's revolving pistols" to enable him to clear the office so that he might attend to his public duties.[62] Most disgusting of all were those who, on hearing a report of an officer's illness, rushed to the President with an application for the sick man's position, "if he should die." Nearly all of them were "mere loafers who are too lazy to work and wish to be supported by the public"—in a word, "the most contemptible race on earth."[63] So far as members of Congress were concerned, Senator Breeze, of Illinois, enjoyed the distinction of being the champion pest. "He has," said the President, "no sooner procured an appointment than he sets to work to procure another," and his recommendations were governed by his political interests and not by the public good.[64]

Although Polk fully realized at the time of his inauguration that he was entering upon four years of incessant toil, he undoubtedly, like all who have not held the office, believed the Presidency to be a position of dignity as well as power. The political intrigues and factional jealousies with which he was beset soon

---

[60] Polk, *Diary*, III, 250.
[61] Polk, *Diary*, II, 360–361, 383.
[62] Polk, *Diary*, IV, 246.
[63] Polk, *Diary*, III, 331, IV, 79.
[64] Polk, *Diary*, II, 426.

divested the office of much of its glamour; the political necessity
of enduring the importunities of the office-seeking horde made it
even contemptible.  On this subject we may quote his own words:

> The office of President is generally esteemed a very high dignified posi-
> tion, but really I think the public would not so regard it if they could look in
> occasionally and observe the kind of people by whom I am often annoyed.
> I cannot seclude myself but must be accessible to my fellow-citizens, and
> this gives an opportunity to all classes and descriptions of people to obtrude
> themselves upon me about matters in which the public has not the slightest
> interest.  There is no class of our population by whom I am annoyed so
> much, or for whom I entertain a more sovereign contempt, than for the pro-
> fessional office-seekers who have besieged me ever since I have been in the
> Presidential office.[65]

Scarcely less obnoxious than the office-seeker was the casual
visitor who had no business to transact but who nevertheless
wasted the President's valuable time.  Even though he begrudged
the time spent in pointless conversation he realized that a refusal
to meet callers would cause adverse criticism and weaken his
administration.  ''I feel,'' said he, ''that I am compelled to yield
to it, and to deprive myself of the ordinary rest, in order to attend
to the indispensable duties which devolve upon me.''[66]

Ceremonious notifications of royal births and deaths added
their share of irritation to the busy and democratic President.
''I confess,'' he noted on one occasion, ''the practice of announcing officially the birth of Foreign Princes to the President of the
United States, has always appeared to me to be supremely ridiculous.''[67]  When his attention was called by Buchanan to a grave

---

[65] Polk, *Piary*, IV, 160–161 (Oct. 19, 1848).

[66] Polk, *Diary*, II, 280–281.

[67] Polk, *Diary*, I, 237.  When not too much absorbed in affairs of state,
he sometimes saw the funny side as well.  E.g. ''These ceremonies seem
to be regarded as of Great importance by the Ministers of the Foreign
Monarchies, though to me they are amusing & ridiculous'' (*ibid.*, II, 215–
216).  The solemn notification of the death in the royal family of Russia
struck him as being so ridiculous that he could ''scarcely preserve his
gravity.''  ''I simply remarked [to the Russian minister] that such
occurrences would take place, and at once entered into familiar conversation'' (*ibid.*, 374).

communication from the French Minister of Foreign Affairs relating to a dispute between American and French consuls over
their claims to precedence, Polk related with approval a story
of Jefferson's ''pell mell'' etiquette, and told Buchanan that ''I
was not a man of ceremonies, that he and Mr. Guizot might settle
the dispute between the consuls in any way they pleased.''[68]

Although Polk was not, as is generally believed, devoid of all
sense of humor, the austerity of his bearing when President of the
United States very naturally gave rise to this belief. His habitual
gravity was caused in part by ill health, but still more by the
weight of responsibilities. Official cares so filled his mind that
no room was left for amusement. This fact is well illustrated
by an incident which he has noted in his diary. One day a
magician gave an exhibition before a select company at the executive mansion and the President was persuaded by Bancroft and
Mrs. Catron to attend. The rest of the company derived much
enjoyment from the entertainment, but Polk felt that his time
had been unprofitably spent. ''I was thinking,'' he wrote,
''more about the Oregon & other public questions which bear on
my mind that [than] the tricks of the juggler, and perhaps on
that account the majority of the company might think my opinions entitled to but little weight.'' He could not, like Lincoln,
find relaxation in a homely anecdote or in a chapter from some
humorous writer. Official cares were constantly on his mind and
he had no time for amusements.

The cares of office added much to the gravity of the President's naturally serious disposition. Indeed, he had become, as
Claiborne has said, ''grave almost to sadness.''[69] While he willingly spent his energies in the public service, he longed for the
day to arrive when he might relinquish the helm of state; it
needed no one-term pledge to prevent him from standing for
reëlection. ''I have now,'' he wrote on his fifty-second birthday,

---

[68] Polk, *Diary*, II, 175.

[69] Claiborne, *Life and Correspondence of John A. Quitman,* I, 228.

"passed through two-thirds of my Presidential term, & most heartily wish the remaining third was over, for I am sincerely desirous to have the enjoyment of retirement in private life."[70]

Polk's success as an executive and as a constructive statesman will, we believe, be made manifest in the chapters which follow. The topics to be considered cover the fields of war, diplomacy, finance, industrial development, and constitutional law. In all of these fields, the President formulated his own policies and, in the main, succeeded in putting them in operation. Soon after his inauguration he announced to George Bancroft that the "four great measures" of his administration would be: reduction of the tariff, establishment of an independent treasury, settlement of the Oregon question, and the acquisition of California.[71] He carried out this program in spite of vigorous opposition. And if we except the coercion of Mexico, upon which there is still a difference of opinion, it is the verdict of history that his policies were both praiseworthy and sound.

[70] Polk, *Diary*, III, 210.
[71] Schouler, *History of the United States*, IV, 498.

## CHAPTER XVI

## COMPLETION OF ANNEXATION

As we have noted in a preceding chapter, the joint resolution adopted by Congress on February 28, 1845, authorized the annexation of Texas by either of two methods. Under the first—the House resolution—Congress consented to admit Texas as a state as soon as the government and people of that republic had agreed to annexation and had conformed to certain requirements specified in the resolution. The second method—the so-called Benton plan—provided:

> That if the President of the United States shall in his judgment and discretion deem it most advisable, instead of proceeding to submit the foregoing resolution to the Republic of Texas, as an overture on the part of the United States for admission, to negotiate with that Republic.

Three days before Polk's inauguration Tyler, as we have seen, approved the joint resolution and selected the first method —the one specified in the House resolution. On March 3 President Tyler dispatched a messenger with instructions to Donelson, the American *chargé d' affaires,* who was residing temporarily in New Orleans.

The action taken by Tyler did not, of course, effect the annexation of the lone-star republic. There was a possibility,[1] at least, that the new President might recall the messenger and select the Benton alternative of negotiating with Texas. Besides, annexation in any case was contingent on the acceptance of the proposed terms by the government and people of the Texan republic.

---

[1] See p. 318 and note 96.

When Calhoun called upon Polk to inform him that Tyler had decided to select the House resolution, the President-elect declined, as we have seen, to express an opinion. And, if we except the seemingly incredible statements made by Tappan and Blair, he did not reveal his opinions concerning the method of annexation up to the time of his inauguration. He says in his diary[2] that his mind was not fully made up as to the choice of method until he met his cabinet on March 10, 1845; he then decided to select the House resolution, or in other words, to acquiesce in the choice made by Tyler. Additional evidence that he arrived at no decision until he had consulted the cabinet is contained in a private letter written to Donelson on the seventh of March. He said:

A despatch was transmitted to you by the late administration on the 3rd Ins. In two or three days another will be forwarded to you on the same subject by a special messenger. But five members of my Cabinet have been confirmed by the Senate; the remaining members I hope will be confirmed at the next meeting of the Senate. I write now to say that I desire you, not to take any definite action in pursuance of the instructions given in the despatch of the 3rd Inst. until after you receive the one which will be forwarded in two or three days, and by which the instructions will probably be modified. I write you this informal note for the reason that *Mr. Buchanan* the Secretary of State has not entered the duties of his office, and because I desire to have the Cabinet complete before definite action is had on my part.[3]

Just what the President meant by saying that Tyler's instructions would probably be modified we can only conjecture. *Possibly* he may have been contemplating a reversal of Tyler's action, although his statement does not seem to warrant such an inference. More likely he was thinking of the reasoning contained in the instructions sent by his predecessor, for this, as we shall see, was criticized in the official dispatch which soon followed.

[2] Polk, *Diary*, IV, 44.

[3] Polk to Donelson, March 7, 1845, ''Polk-Donelson Letters.'' The endorsement on the letter reads: ''The President March 7. Recd. from Mr. Pickett on the 19th at New Orleans.''

As soon as the decision to proceed under the House resolution had been reached Buchanan, by the President's order, delivered to Almonte, the Mexican minister, an answer to the protest against annexation which that official had addressed to Calhoun. In his letter Almonte characterized annexation as ''an act of aggression the most unjust which can be found recorded in the annals of modern history—namely, that of despoiling a friendly nation like Mexico, of a considerable portion of her territory.'' After asserting that Mexico would exert all of her power in recovering her province of Texas, he concluded by demanding his passports. In reply Buchanan informed Almonte that while President Polk desired to continue friendly relations with Mexico, annexation was ''irrevocably decided'' so far as the United States was concerned, and that it was too late to raise the question of Texan independence.[4]

On the same day, March 10, Polk sent out another messenger, Governor Archibald Yell, with new instructions for Donelson. The instructions from both Presidents reached the *chargé d' affaires* at New Orleans on March 24, and he set out immediately for Texas.[5]

In the new instructions, Buchanan informed Donelson that Polk did not concur with Tyler in the belief that procedure under the Benton alternative would necessitate the conclusion of a treaty which must be ratified by the Senate, ''yet he is sensible that many of the sincere friends of Texas may entertain this opinion.'' Should this prove to be the case, dissension and delay must be the inevitable result. From all points of view, said Buchanan, the House resolution was to be preferred, therefore he urged Texas to accept it without modification and to trust to sister states for desired adjustments. He desired especially that the public lands of Texas should be transferred to the United

---

[4] Almonte to Calhoun, March 6; Buchanan to Almonte, March 10, 1845 (Buchanan, *Works*, VI, 118–120).

[5] Donelson to Buchanan, March 24, 1845 (*Sen. Ex. Doc. 1*, 29 Cong., 1 sess., 45, 46).

States so that the federal government might extend its laws over the Indian tribes.[6]

Donelson reached Galveston on March 27 only to find that a British vessel had arrived there a short time before and that the British and French ministers had gone to Washington, Texas, to confer with the government of that republic. As it was rumored that these diplomats carried with them the promise of Mexico's recognition of Texan independence and an offer from England of a favorable commercial treaty, Donelson "put off in a hurry after them." When reporting this information to Polk, Yell said that should General Houston espouse the cause of annexation, President Jones would also support it. Yell had conversed with many Texan leaders, including Memucan Hunt. They talked, he said, of getting the people to demand that congress should be called for the purpose of considering annexation.[7]

Not all of the leaders, however, were pleased with the terms of annexation offered by the United States. Donelson did not believe that the people would acquiesce in annexation unless the proposition were presented to them by their own government, and he thought that President Jones was not in favor of the measure. He was not encouraged by the apparent attitude at the capital when he first reached there, but within a month he was able to report that he considered the question as settled, so far as Texas was concerned.[8]

The people proved to be in favor of annexation, and the leaders could not ignore their wishes;[9] nevertheless, the Texan government could not afford to disregard the wishes of General Houston, and he, at first, assumed a hostile attitude. On his arrival, Donelson found the Texan government disposed to offer objections to the American terms of annexation, and he had

---

[6] Buchanan to Donelson, March 10, 1845, *ibid.*, 35–38.

[7] Yell to Polk, Galveston, March 26, 1845, *Polk Papers.*

[8] Donelson to Buchanan, April 1, 3, May 6, 1845 (*Sen. Doc. 1*, 29 Cong., 1 sess., 47, 51, 56).

[9] Smith, *Annexation of Texas*, 434–435.

reason to believe that, in no small degree, this attitude was due to the hostility of Houston. The ex-President was sojourning at some distance from the seat of government. Donelson paid him a visit in the hope that he might overcome his objections to immediate annexation.

In a letter to Donelson, Houston had said that in the House resolution ''the terms are dictated and conditions absolute.'' Believing that Texas should have something to say about the terms of union, he therefore preferred the Benton alternative of negotiation. The proposed method, in his opinion, left too many things uncertain. He opposed, especially, the cession of Texan property to the United States and the ambiguous character of the northwestern boundary.[10] Donelson reminded Houston that the specifications in the House resolution regarding property, debts, and public lands, were substantially those which had been suggested by Houston himself only a few months before, still the ex-President gave no intimation that he would withdraw his opposition.[11]

However sincere Houston's objections may have been, forces were at work which were likely to modify them. Donelson had brought to Houston a letter from General Jackson which praised the work he had already done and assumed that he would aid in its completion.[12] The immediate effect of this letter was not apparent, but Houston, like Benton, always wished to stand well with ''the chief.'' In addition, he could never quite overcome a lingering desire to be once more under the folds of ''old Glory.'' Then, too, the Washington *Globe* and other newspapers intimated that he might be chosen President of the United States in the

---

[10] Houston to Donelson, April 9, 1845 (*Tex. State Hist. Assn. Quar.*, Oct., 1897, 79 ff). Donelson to Buchanan, April 12, 1845 (*Sen. Doc.* I, 29 Cong., 1 sess., 52).

[11] Donelson to Calhoun, April 24, 1845 (*Rep. Am. Hist. Assn.*, 1899, II, 1029). Houston's memorandum of suggestions is given in Jones, *Republic of Texas*, 414–415.

[12] Jackson to Houston, March 12, 1845 (Yoakum, *History of Texas*, II, 441). See also, Duff Green to Calhoun, Dec. 8, 1844 (*Rep. Am. Hist. Assn.*, 1899, II, 1007).

event of annexation.[13]  For the present, however, Houston was obdurate, and Donelson returned to the seat of government to continue the struggle with President Jones and his cabinet.

Although Jones was noncommittal and spoke of offers from Mexico, already there were indications that popular pressure would be brought to bear upon the government.[14]  Some, it is said, even threatened to lynch Jones if he should attempt to prevent annexation.[15]

On the first of April Donelson transmitted the proposals of his government to Allen, the Texan Secretary of State, and with them a letter explaining why the House resolution had been selected.  President Jones complained about the terms offered in the resolution, but on April 15 he issued a proclamation summoning the Texan congress to convene on the sixteenth of June.[16]

As public opinion in favor of annexation rose to a high pitch, Houston's attitude experienced a noticeable change, and early in May he set out for the Hermitage to visit General Jackson.  After conversing with him at Galveston, Yell reported to Polk that the ex-President was now friendly and not the least opposed to annexation—that *"he is now safe."*  He is, said Yell, the "Power behind the Throne, greater than the Throne itself."  Donelson, in Yell's opinion, deserved much credit for the "heroic work" he had been doing; his relationship to the "old hero" had greatly assisted him in dealing with the Texans.[17]  Whatever the reason may have been, Houston's conversion to annexation seems to have been complete, and late in May Jackson wrote with enthusiasm that "Texas comes into the union with a united voice, and Genl

---

[13] Smith, *Annexation of Texas*, 439.

[14] Letters to Jones from Underwood, Norton, Lubbock, Ashbel Smith, *et al.* (Jones, *Republic of Texas*, 442, 444, 446–449).  Jones's endorsements on these letters claim that instead of being opposed to annexation, he was "its chief author.'  This may be doubted.

[15] Smith, *op. cit.*, 441.

[16] Donelson to Allen, March 31;  same to Buchanan, April 12;  Proclamation of April 15, 1845 (*Sen. Doc. 1*, 29 Cong., 1 sess., 48, 52, 54).

[17] Yell to Polk, May 5, 1845, *Polk Papers*.

Houston, as I know, puts his shoulders to the wheels to roll it in speedily. I knew British gold could not buy Sam Houston *all* safe & Donelson will have the honor of this important Deed.''[18]

Houston's conversion did not settle the matter. Another difficulty now presented itself. The House resolution required that a convention should be assembled in Texas for the purpose of framing a new state government, but the Texan constitution had, of course, made no provision for such proceeding. President Jones could block annexation by declining to exercise extra-legal authority, and for a time it was feared that he might do so. On May 5, however, Jones issued another proclamation. Admitting his want of authority, he nevertheless *recommended* that delegates be chosen to meet at Austin on July 4 for the purpose of considering the offer made by the United States.[19]

Allen now pointed out to Donelson that acceptance of the American proposal of annexation would very likely result in an invasion from Mexico. He therefore requested that an American army should be brought to Texas so that it might be ready to repel such an invasion.[20] Donelson submitted Allen's request to his government; but Polk and Buchanan had already anticipated the wishes of Texas, and a promise of protection had been forwarded to Donelson. Buchanan was instructed by the President to say that as soon as Texas shall have accepted the American proposal, ''he will then conceive it to be both his right and his duty to employ the army in defending that State against the attacks of any foreign power.'' A force of three

---

[18] Jackson to Polk, May 26, 1845, *ibid.* Smith thinks it likely that Houston was influenced to some extent by the belief that the United States might seize Texas as it had seized West Florida (Smith, *op. cit.,* 443).

[19] *Sen. Ex. Doc. 1,* 29 Cong., 1 sess., 63–64.

[20] President Jones maintained later that Donelson, by a ''trick,'' had induced Allen to make the request for troops. This may be a misrepresentation, yet it is interesting to note that Polk and Buchanan made an offer of troops before they had received Allen's request (Jones, *Republic of Texas,* 53, 457–458). As to misrepresentation, see Smith, *Annexation,* 445, note 21.

thousand men, he said, would immediately be placed on the border, prepared to enter Texas and to act without a moment's delay.[21]

Shortly after this promise to protect Texas had been sent to Donelson a significant article appeared in the Washington *Union*. It may not, of course, have been inspired by the President; but the coupling of the American claims against Mexico and the desire for California with the question of annexing Texas accords so well with Polk's previously announced policy that one is tempted to assume that Ritchie voiced faithfully the views of the administration. Polk and his cabinet, said the article, are fully capable of handling the Texas and Oregon questions. It is uncertain what course Mexico will pursue, but

> Her true interest will be found in peace. Let the great measure of annexation be accomplished, and with it the questions of boundary and of claims. But if she madly rushes on to the alternative of war, who shall pretend to set bounds to the consequences?
>
> We infinitely prefer the friendly settlement of the great question now pending. It will secure the peace and welfare of the Mexican nation. It can now be done, and it should now be accomplished. For who can arrest the torrent that will pour onward to the West? The road to California will open to us. Who will stay the march of our western people? Our northern brethren also are looking towards that inviting region with much more interest than those of the South. They, too, will raise the cry of "Westward, ho!" However strongly many of them may now oppose annexation, yet let California be thrown open to their ambition and the torrent even of their population will roll on westwardly to the Pacific.[22]

The preliminary treaty between Texas and Mexico, which had been arranged by Captain Charles Elliot, the British *chargé*, was signed by the executive officers of the former country on the twenty-ninth of March. Under pretext of making a visit to South Carolina, Elliot had, in April, set out for the Mexican capital.[23] His artifice, for the time being, was successful.

---

[21] Donelson to Buchanan, May 6; Buchanan to Donelson, May 23 (*Sen. Ex. Doc. 1*, 29 Cong., 1 sess., 40, 56, 69, ff.).

[22] *Union*, June 2, 1845.

[23] "I shall go out in the 'Electra,'" Elliot wrote to President Jones on April 5, "*but change ships out of sight of land*, and go down in the

Having sent (May 6) to Buchanan the letter in which he stated that Texas desired military protection, Donelson left for New Orleans—partly to get news of conditions in Mexico, and partly to keep track of Elliot. At New Orleans he heard it rumored that a British fleet was coming to aid Mexico. He notified Buchanan immediately and urged that the United States should take steps to protect Texas. "Of course," said he, "if war should be declared against us, Texas will be its theatre, and the earlier we are in possession of the commanding points on the Rio Grande the sooner we shall be able to bring it to a close."[24]

While at Iberville, Donelson read in a New Orleans paper that Captain Elliot had induced Mexico to recognize the independence of Texas if she would agree to remain a separate nation. He returned immediately to Texas. Before starting, however, he dispatched another letter to Secretary Buchanan in which he prophesied that

Texas will be sure to call the proposal recognizing her independence as nothing but a *ruse* on the part of the British government, by which it is hoped that the people of Texas will be led to reject annexation; and the effect will be, still greater unanimity in favor of the United States, and against all interference on the part of Great Britain in a question *truly* American.

He believed that the United States should be prepared for "an immediate blow upon Mexico" in case that country should declare war, and that "Texas will be as ready as we are to defend the 'star spangled banner,' and denounce British dictation."[25]

On his arrival at Galveston, Donelson learned that Elliot was about to leave for Washington, Texas, for the purpose of submitting to the Texan government the plan of recognition to which Mexico had consented. The two men discussed the plan freely,

'Eurydice.' By this means I shall be reported as gone to 'Charleston' in the 'Electra,' and so hope to arrive unobserved'' (Jones, *Republic of Texas*, 443). The preliminary treaty is printed on pp. 473–475 of the same volume.

[24] Donelson to Buchanan, May 11, 1845 (*Sen. Doc. 1*, 29 Cong., 1 sess., 56).

[25] Donelson to Buchanan, May 22, 1845 (*ibid.*, 58–59).

and Donelson was disgusted by the hypocrisy displayed in the representation that the overture for an agreement had come from Texas. "Stripped of diplomatic phrase," he wrote, "this recognition is nothing more nor less than a contrivance of Great Britain to defeat the measure of annexation, or involve Mexico in a war with the United States." Since Mexico was reported to be concentrating troops on the Rio Grande "where Texas has, as yet, established no posts," Texas would probably send a force to remove these intruders and Captain Stockton would be ready to coöperate after the acceptance of annexation. In "addition to the suggestions before made on this subject, I would remark that the route for the infantry or artillery in our service which may be thought requisite on the Rio Grande, should be by *water* and not by *land*." Two days later he wrote again to the Secretary of State. He had just received Buchanan's letter of May 23 which promised protection, but it did not cover the whole ground. If Mexico should invade Texas to the Nueces or farther *before* the convention has had an opportunity to accept the American proposal, "are the United States," he asked, "to stand still and see the country thus invaded, without interposing protection?"[26]

In the same mail with Donelson's dispatches went a letter from Charles A. Wickliffe, Polk's confidential agent in Texas. It informed the President that Captain Elliot was boldly asserting that annexation would be followed immediately by a declaration of war by Mexico. Mexico, said Elliot, would declare war instantly; the United States would blockade the Mexican ports; but Great Britain would not submit to this, and, consequently, there would be war for twenty years. Nevertheless, said the agent, Elliot was fully aware that a majority of the Texans were in favor of annexation. Wickliffe urged that any attempt on the part of Mexico to invade Texas while negotiations for annexation were pending should be repelled with vigor by the United States.[27]

---

[26] Donelson to Buchanan, June 2, 4, 1845, *ibid.*, 64–66.
[27] Wickliffe to Polk, June 4, 1845, *Polk Papers*.

The letter just received from Buchanan authorized Donelson to guarantee protection *after* the American proposal had been accepted, and on June 11, he gave this qualified promise to the Texan Secretary of State.  Elliot's bluster thoroughly aroused his indignation, and in his letter to Allen he said that

if Texas cannot be allowed to enjoy the blessings of peace and independence, as one of the sovereign members of the American Union, without asking permission of Mexico or of the monarchies of Europe, the fact is worth volumes of argument in explaining the duty of those who are struggling to maintain a system of government founded on the will and controlled by the authority of the people.[28]

The tone of this letter had a reassuring effect upon the Texans and lessened the hazard of an exercise of independent judgment.

The letters which Donelson and Wickliffe had written on the second and fourth of June procured prompt action on the part of their government.  These communications reached Washington on the evening of June 14, and on the following day Polk wrote an interesting and important letter to Donelson.  The threatened invasion, said the President,

increases our solicitude concerning the final action by the Congress and Convention of Texas upon our proposition of annexation.  In view of the facts disclosed by you, not only as regards the approach of an invading Mexican army—but of the open intermeddling of the British Charge d' affaires with the question of annexation, I have lost no time in causing the most prompt & energetic measures to be adopted here.  I am resolved to defend and protect Texas, as far as I possess the power to do so.

This statement makes it clear that Polk did not doubt the genuineness of the British menace, and that he was prepared to meet it at all hazards.  He informed Donelson that General Besancon, the bearer of this letter, would be dispatched that night with instructions and that another messenger would be sent at the same time to Fort Jessup, bearing orders for the troops to march at once to the mouth of the Sabine.  These

---

[28] Donelson to Allen, June 11, 1845 (*Sen. Ex. Doc. 1*, 29 Cong., 1 sess., 71).

troops were to act as Donelson might direct, under his instructions from the Department of State. The *chargé* was told that the steamer *Spencer* had been ordered to leave New York to report to him at Galveston, and that an additional naval force would be sent immediately to the Gulf of Mexico. Polk urged that the Texan convention should, on the day of meeting, pass a general resolution accepting the offer made by the United States. ''The moment they do this,'' said the President,

I shall regard Texas as a part of the Union; all questions of Constitutional power to defend & protect her by driving an invading Mexican Army out of her Territory will be at an end and our land and naval forces will be under orders to do so.

The convention could then proceed with its deliberations in safety, without fear of Mexican invasion or of ''British intrigue'' . . . . ''The assent of the Convention is all we want.'' The question of employing the army and navy of the United States to repel a Mexican invasion during the interval between the acceptance of annexation by the Texan congress and the meeting of the convention, Polk left to the discretion of Donelson. He expressed the hope that there might be no necessity for exercising such discretion, nevertheless, should anything occur which was calculated to overawe or interfere with the peaceful deliberations of the convention—

then in my judgment the public necessity for our interposition will be such that we should not stand quietly by & permit an invading foreign enemy to occupy or devastate any portion of Texan Territory. Of course I would maintain the Texan title to the extent which she claims it to be & not permit an invading enemy to occupy a foot of the soil East of the *Rio Grande*.[29]

The troops stationed at Fort Jessup could not, as the letter pointed out, reach Texas in time to afford immediate protection to the convention which would assemble on July 4; nevertheless, as a definite statement of Polk's plans and purposes, this letter

---

[29] Polk to Donelson, June 15, 1845, ''Polk-Donelson Letters.'' Also, a copy in *Polk Papers*.

is extremely interesting. Writing to Donelson on the same day, Buchanan said that Captain Elliot, by obtaining Mexico's consent to annexation, had "deprived that power of the only miserable pretext which it had for a war against the United States."[30]

The troops to be sent from Fort Jessup were commanded by General Zachary Taylor. By a confidential dispatch dated May 28, Marcy had given instructions for the general's guidance, should annexation be accepted by Texas. Taylor sent a messenger to consult with Donelson concerning the necessity of sending troops into Texas and to investigate the resources for their subsistence. Donelson reported to him that all branches of the existing Texan government had assented to annexation, and that the convention would do so on the fourth of July. If any reliance, said he, is to be placed upon the threats made by Mexico and the advice which it may be presumed will be given to her by the British and French governments, "an invasion of Texas may be confidently anticipated"; at all events, the General would be justified in moving to the western frontier in order to give the protection authorized by President Polk. He advised Taylor to transfer the troops from New Orleans directly to Corpus Christi, which is a healthy place and convenient for supplies, "and is the most western point now occupied by Texas." In the same letter Donelson remarked that the "occupation of the country between the Nueces and Rio Grande, you are aware, is a disputed question. Texas holds Corpus Christi; Mexico, Santiago, near the mouth of the Rio Grande."[31]

Von Holst has made much of the phrases just quoted. Isolating them from their context and giving to them an erroneous, or at least an ambiguous, translation, he has used them to substantiate his assertion that Donelson, in this letter which was forwarded by Taylor to Washington, "emphasized the fact that

---

[30] Buchanan to Donelson, June 15, 1845 (Buchanan, *Works*, VI, 174).
[31] Taylor to Adj. Gen., June 18; Donelson to Taylor, June 28, 1845 (*H. Ex. Doc. 60*, 30 Cong., 1 sess., 800, 805).

it was an open question to whom the land between the Nueces and the Rio Grande belonged.''[32]  His purpose is to show that Polk provoked a war by claiming unjustly a strip of land the ownership of which even his own subordinates had questioned. Whatever may have provoked the war, Donelson's letter conveys no such meaning.  As a matter of fact his chief emphasis was placed on the healthful conditions at the places designated and his desire to avoid taking ''an offensive attitude in regard to Mexico, without further orders from the government of the United States.''  Taylor was advised to limit his activities to the defense of Texas unless attacked, in which case he was to drive the Mexicans beyond the Rio Grande.  Donelson spoke of *occupation,* not of *ownership;* but even if he had meant the latter, it is clear enough that it was not a ''disputed question'' so far as he was concerned.  The paragraph which contained these phrases was followed by another which said that ''the threatened invasion of Texas, however, is founded upon the assumption that Texas has no territory independent of Mexico.''  Von Holst found it convenient to omit this paragraph, for it did not harmonize with the thesis which he had set out to prove.[33]  Donelson's views on the subject had already been expressed very clearly in his letters of May 11 and June 2, above quoted, in which he advised an early occupation of posts on the Rio Grande.

In this same connection, von Holst represents Taylor to have spoken of San Antonio as being situated on the *western boundary* (''redete gar von San Antonio als an der westlichen Grenze gelegen'') ; whereas the General simply spoke of the immediate occupation of ''the western *frontier* (italics mine) of Texas,

---

[32] von Holst, *History of the United States,* German ed., II, 72, Eng. trans., III, 90.

[33] His remark concerning Polk's suppression of facts might well be applied to his own writings: ''That his silence about them was deliberately designed is made clearer than day by the false coloring by means of which he manages, without exciting distrust by bold misrepresentations, to give to things which supported his assertion a weight which they did not remotely deserve'' (*ibid.,* Eng. trans., III, 89).

from the coast to San Antonio, and ultimately further north.''[34]
On the same page we are told that the Texan Secretary of War
asked Taylor to protect Austin, on the Colorado ''da es an der
Grenze ist,'' which the translators have made to read ''because
it is on the boundary.'' But the Secretary had written that

The town of Austin where the convention will assemble, and the most of the
archives of our government are now deposited, being on the frontier, and
exposed to Indian depredations and Mexican invasion, would require protection, as would also San Antonio de Bexar and Corpus Christi.[35]

In justice to von Holst it may be said that *Grenze* is the German equivalent of *boundary,* and that he may have been ignorant
of the distinction drawn by Americans between the words
*boundary* and *frontier;* and yet, it seems incredible that he could
have so misunderstood the letters as a whole as not to have known
that the American officials were speaking of a general region,
and were not attempting to fix a boundary line. That von Holst
himself meant *boundary* when he used the term *Grenze* is shown
by the context, and his translators in converting his writings
into English have invariably written *boundary* instead of *frontier,* which had been used in the original documents. Were it
not for the fact that this writer's version of Polk's policy has
influenced both writers and teachers of history, it would hardly
be worth while to dwell on his misuse of official documents.

Donelson's belief that Captain Elliot and his government
were striving to prevent annexation was by no means unfounded.
Great Britain was not willing to extend her interference to the
point of risking a war with the United States, but she was determined to apply every possible pressure that stopped short of
this limit which she had set for her activities.[36] However, the

---

[34] *Ibid.,* Ger. ed., II, 72. Taylor to Adj. Gen., July 8, 1845 (*H. Ex.
Doc. 60,* 30 Cong., 1 sess., 802).

[35] von Holst, *op. cit.,* Ger. ed., II, 72, Eng. trans., III, 90. Cook to
Taylor, June 27, 1845 (*H. Doc. 60,* 30 Cong., 1 sess., 804).

[36] E. D. Adams, *British Interests and Activities in Texas,* chap. ix. It
has been considered unnecessary, in a biography of Polk, to discuss in
detail the acts and the motives of England, France, and Mexico, except
in their bearing on Polk's policy. The part played by England is well
presented in the volume by Professor Adams just cited.

officious meddling of Captain Elliot and the Mexican threats of invasion caused anxiety in Texas, and fear of the latter led the government to solicit the protection of the United States. By instructing Taylor to send dragoons to San Antonio and infantry to Corpus Christi, Donnelson had inspired the people with a feeling of safety, even though Taylor could not reach these points before the meeting of the convention.[37]

The preliminary treaty which Elliot had arranged between Texas and Mexico[38] provided for the suspension of hostilities until the people of Texas had either accepted or rejected the terms of the agreement. Accordingly, on June 4, President Jones issued his proclamaation declaring a truce. The general effect of this proclamation and of the mystery and secrecy employed by Elliot in bringing the two governments together[39] led the people still more to distrust both men, and, consequently, aided the cause of annexation. Donelson handled the question most skilfully and did much to solidify the sentiment in favor of joining the United States. On the other hand, he very sensibly refrained from doing anything which might antagonize the Texan officials who were still trying to maintain a neutral position.[40] Then, too, the apparent insincerity of Mexico added strength to the annexationists. As soon as President Jones had proclaimed a truce, Bankhead, the British minister in Mexico, pressed that government to issue a similar proclamation. Instead of complying, Cuevas, the Minister of Foreign Affairs, made dire threats of war on Texas.[41] Even those in the lone-star republic who were inclined to oppose annexation could no longer contend that Mexico would peacefully concede independence.

---

[37] Allen to Donelson, June 26; Donelson to Allen, June 30, 1845 (*Sen. Ex. Doc. 1*, 29 Cong., 1 sess., 92, 94). Smith, *Annexation of Texas*, 451.

[38] For a copy of this document see Adams, *op. cit.*, 210–211, or Jones, *Republic of Texas*, 473–475.

[39] Elliot was later reproved by the British Foreign Secretary for the secrecy of his proceedings because they ''laid Great Britain open to the charge of intriguing in Texas'' (Aberdeen to Elliot, July 3, 1845; cited by Adams, *op. cit.*, 220).

[40] Smith, *Annexation of Texas*, 452–454.

[41] Adams, *British Interests and Activities in Texas*, 221–222.

On June 16 the Texan congress assembled, and President Jones submitted the American joint resolution; two days later he placed before this body the terms of the conditional recognition of independence which Elliot had negotiated with Mexico. On the congress now devolved the duty of choosing between the two proposals; but as Mexico was already threatening war, there was little probability that any arrangement made with that country would be selected. Without loss of time the congress by a unanimous vote agreed to accept the offer made by the United States, and by a similar vote it rejected the proposed treaty with Mexico.[42]

As the time for the meeting of the popular convention approached, it appeared that there might be greater difficulty in winning the approval of that body. In several respects the terms offered by the United States were unacceptable to the Texans. The American joint resolution had not specified a definite boundary, and there were uncertainties regarding public lands, Indian policy, and other details. Some suggested, also, that before it had entered the Union the republic ought to be divided into several states, in order to increase its political importance.[43] On the other hand, Donelson had been instructed by his government to urge upon Texas the wisdom of accepting the proposed terms without modification, and before the meeting of the convention he had spared no effort in shaping public opinion to sanction such a course. In this connection he pointed out that many of the unsatisfactory matters could be adjusted after annexation, while haggling over terms would result in discord and delay.

---

[42] Donelson to Buchanan, June 23, 1845 (*Sen. Ex. Doc. 1*, 29 Cong., 1 sess., 83).

[43] Smith, *Annexation of Texas*, 456–457. General Houston, as we have noted, had had misgivings regarding the boundary question, and although he had left the scene of action Polk deemed it worth while to reassure him on the subject. ''You may have no apprehensions,'' wrote the President, ''in regard to your boundary. Texas once a part of the Union & we will maintain all your rights of territory & will not suffer them to be sacrificed'' (Polk to Houston (copy), June 6, 1845, *Polk Papers*).

An interesting account of the part played by Donelson and of the attitude of the Texan officials is given in a letter written to Buchanan from Washington, Texas, by John G. Tod. Tod had evidently just arrived in Texas from Washington (D. C.), and his letter is in the form of a daily journal of events from July 1 to July 11, 1845.[44] Donelson, according to Tod, had no doubt whatever that annexation would be consummated, and he could not understand why officials in Washington were so excited about the question. " 'There has,' said he, 'never been any difficulty about it at all. President Jones has always been open and candid upon this subject and there was no room to apprehend trouble and difficulty if it is not created by the management of the matter in Washington.' "[45] Under date of July 2, Tod recorded that Jones, Allen, and Raymond[46] had called on Donelson. "The President and the latter laughed and joked a good deal about the excitement on the Potomac." After this meeting Tod had a long conversation with Jones and told him that Polk and his cabinet had become suspicious because Ashbel Smith, on his way to England, had passed right by Washington without calling on the President. With a remark that he was not responsible for Smith's acts, Jones proceeded to say that there never had been any doubt of or opposition to annexation. With apparent contradiction, however, Tod reported Jones to have said that "Major Donelson had conducted the affair very ably, and if it had not been for his prudence and good management, the last Congress would have involved the measure with much greater obstacles and probably defeated it." After predicting that there would be no war if the United States would "only keep quiet and cool," Jones said that there were two very

---

[44] *Buchanan Papers.* Tod was a Texas army captain and served as bearer of dispatches. Later, he was employed by Polk as special messenger to carry to President Jones a copy of the joint resolution of Congress which admitted Texas into the Union (Polk, *Diary,* I, 148).

[45] This was written on July 1. Evidently Donelson's opinion of Jones had undergone a change.

[46] Recently the Texan *chargé* at Washington.

unaccountable things connected with annexation: first, that the United States should feel any uneasiness, when the government as well as every man, woman, and child in Texas desired annexation; and second, that Elliot should have entertained any hope that the offer of independence or anything else would prevent Texas from joining the United States. He had, he said, told Elliot that he would lay his offer before the congress and the convention, but that he did not doubt that Texas would be annexed. " 'His object in obtaining the offer which he did from Mexico, was to strengthen the cause of Annexation, and place us on higher grounds with the world. It was truly a great advantage to our cause, that it disarmed Mexico entirely in the estimation of other Nations, and Mexico was fully aware of it.' "[47] Jones's statement that no attempt had been made to deceive Elliot accords with the reports which the British diplomat made to his own government.[48] Houston, also, testified that President Jones had not been guilty of double dealing and denied that European governments had been intriguing in Texas.[49] This denial does not, of course, mean that the ministers of England and France had not done all in their power to prevent annexation; but whether or not their activities amounted to *intrigue* depends upon the definition of the term. "At no time, in no manner," said Ashbel Smith long afterwards,

did the British government attempt to exercise or even hint the remotest wish to exercise any political influence in the affairs of Texas, or to possess any advantage, obtain any facility, enjoy any privilege that was not equally and as fully accorded to every other power in amity with Texas.[50]

On the day preceding that set for the assembling of the convention, some of the delegates, at an informal meeting,

---

[47] Under date of July 9, Tod said that the people of Texas were surprised because articles in American newspapers—even the Washington *Union*—expressed doubts that Texans sincerely desired annexation.

[48] Adams, *British Interests, etc.*, 216.

[49] J. Geo. Harris to Polk, June 12, 1845, *Polk Papers*. Harris had just seen Houston in Nashville.

[50] Smith, *Reminiscences of the Texas Republic*, 38.

drafted an ordinance expressing assent to the American joint resolution. Thus prepared, the convention, which formally organized on July 4, promptly voted to enter the Union, and by another vote agreed to wear crape for a month in memory of General Jackson. On the tenth, Allen, the Secretary of State, notified Elliot of the action taken by both the congress and the convention. When doing so, he pointed out that "these manifestations hardly admit of a doubt that the incorporation of Texas with the Federal Union is destined to an early consummation."[51] By the end of August the convention had finished drafting a constitution for the new state, and the second Monday in October was fixed as the day on which this constitution as well as the question of accepting the American offer of annexation should be submitted to a vote of the people. By November 10 President Jones was able to announce that the people had approved both annexation and the state constitution.[52]

Since both the government and the people of Texas had accepted the American offer, nothing remained to consummate annexation except formal admission into the Union by the Congress of the United States. When, therefore, Congress met in December, 1845, Polk announced that Texas had agreed to annexation and had submitted her new state constitution. Since this had been done, "the public faith of both parties is solemnly pledged to the compact of their union," and "strong reasons exist" why the new state should be admitted without delay.[53]

On December 10 Douglas reported from the House Committee on Territories a joint resolution which declared Texas to be a

---

[51] Allen to Elliot, July 10, 1845 (*Texas Diplomatic Correspondence*, III, 120). No further action was taken by Great Britain or her representatives, and Mexico was made clearly to understand that England would not support her in the event of trouble with the United States (Adams, *op. cit.*, 224–225).

[52] Smith, *Annexation of Texas*, 459–460. As late as September, W. D. Lee presented credentials as *chargé d' affaires* from the government of Texas, but Polk declined to recognize him in that capacity. Instead, he instructed Buchanan to deal with Lee as the agent of a state (Polk, *Diary*, I, 17–20).

[53] Richardson, *Messages*, IV, 386.

member of the Union on an equal footing with the original states. Although this resolution met with vigorous opposition, it was adopted eventually by a majority of nearly two-thirds. It was transmitted to the Senate where it encountered still further opposition, although there was small prospect that the dissenters would succeed in defeating it. Some of the Senators who had originally opposed annexation now agreed with the President that the national faith had been pledged, and the measure was adopted by a vote of thirty-one to fourteen. Within a short time the laws of the Union were extended over the new state, and the Republic of Texas ceased to exist. One important question, however, remained to be answered: What will Mexico do about it?